Contents

Part II
Case Studies

Website Resources

For Lecturers:

• A secure, password protected site with teaching material
• Complete, downloadable Instructor's Manual and case teaching notes
• Powerpoint slides that can be downloaded and used as OHTs

Also: This site has a syllabus manager, search functions, and email results functions.

List of Maps

Preface

The need for an updated edition of *The Business Environment:* is a reflection of the importance of the subject in undergraduate and professional educational programmes. A clear understanding of the theories and models outlined in the text is valuable in itself for a clearer understanding of modern business – and it also provides a fundamental building block for the study of corporate strategy, a subject which is included at more advanced levels of the business curriculum. Although the overall structure of the book remains much the same as before, the change in title to *The International Business Environment: Challenges and Changes* reflects the increasingly international nature of areas studied. As before, we try to blend theory with practical examples to allow students to apply those theories.

However, some changes have been made in response to requests and observations by readers. The most important of these is the much greater emphasis given to the international aspects of the environment; not only is the title of the book different, this aspect of the environment has been greatly enhanced throughout the text. Attention has been given to the development of material to do with information technology, social dynamics, Europe and globalisation. All case studies are new; they have been carefully selected to illustrate an array of organisational types, policy issues and operating environments. Practical examples, throughout the text, have been replaced or updated. The structure of the book is explained and explored in Chapter 1, but we provide a brief outline here.

Chapter 1 sets the scene on the business environment and delineates the scope of the book. It recognises that a number of interrelated environmental forces act upon a variety of types of organisation which can be differentiated by, for example, their prime objectives or their legal status; the environment influences different types of organisation in different ways. These forces are grouped under the acronym PESTLE C (for political, economic, social, technological, legal, ecological and competitive), but form an interrelated and complex whole acting at a number of geo-political scales. Additionally, the impact of individual perception and organisational filters and the influence they have on the business environment and forecasting is explored.

Chapter 2 seeks to identify the nature and complexity of the competitive environment and to determine how its dynamic nature and structure affects both the level of competition that an organisation faces and the future profitability of organisations. The international character of competition and the importance of the European Union are identified as key issues. We introduce some of the tools and models that organisations can use to understand their own position and that of their competitors.

Markets left to their own devices may become anti-competitive; intervention may be necessary. Governments can also provide support for new, fledgling industries to allow them to grow and become competitive in the international arena. We look at this role at national level and in the EU.

Chapter 3 explores the four main macroeconomic goals of employment, economic growth, low inflation and the balance of trade in some detail and we consider the changes in government priorities within the macroeconomic environment in recent decades. We discuss the international macroeconomic environment, with particular reference to the EU and the internationalisation of markets and how organisations are required to respond to macroeconomic factors, such as interest rate changes and the removal of trade barriers, which are outside of their direct control.

Chapter 4 takes a broad view of the technological environment. It begins by defining technology and draws distinctions between knowledge and innovation. Considerable attention is given to the funding of research and development (R&D) in major industrial economies and the relevance of R&D to different sectors is considered. Some general technologies affecting organisations are considered, including advanced manufacturing technology and information-based technologies. The effects of technology on organisations and people are discussed. The chapter concludes by considering the management of technology and of technical professionals.

Chapter 5 looks at three broad aspects of the dynamic and multi-faceted social environment – national culture, demographic restructuring and various social changes. It also examines the complex interactive relationship between organisations and a social community or society. This relationship takes place within a local, national and regional cultural context.

The chapter discusses national culture which, it is argued, influences all organisational and environmental activity. It investigates demographic issues at a local, national and international scale and assesses their influence upon organisations. Finally, it takes a closer look at a number of critical social phenomena and identifies some of the key consequences of social dynamism for commercial and other organisations. Issues such as crime, health, the family and the changing face of organised labour are considered.

Chapter 6 is set in the context of actions taken at a global, national and local scale and looks at ethical as well as environmental issues. Environmental campaigners and business people are increasingly recognising the importance of agreeing trade-offs between economic development, company performance and wider ecological issues. As it is often difficult, perhaps impossible, to confine ecological problems to issues that can be dealt with by individual countries, it is becoming increasingly apparent that 'world solutions' need to be sought.

The more serious ecological concerns are looked at and the extent of their impact is investigated. The basic economic arguments which help us understand how firms are able to pollute the environment are explored and the range of actions which can be taken by governments to monitor and regulate the output of pollutants from economic activity identified. We end the chapter by examining the different approaches adopted by businesses towards environmental and ethical issues, discussing the impact of these upon consumers and noting the extent of consumer power in respect of ecological issues.

Chapter 7 focuses on key political issues and examines the potential impact of governments and international bodies on organisations. The chapter includes an examination of different political philosophies regarding the role of government and the amount of democratic representation that exists in various bodies. We also consider how different political philosophies, from interventionist to laissez-faire, link with economic policies and attitudes to business activities.

Political decisions are made at all geo-political levels from local authorities to national government, regional groupings (such as the EU) and on to international agencies such as the United Nations and the World Bank. The role and interaction of these bodies with each other are examined, along with their impact on business and other organisations. The chapter concludes by considering the importance of stability and government attitudes to international business and their investment decisions and how global political threats may impact on all organisations.

Chapter 8 reflects the fact that businesses of the twenty-first century operate at a global level and are becoming increasingly involved in Internet-based trading. The legal environment within which such businesses now operate is of necessity far broader than was once the case. Thus, once the chapter has outlined and discussed both the nature of law and the broad legal requirements of which businesses need to be aware, it proceeds to examine other equally, if not more important, issues controlling business behaviour. We examine whether businesses operate in a socially responsible manner when dealing with their numerous stakeholders, and whether codes of conduct assist, or detract from, that process.

The chapter then considers whether multinational enterprises have a positive or negative impact upon the economies in which they operate. It examines the role of whistle-blowing and discusses whether the presence of whistleblowers indicates a weak company or one which is simply more accountable than most. Finally, the chapter explores the responsibility businesses owe, in terms of the security of their computer infrastructures, to their immediate stakeholders in particular and to the wider public in general. To this end, the chapter examines issues such as password security, security processes and the potential dangers posed by less developed economies connecting to the Internet economy.

Chapter 9 focuses upon the nature of change in the business environment and organisational, individual, group and government responses to environmental dynamism. The chapter notes that the business environment is increasingly complex, dynamic, and uncertain for many organisations, individuals, groups and governments. Major economic, political, technological and social changes have transformed and internationalised the business environment in the last two decades, necessitating organisational change and increased flexibility. Some argue that there is a trend towards high profile 'shock events' and non-linear chaotic patterns in many areas of the natural world (to some extent such patterns are also observable in the business world) which suggests that organisations might do well to make contingency plans. The nature of the business environment calls into question the validity of organisational approaches to long-term planning and suggests the need for processes which build in flexibility and adaptability. Turbulent environments demand government attention. The future role of government is likely to remain a fiercely debated issue for some time.

Thanks to all those who have helped to put the book together by providing chapters, case studies and information.

Acknowledgements

We are grateful to the Financial Times Limited for permission to reprint the following material:

Getting out of the growth doldrums: Only a disaster can save Japan and Germany, © Financial Times, 27 December 2002; Deflation: Stubborn deflation challenges Tokyo to break with orthodoxy, © Financial Times, 21 November 2002; Unemployment: Threat to high growth posed by rising value of the crown, © Financial Times, 12 December 2002; Trade disputes: Daewoo must charge more for six ships, © Financial Times, 11 November 2002; Migration and EU enlargement: Fears of big move west may be unfounded, © Financial Times, 10 December 2002.

We are grateful to the following for permission to reproduce copyright material:

Figure 2.5 (1.1 p. 4) Chapter 2 Reprinted with the permission of The Free Press, a Division of Simon & Schuster Adult Publishing Group, from COMPETITIVE STRATEGY: Techniques for Analyzing Industries and Competitors by Michael E. Porter. Copyright © 1980, 1998 by The Free Press. All rights reserved. We are grateful to Greenpeace for permission to reproduce an extract adapted from their web site, www.greenpeace.org.uk

In some instances we have been unable to trace the owners of the copyright material, and we would appreciate any information that would enable us to do so.

Guided tour

At the start of each chapter **Learning Outcomes** and **Key Concepts** outline the knowledge and topics which will be covered

Minicases in each chapter illustrate and elicit analysis of specific issues

A narrative **Conclusion** and **Summary** of main points list and review the key themes of the chapter

A set of **Discussion Questions** encourage critical reflection on the chapter as a whole

A list of relevant **Weblinks** provides a starting point for research into relevant information online

Suggested **Further Reading** and **References** facilitate more detailed study of particular topics

A bank of longer integrative **Case Studies** provides a flexible resource for seminar and other out of class study

To David,
to Jack, Dawn and Alice,
and to Vera, Jack, Ronnie and the lads

Part One

The International Business Environment

1

The International Business Environment

Ian Brooks

Learning Outcomes

Upon completion of this chapter the reader should be able to:

- define the term business environment and know a number of models of the contextual environment of organisations;

- recognise that environmental forces, acting at a variety of geographical scales from global to local, influence organisations;

- understand that the business environment is unique to each organisation and that human processes influence our understanding of the business environment;

- understand the prime sources of complexity and dynamism in the business environment;

- critically assess the nature and value of environmental forecasting techniques and styles;

- understand the nature of the strategy formulation process;

- map environmental stakeholders' power/interest and conduct a sector impact analysis.

Key Concepts

- business environment
- PEST and PESTLE analysis
- environmental stakeholders
- geo-political scales

- dynamism and complexity
- environmental determinism and enactment
- perceptual and organisational knowledge filters
- subjective and objective forecasting
- impact analysis, brainstorming, Delphi, scenario planning
- strategy, structure and strategic planning
- SWOT analysis

Environmental forces

Whether it is an international banking organisation, a university or a multinational motor manufacturer, no organisation exists within a vacuum. It is very likely to have a number of competitors, to be subject to international, national and local government regulation and control, obliged to comply with national or European pollution regulations and subject to fluctuations in the fortunes of the global economy. The business environment comprises an array of 'forces' acting upon organisations, often with far-reaching implications.

This introductory chapter explains the rationale and scope of the book and demonstrates the fundamental characteristics of the business environment, its relationship with organisations and the implications for organisational structure and strategy. We start by defining the business environment and by classifying the forces at play. The chapter then develops a model of the international business environment which forms the basis of our approach. We briefly explain the diverse nature of organisations and take a closer look at various approaches to environmental forecasting before discussing the relationship between the business environment and organisational activity. The role of the business environment in influencing the strategic direction of organisations is addressed and some of the complex issues are debated. Naturally, many of the issues raised are further developed in later chapters.

The focus of this book is on the organisation in its environment rather than on the individual, group or government and their external environments, although Chapter 9 examines the implications of environmental change for individuals, groups and governments. Figure 1.1 demonstrates that focus.

The international business environment: a definition

The word 'environment' does not merely refer to the natural or ecological environment, although that may be an important consideration for many organisations. It is a general concept which embraces the totality of external environmental forces which may influence any aspect of organisational activity. Similarly, the word 'business' is used to imply any type of organisation, whether it be a commercial profit-making enterprise, a government agency or a non-profit-making charitable trust. Consequently,

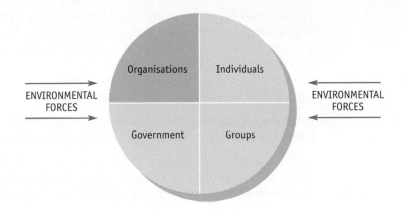

Figure 1.1 Focus on the organisational external environment

we will use the terms 'business' and 'organisation' interchangeably. Hence 'the business environment' is a broad and all-embracing term which encompasses any and all influences which are external to the organisation in question.

In this book, we refer to the 'international' environment suggesting that most, if not all, organisations are influenced by forces often outside of their control. These forces emanate from beyond their locality or even the nation(s) in which they operate; many are truly global or international in scale. For example, the causes and effects of global warming do not respect national boundaries. It is a global concern. Similarly, terrorism, even when inspired by narrow nationalistic extremism, is truly international in its influence. Terrorism can strike in any country of the world. In the commercial world, economic, political or social phenomena in one country can influence the behaviour of organisations in another part of the world. The downturn in the Japanese economy in the 1990s adversely effected some manufacturers in the electronics sector operating from S. E. Asia to N. E. England. A devastating bomb in a Bali nightclub not only decimated victims' lives but also the tourist industry in Bali and reduced holiday bookings in most world locations. Hence, this book takes a holistic view of the business environment, concerning itself with the range of geo-political scales from global, through international, regional, national and local influences.

Defining the environment poses an intellectual problem although a number of eminent researchers have categorised the different approaches (see Smircich and Stubbart, 1985; Mansfield, 1990). Wilson (1992) has suggested three broad conceptions of the business environment, each of which is covered in some detail in this book. He argues that the business environment may be viewed as:

- an objective fact, a clear measurable and definable reality;

- a subjective fact, its particular characteristics being dependent on individuals' interpretation and perceptions;

- enacted (Weick, 1979), where the division between organisation and environment is not clear and where the environment is created and defined by individuals.

This complex argument is explained further in the section on perceptual filters. It need not overly complicate our understanding of the business environment at this stage, although awareness of the role of human perception when defining environmental opportunities or constraints is useful.

It is important for students of business to study the environment and for managers to analyse their organisation's environment for many reasons:

- the nature of the business environment fundamentally influences the activities of business – it affects its markets, its technologies and its workforce;

- operational activities, like new product launches, staff recruitment drives and manufacturing technology reviews need to recognise environmental factors and changes in order to better ensure success of the venture;

- it is likely that profit and organisational well-being are fundamentally related to global, national and local environmental conditions;

- strategic planning needs to take into consideration likely changes in the international business environment.

A classification of environmental forces

The simple acronym 'PEST' (standing for Political, Economic, Social, Technological) serves well as an *aide-mémoire* when considering the array of environmental forces influencing business activity. In fact if the acronym is enlarged to 'PESTLE' (to include Legal and Ecological) it encompasses most areas of concern in this field. We add to this consideration of the competitive environment the interplay between organisations competing, directly or otherwise, with one another (see Chapter 2). Figure 1.2 illustrates this categorisation of the business environment. This text concentrates on each of these forces and the interaction between them.

PEST analysis enables students or managers to assemble a logical and comprehensive picture of their environment. However, it is the interrelationship between the apparently different factors which adds not only complexity and uncertainty but also richness and greater accuracy to the analysis. Minicase 1.1 illustrates a simple PEST analysis of Scania, a multinational, Swedish-owned truck manufacturer.

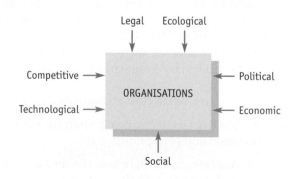

Figure 1.2 PESTLE

Minicase 1.1   PESTLE analysis of Scania (GB) Ltd

Legal

- Block Exemption – the EU removed regulation 123/85 so enabling dealers to seek multi-franchises (2000), that is, one dealer can market products from different manufacturers. This is also the case in the car industry.

- EU transport regulations/harmonisation; working hours directive (drivers); emissions standards (Euro 1, Euro 2, Euro 3); maximum truck sizes.

- Maximum legal truck sizes, likely to increase, may reduce truck demand due to scale efficiencies.

Ecological

- Euro 1, 2 & 3 regulations impose increasingly stringent emissions and noise limits requiring costly R&D spend on redesign of engines and other parts.

- Environmentalist transport lobby aim to increase rail freight and reduce the numbers of large trucks on the roads.

- Stringent standards require more frequent engine service and emissions checks.

- Increasingly aware and active public concern over health issues, quality of life and road congestion.

Political

- National and European government transport policies.

- Investment in rail freight terminals and other infrastructure following privatisation.

- Pressure to regulate road haulage companies further, e.g. driver hours, registration requirements.

- Reductions in centrally funded road building; toll roads.

- Excise duty on diesel; levels of road tax on trucks.

Economic

- Effects of economic cycles are pronounced in this industry, dramatically effecting new truck sales.

- Currency fluctuations: especially of Swedish krona/euro against sterling and non-European currencies.

- Single European Currency – UK entry?

- Interest rates (many trucks purchased on financing arrangement often organised through Scania Finance Ltd – the lower the rates, other things equal, the higher the sales.

Social & demographic

- Societal lobby of governments to reduce or control road traffic and congestion.

- Changing shopping habits influencing rates of growth and geographical distribution of retailers.

Technological

- Complexity in truck design and on-board aids, e.g. on-board computers – engine management systems, trans-European navigation, communications.

- Continual improvements in fuel consumption and emissions control as manufacturers seek competitive advantage while complying with Euro standards.

- Alternative fuels.

- Alternative transportation systems.

- Improved technologies and quality increasing service intervals.

Competitive

- Changing customer base: from small haulage operators to large fleet management organisations – increased buyer power.

- Growth of rental market; non-manufacturing suppliers, e.g. Ryder, BRS.

- Convergence in design and 'quality' characteristics among main players leads to increasing competition.

- Marque loyalties of declining importance; lifetime cost considerations; after-sales market of increasing importance.

- Whole package concept (e.g. trucks, financing and after-sales services).

- Possible future Japanese or Far Eastern incursion into European truck market.

- New entrants' excursion into large & lucrative after-sales market (as in motor car industry, e.g. Kwik Fit).

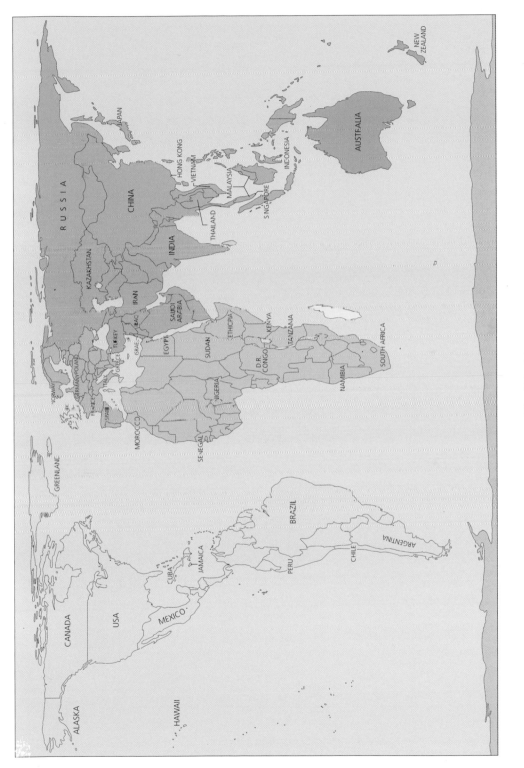

The World

The European Union

Europe

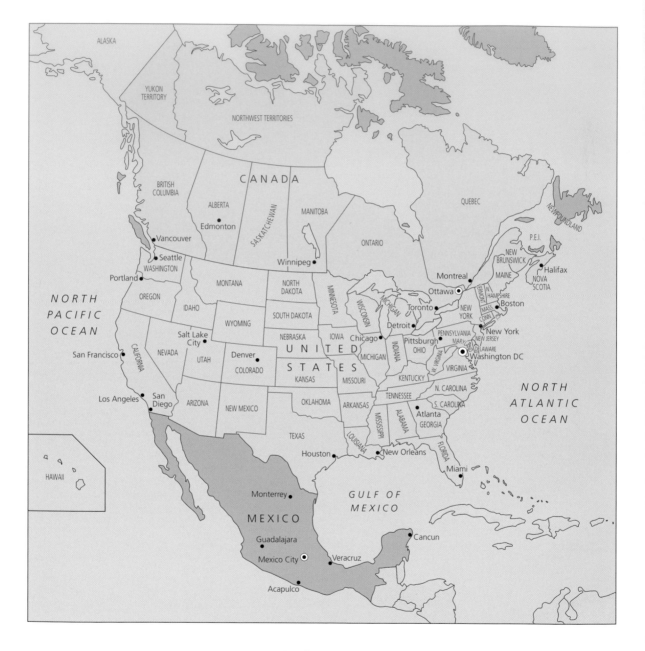

North America

Latin America

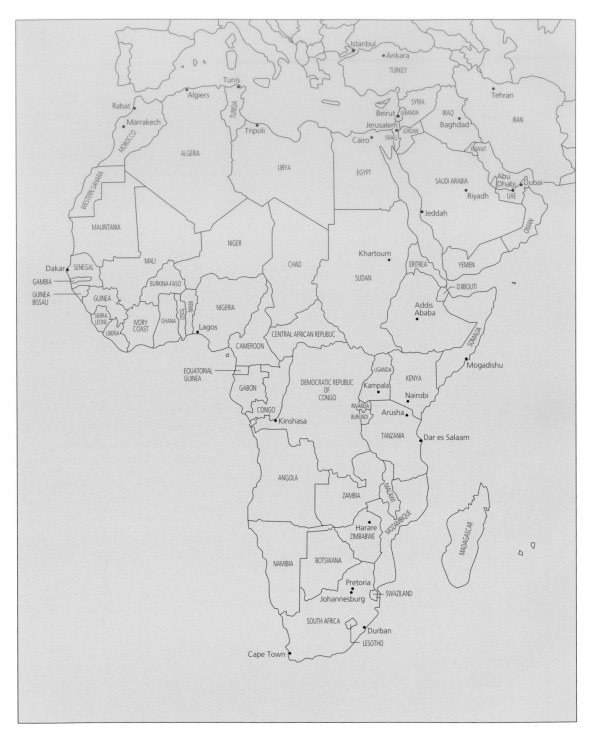

Africa & the Middle East

South East Asia

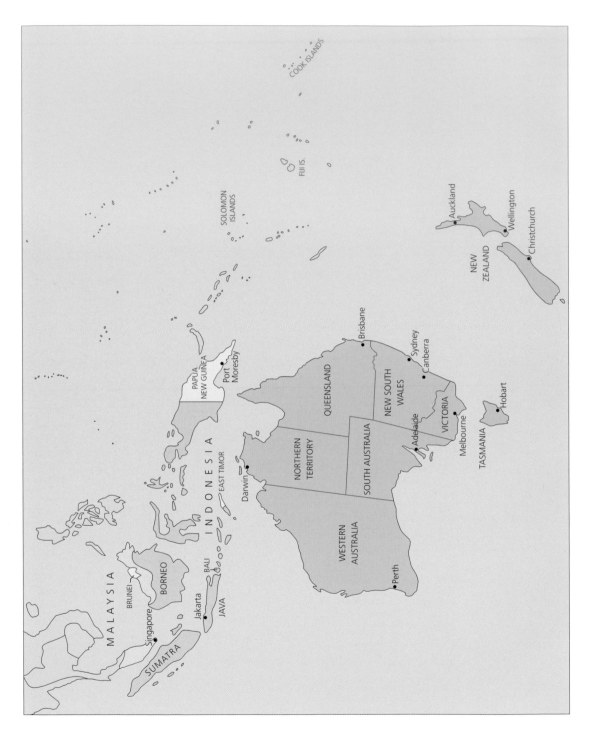

Australasia

Questions

1. Identify those factors which influence the activity and well-being of Scania in the UK which have their origins in an international context. For example, 'Block Exemption' derives from European Union legislation.

2. Which environmental forces facing Scania are confined to the UK?

There are a number of important aspects of Scania's environment which will influence the company's strategic and operational decision making. Some of these factors lie within Scania's control, such as aspects of truck design to meet Euro standards and fuel efficiency targets, while many others, such as fluctuations in the value of the Swedish krona, are beyond its influence.

There are numerous other, sometimes graphic, representations of the business environment. Daft (1992) demonstrates pictorially his typology of environmental forces (Figure 1.3). This 'dartboard' configuration gives the organisation pride of place in the centre while radiating from it are eight categories of environmental concerns. This

Figure 1.3 The 'Dartboard' model
Source: adapted from Daft (1992)

typology is similar to the 'PESTLE' acronym suggesting, as it does, that all environmental forces fall within one or more of these specified categories.

Other studies separate a firm's external environment into three categories although it is not the intention of this book to focus, in any detail, on the internal or operating environment of the organisation. They are:

- the 'remote environment', such as global and domestic political, social and technological concerns – this is akin to the contextual environment outlined above;

- the 'industry environment' or its competitive forces; and

- the 'operating environment' which comprises a rather mixed group of actors including suppliers and customers.

The day-to-day activity of organisations includes interaction with the 'task environment', including an organisation's relationship with its customers, suppliers, trade unions and shareholders. However, this book focuses on the broader contextual environment which permeates and extends beyond the immediate task environment.

Robbins (1992) suggested that the prime forces for change within organisations derive from forces acting within their environment. Specifically, he suggested the following typology of forces: the nature of a workforce, technology, economic shocks, social trends, world politics and competition. These still hold true today and together with other dynamic environmental forces will be explored within this book.

Classifications of the type outlined above attempt to model the environment and although they tend to simplify reality, they help us in identifying and understanding what are complex environmental processes and forces. They serve as useful tools to aid our analysis of the environment. The 'real' environment is a complex array of interrelated forces; we merely compartmentalise them for simplicity and to gain insight. Often a number of forces within the environment combine to influence an organisation. It is when reading case studies or analysing real organisations that the complexity of the business environment becomes apparent, yet understanding the individual elements of that environment will enable you to better appreciate the nature and dynamism encountered.

Environmental stakeholders

All organisations, whatever their size, have a number of stakeholders. A stakeholder is a person, organisation, interest group or other body which holds a 'stake' in the business. In addition to having an interest in the activities of the organisation, some stakeholders have power to influence those activities. Institutional shareholders such as large insurance companies, for example, are powerful stakeholders in many commercial companies and consequently have considerable influence, if they wish to use it, upon the nature of company objectives.

Governments often hold a controlling influence over public sector bodies and hence are vital stakeholders in those organisations. In the National Health Service (NHS) hospital management and medical personnel regard the Department of Health and the particular government of the day as very important and powerful stakeholders. Whether they as managers or medical professionals like it that way is a debatable issue but the fact remains that the UK government, via the Department of Health, provides the funds and the legal framework within which hospitals and other NHS facilities operate. However, in addition to a government department, a general hospital has other 'environmental stakeholders'. These include the local community which the hospital serves. One might argue that this customer base is the most important stakeholder. Of course not all stakeholders will hold equal power or influence over the affairs of the organisation, and the community may have less influence over hospital strategic activities than does the government. For example, many regional health authorities in the UK do not now undertake free cosmetic surgery, except in severe cases, despite considerable demand from the general public.

By way of further illustration, Table 1.1 lists some of the environmental stakeholders of a typical university. It indicates whether the stakeholders have high, medium or low power over the university and whether they have a relatively high, medium or low interest in the activity and strategic direction of the organisation. The analysis involves judgement; however, it can be carried out for any organisation with which you are familiar. It should also be noted that, due to volatility in the business environment, stakeholder power and interest is itself dynamic. Figure 1.4 shows how one might 'map' stakeholder power and interest in an organisation using the data from Table 1.1. This graphically illustrates which stakeholders wield most power and influence. Such an analysis provides a useful analytical tool for managers to assess the relative power and influence of each of their environmental stakeholders. It may prove invaluable in the strategic management process.

Geo-political scales

This book studies the business environment at a range of geo-political scales. The 'geo' in this case refers to 'geographical' scale while the 'political' implies levels or tiers of government. Hence at the local level in most countries there is a tier of government

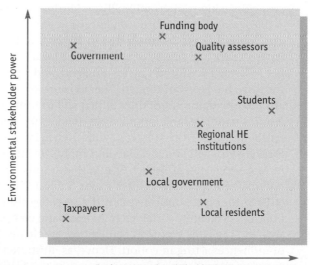

Figure 1.4 Stakeholder mapping: a university

Table 1.1 Environmental stakeholders: higher education

Environmental Stakeholders	Power to Influence Strategy	Level of Interest in Activities
Government	HIGH	MEDIUM
Students	MEDIUM	HIGH
Quality assessment bodies	HIGH	MEDIUM
Local government	LOW	LOW
Local residents	LOW	MEDIUM
Funding body	HIGH	MEDIUM
Other regional HE institutions	MEDIUM	MEDIUM
Taxpayers	LOW	LOW

which is responsible for certain activities within a relatively small area. Similarly there is a tier of government, often very important and influential, at a national scale. In Europe the European Union (EU), and in South-East Asia ASEAN, form a further level of governance. The EU, for example, has created enormous change, not least in trading relations, patterns of trade and alterations in product specifications. It is a dynamic force in organisations across Europe and indeed elsewhere. Furthermore, very many forces acting upon business today have their origins in a global context. Major political disturbances leading to war or terrorism, changes in oil prices and availability, agreements to reduce CO_2 omissions and innovations in information and communications technology do not respect national boundaries; they are global in reach, operate across nations internationally and influence all organisations directly or indirectly.

Most organisations are influenced by environmental forces operating at different geo-political levels, as illustrated in Figure 1.5. For example, Scania interacts with its environment at a variety of scales. At the local level in the United Kingdom its head office is located in Milton Keynes, England, and a move to an alternative location within the town has been considered. The decision where to locate will be subject to local government planning restrictions which will in turn be influenced by national laws. Also, Scania employs a large number of skilled, experienced and professional staff who currently live in or near Milton Keynes. Hence factors within the local environment (i.e. local government and local labour supply) are important to the activities of Scania (GB) in Milton Keynes. However, Scania is also subject to environmental dynamism at the national, European and global scales. Table 1.2 illustrates two influences upon Scania (GB) at four geo-political scales. It also categorises these forces into legal, ecological, political, economic, social, technological and competitive. Many environmental issues, such as EU engine emission regulations, are themselves the outcome of a diverse range of influences acting in cohort. Hence, as illustrated in Table 1.2, the nature of the laws governing truck engine emissions within the EU is influenced by a complex consortium of ecological, social, technological, political and legal forces. Conflicting pressures

Table 1.2 Factors operating in Scania's business environment at four geo-political scales

Geo-Political Scale	Environmental Issues (examples)	Environmental Forces
Local	A: Milton Keynes town planning regulations (Scania GB headquarters)	A: Political, legal, social, ecological
	B: Local skilled labour supply conditions	B: Social, economic, competitive
National	A: Value of sterling against the Swedish krona/euro	A: Economic, political
	B: Government freight transport policy	B: Political, social, competitive
European Union	A: Emissions control and truck size regulations	A: Ecological, technological, political, social, legal
	B: Trading relations and concessions to non-EU countries	B: Political, competitive
Global	A: GATT negotiations to pursue free trade agreements	A: Political, legal, competitive
	B: CO_2 emission targets	B: Ecological, social, political

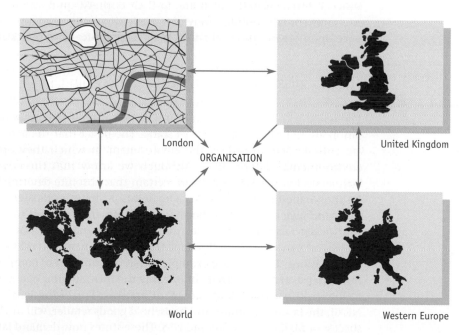

Figure 1.5 Geo-political scales

are brought to bear on the European government from ecological pressure groups, social and political philosophies and organisational lobbyists. The outcome is, in this case, a compromise 'solution' enshrined in law.

Unfortunately, it is not always simple or practical to distinguish between the business environment at various geo-political scales as these influences are often so inter-related and complex that they can only be fully appreciated collectively. Some forces will operate at a number of different levels and manifest themselves in a variety of ways. Hence it may fall upon local government to enforce pollution controls that originated at global inter-governmental conferences. Even many small, local companies are increasingly aware that forces operating at the European level, such as product specification directives emanating from Brussels, have a direct and often profound influence on their business. For example, many local butchers' shops in the UK are finding it increasingly difficult to comply with European Union health and safety regulations. For some it is proving to be the proverbial last straw.

Not all organisations are influenced equally by the international business environment. In fact what may prove to be a real threat for one organisation could be a wondrous opportunity for growth and profitability for another. For example, the technological advances made in the design, production and marketing of personal computers and the consequent reduction in their cost and improvement in quality have led to enormous increases in their demand for household and business use. These technological forces have, however, virtually proved a death-blow to the manufacture of mechanical and electronic typewriters and have reduced the demand for mainframe computers for certain applications.

In reality every organisation has a complex array of environmental influences with which it interacts and which are, in their entirety, quite unique. Hence the business environment is a complex array of forces acting with often unpredictable and unequal force upon organisations at a variety of geographical and political scales.

The organisation–environment relationship

The relationship and direction of influence between the environment and an organisation are not one-way, simple or static. The belief that the activities of organisations are entirely determined by the environment in which they operate is described as environmental determinism. Although we know that the environment influences business activity it is by no means certain that absolute determinism is apparent even for the smallest of organisations. Organisations have tentacles of influence which help form and give shape to the business environment. In other words there is not a one-way causal relationship between environment and organisation. The reality is that many companies profoundly shape their environment and that facing numerous other organisations. The simplest example is that of a number of competing companies in an industrial sector. The activity of one, say the introduction of a new product range, will influence the activity and success of another. For example, the planned growth of NEXT, the fashion clothing and household goods retailer, will influence the activity and success of Marks & Spencers and DFS. These stores now demand large-scale retail outlets which in turn influences the planning decisions made by town-centre planners: town-centre growth and prosperity may depend on the scale of outlets available to retailers. For example, as major high street names (like M&S, NEXT, John Lewis) in the UK demand large-scale outlets in prime positions, Northampton plans to build a £250 million extension to its shopping centre to be completed in 2008 in order to maintain or improve its status as a shopping centre. Without such a move, it is argued, the town-centre shopping facilities would actually decline as major multinational retail chains withdrew. Shoppers would be attracted to nearby centres offering a wider range of outlets, such as Milton Keynes, and a spiral of decline would set in. What Northampton aims to do is to create an attractive business environment for major retail outlets, encouraging them to expand in the town, and in so doing increase the popularity of the town for shoppers. Figure 1.6 indicates this two-way influence between organisation and environment.

Each organisation forms part of the business environment of other organisations, as competitors, allies, suppliers, buyers and so forth. No organisation is isolated and without any influence on its own environment and that of others. Many organisations, especially sizeable and/or influential ones, exert considerable pressures for change in their business environment. Hamel and Prahalad (1994) argued that companies can only control their future if they know how to influence the destiny of their industry. For example, the Direct Line company in the United Kingdom has revolutionised the insurance and financial services industries. They have effectively marketed and delivered a quick and efficient 'telephone line' service. This has reduced their overheads, when compared to normal broker services, rapidly increased their market share and enabled them to maintain highly competitive rates which have 'squeezed' more traditional competitors. They, and the numerous companies now mimicking them, have changed the business environment for all insurance and financial services companies.

A similar process is likely to occur as the Internet is used for marketing and purchasing consumer goods; for example, the 'virtual' supermarket may rapidly lead to fundamental changes in shopping habits in the next decade with enormous potential knock-on effects on current businesses and their operations. Internet providers of household electrical goods, for example, are already significantly affecting the business of major UK electrical retailers like Dixons and Curry's. For the customer this increased competition is largely welcomed as it tends to lead to reduced prices, but for the retailer it cuts their profit margins and demands greater efficiency in operations. Many retailers are attempting to secure their futures by operating both retail outlets and Internet and/or catalogue sales simultaneously.

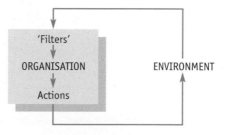

Figure 1.6 Organisation and environment: two-way influence

Sometimes organisations within a business sector collaborate with each other in order to maintain a stable environment within known competitive conditions. For example, many European motor manufacturers had for some time succeeded in persuading the European Union to extend the 'block exemption' scheme for motor distributor dealerships enabling manufacturers to demand that their dealerships distribute, service and repair solely their vehicles. Hence motor manufacturers maintained control over their distribution channels which acted as a strong barrier to entry for any new makes that might want to enter the market. The investment required to establish a comprehensive distributor network is immense and effectively deters many potential entrants and limits the penetrative capabilities of others. The conditions of competition are thus maintained – business as usual. Now that the removal of block exemption has been achieved, competitive conditions in that industry are changing.

A model of the business environment

The model of the business environment illustrated in Figure 1.7 indicates how the various environmental forces, acting at a variety of scales, pass through what we refer to as 'perceptual filters'. These filters, which are explained more fully below, comprise all the internal mechanisms within organisations which enable managers to construct their own view of environmental realities. For example, an organisation may not have an active environmental scanning capability and hence may miss numerous potential opportunities, while others may be managed by eternal optimists who are convinced of their organisations' invincibility even when faced with hostile environmental influences. For all intents and purposes, these perceptual filters actually change and shape 'reality' for organisations. They influence the way organisations look at their environment and what

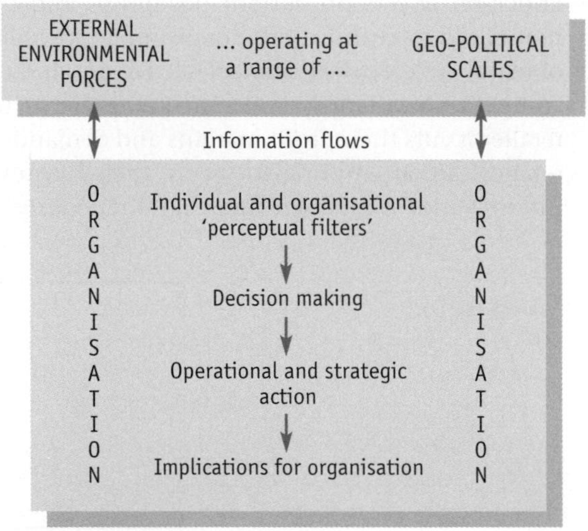

Figure 1.7 Model of the business environment

they see. Consequently, we must not underestimate their power and influence. The failure of the UK motorcycle industry, which has been virtually wiped out, was in large part due to its inability to accept that the business environment was rapidly changing. Design, product and process changes, largely developed in Japan, were ignored by British manufacturers who failed to perceive and react either to these environmental changes or to evolving customer requirements. The 'new' developments were viewed as distant and faddish; manufacturers were focused on past glories not future realities. The business environment in all countries is littered with similar examples.

Information about an organisation's environment may take a variety of forms: for example, it may comprise sophisticated data from a strategic management information system or, conversely, an apparently minor snippet of information gleaned by a powerful senior manager. There is little evidence to suggest that organisations are more likely to act on concrete data than on the opinion or impression of its senior personnel. Environmental information is always the result of 'human' analysis. It has passed through the complex perceptual filters which exist within every organisation. However, this information will not influence all organisations equally.

Managers at all levels utilise environmental information to facilitate their decision making in order to enable the organisation to operate successfully. A thorough awareness of the nature of an organisation's environment is an essential prerequisite for strategic management. The environment often determines, and always influences, the future course of action of organisations and acts as a force for change in organisations.

Perceptual filters

Organisations and their employees assist in the 'creation' of their own business environment such that the actual nature of that environment remains as much one of human interpretation as of hard 'reality'. Different organisations in the same industry often view environmental forces quite differently from one another, even though those forces may in fact be very similar. Additionally, organisations filter and interpret incoming information about the environment and managerial cognition, organisational culture and politics all influence this process. These statements require further explanation.

Decision-makers in organisations receive and assimilate incoming data from the environment. That data is, however, incomplete. Even the most sophisticated environmental scanning and forecasting activities can only collect and process a small proportion of all important environmental information. Most strategic decision-makers are primarily concerned to learn about those changes which might influence their activity and as such they continuously make decisions regarding the importance or significance of 'new' information. It is quite possible, therefore, that person A will ignore data or dismiss it as unimportant while person B, even in the same organisation, may take this same information on board and 'allow' it to influence their decision-making process. This difference in 'reception' may be attributed to differences in the individuals' backgrounds, their position in the organisation, or how welcome or potentially threatening the information is to the receiver. Just as individuals differ, so do organisations and whole industrial sectors.

Our individual and collective perception only enables us to 'see' and interpret in certain ways. It is these perceptions that drive individual and business actions. Weick (1979) suggests that individual and organisational actions might in turn influence change within the environment. A hypothetical example (Minicase 1.2) will help illustrate this phenomenon.

Miller (1988) argued that managers' perception of their environment has a greater influence on organisational decision making and eventual strategic direction than does more objective information. He is not alone in this belief. Boyd *et al.* (1993) suggested that this raises some major concerns regarding the reliability and validity of managers' perception. They argue, for example, that managers often make broad generalisations

---

Minicase 1.2   Enactment – a self-fulfilling prophecy

Let us assume that *Forefront*, a computer software house, perceive that the competitive environment in which they operate is changing. These perceived changes encourage them to develop a technologically superior Windows™ environment software product. They also perceive that numerous smaller software companies may begin to encroach on their other activities if they do not focus research and development (R&D) activity in these areas. Faced with a decision, Forefront decide to increase their efforts in R&D in the Windows™ market. This entails reducing their R&D spend and management attention elsewhere. After two years Forefront have successfully produced and marketed their Windows™ product and remain the market leaders. However, there has been a cost. The neglect of their other software products has meant that competitors have overtaken them in market share terms in these other product lines.

Their original perception of their environment led them to a particular strategic management decision. As a result of that decision Forefront have enacted their environment. That is, their actions have assured that their perceptions became a reality. Their actions, to focus on the Windows™ environment at the expense of their other products, have led other 'environmental actors' (that is, their competitors) to adjust their strategic policy to take advantage of the opportunity. Forefront's perceptions and subsequent actions have become a self-fulfilling prophecy.

Questions

1. What is it about Forefront's activity that has made them 'enact' their environment?

2. Discuss why two organisations in the same sector might 'see' their environment in quite different ways.

based on a small number of cases. Huber (1985) contended that these and other short-comings are inevitable due to the perceptual and cognitive limitations of managers.

Some managers and organisations, in facing an uncertain business environment, perceive their environment as more certain than it actually is. This is particularly true of those managers who have a low tolerance for confusion or ambiguity.

In summary, the main influences upon individual and organisational perception are:

- characteristics of individuals, such as background, education and duration of employment within the organisation;

- organisational culture;

- organisational politics, structures and control mechanisms;

- history and development of an organisation;

- industrial sectors and their norms.

Dynamism and complexity

Throughout this book we stress the dynamic nature of environmental forces; however, we recognise that the degree or extent of dynamism is not equal for all organisations or environments. For example, at present the extent of environmental flux affecting a high street solicitor, although not negligible, is less than that influencing BP or General Motors. It may be the case, of course, that BP have a far greater influence over their environment than does the solicitor's office, so dynamism is not necessarily a handicap, especially if that very dynamism preserves and enhances the competitive strengths of the firm.

Complexity in the environment is a product of a number of interrelated factors and the degree of environmental uncertainty, possibly caused by dynamism, plays a major part. An organisation faced with an uncertain environment is, other things being equal, in a far less advantageous position than one facing stability. However, yet again all is not straightforward, for many organisations become complacent when faced with a set of known environmental parameters. A significant change in one or more of those characteristics often leaves the inflexible organisation unable to cope. Environmental complexity also tends to increase for organisations operating at a variety of geo-political scales. A transnational manufacturing and marketing organisation is likely to encounter dynamic environmental forces at local, national and global scales. Figure 1.8 can be used to 'map' an organisation's position according to the levels of complexity and dynamism in its environment. By way of illustration we have located the approximate position of a number of 'generic' organisations.

When faced with a complex, uncertain and dynamic environment some organisations and many individual managers attempt to simplify that environment; at least in their own minds. This is probably not a wise course of action. Researchers have argued that attempts to reduce environmental uncertainty may lead to poor long-term organisational performance. The themes of dynamism and complexity will be developed throughout this book and the consequences for organisations, government, individuals and groups further explored in Chapter 9.

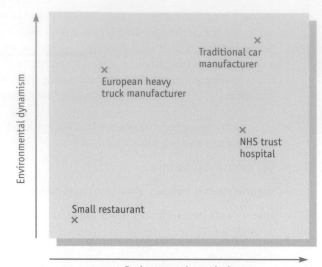

Figure 1.8   Complexity and dynamism in an organisation's environment
Source: adapted from Johnson and Scholes (2002)

The organisation

Types of organisations

The term 'organisation' or 'business', as used in this book, embraces a wide range of legal entities with diverse objectives. Table 1.3 lists, with examples, the main types of organisation in the UK. Each country will have variations upon these, yet in many ways they will be similar.

As organisations differ fundamentally from one another in their legal status and primary objectives it is not surprising that the environmental forces which influence them also vary. In fact environmental pressures may encourage some organisations to actually change their legal status and objectives. For example, deregulation and increasing competition in the financial services industry is influencing the activity and success of building societies and life assurance companies. Due to overcapacity, technological changes and further potential for economies of scale some have merged while others have been swallowed up by larger companies. Merger activity may in turn lead to a change in legal status. For example, in August 1995 the Halifax Building Society and the Leeds Building Society formally merged and later became a public limited company with its shares quoted on the London stock exchange. This has now enabled the Halifax to acquire, for example, the Birmingham Midshires Building Society in 1999 and become a thriving UK bank in the twenty-first century.

Table 1.3 Types of organisation

Types of Organisation	United Kingdom Examples	Global Examples
Government Civil Service Departments and Agencies	Ministry of Agriculture Food and Fisheries	Ministero Scuola Ed Educatione (Italy)
Local Government Organisations	Gloucestershire County Council	California State Legislature
Incorporated by Royal Charter or by Act of Parliament (Public Corporations)	BBC (by Royal Charter) Post Office (by Act of Parliament)	Air France
Quasi Autonomous Non-Governmental Organisations (Quangos)	Higher Education Funding Council Executive (HEFCE)	UMNO (Malaysia)
Sole Trader	The King of Baltis	Kobayashi Electronics (Japan)
Partnership	PricewaterhouseCoopers	PricewaterhouseCoopers
Charity Organisations	Oxfam	International Red Cross
Private Limited Company	Virgin Atlantic	Joe's Garage
Co-operative	Co-operative Retail Society	Cooperativa Di Consumatori (Italy)
Public Limited Company (PLC)	Manchester United plc	Heineken (Holland)
Building Societies and Friendly Societies	Bradford & Bingley Building Society	

Organisational objectives profoundly influence an organisation's activity and strategic direction. Knowledge of these objectives will help determine the importance of different environmental forces and changes. Table 1.4 gives a flavour of the range of objectives that exist in just three types of organisation.

In addition to the legal status and prime objectives of organisations there are numerous other factors which may profoundly affect the nature of the organisation–environment relationship. These include:

- organisational structure;
- size of the organisation;

Table 1.4 Organisational objectives

Type of Organisation	Prime Objective
Commercial company (e.g Shell plc)	To maximise shareholder value
Charity (e.g. Oxfam)	To relieve poverty, distress and suffering in any part of the world
General hospital	To provide quality health care for the local community

- type of technology used;
- organisational and individual perceptual filters.

These and other factors will, subtly or otherwise, alter the importance of any particular environmental variable. For example, a large and diversified organisation may cope better with a proposed new EU regulation (because of its ability to influence the outcome by lobbying) than a smaller, more specialised firm. Conversely, it is frequently argued that small firms tend to be more flexible and able to cope with environmental uncertainty than large, sluggish organisations.

Environmental forecasting

Forecasting in a dynamic and complex environment

We have argued that managers' perception influences their vision and assessment of the business environment. These processes are based on subjective judgements of the environment. However, many organisations attempt to use more objective environmental measures. The following section explores some of these objective, and other more perceptual, measures, while the role that organisational culture and outlook play in influencing views of the environment is discussed in the final section of this chapter.

Managers with strategic responsibilities in organisations are often frustrated by the difficulty of predicting changes in the environment. It is frequently the case, especially in smaller organisations, that little formal long-term forecasting takes place. It is viewed as such an uncertain science that time is not spent attempting to foresee what is often regarded as the unforeseeable. Instead managers prefer to be influenced by a combination of information resulting from their accumulated experience in business and a variety of perceptual measures of their environment. This may, however, prevent organisations from acting proactively, so that they are often in a position of having to react to a change thrust upon them.

There are many examples of companies which have failed due to their reliance upon incorrect forecasts or the inability of management to react appropriately to environmental evidence. A good example is that of the car industry in the USA in the 1970s. Over 20 per cent of its market share (that is an awful lot of cars!) had, by 1980, been lost to foreign manufacturers who produced smaller, more fuel-efficient vehicles. The American manufacturers had failed to appreciate that global political and economic conditions would lead to large increases in oil prices, and that social factors, such as greater female economic and geographic mobility, were 'conspiring' to create a preference for smaller cars. In the early 1980s US car companies made losses in excess of $5 billion (£3.1 billion). Japanese car manufacturers, on the other hand, had anticipated the future need for fuel-efficient cars with lower servicing costs or, as many commentators have argued, they planted the idea in consumers' minds. More recently, the closure of a number of plants around the world, including Scotland and the north-east of England, manufacturing semiconductors was the outcome of a dramatic fall in global prices because of massive over-supply. Should this have been predicted? Closures of relatively new plants in the UK were costly mistakes for both the producing companies and the workforce.

At best, assessing the potential impact of likely changes in the environment offers organisations an advantage over their competitors by enabling decision-makers to narrow the range of options. Measures will always entail some element of subjectivity, if only in the processes involved in collecting the data. The accuracy and, therefore, the value of such forecasts will often depend on the 'richness' of data, itself a product of managers' choice of communication media. Boyd *et al.* (1993) argued that 'richness' is a product of the speed of feedback, variety of communication channels utilised, and the 'personalness' of the information. Nevertheless, it is clear that, in a dynamic and complex business environment, attempting to forecast sometimes discontinuous trends is fraught with difficulty. One need only look at the frequent inaccuracies of Organisation for Economic and Social Development (OESD) and national government forecasts of medium- or long-term economic indicators such as GDP growth despite their 'closeness' to the economy and privileged access to data. However, to do nothing is also a dangerous course of action for an organisation, as is over-reliance on internal sources of information rather than external channels. It is quite possible, under such circumstances, that a state of inertia could set in, which would ill equip organisations to accurately forecast changes in the environment and which may lead to poor quality decision making and organisational underperformance.

Approach to forecasting

Peace and Robinson (1994) suggest that strategic decision-makers need to take a step-by-step approach to forecasting (see Figure 1.9). Their model outlines five steps:

- selection of environmental variables that are critical to the organisation;
- selection of sources of information about those variables;

- evaluation of forecasting techniques;
- integration of the results of forecasting into the strategic management process;
- monitoring and evaluation of the critical aspects of these forecasts.

Some variables may be so obviously important to the well-being of the organisation that they become, in a sense, self-selecting. For example, a company which smelts aluminium will be concerned about likely changes in the price of electricity as this forms a major cost in the production process. Other variables will be identified, usually by senior managers with experience in the organisation and within the sector. However, it is critical to select variables that may be important in the future and not just rely on those which have been critical in the past. It is not a difficult task to select the key variables, although a little lateral thinking may prove useful. It is likely that you could select many key variables for each of the case study organisations at the end of this book. In order to keep the list of variables manageable it is recommended that you omit factors that have little chance of occurring.

There are numerous sources of information about the business environment. These include government and international organisations' statistics and forecasts regarding economic variables such as inflation and growth rates, research findings estimating changes in commodity prices, informed opinions on political, social or technological changes, and so forth. A considerable amount of information is merely 'picked up' by managers keeping their eyes and ears open and continually scanning their business environment for opportunities or threats resulting from imminent change. Although quantitative measures of environmental variables carry a certain credibility, more judgemental and subjective approaches are likely to prove practical and sometimes more accurate. You will note from our discussion of perceptual filters that subjectivity impinges on all human activity – not least upon the manager sensing changes in the business environment.

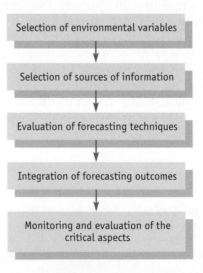

Figure 1.9 Step-by-step approach to forecasting

Forecasting techniques

Using sophisticated computer techniques and relying primarily on numerical data, some companies and many governments attempt to model changes in the environment. These models often utilise economic data and attempt to estimate future economic variables, such as interest rates and the external value of currencies. There are many private consultancy companies that specialise in developing such models for government and commercial clients. However, as environmental stability is very much a phenomenon of the past, modelling of this type has been subject to considerable 'bad press'. Such models find environmental flux and discontinuity difficult, if not impossible, to predict. For example, models of this nature could not possibly have predicted the terrorist attack on New York in 2001 (9/11) and, for example, the catastrophic effect this had on US and European airlines.

Far less expensive to develop, and often just as accurate, are time series and judgemental models. Time series models attempt to identify trends in variables based on historical data or cyclical factors and extrapolate them into the future. For example, a simple time series model may look at the population of a country at five-year intervals over the past hundred years then use this evidence to predict future demographic changes. This method does not, however, allow for environmental discontinuity where the 'rules' of the past no longer apply. A slightly more sophisticated model may add additional variables, such as likely changes in birth rates and predictions concerning the migration of people, which may have a bearing on the population of the country in question. The resulting demographic forecasts may prove useful for strategic planners in government and some organisations (see Chapter 5 and Case Study 5).

Judgemental models are those based upon the informed opinion of people in the relevant field. For example, sales force personnel may be asked to estimate likely future trends in sales potential, taking into consideration all likely variables. Their experience 'on the ground' may prove invaluable and lead to more accurate forecasts than sophisticated modelling techniques could achieve.

Table 1.5 illustrates a United Nations (UN) prediction of world population growth to the year 2150. This prediction combines knowledge of historic trends, including more recent signs of a reduction in the rate of world population growth, with educated guesswork. It shows population growth only increasing slightly after about 2050. Whereas the UN estimate that an extra one billion (1000 million) people will inhabit the world between 1999 and 2013 (just 14 years), they believe that it will take 129 years for an extra billion people to live between the years 2054 to 2183. Will it be proven correct?

How can anyone predict population growth in the next millennium using 'scientific' means? Well, demographers (those who study population) are luckier than many as trends in population are partially predictable over reasonably long time periods. For example, if world population growth slows shortly (as they predict) this will mean that there will be fewer young adults in a generation's time, and therefore fewer mothers and fathers to have children.

The UN believes that because world population growth is slowing now, it will continue to do so indefinitely. What they cannot predict is an event or events which cause current trends to radically alter. For example, there may be dramatic new technological inventions which vastly increase longevity and/or fertility rates or, conversely, there may be

Table 1.5 World population growth

Year	Population in Million
1000	310 million
1250	400 million
1500	500 million
1750	790 milion
1900	1650 million
1950	2520 million
2000	6060 million
2050	8910 million (est)
2100	9461 million (est)
2150	9750 million (est)

Source: UN Secretariat, The World at Six Billion, 1999

new viruses which threaten the lives of billions. However, as suggested, some important demographic factors can be predicted with reasonable accuracy and the predictions are vital to certain business sectors. For example, we know that in most of the Western world, with the possible exception of the USA (see Chapter 9), the population is ageing. We can make what may be reasonably accurate estimates of the number, even the proportion of the total population, which will be of pension age in the year 2050 for the simple reason that these people already exist. So, whereas about 9.4 per cent of the population of the UK in 2004 is of pension age (65+ years old), it is predicted that that figure will rise to 13.5 per cent by 2050. The accuracy of this prediction is highly important for all of us and especially for government and the pension business. It will also have highly significant implications for the NHS and healthcare industry.

Brainstorming is another common, rather creative, method of generating ideas and forecasts. Brainstorming can usefully be employed to estimate future trends in technology development, for example. A number of informed people are encouraged to generate ideas and forecasts in a group setting. Many of these ideas may appear fanciful but technological developments often do lead to 'fanciful' outcomes! Such techniques can generate useful judgemental ideas about potential future events.

The Delphi method of forecasting is a more systematic technique than brainstorming. This method attempts to gain consensus among a group of people, such as a senior strategic management group. For example, a company senior management team may meet and aim to forecast their likely competitive position in five years' time. They will discuss all relevant variables and start to agree on as many points and issues as possible in an attempt to develop the most likely and most widely held view. This can then be used in the strategy process.

It is interesting to note some of the predictions made in the past from reputable sources which turned out to be somewhat misguided. *The Quarterly Review* (1825), an English journal, noted 'what could be more palpably absurd than the prospect of loco-motives travelling twice as fast as stagecoaches'. Henry Ford's lawyer advised (1922) that 'the horse is here to stay, but the automobile is only a novelty – a fad' while an editorial of the *Boston Post* in 1865 wrote, 'well informed people know that it is impos-sible to transmit the voice over wires and were that it were possible to do so, it would be of no practical value'. Finally, the Chairman of IBM in 1943 wrote, 'I think there is a market for about five computers'.

Scenario development recognises judgemental and non-quantitative information such as changing fashions. Scenarios are 'pictures' or 'stories' of what might be the case some time in the future. They draw upon both subjective and more objective data. Hence a company may develop two or three likely scenarios for some future date and take these into consideration in their planning process. They may develop contingency plans to cope with each scenario should it arise. The multinational oil giant, Shell, has made extensive use of scenario 'planning'. Let us take an example, that hydrogen fuel cells rapidly replace traditional fossil fuelled engines for road transport between 2020 and 2030. If this scenario occurs, what will be the implications for business (refer to Minicase 1.3)?

Finally, a number of organisations and consultancies have developed 'political risk' ratings for countries around the world. These take into consideration the stability and predictability of nations and their governments, and advise commercial organisations and governments on the risks involved in overseas investment.

Impact analysis

One simple, yet effective, way of forecasting the effect of environmental changes on organisations is to conduct an impact analysis. This involves ascertaining a series of potential environmental changes and assessing the probable effect of these on a range of organisations, usually direct competitors. Table 1.6 illustrates a simple impact analy-sis of the heavy truck industry. The effect of a change is first assessed as either a positive (+) or negative (−) influence. Positive influences are those where there will be a benefit to the company financially or otherwise. Changes which may lead to strongly positive effects are given a ++ or even +++ rating. The impact analysis may then involve a brief explanation of the plus/minus score.

It can be seen from the impact analysis in Table 1.6 that changes in environmental regulations will adversely effect all truck manufacturers; however, some are better prepared due to their scale and a history of concern for such issues. A realignment of exchange rates will not affect all three companies in the same way.

Impact analysis enables managers or analysts to assess the effects of environmental change on an organisation and upon its competitors. Clearly, where such changes are likely to adversely affect an organisation more than its competitors then contingency planning needs to be considered.

Minicase 1.3   The hydrogen economy

Major car manufacturers like Ford, General Motors, Toyota and DaimlerChrysler are currently embarking on major investments in hydrogen technology and forging alliances in the process with Shell, BP and Exxon. Shell launched a new company in 2003 – Shell hydrogen – with an initial budget of about €100 million (£65m/$100m). Buses powered by fuel cells are already in service in Chicago, Vancouver and Oslo on an experimental basis.

The development has been stimulated by:

• tightening in air quality standards and targets to reduce CO_2 omissions in the light of concern over global warming;

• increasing security threat over oil reserves and consequent fluctuations in oil prices.

The 'obvious' impact of the use of hydrogen fuel cells is a cut in gasoline by up to 100 percent!

Hydrogen is easily made. For example, one large oil refinery, BP's Grangemouth in Scotland, produces about 150 tonnes of hydrogen a day – enough to fuel 500 000 cars. Currently, however, hydrogen is difficult to store and transport. The Daimler-Chrysler buses currently being tested are five times more expensive than conventional buses and prices are unlikely to fall until fuel cells can be mass produced. Pure hydrogen is especially difficult to store as it does not liquefy until its temperature reaches absolute zero and it is highly combustible. Currently, fuel tanks have to be bulky and take up considerable space and allow only small distances between refuelling. If the technology is to be used in cars it may be necessary to store the gas at around 5000 psi (an average car tyre 'stores' air at around 30 psi). The technology to do this is yet to be developed. To build a low carbon economy, governments, investors, business and consumers will need to sustain change. Consumers will need to lobby government ('green votes') and engage in 'green purchasing'.

Questions

What are the likely implications of this development for:

• car manufacturers;

• major oil companies, like BP, Exxon and Shell;

• the countries of Saudi Arabia, Iraq, Venezuela and Qatar;

• political stability in the Middle East;

• petrol retailers?

Table 1.6 Impact analysis in the truck industry

Environmental Scenario	Scania	ERF	Mercedes Trucks
Ecological	-	---	--
Strict new European Union environmental protection legislation (i.e. Euro standards 3 and 4)	Track record in R&D on environmentally friendly engines and truck design, nevertheless changes will require extra investment	UK company, too small to invest sufficiently in environmentally friendly R&D	R&D expenditure on environment-orientated technology but without outstanding quality reputation of Scania
Economic	++	-	++
Sweden adopts the euro; UK and sterling remain out of euro	Reduces transaction costs and uncertainty in euro countries	Little effect on UK market but uncertainty and transaction costs remain with exports	Reduces transaction costs and uncertainty in euro countries
Political	--	--	-
Governments enforce movement of 'heavy' freight to railways and restrict the use of heavy trucks	Will adversely affect the sale of trucks, servicing and parts sales as Scania do not produce light trucks and vans	Will adversely affect the sale of trucks, servicing and parts sales as ERF do not produce light trucks and vans	Mercedes is protected to a degree by having sizeable market shares in motor vehicles of all sizes but heavy truck sales would suffer

Environmental analysis and strategic process

Strategy and structure: environmental influence

Most early organisational theory and management research assumed a largely stable business environment. Proponents of the Classical School and of Scientific Management argued that organisations should be machine-like and feature centralised authority, clear lines of command, specialisation and the division of labour and numerous rules and regulations. However, such mechanised and bureaucratic organisations, typified by hierarchical structures and a fervent adherence to the power-control role of management, are poorly suited to dynamic and complex environments. By the 1940s in North America and increasingly also in Europe, the deficiencies of the 'classical' organisation became apparent. Technological changes, increasingly complex markets and social, political and cultural changes created new demands on organisations which many were ill-equipped to manage. Although many of the basic principles identified by classical management theorists, such as Fayol and Taylor, remain entrenched within many 'modern' organisations, other environmentally sensitive changes have occurred. The Human Relations School (late 1930s onwards), typified by the work of Chester Barnard and landmark studies by the Tavistock Institute, together with the Hawthorne studies, signalled change. In the search for greater effectiveness and flexibility within organisations, emphasis has shifted towards the consideration of 'people' issues such as motivation and leadership. A better motivated and well-led workforce will prove to be more flexible and capable of coping with environmental change and complexity.

A study of electronics companies in the UK by Burns and Stalker (1961) attempted to establish why some companies were able to cope with changes in their environment, specifically dynamism in their product markets, while others were inept in this regard. They argued that successful innovators had developed an 'organic' structure while those with 'mechanistic' structures were less able to adapt. Lawrence and Lorsch (1967) found a similar relationship between the business environment and the internal structure of the firm in the USA. Where they differed from earlier researchers was that they did not believe that organisations or their environments were uniform or unchanging. They postulated that the more turbulent and complex the environment the greater the degree of difference between sub-parts of the organisation. Hence they argued that successful companies were those that developed appropriate degrees of differentiation between specialist departments while simultaneously promoting integration calling on common goals.

In environments that are certain and stable, organisations will tend to develop a form and structure which is most efficient in relation to that environment, probably one with a high degree of managerial control and mechanistic structures and systems. If an organisation's environment is uncertain and complex, managers design structures with greater in-built flexibility. However, perception may play a part in this process – that is, managers in organisations which have an organic structure may perceive the environment as being dynamic and uncertain while those in more mechanistic structures may perceive their environment as being more certain; the reality may be quite different. Nevertheless, there are many firms in the company graveyard whose managers 'perceived' their environments as being stable and certain when in fact they harboured destructive dynamic forces.

There has been research concerning the relationship between groups of organisations and their collective environment. Grinyer and Spender (1979), for example, argued that organisations in a particular industry sector, such as the motor vehicle industry or the higher education sector, have a tendency to develop 'recipe knowledge' about how to operate in that business. This recipe knowledge influences their collective view of the industry environment. They argue, however, that companies who continually develop their recipe knowledge in line with changes in the environment are likely to succeed and prosper at the expense of their more sluggish competitors. These organisations are not imprisoned by the recipe.

As argued in the section above on environmental forecasting, it is often suggested that the success of commercial firms depends on their ability to foresee and subsequently act upon environmental information. Miles and Snow (1978) have identified various types of organisation which possess quite different capabilities and motivations in this respect. Their typology of organisations refers to the 'style' in which they operate strategically. This style influences their relationship with the business environment and is, in turn, influenced by that environment. Hence 'defender' organisations, they argue, attempt to create a stable environment which suits their non-dynamic structure and strategy, while 'prospectors' view their environment as ever-changing and seek continual strategic and structural adjustments to cope with changes. They are continually searching for new opportunities and in the process may create change and uncertainty for others within their competitive environment. They identify two other categories of organisation, 'analysers' and 'reactors'. The former are capable of acting in both stable and unstable environments, a quality of considerable value. 'Reactors' act only when environmental change 'forces' them to do so. They are not 'proactive' organisations. Boyd *et al.* (1993) state that 'given these differences in internal versus external focus, one would expect a greater potential for environmental misperception among defenders or reactors, relative to analysers'.

All four types of organisation, it is argued, 'enact' or create their environment. What they choose to see and how they choose to interpret that environment is quite unique to each organisation. Hence a defender may view ostensibly the same environment as a prospector yet see stability and continuity all around while the prospector sees only change and opportunity. Clearly each organisation filters data to suit its own capabilities and concerns. Executives selectively misinterpret aspects of their environment. These filters include individual managers' cognitive processes, organisational culture and politics, other group or team factors and the strategic orientation of the organisation. Therefore, as stated above, it is quite possible for two organisations to view the same environmental change as either a glorious opportunity for growth and prosperity or, depending on their perception, a catastrophe threatening organisational survival.

More recently the development of chaos theory has stressed that, because of the unpredictability and constant flux which characterise the business environment, organisational structure and strategy need to be fundamentally reappraised.

Strategic planning

The strategic planning process in organisations is the subject of considerable attention in the field of business and management. The academic and, increasingly, the practitioner worlds are engaged in lively debate over issues such as the nature of strategy formulation. To put it rather simplistically there are two broad schools of thought – the rationalist and subjectivist approaches.

The rationalist approach argues that strategic planning is, or certainly should be, undertaken in a logical and largely linear fashion. It is suggested that organisations monitor their business environment and analyse their internal resource position in order to assess what strengths and weaknesses they have which might facilitate the exploitation of environmental opportunities and the avoidance of environmental threats. A stakeholder analysis is also important at this stage.

PESTLE analysis, or the many variants upon it described above, is usually undertaken within organisations as a prelude to a more strategically orientated technique – a SWOT analysis. This acronym stands for Strengths, Weaknesses, Opportunities and Threats. As part of a strategic process of analysis an organisation may assess its strengths and weaknesses from an internal resource perspective. For example, it may conclude that it is in a sound financial state and that it utilises modern, effective technology. Its weaknesses may, for example, be an under-trained and poorly motivated staff.

It is the latter two elements of this acronym which are of particular relevance here for it is in the business environment where both opportunities and threats can be found. As a vital strategic tool businesses often attempt to identify such opportunities that they may seek to exploit and threats that they attempt to avoid.

Similarly, a popular model suggests that the initial stages of strategy formulation lie in gaining an appreciation of the degree of uncertainty in the organisation's environment. This is preceded by an audit of environmental influences. The strategic planner then conducts a structural analysis of the immediate competitive environment of the organisation before analysing the organisation's strategic position. Johnson and Scholes (2002) explain that the aim of such analysis is to develop an understanding of opportunities which can be built upon and threats which have to be overcome. Organisations can then adapt to their environment and by actively managing environmental relationships can in turn shape the changes that are occurring. The task of rational strategic management in this scenario involves reading the environment and then 'creating initiatives that will resonate with the changes that are occurring' (Morgan, 1989).

Senior management generate a series of strategic options from which choices are later made after due analysis and consideration of all parameters. The chosen strategies are then implemented.

Thus it is assumed that actual or predicted changes in the environment lead to planned strategic change in organisations. Strategic planning, therefore, is an attempt to match organisational capabilities with environmental opportunities. Hence the dominant paradigm is that organisations are in a state of 'dynamic equilibrium', continually adapting to their environment. These planning activities, it is argued, are essential for organisations to cope with environmental dynamism.

Strategic planning often tends to adopt a three- to five-year time scale, during which time the business environment of most organisations will alter significantly. However, it should be stressed that proponents of the rational approach do stress the need for 'reality embellishments' such as feedback loops (for example, to enable further environmental scanning to influence decisions at a later stage) and consideration of the role of organisational culture, politics and other contextual, non-rational, issues in the planning process.

This argument brings us to an alternative perspective on strategy formulation, the subjective approach. These alternative views are often based both on empirical research and intuitive judgement and attempt to explain the actual processes that take place in organisations. They tend to be less prescriptive. As argued above, organisations are not entirely rational or logical in their environmental-sensing or decision-making processes. Organisation-level filters of an intensely 'human' nature disrupt mechanical linear planning processes. They influence the nature and quality of information available and severely limit the range of strategic choices likely to be entertained. They also add an inescapable richness and reality to organisational activity. It is rather pointless to assume, as some traditional rational models imply, that organisational culture, politics and other human processes can, somehow, be easily managed, ignored or stopped from fundamentally influencing organisational activity.

Many academics and management writers question the almost taken-for-granted assumption that successful organisations adapt or seek to 'fit' their environment. They argue that firms that do seek adaption to their environment are prone to imitation and repetition as competitors do likewise. Many successful organisations use resources more creatively and challenge environmental assumptions. They are able to influence the environment of their competitors and, in part at least, create their own environment. This process, referred to as 'enactment', is discussed above. However, the simple rational model of strategic planning pays little attention to the notion of enactment or the way in which organisations influence their business environment.

We have argued above that organisations and individuals enact their environment and may view similar information in quite different ways. This is a non-rational process. When we make this assumption we suggest that environments are not fixed and measurable in a strict sense. They are open to multiple interpretations. Additionally, internal processes of strategic planning are not as the Rationalist School would suggest. Often crucial business decisions are based on very limited data, moulded by personal considerations or cultural norms and implemented by political expediency. Some organisations will have sophisticated planning departments; others will be strategically 'led' by a dominant stakeholder such as the managing director. There is not a great deal of evidence to suggest that one style is a guarantee of greater success than the other.

Although interesting, this subject is complex. You are very likely to investigate it in further detail if you are engaged on a structured business or management course which leads to considerations of strategic management or corporate policy. It is, however, wise at this stage to appreciate the arguments of both schools of thought and develop a broad understanding of organisational processes and academic debates.

Conclusion

It is hoped that you now have a better understanding of the business environment facing all organisations. That environment is often very complex and rapidly changing. It operates, sometimes, internationally and often nationally, as well as locally. The small local bar or mobile phone retailer, for example, may only employ a few staff and have a small turnover but will be influenced by large-scale changes in the environment. For example, changes in telecommunication and financial transaction technology operate on a global scale and will affect the way these micro companies do their business. Employment laws at a national and international level (such as the maximum working week or minimum wage enshrined in EU regulation) will influence the manager's decisions regarding staffing arrangements. Changes in competitors' behaviours and new products will influence what the two micro businesses actually sell; these products and behaviours might originate from the USA or Europe or the Far East, for example. A downturn in the fortunes of the economy, perhaps caused by rises in oil prices and uncertainty due to terrorism and war, might make potential customers think twice about buying a new mobile or going out drinking, particularly if they have become unemployed, and the small business might, in turn, struggle to survive. We have learned that the business environment represents an integrated set of forces operating at a variety of scales and impacting on all businesses. We also know that although attempts to forecast change might prove useful, there are real difficulties in predicting the future and the likely impact of even well-understood changes.

Having set the scene and defined the parameters within which we will study the international business environment, this book now takes a closer look at the individual environmental forces which influence organisations. Chapters 2–8 run through the PESTLE factors and competitive forces. Each chapter will explore the forces at play and the implications of these for organisations. The final chapter revisits many of the themes discussed above and further develops and explores them, focusing in particular on the influence of the business environment on organisations, individuals, groups and governments. The case studies which form Part II of this book support this material.

Summary of main points

This chapter has aimed to 'set the scene' on the international business environment and to delineate the scope of this book. A number of vital issues and concepts have been covered. The key points are:

- There are a number of interrelated forces acting upon organisations which emanate from the external environment of the organisation.

- For the purpose of analysis, these forces can be placed in distinct categories, but in reality they form an interrelated and complex whole.

- Environmental forces act at a number of geo-political scales, very many at the global or international level.

- The relationship between organisation and environment is not clear-cut, as information flows from the environment to the organisation but also from the organisation to the environment.

- There are a variety of types of organisation which can be differentiated by, for example, their prime objectives or their legal status – the environment influences different types of organisation in different ways.

- Individual perception and organisational filters influence how the business environment is viewed.

- Forecasting the business environment is problematic due to change and complexity, yet many methods exist and are widely used.

- There is a relationship between the business environment and both the structure and strategy of organisations.

- There is considerable debate concerning the nature and process of strategic policy formulation but an understanding of the international business environment is essential for successful strategic management.

Discussion Questions

1. For an organisation with which you are familiar (e.g. your workplace, university or a case study from this book) identify two environmental forces for each of the PEST categories. Establish the geo-political scale(s) at which each force may operate.

2. Carry out an environmental stakeholder analysis of a organisation with which you are familiar. Place this information on a grid as shown in Figure 1.4. What does this tell you about management priorities and their chief concerns?

3. Discuss the range of forces that might act on a small or medium business in your local area, such as a café or the pub across the road or the university.

4. Select an organisational case study and identify an array of environmental variables which influence the company.

   a. Which of these variables may management be able to forecast?

   b. What are the likely sources of information to facilitate forecasting?

   c. What approaches and methods of forecasting might be employed?

   d. What would be some of the difficulties in accurately forecasting changes in these variables?

5. Conduct an impact analysis for a sector of industry with which you are familiar.

6. Discuss a scenario and the potential implications for business. The scenario could be (a) a sustained fall in birth rates, such as has been experienced in Italy in the past forty years, (b) an increase in the threat of global terrorism, or (c) a requirement for business to offer flexible working to parents of school age children.

7. Read the headlines on the front page of today's newspaper (preferably a broadsheet newspaper!). What are the implications of these news stories for business?

Web Links and Further Reading

You should refer to the web links section at the end of each chapter for useful sites related to each area discussed above. Also, many university lecturers put 'business environment' notes and other materials on their web pages, and many of these can be accessed with ease.

References

Bourgeois, L.J. (1985) 'Strategic goals, perceived uncertainty and economic performance in volatile environments', *Academy of Management Review*, 28, 548–73.

Boyd, B.K., Dess, G. and Rasheed, A.M.A. (1993) 'Divergence between archival and perceptual measures of the environment: causes and consequences', *Academy of Management Review*, 18(2), 204–26.

Burns, T. and Stalker, G.M. (1961) *The Management of Innovation*, London: Tavistock.

Daft, R.L. (1992) *Organisational Theory and Design*, West Publishing.

Grinyer, P. and Spender, J.C. (1979) 'Recipes, crises and adaption in mature businesses', *International Studies of Management & Organisation*, 9, 13.

Hamel, G. and Prahalad, C.K. (1994) *Competing for the Future*, Cambridge, MA: Harvard Business Press.

Huber, G.P. (1985) 'Temporal stability and response-order biases in participant descriptions of organizational decisions', *Academy of Management Journal*, 28, 943–50.

Johnson, J. and Scholes, K. (2002) *Exploring Corporate Strategy: Text and Cases*, 6th edn, Hemel Hempstead: Prentice Hall.

Lawrence, P.R. and Lorsch, J.W. (1967) *Organisation and Environment*, Cambridge, MA: Harvard Graduate School of Business Administration.

Miles, R.E. and Snow, C.C. (1978) *Organizational Strategy, Structure and Process*, New York: McGraw-Hill.

Miller, D. (1988) 'Relating Porter's business strategies to environment and structure', *Academy of Management Journal*, 31, 280–308.

Morgan, G. (1989) *Creative Organisational Theory: A Resourcebook*, Sage.

Peace, J.A. and Robinson, R.B. (1994) *Strategic Management: Formulation, Implementation and Control*, 5th edn, Chicago: Irwin.

Robbins, S.P. (1992) *Essentials of Organisational Behaviour*, 3rd edn, Hemel Hempstead: Prentice Hall International.

Smircich, L. and Stubbart, C. (1985) 'Strategic management in an enacted environment', *Academy of Management Review*, 10(4), 724–36.

Weick, K. (1979) *The Social Psychology of Organizing*, Reading, MA: Addison-Wesley.

Wilson, D.C. (1992) *A Strategy of Change*, Routledge.

2

The Competitive Environment

Jamie Weatherston

Learning Outcomes

On completion of this chapter you should be able to:

- recognise the difficulties that businesses face in a dynamic competitive international environment;

- understand the traditional microeconomic view of competition and be able to apply its models to a business situation;

- be aware of the classification of markets and appreciate how competition in markets differs;

- appreciate the factors on which competition is based;

- distinguish between the various tools of competitive analysis and apply them to commercial examples;

- be familiar with the role of government and regulatory authorities in the market at different geo-political scales and be able to assess measures of intervention;

- illustrate how public interest is served in market activities.

Key Concepts

- market economy
- price mechanism
- market structures
- monopoly

- oligopoly
- monopolistic competition
- nature of products and services
- concentration
- market entry
- barriers to entry
- economies of scale
- experience curve
- competition
- collusion
- contestable markets
- Porter's five forces

Introduction

In this chapter we will seek to identify the competitive environment and determine how its dynamic nature affects both the level of competition that an organisation faces and the future profitability of organisations. It has been suggested by Thompson and Strickland (1995) that when crafting an organisation's strategy one of the major tasks facing decision-makers is an assessment of the company's external environment, in particular the industry and competitive conditions in which the organisation operates. The structural characteristics of an industry play a key role in determining the nature and intensity of competition within it (Grant, 1995). Using the traditional microeconomic approach we will outline the basic economic problem and the approach of economic systems to that problem, and examine how resources are allocated in differing economies. We will identify the conditions that determine the level of complexity in a market and investigate each of the market structures to which these conditions apply. An exploration of market structures and an understanding of the differences between the structures presented by economists provide a useful starting point for this analysis.

Organisations will always attempt to reduce the dynamism and uncertainty of the market in which they trade. Many tactics, some legal, others not, can be employed to this end. A major part of this chapter will be devoted to the identification and analysis of the tactics exhibited. The huge sums of money that some organisations invest in research and development and advertising may be necessary to maintain the organisations' position in the market and raise a barrier to prevent others from entering that market. Coca-Cola and Nike, for example, spend huge sums of money on marketing. Similarly, the need for research and development spending in the pharmaceutical industry limits entry by other organisations. Other activities, for example entering into agreements that restrict competition, evidenced by the vitamin cartel, may have a similar effect.

The Competition Commission in the United Kingdom reports that throughout much of the 1990s there appear to have been a variety of cartels operating in the vitamins industry, where collusion among the major manufacturers maintained prices and allocated markets for individual vitamins. These activities have led to prosecution, fines and imprisonment of executives.

The European Commission has sent statements of objections to 13 producers of bulk vitamins with regard to suspected price-fixing cartel activity. Companies have pleaded guilty to the US Department of Justice on charges of participation in various cartels in the USA and elsewhere. Canadian and Australian authorities have also imposed fines on certain vitamins producers for cartel activity. In the case of both vitamins C and B2, the Competition Commission were told that these cartels operated from around 1991 to 1995. BASF, and some other producers, said that the reason for the breakdown of the cartels was emerging competitive pressures and the desire of certain companies to respond aggressively to these rather than to surrender market share (Competition Commission, 2001).

This type of collusive activity may be against the interests of consumers. If that is the case then regulatory authorities need to become involved, as in the case above. We will examine the role and the activities of these bodies at three geo-political levels: local, national and global. The concept of contestable markets will also provide the reader with an additional interpretation of the market.

Michael Porter's (1980) structural analysis of competitive forces (the five forces model) establishes the factors which determine industry profitability and competitiveness. This model originates from the traditional approach and provides a useful basis from which strategists can begin to build a picture of their competitive position. Competitor analysis can also be used in conjunction with the five forces model to create a more in-depth analysis of the position. Throughout the chapter we will be identifying the tools and techniques which are needed to carry out an investigation of the competitive environment. The starting point for our analysis is the traditional economic view.

The traditional economic view

The basic economic problem is how to allocate scarce resources among the almost limitless wants of consumers in society. Choices have to be made about what and how to produce and for whom goods and services should be produced.

An examination of the theory as it applies to two theoretical types of economy is useful, that is, the command economy and the market economy.

The command economy

In a command economy the questions of allocation are answered by the state. The state decides on the volume of production, the types of goods and services produced, the type of work each citizen will do, the ways in which they will be rewarded, the level of pollution control and many other aspects of life. Individual citizens must accept a large measure of direction in their daily life.

The market economy and the price mechanism

The market economy is at the other end of the spectrum. Within this system the consumer is 'king' – consumer sovereignty. Choices made by consumers directly affect the allocation of resources in the economy. Consumers aim to gain the maximum 'utility', or satisfaction, from the goods that they purchase, and are, therefore, concerned about the price they have to pay for items they consume. They express their choices by the prices they are willing to pay for goods.

In the market economy firms choose the methods by which to produce goods and services. They are concerned, primarily, with the costs of making their products or providing their service and the revenues they receive. In this situation firms aim for the greatest return on their investment.

Ideally, the price mechanism allows people to buy what they want, subject to income constraints. The nature and quantity of what is produced will be influenced by consumer preference, expressed through buying behaviour. The ways in which goods are produced will be decided by competition between producers who will seek to produce at lowest cost. The number of people who are able to buy the goods and services will also be decided by the market. Those whose services are in greatest demand will receive the greatest rewards, in terms of wages, and so have the greatest buying power. Graduates would come into this category. This mechanism registers people's preferences and transmits them to the firms who produce the goods for consumers to buy.

The consumer is central to the system via the operation of supply and demand. Demand influences price and price influences supply (a fuller analysis of demand and supply is given in Chapter 6). Ultimately the use of scarce factors of production – that is, land, labour and capital – is dictated by the demands or wants of individuals. When consumers want more of a product than is being supplied, price increases, resources are attracted to the industry and supply expands. When demand falls the opposite effect occurs. There is obviously a time lag involved in the operation of the price mechanism. The speed of the effect varies depending on the situation. In a manufacturing context it is very difficult to transfer production quickly from one good to another, in response to a change in consumer demand, because of the specific nature of machinery or the need to re-train labour. However, the situation is not quite so clear cut as it seems, as Minicase 2.1 shows.

The traditional microeconomic view of competition emphasises the role of market structures in the market economy:

> A market is a set of arrangements by which buyers and sellers are in contact to exchange goods and services.
>
> (Begg *et al.*, 1994)

This view is based on the structure–conduct–performance (s–c–p) paradigm which tells us that demand and supply establish the basic conditions of the market. This, in turn, prescribes the market structure, the conduct of the organisation in the market and its performance, for example its turnover and profit (see Figure 2.1).

Readers may be unfamiliar with economic theories relating business activity to market structure. As competition is based on these theories it is necessary to have an understanding of some of the concepts raised by microeconomics.

Minicase 2.1   Coffee: plaything for speculation

In the past years the price of coffee has been subject to regular fluctuations. In 1997, the prices increased considerably; later the same year, the prices collapsed. In the first half year of 1997, the price of arabica coffee, the most important coffee sort, tripled on the forward market of New York.

More than other cash crops from developing countries, coffee has attracted the interest of investors and speculators. Large financial investors have, since the dissolution of the International Coffee Agreement in 1989, a mounting influence on coffee prices. When the coffee prices were low, investors fell with large fortunes on the coffee market. They are not interested in coffee itself; they speculate only in the expectation of selling the coffee after a lapse of time with great benefits. At the moment they decide to take their profits, the coffee price collapses like a house of cards. Speculators thus intensify the 'price tendencies', one moment up, the other down. The cynical thing about this price story is that coffee farmers hardly get anything out of it.

Coffee farmers hardly profit from higher prices

The profits from higher coffee prices end up for the greater part with the trade companies and the speculators who dispose of the coffee. Most of the time they are not the small-scale farmers. Because of a lack of money, they sell the coffee as soon as possible, sometimes when the berries are still on the bushes. The farmers are not in a position to bargain for the best prices, let alone that they can wait for better times. For the coffee pickers on the plantations the situation is somewhat different. The large landowners do not pay any more pick wages when there are higher yields. So, also the coffee pickers hardly benefit from higher prices.

Gordon Nyendwoha, a coffee farmer in Uganda

Uganda and coffee are inextricably linked. Coffee is the main source of income for farmers and it forms the heart of the Ugandan economy. Three-quarters of the population earn money from the cultivation of or the trade in coffee. Gordon and Monica Nyendwoha form one of the millions of Ugandan families who rely on coffee. They grow their own food on their 'shamba', but coffee is their only source of income. The fluctuations of coffee prices on the world market therefore have a direct impact on the everyday life of peasant families. Gordon Nyendwoha: 'Today I receive only half of last year's price! The year before I had enough money to pay secondary school fees for my eldest child. Nowadays, not any more. What would I do if the coffee price was higher? Send all my children to school, of course! To allow them to do better than me.'

Doors closed for processed coffee

Coffee cannot be transported across the globe without restrictions. The European Union, for example, applies a range of regulations to control the coffee trade. All coffee entering the EU is subject to an import duty. The higher the level of processing, the higher the tariff. This so-called 'tariff escalation' protects coffee roasters in the EU against competition from outside the EU.

Source: Fairworld [Online], 'Pangea', available from: http://www.citinv.it/equo/newsletter/news3/Inglese/food7.html [accessed 9 December 2002]

Questions

1. Explain why coffee growers and pickers have to take the price on offer (refer also to Chapter 6).

2. Identify and comment on other trade or non-tariff barriers that operate against the interests of the developing world.

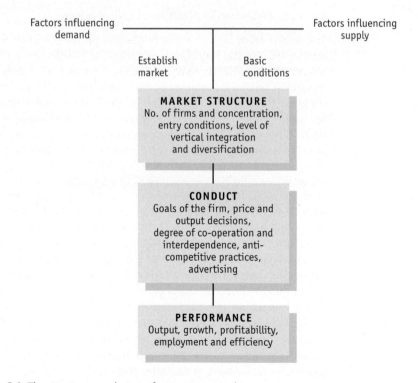

Figure 2.1 The structure–conduct–performance approach

Economists distinguish between various types of market which are classified into four general types: perfectly competitive, monopoly, oligopoly and monopolistic competition. The classification and correspondingly the level of competition is based largely on:

- the nature of the product that is supplied, which in turn is determined by demand and cost conditions facing the market;

- the number and concentration of firms in the market; and

- market entry conditions including the existence of barriers to entry and the level of information available to firms and customers.

We will now look at each of these factors.

The nature of the product or service

It is important to differentiate between products or services offered as their nature will affect competition. It is usual to distinguish between homogeneous and heterogeneous products, that is, products of the same sort and those of different sorts.

If a number of organisations are selling an identical or homogeneous product then the ability of producers to set the price of that product is reduced. For example, the price that a pub can charge for a standard pint of lager may be constrained by other pubs in the locality. Competitive behaviour is limited because the individual organisation has no market power. If the product is differentiated in some way – for example, a bottled international brand lager – then the seller has an increased ability to decide the price, and other aspects of competition, because the product is differentiated. Would you pay more for this type of product, over the standard offering?

This ability to differentiate products is recognised as essential and is used widely by organisations. The brewing industry produces heterogeneous products, e.g. lager. Each brew is different, though each still has the fundamental characteristics that distinguish it as a lager. Even if different brews look and taste very similar it may be possible for brewers to create a difference through marketing. Marketing is an important differentiating tool that is effective in promoting brand image. Brand recognition and customer loyalty are often important advantages held by incumbents (that is, organisations that already have an established position in the market). The biggest lager brands are still getting bigger, by both volume and value, with Carling still the largest overall, while Stella Artois is making impressive strides in the premium sector. Mintel's own research shows that 58 per cent of lager consumers prefer to buy a well-known brand, which endorses the brand owners' strategies to focus on their core brands (Mintel, 2001).

Number of firms and concentration

If there is just one organisation in the market then there is no competition. That organisation is a monopolist and, if not restrained by regulation, capable of making substantial profits. On 20 March 2001, the European Commission issued its first decision under Article 82 of the EC Treaty in the postal sector. It found that the German postal operator, Deutsche Post AG (DPAG), had abused its dominant position in the market for business parcel services by granting fidelity rebates and engaging in predatory pricing. In view of the long-standing market foreclosure caused by its practices, a number of requirements were imposed on DPAG including a fine of €24 million (European Commission, 2001).

It is evident from looking at the former activities of companies such as BT in the United Kingdom or Enron in the United States that the level of profit in the home market can increase an organisation's ability to compete in international markets, with companies able to utilise their resources in an extremely competitive environment.

As the number of organisations in the market rises, competition increases and the ability of organisations to protect their profits declines. Hamburger stalls at any festival or sporting event, or ice-cream sellers on a beach, for example, face intense competition as consumer choice is multiplied.

It is not only the number of organisations that decides the extent of competition in a market. The level of concentration also affects the nature of competition. Concentration measures the share that the largest companies have of the total market output and reveals the extent of the domination by those large companies. Market concentration can be measured by the concentration ratio (CR):

The *n*-firm concentration ratio is the market share of the *n* largest firms in an industry.

Let us take an example of an industry with a turnover of £350 million where the four largest organisations have a combined share of £245 million. The concentration ratio of the four largest organisations is the output of the four largest firms divided by the total market, that is

245/350 × 100 = 70%

The four-firm concentration ratio is 70 per cent, that is CR4 70. The most commonly used measures are the four- and five-firm concentration ratios. In the Belgian Horeca sector (hotels, restaurants and cafes) for example, Interbrew, the largest Belgian brewer based in Brussels, holds an overall market share of roughly 56 per cent. The second brewer Alken-Maes (now part of Scottish Courage, previously part of Danone) has around 13 per cent of this market. The share of the third-largest brewer Haacht is somewhere around 6 per cent. The fourth brewer, Palm, holds roughly 5 per cent of the market. Together, the four main brewers represent around 80 per cent of the Belgian Horeca market CR4 80 (European Commission, 2002).

The concentration ratio should give an indication of the amount of competition within an industry. Industries with low concentration ratios may be more competitive because each organisation is competing with similarly sized rivals. No one organisation in this market wields more market power than the others. It is also apparent that the less concentrated an industry, the lower the barriers to entry (and vice versa). If there are few barriers to entry then new organisations can enter the market relatively easily and capture market share. This effectively increases competitive pressures in that industry. (See below for further explanation of barriers to entry.)

Alternatively, a high concentration ratio may indicate a smaller degree of competition, as in the retail sector, where it should be possible for each organisation to protect its share. This is particularly likely to occur if the market is still growing. We will analyse this in more detail when looking at the market for goods and services.

Evidence suggests that market concentration increased sharply until the 1980s and it is still continuing. One sector which has seen substantial change in market concentration is the United States textbook market which is now dominated by three main suppliers. These three now account for approximately 62 per cent of the industry whereas in 1990 it was only 35 per cent.

The number of organisations and their concentration is not the only important factor to consider when analysing an organisation's competitive position. Table 2.1 shows two markets, each with a similar CR4. In the Belgian Horeca market the second-largest organisation has a market share of just 23 per cent of that of the largest organisation. In the United Kingdom, the two largest supermarkets are much closer in size, and the rest of the market is more evenly distributed amongst the top four.

The competitive nature of these markets is likely to be very different, even though the CR4 is very similar. If this concentration ratio is used as the only measure it could be inferred that the Belgian Horeca market was not particularly competitive. However, this could not be further from the truth.

The concentration of a market is only one indicator which should be appraised in conjunction with others when assessing the competitiveness of a market. These examples illustrate a basic problem with the concentration ratio measure, that it gives no information about inequality or the relative market share within the group of organisations selected.

Table. 2.1 Relative size within a market (%)

UK Supermarket	Market Share	Belgian Brewers	Market Share
Tesco	24.2	Interbrew	56
J.Sainsbury	18.6	Alken-Maes	13
Asda	16.3	Haacht	6
Safeway	10.1	Palm	7
4 firm concentration ratio	69.2	4 firm concentration ratio	80

Source: European Commission (2002) and http://www.corporatewatch.org.uk/pages/whats_wrong_supmkts.htm [accessed 4 December 2002]

Herfindahl–Hirschman Index (HHI)

The Herfindahl–Hirschman Index (HHI) is an alternative measure of market dominance and concentration which attempts to overcome the problem of the concentration ratio measure. It was developed in the United States and is used by many regulatory authorities, including the US and UK, particularly when considering merger activity. The HHI formula is shown below and an example is shown in Minicase 2.2.

$$\sum_{j=1}^{n} (\% \text{ market share})^2$$

The HHI measures not only the number of organisations in the market but also the inequality between them, in terms of market share. A score of over 1800 points on the HHI represents a highly concentrated market. A merger which creates a market with this level of concentration will raise concerns (Fishwick, 1993). The lower the index, the more competitive the market.

The 1992 United States guidelines specify that the score on the post-merger HHI has to be less than 1000 for the merger not to have an adverse effect on competition in the market.

Market entry conditions

Many markets present severe barriers to entry to prospective competitors while in others barriers are almost non-existent. It is clearly easier to open a small restaurant than to establish a Formula One racing team! The barriers in each case are very different. Barriers to entry can be categorised into two groups, so-called innocent barriers and those deliberately erected to prevent entrants.

Barriers erected deliberately

In some cases incumbents may take action to restrict entry. This could involve increasing expenditure on R&D, the introduction of new technology, advertising, legal action or rewarding customers through fidelity rebates. Barriers founded on reputation – for example, the use of predatory pricing which lowers the price paid by the consumer – can be very effective in making new entrants think twice about the attractiveness of the market or be used to force competitors out. Northcliffe Newspapers have been punished for alleged predatory pricing of advertising at its Aberdeen-based newspapers. The Office of Fair Trading said Northcliffe slashed advertising rates at the *Herald & Post* in an underhand attempt to stop advertisers from taking their business to the *Aberdeen & District Independent*, a rival freesheet, in an attempt to 'expel' its only competitor (Milmo, 2002).

Brand proliferation also acts as a barrier to entry. Multiple brands, produced by the same manufacturer, compete against each other but also present an effective barrier to new products. It is difficult for a new entrant to establish a large market niche with

Minicase 2.2   Analysing the Safeway takeover
using the HHI

It was clear in January 2003 as Tesco, the sixth contestant, entered the area, that
the fight to take over Safeway would be a hard-fought battle. Using the approaches we have already outlined it is possible to undertake an analysis of the
market that the takeover may create.

Grocery market shares from 1998/9–2000/1

	1998/99 %	1999/00 %	2000/01 %
Tesco	22.8	23.6	24.9
Sainsbury's	18.6	18.2	17.7
Asda	12.8	14.0	14.5
Safeway	10.4	10.5	10.7
Somerfield	4.8	4.5	3.7
Kwik Save	4.7	3.5	2.6
Wm Morrison	4.3	4.9	5.4
Iceland	2.8	2.8	2.8
Waitrose	2.7	2.7	3.1
Lidl	1.0	1.3	1.4
Aldi	1.6	1.5	1.3
Netto	0.6	0.6	0.6
Other multiples	0.8	0.9	0.8
Total multiples	**87.9**	**89.0**	**89.5**
Co-ops	6.2	5.4	5.0
Symbols	1.3	1.2	1.3
Other independents	4.6	4.3	4.2
Total	**100.0**	**100.0**	**100.0**

*Source: adapted from 'Food Retailing', August 2001, Retail Intelligence UK –
Retail Plus
http://reports.mintel.com/sinatra/mintel/reports/ [accessed 21.1.03]*

Using the formula above and the assumption that there are five other multiples in the market the HHI in 2001 is:

$$1(24.9)^2 + 1(17.7)^2 + 1(14.5)^2 + 1(10.7)^2 + 1(3.7)^2$$
$$+ 1(2.6)^2 + 1(5.4)^2 + 1(2.8)^2 + 1(3.1)^2$$
$$+ 1(1.4)^2 + 1(1.3)^2 + 5(0.8)^2 = 1329.07$$

If Safeway is acquired by one of its Supermarket competitors it is possible to see the effect that this will have on the competitiveness within the market. We can show the position if the takeover by Morrisons is successful:

$$1(24.9)^2 + 1(17.7)^2 + 1(16.1)^2 + 1(14.5)^2 + 1(3.7)^2$$
$$+ 1(2.6)^2 + 1(2.8)^2 + 1(3.1)^2 + 1(1.4)^2$$
$$+ 1(1.3)^2 + 5(0.8)^2 = 1444.63$$

We can also see that the CR4 rises from 68 to 73.

The takeover of Safeway by Morrisons would clearly send the HHI still higher, representing a more highly concentrated market, with little room for further merger activity.

Questions

1. Calculate the HHI assuming that Safeway were taken over by Tesco. Carry out the same process assuming the takeover is by Sainsbury. Comment on your findings.

2. A takeover by either Tesco or Sainsbury is likely to be referred to the Competition Commission. Why is this the case? Would a takeover by either of these companies proceed?

only one product. The world market for soap powders is dominated by two companies, Procter and Gamble (P&G) and Unilever. They do not sell only one homogenous product each, but have a range of differentiated products, targeted at particular segments of the market. This process of differentiation has increased recently. From 1937 to 1980 P&G launched only seven detergents onto the market. This compares with the introduction of fourteen new lines from 1989 to 1994. By 1998 P&G had twenty-six detergents available on the United Kingdom market.

Hotel development in the United States over the last decade has demonstrated an acceleration of brand proliferation. Research indicates that franchise or chain branded hotels command an overwhelming market share versus independent hotels. The percentage of United States independent hotel rooms versus total supply slipped from

38.9 per cent in 1990 to 30.3 per cent in 1999 due to significant growth in the economy and mid-scale chain sectors. However, independents have made an impact in major markets and specialised resort locations (Swig, 2000).

Proctor and Gamble and Unilever could be described as having created barriers to entry by the scale of advertising that they undertake. In 1998 they were first and second highest in worldwide advertising expenditure – Proctor and Gamble's advertising expenditure was $4747.6 million and Unilever's $3428.5 million. It is interesting to note that in the soft drinks market the two leading firms in the United States in 2001, Coca-Cola with a market share of 47.3 per cent and Pepsi with 31.6 per cent, were also the biggest advertisers.

Innocent barriers

Innocent barriers arise when an organisation has absolute cost advantages. In this case the incumbent organisation is able to produce at such a cost that it is uneconomical for another organisation to try and enter the market because their unit costs are, in comparison, much higher. The unit cost is the cost of producing one unit of output. In this situation organisations are said to benefit from economies of scale.

Barriers to entry will be investigated in more detail below.

Economies of scale

Figure 2.2 shows a situation where an increase in size of plant from 10 000 to 30 000 units results in a fall of average total cost (ATC) from £1000 to £500 per unit (average

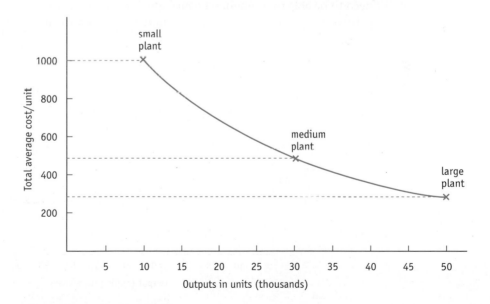

Figure 2.2 Absolute cost advantage

total cost is total cost divided by output, i.e. TC/O). A large plant with a capacity of 50 000 units reduces ATC even further, to £300 per unit.

Figure 2.3 shows that average costs per unit of production fall as output rises. Costs fall not at a uniform rate but at a declining rate, producing the typical U-shaped long-run average cost curve. When the curve becomes horizontal this output is known as the minimum efficient scale of production (MES), in this case, approximately 80 million tons per year. In some industries economies of scale are substantial, for example in telecommunications and car manufacture.

If the MES is large in relation to the total market demand then it will be almost impossible for a new entrant to successfully enter the market. An organisation trying to enter the market at lower levels of output, e.g. 30 million tons per year in the example in Figure 2.3, would be at a severe cost disadvantage to the incumbents. The price that the new entrant would have to charge to break even would be much higher than those charged by the incumbent organisations that are experiencing economies of scale, and so it would be very difficult for the new organisation to set a price to attract customers.

The possibility of successful entry into the market is slim, unless the organisation were able to target a particular segment of the market that is regarded as unimportant by the incumbents. The new entrant would still face a tough struggle as it would be a formidable task to establish a brand image and customer recognition over a very narrow product range. For ten years now, China has attempted to develop its automotive industry through an industrial policy approach closely modelled on that of the Korean government in the 1970s. However, the size of the typical Chinese firm is small in a sector with well-known economies of scale and even the largest firm operates far below the minimum efficient scale (Huang, 1999).

Global competition can wipe out previously concrete advantages. Organisations need to be able to respond to change quickly if they are to survive in the fiercely competitive global market. Lean production methods and flexible manufacturing have

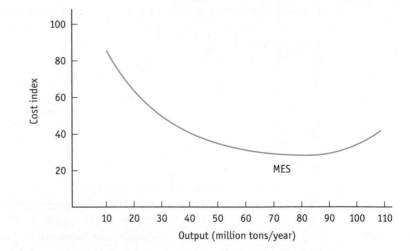

Figure 2.3 Minimum efficient scale

helped Japanese industry. The importance of innovation to support competitiveness by reducing costs and increasing quality should be recognised. The technological revolution of the past few decades has transformed retail services. Computerised information technology has facilitated the reorganisation of distribution systems and increasingly efficient stock-handling methods have enabled retailers to benefit from economies of scale.

In the pharmaceutical sector Simpson (2002) suggests the minimum efficient scale of organisation needed to discover new medicines has fallen due to a number of factors:

- advances in technology;

- the existence of a pharmaceutical industry with an insatiable demand for such discoveries;

- a capital market, in particular venture capitalists, willing to finance high risk biotechnology start-ups.

Together, she adds, these factors have provided some research scientists with a new opportunity to establish small biotechnology businesses, outside existing, large pharmaceutical companies and outside universities. Many 'scientist entrepreneurs' have taken this opportunity. From zero in the early 1980s, the United States biotechnology industry, which was the first to develop, had grown to nearly 1300 companies employing 140 000 people by 1997. The European biotechnology industry, where the United Kingdom is the largest player, started up later but has also grown rapidly: to 1000 companies with nearly 40 000 employees by 1997.

It must also be recognised that capital investment in plant and equipment can lead to overcapacity if market growth is slow. The result could be severe for some companies and industries. A number of Japan's large-scale steel plants faced closure in 1998 due to the severe recession being experienced in Japan and the Far Eastern 'tiger' economies (see Case Study 3).

It is not only economies of scale that confer advantages on organisations. We can use the experience curve phenomenon to further illustrate how advantages of incumbency can accrue to organisations.

Experience curve

The experience curve effect provides additional insight into the problems of entering a market. The experience curve was first described and popularised by the Boston Consulting Group (BCG), an American consultancy company, in 1968.

BCG observed, during studies of company performance, that incumbents in any market segment benefited from the experience that they had accumulated. The study showed a direct and constant relationship between aggregate growth in volume of production and declining cost of production. That is, as production volume increased the company became more efficient at producing the product or service, and the cost per unit of that activity therefore declined. At first cost per unit fell rapidly and then more slowly as learning opportunities were exhausted. This resulted in a progressively

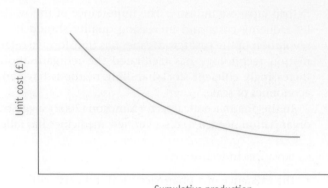

Figure 2.4 The experience curve effect

declining gradient exhibited in the experience curve (see Figure 2.4). It has been claimed that costs fall by around 15 to 30 per cent with each doubling of output.

Experience curve savings are particularly important if price levels for a product are relatively similar, because what makes a company more profitable than its competitors is the level of its costs. If an organisation can increase output relative to its competitors then it will move down the experience curve more quickly, reducing costs, and thus widening cost differentials.

BCG put forward three reasons why this fall in unit costs may occur. These were due to economies of scale, specialisation and learning. We have examined the first of these reasons above and will explore the other two next.

Specialisation

It usually becomes increasingly possible to design narrow and focused jobs as scale of production grows. Ford's car plants were at the forefront of this move in the 1920s and 1930s. Increasing specialisation through the division of labour should bring advantages. More recent use of call centres also brings in many advantages. These are summarised by Beardshaw (1992):

- increase in skill and dexterity means the task can be carried out more expertly;

- time saving through reduced down time, the time in which a worker is idle, and the time saved on training;

- individual aptitudes can be utilised so individuals can concentrate on what they do best;

- machinery can be further utilised – modern production techniques, starting with the Ford Motor Company's own production line, are able to make full use of machinery because of specialisation of the workforce;

- breaking down the process into separate tasks allows for closer management control.

Learning

It is important to understand that organisations as well as individuals learn. As tasks are undertaken more frequently, individuals can learn and become more proficient at their work. Labour costs should decline. Similarly, an organisation should be able to learn and put in place efficient systems and procedures which should also translate into cost savings. Learning is likely to be the most important component in the experience curve for organisations in high-technology industries. Maintenance of learning and its conversion into organisational knowledge is a key element of competitive advantage for many high-tech companies. Japanese companies have been at the forefront of the global learning process, adapting the American philosophy of total quality management and advancing the ideas. This has led to the development of 'quality circles', 'kaizen' or continuous improvement, 'just-in-time manufacturing', 'right first time, every time' and many more management techniques which some Western companies are still coming to terms with.

The experience curve has been shown to hold for such diverse products as photovoltaic solar cells, B17-bombers during the second World War, AT&T long distance voice tariffs over a 50-year period, the Ford model T car, shipbuilding, airframe construction, software project management and semiconductors. The advantages of high volume and rapid movement down the experience curve are advantages that large businesses, by definition, possess. Competitors in the credit card industry – including American Express, Capital One and Providian – are developing customised online offerings and integrating them closely with other delivery channels. They are using their experience as established experts at remote marketing and customer management, swiftly incorporating and utilising client information to hone tailored offerings to select individuals (Olson *et al.*, 2001).

Boeing's domination of the world aircraft market is in part due to learning by experience, gained from early entry into the market, which has been translated into more efficient operations. That Boeing's dominant position in the market seems to be under threat may, in turn, be due to other manufacturers, particularly the relatively young European competitor Airbus Industrie, having closed the gap on Boeing in terms of learning and experience. The combined effects of experience and economies of scale mean that many big companies gain substantial advantage. Not only are costs lower but visibility in the marketplace is also greater.

Smaller companies may find that their ability to control overhead costs and maintain a lean organisation, while significant, can be matched by well-managed, larger companies that understand and exploit economies of scale and scope (Camillus, 1998).

The ease of entry into a market is probably the major factor influencing competition. If organisations can enter a market at relatively little cost they are likely to seize the opportunity. Various strategies, as we have seen, are available to organisations that enable them to construct barriers that prospective competitors find difficult to overcome. One of the main deterrents to organisations entering a market is the risk of losing valuable funds in the venture. We explore this further by examining the contestable market approach below.

At this stage it is useful to undertake a closer examination of the market for goods and services. As in the business world very few organisations operate within perfectly competitive markets, we can concentrate our analysis on the monopolistic, oligopolistic and monopolistically competitive markets. We will draw on the ideas introduced in this section.

The market for goods and services

In this section we will investigate the different competitive environment that organisations will face in monopoly, oligopoly and monopolistic competition and probe some of the issues surrounding each configuration. Table 2.2 summarises the characteristics of these markets.

Monopoly

The economists' view

Economists view monopolists as the sole supplier of an industry's output, producing goods and services for which no substitute is available. In this extreme case a monopoly is said to have a concentration ratio of 100, it being the only organisation supplying the market. Those monopolies that enjoy massive economies of scale are called natural monopolies; in this case there is only room for one firm producing at minimum efficient scale – for example, water, gas and electricity suppliers. The market power of these organisations is controlled by regulatory authorities (see below). Monopolies can arise because of barriers to entry that prevent competition. These

Table 2.2 Models of market structure

Characteristics	Perfect Competition	Monopolistic Competition	Oligopoly	Monopoly
No. and size of sellers	Many, small	Many, small	Few, large	One, no close substitutes
Type of product	Homogeneous	Differentiated	Differentiated or homogeneous	One
Entry barriers	None	None	Low, some	High
CR (%)	0	Low	High	100
Example	Fruit and vegetable markets	High street clothes retailers	Airlines, car manufacturers	Saudi Telecommunications Co

barriers may be due to actions taken by incumbents or innocent barriers. De Beers' very strong position in the supply of diamonds relies on its central selling organisation controlling 80 per cent of world trade in rough diamonds.

Monopolists, because of their protected position, need not be overly concerned by the threat of new organisations entering the industry in the short or medium term.

It is possible for the monopolist to make monopoly or abnormal profits in the long run, unlike in a competitive industry where profits are eroded by new organisations entering the market. Indeed companies which hold monopoly positions, and are able to maintain large profits, are not uncommon. In Morocco the tobacco market is dominated by the state monopoly, which made profits of 173.3 million dirhams ($15 million) in 2000. Saudi Telecommunications Co (STC), set up in 1998 as the first step in a process towards privatising Saudi telecoms, achieved net profit of 3.47 billion Saudi riyals ($928 million) in 2001 (BBC, 2002). The utilities, privatised in the United Kingdom during the 1980s and 1990s, on the whole enjoyed monopoly positions in their home market, though for many this position has been eroded. However, their annual reports are widely reported in the media, and profit announcements are often accompanied by a furore from consumer groups who are concerned that profits are being made at the expense of the consumer.

The view of the authorities

An alternative view of monopoly is employed by the competition authorities. In the United Kingdom a scale monopoly exists where one firm has at least 25 per cent of a market. A complex monopoly exists where two or more firms together account for at least 25 per cent of a market and engage in similar conduct. In the United States federal antitrust policy began with the signing of the Sherman Act in 1890. It was aimed at benefiting consumers. In the words of Senator John Sherman, the act was to outlaw arrangements 'designed, or which tend, to advance the cost to the consumer' (Brozen, 1978). Baçina (2002) shows that sales of games consoles in the three key markets are dominated by three companies: Sony, Nintendo and Microsoft (see Table 2.3). The

Table 2.3 Market share of leading games consoles

	US Market Share%	Japan Market Share %	Europe Market Share %
PlayStation2	61	63	75
Xbox	18	4	14
Gamecube	21	28	11

Source: 'PS2 tops sales ... yet again', Friday, 29 November 2002,
http://www.civicvideo.com.au/index2.php4?page_id=games&&n_id=1322
[accessed 20 January 2003]

position shows that although an organisation does not control the whole of the market, its market position may confer on it enormous power. Look back at the concentration ratio!

Problems associated with monopoly

Lack of competition in the market may mean that there is a danger that a monopolist can take action that may adversely affect the consumer. Results could include:

- restriction of output, as the monopolist can create a shortage, depriving consumers while increasing its profits;

- price fixing, as the monopolist can restrict supply to those who can afford to pay higher prices;

- regulation of terms of supply, as the monopolist can impose harsh terms on consumers;

- removal of consumer choice – for example, the situation for consumers buying cars or any consumer goods in the former Communist states of Eastern Europe was dire.

Minicase 2.3 illustrates some of these potential problems.

Because monopolists may try to manipulate the market against the wishes of the consumer, it is necessary for other forms of control to be applied to the market.

Control of monopoly power

The imposition of strict controls provides a challenge to the monopolist's position and its ability to make profits. Control of monopoly can take a number of forms. In an effort to limit the dangers of monopoly power many monopolies have to be regulated by the government or its agencies. Control of monopolies is not only the province of national government but is increasingly coming under a higher tier of control, that of the European Union. The main regulating body in the United Kingdom is the Competition Commission established by the Competition Act 1998.

The Competition Act 1998, which received royal assent in November 1998 and came into force on 1 March 2000, introduced a new domestic competition regime in the United Kingdom by outlawing cartels and other anti-competitive agreements and the abuse of a dominant position.

'It provides a strong deterrent against cartels and abuses of market power', suggested Margaret Beckett. However, agreements that provide balanced benefits, shared between consumers and business, will be permitted. The Director General of Fair Trading (DGFT) is responsible for enforcing the new legislation and has strong investigatory powers. The working of the new legislation was outlined in a DTI press release (DTI, 1997).

Minicase 2.3   Monopoly references – new cars: a report on the supply of new motor cars within the UK

The brand leaders in this market are Ford, Vauxhall, Peugeot, Renault, Volkswagen and Rover; the main additional brands Volvo, Mazda, Citroën, Nissan, BMW, Land Rover, Skoda and Audi. The combined United Kingdom market share of the top six supplier groups in 1999 was 79 per cent. Most of the 20 or so other suppliers are relatively small in global terms but Fiat, Toyota, DaimlerChrysler and Honda are substantial players in the world motor industry.

On 17 March 1999 the Competition Commission received a monopoly reference from the Director General of Fair Trading sent under the Fair Trading Act 1973 (FTA) on the supply of new cars within the United Kingdom by manufacturers and importers.

The Competition Commission identified a complex monopoly situation resulting from suppliers' practices in distributing new cars in the UK. Most of these practices relate to suppliers' operation of the selective and exclusive distribution (SED) system permitted by the Block Exemption. The 17 suppliers with 1 per cent or more of the total supply of new cars in the United Kingdom in whose favour the complex monopoly situation is said to operate together accounted for 94 per cent of the total number of new cars registered in the United Kingdom in 1999.

Although the United Kingdom car market is relatively unconcentrated, almost all sales fall within the vertical restraints imposed under the SED system. Nearly all suppliers control the entry, growth and exit of franchised dealers in their respective networks. At the core of the SED system:

* the suppliers' refusal to supply new cars to retailers other than their franchised dealers;

* the associated prohibition on dealers from reselling except to final customers and other dealers in the manufacturer's network;

* the granting of exclusive territories to dealers;

* and the requirement that dealers sell exclusively one brand of new car.

Dealer agreements typically impose many additional restrictions and obligations on dealers. This covers such matters as sales targets, standards of showrooms and other facilities, stock levels, organisation and staffing, training, customer service, advertising and promotion, accounting systems and the provision of detailed business information to the supplier.

The overall effect of the suppliers' practices has thus been to raise the United Kingdom price of new cars sold to private customers. How far prices may currently exceed the competitive level is difficult to estimate. On this basis the Commission believes that prices paid by United Kingdom private customers are currently likely to be, on average, about 10 per cent too high even after taking account of discounts, trade-in allowances and financial benefits. This amounts to some £1100 for the average car.

The Competition Commission recommended that:

- Suppliers should be prohibited from refusing to supply, on normal commercial terms, any party wishing to retail the supplier's new cars.

- Retailers should be free to sell the supplier's brand of cars to resellers.

- Suppliers should not be allowed to withhold supplies.

- Suppliers should not be allowed to grant exclusive territories.

About half of the practices which are found to be against the public interest are explicitly allowed by the Block Exemption. In order for them to be prohibited or constrained, therefore, one of three routes would have to be taken:

- the benefit of the Block Exemption would have to be unilaterally withdrawn in the case of individual agreements in the United Kingdom;

- a decision would have to be taken to prohibit acts which are permitted by the Block; or

- the Block Exemption itself would have to be changed or allowed to expire.

The Commission recommended that:

- the Secretary of State should make an order to prohibit suppliers (pending abolition of the SED system) from discriminating by price between fleet customers and dealers and from discriminating in the terms on which new cars are supplied to contract hire companies according to whether the companies' end-customers are fleet or private customers;

- in order to mitigate the adverse effects of RRPs, suppliers should be prohibited from seeking to control the prices at which dealers may advertise new cars.

Suppliers should be prevented from making agreements which cause dealers to pre-register cars and should publish information about the supply of cars which they themselves have pre-registered.

Source: Adapted from 'New cars: a report on the supply of new motor cars within the United Kingdom,' www.competition-commission.org.uk/rep_pub/reports/2000/439cars. htm#.summary [accessed 23 January 2003]

Questions

1. Given the scope of the recommendations, what future developments can you foresee in the industry?

2. Using the Competition Commission website or another suitable source comment on a situation which was said to be against the public interest.

Anti-competitive agreements

Prohibition is based on Article 85. Agreements will be prohibited that have the object or effect of preventing, restricting or distorting competition in the United Kingdom. These prohibitions replace the Restrictive Trade Practices Act 1976 (RTPA) and the Resale Prices Act 1976 (RPA). The DGFT decides if prohibitions are infringed and the level of fines and other penalties to be imposed. Beneficial effects are assessed by DGFT for exemption. Appeal is to the Competition Commission.

Abuse of a dominant market position

Prohibition is based on Article 86. Abuse of a dominant market position in the United Kingdom is prohibited. The kind of conduct that may constitute an abuse is:

- imposing unfair purchase or selling prices, or other unfair conditions;

- limiting production, markets or technical development to the prejudice of customers;

- applying dissimilar conditions to equivalent transactions with other trading parties thus placing them at a competitive disadvantage; and

- making contracts subject to the acceptance of other obligations which are irrelevant to the subject matter of the contract.

Most of the Competition Act 1980 is repealed and the Act also provides for the amendment of the Fair Trading Act 1973 (FTA) to strengthen the DGFT's investigative powers in respect of monopoly investigations, including complex monopolies. The DGFT decides if prohibitions are infringed and, if so, the level of penalties to be imposed:

- *Criteria* – whether either prohibition is infringed is decided upon based on a test on the effect it has on competition.

- *Investigation* – the DGFT has strong investigatory powers, including forcible entry/search powers.

- *Fines* – penalties of up to 10 per cent of United Kingdom turnover can be levied.

Third party rights to challenge companies and seek damages are included and alleged anti-competitive agreements and behaviour may be halted during investigation.

The European Union (Directorate General for Competition) has exclusive powers to act on certain large mergers with a European dimension. It also has powers to deal with restrictive agreements and anti-competitive practices when trade between members of the European Community, or in some cases the European Economic Area (EEA), is affected.

In the United Kingdom the privatisations of the 1980s and 1990s also spawned the growth of a number of Sectoral Regulators (utility regulators and others) that have a specific role to play in promoting or facilitating competition within their sectors:

Ofgem – in the energy markets.

Ofwat – in the water industry.

Oftel – in the telecommunications sector.

ORR – for railway services.

CAA – in relation to air traffic services.

Regulation of monopolies can also have a detrimental effect. Joseph Schumpeter (1883–1950), for example, placed particular emphasis on innovation and the ability of particular types of organisation to achieve technical advances. In this context profits of monopolistic companies can be invested into research and development. It could be argued that Microsoft has used its position to finance R&D, which has helped it to be innovative and create new products.

It is evident from this brief analysis that the authorities worldwide are intent on strengthening competition law by prohibiting anti-competitive behaviour. Monopolists do not have free rein over their market. It is up to organisations within the market to be particularly aware of how changes in the regulatory regime are going to affect them in the future and design organisational responses to meet those changes. Of increasing importance is the response of consumers to monopolists. For example, the periodic floods and droughts in some areas of the United Kingdom have provoked an outcry from consumers and consumer groups. It is in the interests of the water companies to listen to the problems of their consumers or the government may be forced to take action. Being proactive and implementing self-control, as opposed to being constrained by tight regulation, is often considered beneficial in the long run.

Schumpeter also recognised the transient nature of the monopolist's position. He suggests that a monopoly will eventually be circumvented by technology and innovation and that barriers to entry are not a serious problem to a competitive market in the long run. The position of BT, for example, has substantially altered from its position as a monopoly provider of telecommunications in the United Kingdom prior to privatisation in August 1984. Not only have regulations resulted in more competition, but the development of mobile phones, and the Internet, have had enormous implications for BT as it strives to maintain its competitive position.

Oligopoly

Oligopoly is defined as a market in which a small number of producers compete with each other. As firm concentration in markets increases then oligopoly becomes more widespread. This is largely an inevitable consequence of a market system. For example, in 1919 there were 108 car manufacturers in the United States. By 1929 this number had fallen to 44. By the end of the 1950s it had dropped to eight and today there are only three major American car manufacturers (Moore, 2002). Oligopolies can be found everywhere in cars, steel, cameras, aircraft manufacture, beer, cereals, etc. In the United States four appliance manufacturers account for 98 per cent of washing machines and four producers supply 85 per cent of beef output. In the soft drinks market in the United States the leading firms in 2001 were Coca-Cola with a market share of 47.3 per cent and Pepsi with 31.6 per cent. The next nearest competitor was Cadbury Schweppes with only 15.6 per cent (Beverage Digest, 2002).

McChesney (1999) shows how an oligopoly may emerge. The media oligopoly appears to have fewer and fewer players, which means that the companies which are left will have overwhelming market dominance. When the merger between Viacom and CBS was announced it signalled a step toward an overwhelming dominance of the United States media and indeed a global media oligopoly dominated by six giants: Time Warner; Disney; News Corporation; Viacom; Sony; and Seagram. Each company holds huge market power in a range of sectors including film, cable TV, magazines, publishing, music and even sports teams.

The United States film industry is a concentrated oligopolistic market with the big six corporations accounting for 90 per cent of theatre revenues in 1997.

The effect of this type of market dominance is also being felt in journalism. Large corporations now have an ability to affect the way people see themselves and others. The concentration of the United States media is distorting the public's perception of news and leading them to a false sense of knowledge. By any known theory of democracy, such a concentration of economic, cultural and political power in so few hands – and mostly unaccountable hands – is absurd and unacceptable (Barron, 2000). In the United States the term 'shared monopoly' is used by the Federal Trade Commission (FTC) to describe a few firms winning and holding a large share of the business in some product line.

In some cases two organisations dominate – for example in the detergent market where Procter & Gamble and Unilever are dominant. This form of oligopoly is known as a *duopoly*.

Because of the small number of competitors each organisation has to consider how its actions will affect the decisions of its competitors. Organisations are interdependent, which means that action by one organisation will elicit a response from its competitor(s). This is particularly important in regard to pricing decisions. It is likely that any change in price will be copied by competitors, with the effect of reducing profits for all organisations. Freedom of manoeuvre for an organisation is very restricted, not because of fear of entry into the market, but because of this interdependence of organisations within the market. The consequence of this is usually relative price stability in the market, with competition based on quality, branding, advertising and service. However, this is not always the case. The intense price war of 1999 hit United Kingdom supermarket profits hard. Further, in January 2003 Tesco and Asda announced a multi-million pound round of price cuts, prompted by the arrival in Britain of United States retailing group Wal-Mart following its takeover of Asda. Tesco said its customers would enjoy £80 million of price cuts on more than 1000 product lines, while Asda announced deep reductions, mainly on its George clothing range. These actions marked the end of an uneasy truce in the supermarket price war (Bowers, 2003).

Between 1981 and 1998 Walt Disney increased its advertising spend from approximately $100 million to around $1.25 billion. In the same period Coca-Cola's spend increased from $200 million to $700 million and McDonald's rose from $220 million to $1 billion. Between 1987 and 1998 Nike's spend went from $25 million to $500 million (Klein, 2000). Non-price competition has become so important, Phil Knight the Nike CEO explained, that 'For years we thought ourselves as a production-oriented company, meaning that we put all our emphasis on designing and manufacturing the product. But now we understand that the most important thing we do is market the product. We've come around to saying that Nike is a marketing-oriented company and the product is our most important marketing tool' (Willigan, 1992).

The United Kingdom grocery market provides a good example of an oligopolistic market in operation. Four organisations account for the bulk of sales. Each company must take account of the reaction of the others when it formulates its policy since its optimal strategy will depend, in part, on the response of competitors.

Economists usually distinguish further between those oligopolies that sell homogeneous products, for example oil companies, and those producing differentiated products. In reality all oligopolists try to differentiate their products, either in substance or by marketing, advertising and image creation. In markets where products are differentiated by advertising, for example the cigarette market, it is possible to erect substantial barriers that new entrants cannot overcome.

The concentration ratio in this sort of market is typically high, with each organisation holding a substantial share of the market. Market share figures for the leading brewers in the United Kingdom can be found in the Key Note Breweries and the Beer Market Report 2002. From this report it is clear that the market is dominated by a number of large companies and it is also evident that the market has a truly international flavour. The four main groups are:

- Scottish Courage (United Kingdom), which includes such, brands as Foster's, John Smith's Kronenbourg, McEwan's, Miller, Beck's and Courage;

- Interbrew, the Belgium Brewer, which has in its ranks Stella Artois, Heineken, Tennent's, Boddington's, Labbatt, Bass and Hoegaarden.

- Coors Brewers, the United States giant brews Carling, Grolsch, Caffrey's Worthington's and Stones.

- The last of the big four brewers in the market is Carlsberg-Tetley (Anglo-Danish) which was formed by the merger between Carlsberg and Tetley (see case study). Its brands include Carlsberg, Tetley, Castelmaine and Calder's.

The four firm concentration ratio, (CR4), in this market is 76, meaning that the four largest companies have a market share of 76 per cent. This leaves the rest of the competitors, which include some of the big names and brands in brewing such as Guinness and Budweiser, with only 24 per cent of the market between them. It is also possible to calculate the Herfindahl-Hirschmann Index from the data presented in the Keynote

Report, (see earlier for calculation). What other conclusions can be drawn from this calculation?

However, the large brewers do not have it all their own way. As well as the dominant brewers it is also apparent that this market does have room for smaller local brewers such as Young's brewery in Wandsworth, south west London, which is renowned for its real ale and has a substantial local market share as well as distributing more widely, though on a small scale in the rest of the United Kingdom. More recently the market has also seen an increase in the number of so-called micro-breweries, micro because of their limited capacity and small number of employees, such as Mordue brewery just outside Newcastle which have been successful in targeting a small but valuable niche market for its brews.

It is in the interest of firms to erect barriers to entry to make it difficult for new organisations to enter the market. Barriers can be created in many ways (see below). In some markets it may be possible for organisations to enter and exit at no cost, increasing the effect of competition greatly.

One way organisations can manufacture barriers to entry is by entering into agreements, known as collusion.

Collusion

Organisations in an oligopolistic market may have much to gain from some form of collaboration or collusion. This can be implicit or explicit. The aim is to jointly reduce uncertainty, prevent entry into the market and maximise profits. Collusion has a distorting effect on the market. It tends to raise prices and control output, both of which adversely affect the consumer.

In October 2002 the European Commission fined Nintendo and seven of its European distributors a total of €167.8 million for colluding to prevent trade in low-priced products. The fine on Nintendo was calculated at €149 million to reflect its size in the market concerned, the fact that it was the driving force behind the illicit behaviour and also because it continued with the infringement even after it knew the investigation was going on.

Prices for play consoles and games differed widely from one European Union country to another during the period investigated by the Commission, with the United Kingdom up to 65 per cent cheaper than Germany and the Netherlands. 'Every year, millions of European families spend large amounts of money on video games. They have the right to buy the games and consoles at the lowest price the market can possibly offer and we will not tolerate collusive behaviour intended to keep prices artificially high,' European Competition Commissioner Mario Monti said.

Because of the likely impact on consumers, both explicit collusion (the operation of cartels) and implicit collusion are illegal. One of the roles of the Competition Commission and Directorate General (DG)IV, the Competition Directorate of the European Commission, is to ensure that markets do not operate against the public interest.

Explicit collusion

Under this form of collusion, usually referred to as a cartel, prices are fixed and output or sales are allocated to each member of the cartel. The cartel is able to act as a monopolist. Allocation decisions are usually the result of negotiation between the organisations. Often decisions are made in relation to the sales each organisation has had historically, or on a geographical basis.

Cartels are evident across a wide range. A notable example was brought to light in November 2001 when the European Union imposed record fines against drug companies for fixing the price of vitamins. Eight companies colluded to form a cartel, which charged excessive prices for vitamin pills in the European market. This led to the price of vitamin pills being set at an excessive level across the world through illegal practices. Mario Monti commented that 'the companies' collusive behaviour enabled them to charge higher prices than if the full forces of competition had been at play, damaging consumers and allowing the companies to pocket illicit profits.'

Implicit collusion

In the case of implicit collusion a price leader may materialise within an industry and other organisations tacitly follow. Activities include:

- *dominant firm price leadership* – where companies choose the same price as that set by a dominant firm in the industry (the leader);

- *barometric price leadership* – where the price leader is the one whose prices are believed to reflect market conditions in the most satisfactory way. This may be a smaller firm;

- *average cost pricing* – where a firm sets its price by adding a certain percentage on top of the average costs.

Alternatively, agreements may have some form of official sanction. The price of transatlantic air fares from European destinations is fixed through IATA. It has been suggested that the existence of this type of system will encourage anti-competitive behaviour. Evidence seems to suggest that airlines have colluded through IATA to block cut-price fares. Understandings over fares also prompted the Civil Aviation Authority, in 1994, to suggest that collusion and price fixing on transatlantic air routes had blocked competition and held those fares at artificially high levels. Because agreements are often tacit rather than explicit it is difficult to find evidence of such arrangements. The European Commission may be forced to take action to stop this kind of price fixing.

An example of the role of competition policy and how difficult it is to identify implicit collusion can be seen in Minicases 2.2 and 2.3.

The breakdown of collusion

A major problem associated with collusion is the temptation for organisations to 'cheat' and so ignore any agreement. By doing so it is possible for the organisation or country, in the short run, to increase profits at the expense of other parties to the agreement. As a result it may be difficult to sustain any agreement for a prolonged period, particularly if there are a large number of organisations.

Cartels can be vulnerable to pressures. For example, IATA during the 1970s was seriously weakened by price-cutting competition from non-member airlines. It was further weakened by the world recession with lower incomes causing weak demand for air travel (with a high-income elasticity of demand) and therefore causing prices to fall dramatically. In order to fill seats IATA members began to compete amongst themselves. Now, we see the impact of the low-cost airlines, such as easyJet in Europe and Virgin Blue in Australia, who are forcing down the prices of their older and normally more expensive rivals (Bizednet, 2003).

Oligopoly is the dominant form of market structure found in all market economies. We have seen that in some oligopolistic industries competition is intense and organisations have to fight hard to maintain their market share. In others the nature of the industry, or the existence of agreements, means that organisations can come close to joint-profit maximisation. However, high profits will attract competitors, so organisations must devote a lot of time to maintaining and defending the barriers to entry. Competition authorities are also active in limiting the amount of collusive activity.

Monopolistic competition

Monopolistically competitive markets include a large number of organisations, with differentiated products and low barriers to entry. There is, therefore, freedom of entry into a market where firms cannot make excess profits in the long run. Organisations act independently, because their market share is likely to be small and their actions are of little concern to others. If one organisation changes price, for example, this is unlikely to affect prices throughout the market. The large number of organisations, combined with their correspondingly small size, means that the concentration ratio will be low, which increases competitive pressures.

The retail trade is often cited as an example of this type of market. Restaurants, hairdressers and builders are all examples of monopolistic competition. A typical feature is that there is only one firm in a particular location. There may be many Chinese takeaways in town but only one in a particular street, so consumers may be prepared to pay higher prices rather than go elsewhere. They are not all the same, but differentiated by each seller. A price rise in one store will not always result in price rises everywhere else (though it is suggested that neighbouring shops may respond).

One of the features of monopolistic competition is the high level of advertising as organisations attempt to maintain or improve their position in the marketplace. Product differentiation may exist because of imaginary differences in the mind of the consumer brought about through advertising, branding and the service provided by an organisation. Product innovation is also constantly sought after, as new products may provide a temporary competitive edge and an opportunity to raise prices and increase profit.

The health food industry is dominated by numerous small companies and a few large multinationals with health food interests. Because organisations are small, expensive forms of advertising, for example the use of television commercials, are avoided. Organisations concentrate on below-the-line advertising such as competitions and point-of-sale material. Advertising expenditure has increased substantially in the main sector of this market since 1988.

The real or perceived differences created by advertising and innovation mean that it is possible for an organisation to charge a higher price. If organisations in the market are seen to be obtaining high profits, new organisations can enter the market because of the low barriers to entry. The monopolistically competitive market is therefore liable to see high levels of competition between incumbents and entrants to the market. There will be enormous pressure on organisations to reduce their costs and improve their efficiency as a way of preserving margins and thus profitability.

Many economists maintain that this type of market is almost never found in practice. It is suggested that all organisations in the market have to take account of their competitors at some level.

Summary

We have now applied the traditional economic model of industry structure as a basis of analysing competition. To what extent is this model of use? Caves and Porter (1980) suggest that if structural change within an industry, particularly changes of concentration and entry, appears to be slow then the traditional model will be applicable.

However, in other circumstances the model may present only a partial view of the competitive conditions facing an organisation. In some industries the rate of change may be rapid with, for example, technology transforming the industry structure by changing both process and products. One only needs to look at the demise of products like electric typewriters and the changes forced on IBM to cope with the market for personal computers to see the influence of technology (see also Chapter 4). It is under these circumstances that the value of using industry structure as a basis for analysing competition may be diminished.

Other economists too have put the structure–conduct–performance approach under the microscope. The Chicago School has taken an alternative view that concentrated markets are not necessarily evil in themselves. Markets that exhibit extremes of concentration may gain benefits such as economies of scale or greater efficiency. The Chicagoans believe that barriers to entry are more apparent than real and that competition is powerful enough to prevent organisations from controlling markets. The conclusion is that conduct and performance of the market are not related to its underlying structure. Competition in a highly concentrated market could be fierce. This obviously has a significant impact on businesses operating in these types of markets.

Contestable markets

A valuable addition to the theory of industry structure is provided by Baumol (1982). He suggests that it is possible for organisations to enter a market without incurring costs because these costs can be recovered when the organisation exits. There are no sunk or unrecoverable costs. This situation is known as a perfectly contestable market. Sunk costs can include the cost of building, advertising and R&D. If the sunk costs of entry are lower, then the market is more contestable or more competitive. Contestable markets are vulnerable to hit-and-run entry. Supermarkets have been able to establish a major market share in the cola market in recent years. Manufacturing is carried out by a partner and shelf space is readily available. Own brands establish a market partly due to demand for the product being elastic – that is, it is price sensitive, and consumers will increase their demand for the product if the price is sufficiently low. Entry into the market was against a background of increasing consumption of soft drinks, from 6.6 billion litres in 1987 to an estimated 9 billion litres in 1996. This provides evidence of low barriers to entry and exit for supermarkets and low sunk costs.

It is doubtful whether a perfectly contestable market exists. In most cases some sunk costs are incurred in market entry. It is the scale of the sunk costs which may, or may not, dissuade a potential entrant from attempting a hit-and-run entry.

The risk that Virgin Atlantic took to start an air service from London to Japan was lessened because the sunk costs were relatively low. If the route proved to be unprofitable, aircraft could be transferred to other routes, rental of terminal space could stop and ground equipment could be switched to another airport. Football teams, particularly those in the higher European leagues, face sunk costs when they hire a player or manager on a lucrative long-term contract. If the player or manager under-performs his contract will still be paid up even if he leaves the club. This clearly is a big risk for the teams and their PLCs.

Structural analysis of competitive forces

Despite criticism, the structure–conduct–performance model may still be a useful foundation for the analysis of a rapidly changing business environment. Porter (1980) argues that 'understanding industry structure must be the starting point for strategic analysis'. Strategic analysis focuses on identifying the basic, underlying characteristics of an industry, which are rooted in its economics and technology. It is these characteristics that shape the competitive environment that the industry faces.

To enhance understanding it is advisable to examine Michael Porter's 1980 model more closely. The model illustrated in Figure 2.5 brings together many elements discussed above as it is based on the s–c–p paradigm. Porter suggests that the collective strengths of five forces determine the state of competition and therefore the ultimate profit potential within an industry. The five competitive forces identified by Porter are:

- rivalry among competitors;
- threat of entry;
- threat of substitution;
- bargaining power of buyers;
- bargaining power of suppliers.

We will briefly explore each one.

Rivalry among competitors

This is Porter's central force. Increased rivalry will lead to increased competition and reduced profits. Intensity of rivalry between competitors will depend on several factors.

The number and relative size of competitors within an industry

If there are many organisations of a similar size, as in monopolistic competition, or oligopoly, then rivalry will be intense. Organisations in the industry are likely to try to gain market share through all possible means. Witness the situation in the petrol retail market where new deals to consumers are continuously being introduced. In industries

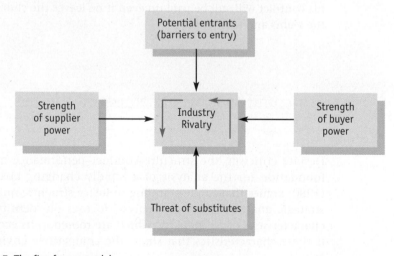

Figure 2.5 The five forces model
Source: adapted from Porter (1980), p. 4

with relatively few organisations, or where one or two organisations dominate, rivalry tends to be much less and the market much more stable.

The rate of growth in an industry

It is important to recognise that the growth rate of an industry is dependent upon a number of factors and that sectoral differences abound. Market growth in industries where product innovation and displacement are dominant is likely to be very different from that of the more traditional sectors, for example shipbuilding. Geographical differences also need to be taken into account. Cigarette smoking is increasing in some areas of the world and declining in others.

When an industry is growing slowly competition will be more intense. The only way an organisation can expand is by taking market share from competitors. The early 1990s saw a fall in European car sales, a phenomenon referred to as negative growth. The only manufacturer to prosper in this cut-throat market was Rover, which managed to increase its market share, albeit from a low starting point.

It is important for organisations to be aware of the product life cycle that their products face, as competitive conditions can be very different at each phase of the life cycle. Figure 2.6 shows four stages in the product life cycle, each with its own characteristics.

Cost conditions

The relationship between fixed and variable cost is important. If organisations operate in a business with relatively high fixed costs it will be in the interests of that organisation to cut its prices in order to sell its output. Train operators are willing to reduce prices at certain times of the day and different days of the week to attract customers. Rail

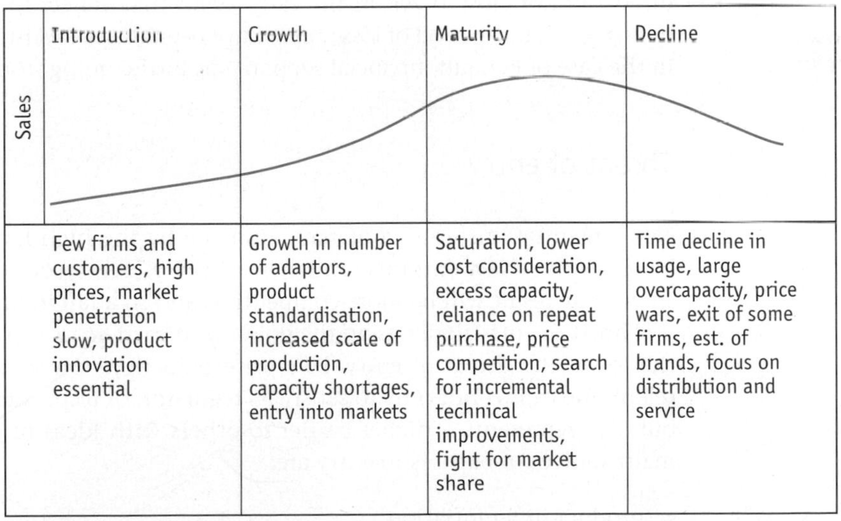

	Introduction	Growth	Maturity	Decline
Sales				
	Few firms and customers, high prices, market penetration slow, product innovation essential	Growth in number of adaptors, product standardisation, increased scale of production, capacity shortages, entry into markets	Saturation, lower cost consideration, excess capacity, reliance on repeat purchase, price competition, search for incremental technical improvements, fight for market share	Time decline in usage, large overcapacity, price wars, exit of some firms, est. of brands, focus on distribution and service

Figure 2.6 The product life cycle: competitive environment

operators offer discounts for off-peak users and a range of discount cards for students, families and pensioners. The discount airlines pricing strategy also reflects this problem. They sell tickets at very low prices to enable them to cover at least a portion of their costs. The variable cost of selling a ticket is very low, the fixed cost of operating a railway or an airline high. Staff have to be employed and trains have to be in service. Organisations in this situation will seek additional business, that is, increased ticket sales, as long as the revenue from sales covers the variable costs of those sales. In January 2003 airlines were selling tickets to Germany for as little as £1.

The battle to attract valuable inward investment from multinational companies is often augmented by substantial offers from governments that cover significant proportions of the start-up cost (see Minicase 2.4).

Lack of product differentiation

If there is little to distinguish one product from another, competition will be intense (see the nature of the product or service above).

High exit barriers

Exit barriers can be measured by the costs organisations incur when they leave an industry. Exit barriers are said to be high if the cost of leaving an industry is high. These costs can include redundancy payments and low scrap value of plant. Exit barriers in the form of emotional barriers and government policy may also be in place. The fact that more football clubs have not been closed down owes much to the emotional as well as financial support that they receive from their often long-suffering supporters. In January 2003 York City Football Club were given financial assistance, worth hundreds of thousands of pounds by supporters, in an attempt to save the club. That more car manufacturers did not close down in the early 1990s may reflect the high cost of leaving the industry. A short period of losses may have been easier to sustain than complete closure. In the case of Renault, financial support was forthcoming from the French government.

Threat of entry

New organisations enter a market, attracted by the high level of returns that incumbents receive. New entrants bring new capacity, new resources and a desire for market share. The result will be more competition and so a fall in profit for all organisations.

Threat of entry depends on the potency of barriers to entry. The higher the barriers, the lower the threat of entry. BT's price reductions on some of its United Kingdom telephone calls is not only to satisfy its regulator, or to pressurise its main competitors, but also represents a higher barrier to others with ideas of entering the market. The main sources of barriers to entry are:

- product differentiation;

- economies of scale and absolute cost advantages;

Minicase 2.4   Investment in Japan through the Development Bank of Japan

The Development Bank of Japan (DBJ) was established on October 1, 1999, as the successor to the Japan Development Bank and the Hokkaido-Tohoku Development Finance Public Corporation and is 100 per cent government owned. The objective of the DBJ is to provide long-term financing and other policy-based schemes to qualified projects as a supplement and inducement to the lending and other services provided by ordinary financial institutions and, by doing so, promote the:

Upgrading, vitalization and sustainable development of the economy and society, the realization of enhanced quality of life, and the creation of self-reliant regions.

The DBJ supplies low-interest, long-term loans and/or debt guarantees for projects in such fields as technology promotion, regional development and urban redevelopment. In addition, DBJ furnishes a wide range of information and promotes the smooth formulation of socially-desirable projects.

DBJ supports the formulation and implementation of a project at every step, starting from its conception and planning. As a fair and impartial provider of necessary skills, the bank helps in the co-ordination of project participants and other tasks on the road to implementation. DBJ is intensifying its efforts to develop new financing methods to use along with traditional ones.

When a project has particular importance in terms of government policy there is a special need to ensure that it brings in a certain degree of profit. This is done while building consensus among all parties involved in order that the project may continue to reflect the policy's intent over the long term. Putting to work the implementation skills it has developed over the years, along with its investment and financing capabilities, the bank provides thorough support at each stage of the project's development.

PFI (private finance initiatives) enhance social capital formation by using private-sector funds and expertise. The bank advises local governments and other public agencies on PFI transactions while also providing the financing necessary for projects.

DBJ is meeting the need for new types of financing for social capital development, including urban development schemes and independent power producer (IPP) projects. One of these is project finance, which ensures the appropriate sharing of risk among project participants and, by limiting repayment security to project earnings, reduces the risk carried by project principals.

Companies that have benefited include:

Universal Studios Japan

Universal Studios Japan has under taken the development of a large-scale movie based theme park in Osaka City which has been built using project finance. The DBJ have aided the project throughout. At the concept stage consideration of the projects financial feasibility was given along with advice on the formulation of the project. At the planning stage the bank co-operated in forming the finance structure of the organisation of a consortium and also assisted in the preparation of the project profitability plan. In the implementation stage they were able to encourage private financing and provide interest-bearing and interest-free loans to project principals

Nagasaki Bayside Mall

This commercial complex was built as part of the Urban Renaissance 2001 Concept, implemented by Nagasaki Prefecture and Nagasaki City. At the concept stage the DBJ gave advice on the planning of district commercial facilities. At the planning stage they gave assistance in the formulation of project profitability and finance plans and then helped co-ordinate with related government ministries and agencies. At the implementation stage low-interest loans were provided to the project principals

Source: The Development Bank of Japan, available from http://www.dbj.go.jp [accessed on 26 January 2004]

Questions

1. Find out and explain the idea of the bubble economy. Why might its collapse have prompted the Japanese government to look more closely at FDI?

2. Identify other companies that have used FDI to enter foreign markets. How has FDI smoothed the way?

- legal barriers;
- capital requirements;
- access to distribution channels;
- threat of retaliation.

Many of these have been discussed above. We will briefly explore those hitherto un-mentioned.

Economies of scale and absolute cost advantages

Economies of scale were discussed in detail above. No matter what economies of scale exist, other cost advantages may also exist, so-called first-mover advantages, which cannot be replicated by potential entrants. These could include:

- access to raw materials – it is extremely difficult to establish a nuclear industry without access to raw material, as many countries have discovered (for example, Iran and Iraq);

- favourable locations – it would be an almost impossible challenge for an overseas bank to set up a wide branch network to compete with the established networks of the home-based organisations, unless, like HSBC, it takes over a United Kingdom bank;

- product know-how and experience curve advantages (see above).

Government subsidies can be used to reduce absolute cost advantages. The launch aid received by Airbus Industrie helped it to compete effectively against America's Boeing. The support for sunrise industries, those emerging new industries of the future, may also be a legitimate use of subsidies, as has happened in New Zealand.

Legal barriers

Legal barriers, such as government licence, charter or a patent, may also be used. A li-cence is required in many fields of business including the taxicab, banking and broad-casting sectors. E-business is said to offer many opportunities to reduce cost and to build new and better relationships with customers. But in particular many SMEs are still reluctant to fully engage in electronic transactions. Among the most cited barriers are uncertainties related to the applicable e-commerce legislation, in particular for cross-border electronic transactions and the lack of trust and confidence in buying and selling over the Internet. Access to simple and practical information on the main legal and regulatory aspects of e-commerce is therefore crucial in order to remove still existing barriers and to help SMEs to 'go digital' (European Commission, 2003).

GlaxoSmithKline and other drug companies are able to protect their new products from competition by use of patents. Environmental and safety standards also place barriers in the way of new organisations entering some industries.

Inefficient public monopolies have in the past been accused of being protected from competition by government funding, especially the power, transport and telecommu-nications sectors in the United Kingdom and telecommunications and postal services in France and Germany respectively. The Japanese government has long been criticised in Europe and North America for imposing barriers that protect Japanese manufacturers and farmers and drastically limit the import of a wide range of goods, such as rice, cars and Scotch whisky, into the Japanese market. Action was taken in mid 1995 by the United States government in response to Japan's conduct, and the increasing trade deficit between the United States and Japan, to limit the number of Japanese exports to the United States. Measures proposed included 100 per cent tariffs on Japanese cars entering the United States market. Minicase 2.4 above shows one way in which the Japanese government has responded.

Capital requirements

The need for capital is linked closely to our earlier discussion of sunk costs. It may be too expensive for an organisation to enter a market.

Access to distribution channels

A barrier can be created by the inability of an entrant to gain access to a distribution channel. Mercury was given the right to rent access to BT's phone lines, otherwise it would have been impossible for them to enter the United Kingdom telephone market. Manufacturers of designer/branded goods have tried to prevent supermarkets from obtaining goods at a cheaper price on the 'grey market' outside Europe and selling them at lower prices to customers. Tesco, for example, imported Levi jeans direct from the USA. A decision on 16 July 1998 by the European Court of Justice found that this was illegal. It was a blow for retailers like Tesco. However, in May 1999 the United Kingdom High Court found in Tesco's favour. In a further twist in November 2001, the European Court of Justice upheld Levi's case that the Trademark Directive allows brand owners to restrict access to branded goods and thus set high prices.

Threat of retaliation

The effectiveness of barriers may be in part reliant on the expectations that entrants have of the possible retaliation of incumbent organisations. Porter (1980) suggests that entrants into an industry can be deterred if:

- there is a history of retaliation against entrants; e.g. it has recently proved difficult to establish new newspaper titles because of the aggressive nature of price-cutting used by incumbents;

- established organisations with substantial resources fight back; e.g. the cross-Channel ferry operators are very aware of the threat posed by the Channel Tunnel and are marshalling their resources in a bid to keep their market share;

- established organisations are heavily committed to the industry and have assets which cannot be employed in other sectors; e.g. British Steel have become one of the most profitable steel makers in the world and it is in their interests to maintain barriers to ensure a continued growth in profits;

- the industry is undergoing slow or zero growth as new organisations cannot be absorbed so easily.

Threat of substitution

Substitutes are those products or services offered by one organisation that can be used in place of the product or service that another organisation supplies. The American Express charge card, for example, faces competition from cash, traveller's cheques, chequebooks and credit cards. The threat of substitutes imposes a price ceiling, as high profits will attract substitutes. The extent of the threat will depend on the propensity of the buyer to substitute, switching costs, and the relative price and performance of substitutes.

The propensity of the buyer to substitute

A critical factor is the propensity, inclination or tendency of a buyer to substitute. If the propensity of a buyer to substitute is high then substitutes will present a great threat. Some products have a low propensity of substitution because of the nature of the product, for example cars. People are reticent to use alternatives such as public transport. It has proved and will continue to prove difficult to encourage people to switch from cars to other forms of transport.

The wider economic environment is also an issue in this case. Car sales across Europe have been affected by weak economic conditions and subdued consumer demand. Western European new-car registrations fell 3.8 per cent in the year to the end of November 2003 and most industry experts expect the European car market to slip 1 per cent to 3 per cent in 2003. Recession can bring job losses and lower real income which must have an impact on the buying patterns of individuals.

The situation is further complicated because substitutes may be difficult to identify and hence keep out. What is the substitute for a beer? It is not another brand of beer from another brewer. That is an example of rivalry among competitors, Porter's central force. Substitutes come from outside the industry. Organisations compete for discretionary expenditure, the spare cash that people have. For example, Jack Rooney, Miller's vice president of marketing, suggests that the promotion budget goes toward devising creative new ways to distinguish the Miller brand from other brands in the marketplace. He says that, 'We're competing not just against Coors and Corona but Coke, Nike and Microsoft' (Stone, 1997). The United Kingdom jeans market has suffered also, with 4 million fewer pairs sold in 1997. In 1999, Levi Strauss in the United States announced factory closures and the loss of over 6000 jobs. Clearly, consumer spending is being directed elsewhere. The problem for the manufacturers is to identify exactly where.

Switching costs

The one-off cost that faces a buyer when switching from one supplier to another is important. Where the switching cost is high then transfer of allegiances is less likely and vice versa. A consumer can quite easily switch to buying a health food product rather than potato crisps, thus reducing the sales of the snack manufacturer. However, the cost of switching from using a car to another form of transport may involve substantial cost and inconvenience to the driver and so discourage change.

The relative price and performance of substitutes

The ability of some of the Japanese high-volume car manufacturers to gain market share in the sports car segment of the car market, for example Mazda with the MX5, largely reflects the relatively lower price of the Japanese vehicles in comparison to their performance and the value that they offer in comparison with competitors.

Bargaining power of buyers and suppliers

Suppliers are those individuals or organisations from whom an organisation purchases items that are needed to carry out business activities. These are the inputs to the organisation and include raw materials and components. Supplier power can reduce prices, increase quality and increase service level demands, all of which will reduce margins.

Buyers are those individuals or organisations that purchase an organisation's outputs. Bargaining power of buyers can reduce prices, increase quality and increase service level demands, putting pressure on profits. Concern over excessive buyer power was one of the factors that prompted the Competition Commission investigation into the United Kingdom supermarket sector. Indeed studies show that buyer power is a feature of food retailing in France, Germany, Spain, and the United Kingdom, but significant differences exist between each country (European Commission, 1999).

The examination of supplier power is analogous to that of buyer power (the factors that contribute to greater buyer power will decrease supplier power) and so we will concentrate on buyer power in this section.

Buyers depend a great deal on the quality and timeliness of information they receive. Full information means that a buyer is in a better position to negotiate a price. Buyers are powerful and more sensitive to price if:

- their switching costs are low – it is easy to go for a drink to the pub next door, no costs are involved;

- the product is important to the buyer. This could be the case if:

  - the product represents a high proportion of total costs – buyers of major pieces of capital equipment are likely to have a strong hand when it comes to contract negotiations;

  - the product is purchased in high volume (see below);

  - the profitability of the buyer industry is low which may mean that the buyer will want to reduce the price of goods that are bought in to protect its own margins.

Products are undifferentiated and substitutes are available

We have already outlined the problems that firms face if products are homogeneous and easily substituted. Buyers can simply play one company off against the other. Competition between suppliers of office stationery is intense. The homogeneous nature of the product means that buyers can shop around for the best prices and, consequently, reduce the sales and profit of their suppliers.

Buyer concentration is high

If your product is bought by only one buyer then concentration is at 100 per cent. In this case buyers have total power, not only over price but all other aspects of the relationship, including quality and delivery time. Marks & Spencer and some supermarkets have entered into exclusive agreements to buy the whole of the output of an organisation. If they withdraw their order then plant closure may be the result.

Threat of integration

In some cases a buyer has the ability to move into that particular business themselves. By using vertical integration companies are able to dominate a sector. Take the example of the Viacom/CBS merger in the United States. The company is now able to produce films at Paramount or a television programme at Spelling studios, air it on ShowTime and CBS, advertise it on 34 TV channels, as well as 164 radio stations and then sell it through Blockbuster (McChesney, 1999).

Porter's five forces model provides organisations with a model for analysing their competitive environment. Unless a company can analyse its competitors it will never be in a position to compete effectively. The benefits to be gained from having an intelligence-gathering system are immeasurable. A capable system may ultimately ensure survival. Minicase 2.5 illustrates the use of the model.

Competitor analysis

The proliferation of different types of washing detergents, such as enzyme-rich, enzyme-free, liquid, automatic, biological and non-biological powders, is not simply a tactic used by the two major manufacturers to put in place a barrier to entry, as described earlier. The multiplicity of types arises from the need of one company to match the innovation of the other. If the companies in the market are unaware of their competitors' direction then a rival may be able to increase its market share.

Competitor analysis is another way of achieving an insight into the activity of competitors. This type of behaviour exists in industries as diverse as the car industry and software design.

Minicase 2.5   A brief structural analysis of the games console market

Competitive rivalry

During the 1990s the market was dominated by three manufacturers; Sony, Nintendo and Sega. The 1995–2000 market share is shown in Table 1. There are still

Table 1 Market share 1995–2000

	Market Share (%)
Sony	47
Nintendo	28
Sega	23
Other	2

three key players in the market. Sony are still the leaders in the three major markets, Europe, Japan and America, the so-called triad. Nintendo occupy second place, with Microsoft, a relatively new player, in third. Sega has lost its position. There are also some smaller players in this industry which account for a very small proportion of sales (see Table 2).

Table 2 Market share in 2002

	USA Market Share %	Japan Market Share %	Europe Market Share %
Sony PS2	61	63	75
Microsoft Xbox	18	4	14
Nintendo Gamecube	21	28	11

Sony's PS2 has taken a substantial share of the games console market. PS2 has benefited from its first-mover advantages by being on the market a year ahead of similar products from Nintendo and Microsoft. Capacity to innovate is clearly a key skill in this market. Sony's strong brand name in the game console, home electronics and entertainment industries makes it well positioned for the market. Sony has also benefited from its partnership with AOL and a number of major game publishers.

Nintendo has always been a strong player in the console industry. It is still second to Sony in terms of total game console unit sales. Its GameCube is targeted at the low end of the market, young children from 7 to 16, who don't require as many features as the more mature age groups.

The Xbox is Microsoft's first entry into the games console market. It has been using an aggressive marketing campaign to compensate for its late entry and gain some market share. However, Xbox is not particularly differentiated from PS2 in terms of features. The fact that Microsoft follows the price set by Sony also makes it vulnerable, although the partnership that Microsoft has with Sega may prove to be useful.

Power of suppliers

In the games console market suppliers have little power. They are hardware and software providers who, to a certain degree, rely heavily on the console manufacturers.

Power of buyers

The final consumer also has little power. The Nintendo case referred to earlier in the chapter demonstrates that the manufacturer can 'call the shots' when dealing with a distributor.

Threat of substitutes

Substitutes, like PCs, have a much smaller market share than consoles in the games market, because they primarily designed for game play. However, it is highly possible that technology will provide opportunities for alternative leisure time activities in the not too distant future. It is possible that the demand for consoles could slow down as players move on to to other activities, choosing to spend their money completely outside the market.

Threat of entry

The number and impact of potential entrants are not totally clear, but as games consoles are likely to evolve into devices that include gaming, home entertainment and PC capabilities, the dominant players in each of these industries may

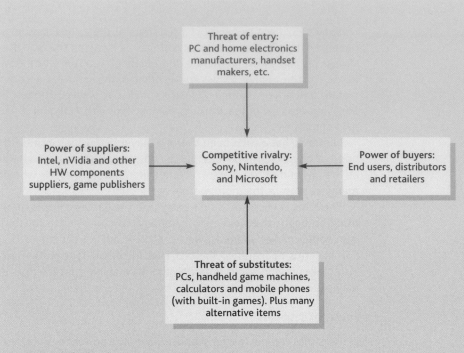

Figure 1 The five forces

want to move into the market. Microsoft's success or failure in this respect may point a way forward.

Question

1. Use Porter's five forces model, along with the other key concepts raised in the chapter, to analyse the competitive environment of an industry of your choice.

Competitor analysis involves an investigation of competitors' goals, assumptions, strategy, and capabilities (Porter, 1980). Not only do existing competitors need to be examined but there is also a need to put potential competitors under the microscope. Add to this a dose of self-analysis and a picture of the behaviour of the market comes into focus. Figure 2.7 shows the competitor analysis model.

Porter (1980) proposes that competitor analysis can answer questions such as the following:

- What are the implications of the interaction of the probable competitors' moves?

- Are organisations' strategies converging and likely to clash?

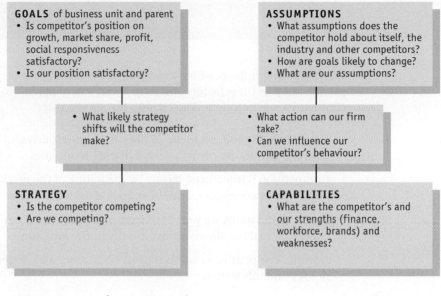

Figure 2.7 Components of competitive analysis
Source: adapted from Porter (1980), p. 49

- Do organisations have sustainable growth rates that match the industry's forecast growth rate, or will a gap be created that will invite entry?

Conclusion

We have seen, in this chapter, that the structure of the market has a direct impact on the competition that an organisation faces. It is, however, evident that market structure does not remain static. Today's monopoly could be tomorrow's competitive cockpit. Organisations face a dynamic and changing competitive environment. International competitors are becoming the barometer by which we measure the success of all organisations.

Organisations cannot rest and remain satisfied with their past achievements. It is important to develop and maintain mechanisms with which to sense environmental change. In this chapter we have introduced you to some of the tools and models that can assist organisations in understanding their own position and that of their competitors. We have also shown that there is a role for government at all scales.

Markets left to their own devices may become anti-competitive, so intervention may be needed. Governments can also provide support for new, fledgling industries to allow them to grow and become competitive in the international arena.

The next chapter explores the macroeconomic environment.

Summary of main points

Competition is influenced by a wide range of factors. In this chapter we have investigated a range of these factors and introduced you to models to aid your analysis of the competitive environment. The chapter has shown that:

- The basic economic problem, of allocation of resources, is resolved in quite different ways within the command and market economies.

- Competition is influenced largely by the nature of the product, the number of firms and their concentration, and the market entry conditions.

- Some organisations are protected from competition by barriers to entry and may be capable of making above-normal profits in the long run.

- A strong competitive position is likely to be eroded by, for example, the use of technology and innovation.

- Oligopolists are interdependent and must consider the actions of rivals when making business decisions; because of the lack of freedom of manoeuvre, competition is based largely on quality, branding, advertising and service.

- Some organisations act to reduce uncertainty by entering into agreements which may be anti-competitive. Regulations need to be in place to monitor such agreements and to protect the public interest.

- Contestable markets exist where there are no sunk costs of entry. In such markets competition will be intense.

- Porter's five forces are:

  - rivalry among competitors;

  - threat of entry;

  - threat of substitution;

  - bargaining power of buyers;

  - bargaining power of suppliers.

- The collective strengths of the five forces determine the state of competition and therefore the ultimate profit potential within an industry.

- Competitor analysis involves the investigation of organisations' goals, assumptions, strategies and capabilities.

Discussion Questions

1. Using published sources analyse the competitive position in a market. Comment on your findings.

2. Explain how a company entering a market may overcome barriers to entry.

3. Identify and give examples of ways in which oligopolies and monopolies may benefit consumers.

4. Using relevant sources explain how the brewing market has evolved and comment on the market structure.

5. Comment on and contrast the activities of two of the sectoral regulators in the United Kingdom.

6. Using appropriate examples discuss the assertion that cartels are vulnerable to pressure.

7. Using examples from published sources, investigate a situation where the sunk costs of companies entering a market are low.

Web Links

http://www.open.gov.uk
The Treasury site and the Competition Commission here is worth a look.

http://europa.eu.int/comm/competition/index_en.html
The Competition Commission of the European Union

http://www.bubl.ac.uk/
BUBL provides a subject-based service. Subjects can be chosen from a subject tree. Includes discussion lists, news pages and access to other sources. It is designed for use by the higher education community.

http://news.bbc.co.uk/
The BBC website provides up-to-date information on business topics from around the world.

http://www1.ifs.org.uk/
Site of the Institute of Fiscal Studies. Includes:

- what's new;
- the Budget;
- surveys;

- publications;
- links to web servers on economics and social sciences.

http://bized.ac.uk/

Business education on the Internet, access to economics and business resources, including:

- company reports;
- data sites, e.g. Central Statistical Office for UK economic data;
- media sites, e.g. *The Economist*;
- government, political and special interest groups, including political parties and Greenpeace;
- key word search facility, latest news.

http://netec.mcc.ac.uk/WebEc.html

WebEc is the virtual economics library. The site gives access to a huge number of areas of economics.

Newspapers

Newspapers are a good source of information on many topics. They can be found on the following sites:

Financial Times	**http://www.ft.com**
Telegraph	**http://www.telegraph.co.uk**
Times Higher	**http://thesis.news.co.uk**
Guardian/Observer	**http://www.guardian.co.uk**
The Times	**http://www.the-times.co.uk**
Sunday Times	**http://www.sunday-times.co.uk**

Further Reading

Porter, M.E. (1980) *Competitive Strategy: Techniques for Analyzing Industries and Competitors*, New York: Free Press.

This is the original text on competitive advantage and useful if you want to look in more detail at Porter's ideas.

Rosen, R. (1995) *Strategic Management; An Introduction*, Pitman, London.

Is an accessible introduction to business strategy which takes the reader on to the next stage.

Rumelt, R.P. (1991) 'How much does industry matter?', *Strategic Management Journal*, 12 (3).

A more academic look at the issues surrounding industry and structure.

Sampler, J. (1998) 'Redefining industry structure for the information age', *Strategic Management Journal*, 19, pp. 345–55.

Looks at some of the more up-to-date matters surrounding industry structure.

References

Barron, J.A. (2000) 'Structural regulation of the media and diversity rationale, May', *Federal Communications Law Journal*, 3, 555–60.

Baumol, W. (1982) 'Contestable markets: an uprising in the theory of industry structure', *American Economic Review*, March.

Bacina, M. (2002) 'PS2 Tops Sales ... Yet Again', Friday, 29 Nov 2002, http://www.civicvideo.com.au/index2.php4?page_id=games&&n_id=1322 [accessed 20 January 2003].

BBC (2002) 'Profit falls at Saudi telecoms monopoly', Wednesday, 29 May 2002, 13:56 GMT 14:56 UK, http://news.bbc.co.uk/1/hi/business/2014682.stm [accessed 25 November].

Beardshaw, J. (1992) *Economics: A Student's Guide*, 3rd edn, London: Pitman.

Begg, D., Fischer, S. and Dornbusch, R. (1994) *Economics*, 4th edn, London: McGraw-Hill.

Beverage digest (2002), available from http://www.beverage-digest.com/editorial/020228sphp [accessed 23 November 2002].

Bizednet, (2003) 'Advanced Economics: Supermarket structure', Weekly Newsletter – 20 January 2003, http://www.bized.ac.uk/current/news/2002_3/200103_ec_apr.htm [accessed 27 January 2003].

Bowers, S. (2003) 'Store wars part two: organic spaghetti vs baby pyjamas', *The Guardian*, 6 January.

Bromley, R. and Thomas, C. (1993) *Retail Change*, London: UCL Press.

Brozen, Y. (1978) http://www.libertyhaven.com/theoreticalorphilosophicalissues/economics/monopolyandindustrialorganization/attackon.html [accessed 10 January 2003].

Camillus, J.C. (1998) 'Focus!', *Praxis Quarterly Journal of Management*, 2 (2), August http://www.blonnet.com/praxis/pr0202/02020160.htm [accessed 12 January 2003].

Caves, R. and Porter, M.E. (1980) 'The dynamics of changing seller concentration', *Journal of Industrial Economics*, 19, 1–15.

Competition Commission (2001) 'BASF AG and Takeda Chemical Industries Ltd: a report on the acquisition by BASF AG of certain assets of Takeda Chemical Industries Ltd', Cm 5209 04/07/01, available from http://www.competition-commission.org.uk/fulltext/456c4.pdf [accessed 20 November 2002].

DTI (1997) 'Competition Bill to benefit consumers and business and the MMC', Press Release P/97/662, 16 October 1997, available at http://www.open.gov.uk/ [accessed 19 November 1999].

European Commission (1999) *Buyer Power and its Impact on Competition in the Food Retail Distribution Sector of the European Union*, available at http://europa.eu.int/comm/competition/publications/studies/bpifrs/ [accessed 23 November 2002].

European Commission (2001) *General Report 2001 – Chapter III: The Community Economic and Social Area Section 6: Competition policy* (27/55), available from http://europa.eu.int/abc/doc/off/rg/en/2001/pt0254.htm#anch0113 [accessed 23 October 2002].

European Commission (2002) 'Notice published pursuant to Article 19(3) of regulation No 17 concerning notification COMP/A37.904/F3 – Interbrew', *Official Journal of the European Commission*, 20.11.2002.

European Commission (2003) *Improving Access of SME's to Information on e-Business Legislation – the European E-business Legal Portal*, available from http://europa.eu.int/comm/enterprise/ict/policy/legal-portal/ [accessed 29 January 2003].

Fenn, D. (2002) *Key Note Breweries & the Beer Market Report 2002*, 21st edn, ISBN 1-84168-352-3.

Fishwick, F. (1993) *Making Sense of Competition Policy*, London: Kogan Page.

Grant, R.M. (1995) *Contemporary Strategy Analysis: Concepts, Techniques, Applications*, Oxford: Blackwell.

Huang, Y (1999) *Between Two Coordination Failures: Automotive Industrial Policy in China and Korea*, Harvard Business School, Working Papers, http://www.hbs.edu/research/facpubs/workingpapers/abstracts/9798/98-099.html [accessed 3 January 2003].

Klein, N. (2000) *No Logo*, London, Flamingo.

McChesney, R.W. (1999) 'Oligopoly – the big media game has fewer players', *The Progressive Magazine*, available from http://www.progressive.org/mcc1199.htm [accessed 3 December 2002].

Milmo, D (2002) 'Northcliffe appeals against OFT fine', *The Guardian*, 16 December.

Mintel (2001) *Lager*, Mintel International Group Limited, June.

Moore, M. (2002) *Stupid White Men*, London: Penguin.

Olson, E. Trascasa, C. and Essayan, M. (2001) *Customization: Making Real Money in a Virtual World*, http://www.bcg.com/publications/search_view_ofas.asp?pubID=609 [accessed 7 January].

Porter, M.E. (1980) *Competitive Strategy: Techniques for Analyzing Industries and Competitors*, New York: Free Press.

Simpson, H. (2002) *Biotechnology and the Economics of Discovery in the Pharmaceutical Industry*, Office of Health Economics, http://www.ohe.org/biotechn.htm [accessed 22 January 2003].

Stone, K. (1997) 'Promotion Commotion', *Report on Business Magazine*, December, 102, found in Klein, N. (2000) *No Logo*, London: Flamingo.

Swig, R. (2000) http://www.hotel-online.com/Trends/Swig/Swig_IndependentBrand.html [accessed 10 January 2003].

Thompson, A.A. and Strickland, A.J. (1995) *Strategic Management: Concepts and Cases*, 8th edn, Chicago: Irwin.

Willigan, G.E. (1992) 'High-performance Marketing: an interview with Nike's Phil Knight', *Harvard Business Review*, July.

3 The International Economic Environment

Mark Cook

Learning Outcomes

On completion of this chapter you should be able to:

* appreciate the changing nature of production in the major international economies;

* appreciate the role of government in influencing macroeconomic activity;

* recognise the changing nature of growth in the major international economies and the implications that flow from this;

* consider the methods of control and impact of inflation;

* understand the reasons for the changes in unemployment within Europe;

* understand the development of trading blocs;

* recognise the importance of international trade between countries and trading blocs;

* understand the interrelatedness of the major European economies;

* appreciate how exchange rate regimes have developed and their possible implications;

* consider the impact of the Single European Market on countries inside and outside of the European Union;

* consider the implications for the European economies of the development of a single currency;

* consider the development of EU enlargement and its impact on the European Union.

Key Concepts

- macroeconomic goals
- the circular flow of income
- growth and structural change
- economic growth
- the costs of growth
- inflation and deflation
- the role of the state
- economic cycles
- unemployment
- international trade
- the Single European Market
- the single currency
- enlargement of Europe

Introduction

On one level it is possible to consider organisations as having control over their own actions. They can decide upon the kinds of resources they require, relate these to forecasts of demand, the current goals of the organisation and the organisation's long-term strategy. However, organisations do not exist in a vacuum. They are affected by and respond to changes in both short-term and long-term economic and business conditions. This chapter concentrates on the economic factors which impinge upon business behaviour. This not only includes changes in the domestic economic environment, but more importantly changes that have taken place in the international economic environment. These changes, such as those in trading relations, international competitiveness, the growing impact of the European Union and the globalisation of markets, affect organisations whether they are involved in international markets or not.

What are the international forces at play and what is their impact on organisations? It is fairly easy to see how interest rates, the level of inflation and competition policy have an effect on organisations, but there are other economic forces to consider. For example, changes in government policy towards training will have a direct impact on organisations both in the short term and the long term and could lead to a shortage of skilled workers, reducing the organisation's productivity and allowing competitors to gain an increasing share of a previously safe market.

Changes in the external environment with regard to the development of trading blocs can affect the ability and desire of organisations to be involved in export markets. Economic issues in the home economy can result in governments altering their policies to influence general economic activity. Poor underlying strength in an economy can lead to changes in interest rates and exchange rates, both of which may inhibit the performance of the organisations in an economy. Countries/governments/organisations also may not be independent in their actions but are influenced by global commitments and rules and regulations pertaining to their own economic or trading bloc. For example, the French government's ability to control their own economy is influenced by their membership of both the World Trade Organisation (WTO) and the European Union (EU). This chapter therefore considers the changes that have occurred in both the domestic and international macroeconomic environment. It will consider the structural changes that have taken place in the major economies of the world, the move towards growing international integration, the development of trading blocs, and the role and evolution of international capital flows. In addition, the chapter will address issues such as growth, the co-ordination of macroeconomic policy and the changing power structures of the major macroeconomic economies. Throughout the chapter it is important to bear in mind the impact such macroeconomic environmental changes have upon the organisations that lie therein.

Any account of the macroeconomic environment needs to be selective. We have included those features which are believed to be most relevant. It should also be borne in mind that although the macroeconomic environment can be viewed from a number of perspectives the emphasis taken here is on a two-tiered approach, concentrating on Europe and then on the international economy.

Macroeconomic accounts

Governments and organisations are often concerned with the performance of international economies both in absolute and relative terms. But can the level of economic activity in the major economies of the world be compared? A standard approach is to consider Gross Domestic Product (GDP) or Gross National Product (GNP), now also known as Gross National Income (GNI), figures of the different countries. GNP/GNI – a measure of the level of economic activity produced in a country in any one year – is a record of the income accruing to a country, some of which may have been produced in the domestic economy (GDP) and some of which may have been produced abroad. GNP can be measured in a number of ways, but the following have come to be accepted as the traditional approaches:

- all the expenditures that are made on final products during the year – National Expenditure;

- all the output of final products/services produced in that country during the year – National Output;

- all the incomes received by the factors of production in the making of the final products during the year – National Income.

Larger countries tend to have higher total GNPs, therefore GNP per head or GNP per capita is a better inter-country comparison of performance. As Table 3.1 indicates, some of the smaller countries, such as Switzerland, have the highest GNP per head.

Table 3.1 GNP and GNP per capita, various countries

Country	GNP 2001 (billions US$)[1] at Current Prices	GNP per Capita 2001 (US$) Based on Current Exchange Rates
Austria	189.6	23 300
France	1309.8	21 500
Germany	1853.4	22 500
Italy	1091.8	18 800
Japan	4141.4	32 600
Mexico	617.2	6 200
Spain	583.1	14 500
Sweden	219.4	24 700
Switzerland	245.4	34 000
Turkey	145.6	2 100
United Kingdom	1426.5	24 300
United States	10019.7	35 200

[1]Current prices and exchange rates
Source: adapted from OECD, April 2003

There are a number of factors to consider when a comparison is made of different countries; see OECD or other suitable texts for details.

How accurate are these figures? Often income is not reported, being part of what has become known as the hidden or underground economy – activity which does not come to the market for tax purposes (see Table 3.2). The inaccuracy of data can pose significant problems for policy-makers, see also Chapter 8.

Macroeconomic goals

In general, the governments of most countries have four major economic goals, not all of which are mutually compatible. These are:

- a high level of economic growth;
- a strong balance of payments;

Table 3.2 Estimates of the underground economy (as a percentage of GDP)

Country/Region	% of GDP
Africa	
Nigeria, Egypt	69–75%
Tunisia, Morocco	39–45%
Latin America	
Mexico, Peru	40–60%
Chile, Brazil, Venezuela	25–35%
Asia	
Thailand	70%
Philippines, Malaysia, Korea	38–50%
Hong Kong, Singapore	13%
Central Europe	
Hungary, Bulgaria, Poland	20–28%
Czech Republic, Romania, Slovakia	9–16%
Former Soviet Union	
Belarus, Georgia, Ukraine	28–43%
Baltic States, Russia	20–27%
OECD	
Belgium, Greece, Italy, Spain, Portugal	24–30%
All others	13–23%
Austria, Japan, USA, Switzerland	8–10%

Source: Schneider and Enste (2000)

- a low level of inflation;
- a low level of unemployment.

Some of the goals may be conflicting. For example, it may not be possible to have a high level of economic growth and a strong balance of payments. Higher levels of economic growth can lead to increases in the rate of inflation. Thus in achieving one goal, governments may have to forego others.

Governments have a range of economic policies which they can use to achieve their targets. For example, a government which wishes to improve the sales of its domestic industries could try and stimulate its domestic economy by:

- reducing taxes (fiscal policy), thereby increasing consumer expenditure;

- increasing the amount of money available or lowering interest rates in the economy (monetary policy);

- erecting trade barriers to encourage domestic consumers to buy more home-produced goods.

These policies may result in a short-term increase in business activity in the domestic economy, but the long-term impact may be different. Reducing interest rates may lead to higher levels of inflation in the domestic economy, which then encourages domestic consumers to purchase substitute foreign goods since these products appear to be relatively cheaper. The introduction of trade barriers may lead to other countries imposing retaliatory trade barriers on the country's exports and so damage business sales abroad. Alternatively the imposition of trade barriers may result in foreign companies seeking entry into the domestic market and producing goods and services there as a means to overcome the trade barriers. This was a strategy adopted by Japanese car makers both in the UK and the US. The resulting firms increase competition in the domestic market and this can damage the performance of incumbent firms. What the above indicates is that policies can be implemented to achieve a particular short-term goal, but the long-term side-effects may well be different.

In this chapter we will explore economic growth, inflation and employment and also refer to the balance of payments as appropriate.

Economic growth

In some countries, GDP has grown at a faster rate than others. This tendency for unequal growth between countries and within trading blocs has implications for government policy, interest rates, exchange rates and the optimal conditions for the growth of businesses within those countries.

Growth brings improvements in real incomes and a greater variety of goods and services to all sectors of the economy. The generation of growth may follow from a highly motivated, highly skilled and highly productive workforce, coupled with innovation, quality capital investment, and a high level of skill training and education.

Table 3.3 highlights the poor growth performance of some major Western industrialised nations; it describes growth in real output per worker, a good proxy for growth in real income per person, of five of the world's major industrial countries, and provides a comparison of the post-war years.

Table 3.3 Growth rate of real output per worker employed (% per annum)

	UK	USA	France	Germany	Japan
1937–1951	1.0	2.3	1.7	1.0	−1.3
1951–1964	2.3	2.5	4.3	5.1	7.6
1964–1973	2.6	1.6	4.6	4.4	8.4
1973–1979	1.6	0.3	2.9	3.1	2.8
1979–1997	1.7	0.9	2.2	1.2	2.3
1998–2001	1.4	1.8	2.1	0.6	1.0

Sources: Matthews, R.C.O., Feinstein, C.H. and Odling-Smee, J. (1982), British Economic Growth, 1865–1973, *Stanford University Press, p. 31; Organization for Economic Co-operation and Development (OECD) (1988)* Historical Statistics, 1960–1987, *Paris: OECD;* OECD Economic Outlook, *April 2002*

The United Kingdom has a long-standing peacetime tendency for a slower growth in labour productivity compared with its major competitors. Moreover, Table 3.3 reveals that there has been a general slow-down in productivity growth since 1973 compared with the two decades after the Second World War.

The pattern of growth has been very uneven since the oil shocks of 1974 and 1979. These differences in economic growth rates could also indicate that some of the EU economies are in different phases of their economic cycles, and this has been put forward as one of the reasons why the UK has opted not to be among the first-wave entrants into European monetary union. The beginning of the new millennium has also seen a growth in the output per worker in the US economy. The burst in the dot.com bubble has now slowed US output growth. Following on from the dot.com experience however, there has been an upsurge in entrepreneurship. Both Germany and Japan now appear to perform relatively less well. The former because of monetary union and the reconstruction of the east of Germany, whilst in Japan increased saving and a drop in consumer confidence have slowed rapidly the performance of the Japanese economy.

Not all countries have experienced slower growth rates during the 1980s and early 1990s. South-East Asian countries (the 'tiger economies') performed remarkably well until 1997/8, shown in Table 3.4 (and Case Study 3).

Some commentators saw growth in Asian countries as result of a much more laissez-faire approach by governments – allowing markets to operate without government interference – and unfettered, cheap labour. However, all this was to change during the later part of the 1990s. Their growth performances have been severely dented following the banking and financial crisis that has hit South-East Asia. In fact both Indonesia and Thailand registered negative growth performances in 1998. China and India appeared to be unaffected by the South-East Asian crisis. By the early part of the new millennium all the countries had returned to positive real growth rates, though for many South-East Asian economies these were less spectacular than those experienced in the previous decade.

Table 3.4 Estimates of real GDP growth rates for selected Asian countries

Country	Annual Average Growth Rate 1984–91	GDP Growth Rate (%) 1992	GDP Growth Rate (%) 1994	GDP Growth Rate (%) 1998	GDP Growth Rate (%) 2001
India	5.0	6.0	6.8	5.8	4.3
China	9.8	13.2	11.8	7.8	7.3
Indonesia	6.0	6.5	7.4	−13.1	3.3
Malaysia	6.2	7.8	8.5	−7.4	0.4
Philippines	1.1	0.3	4.3	−0.6	3.4
Thailand	8.9	7.9	8.5	−10.5	1.8

Sources: World Bank, The World Bank Atlas 1995; *Asian Development Bank,* World Economic Outlook, *May 1998 (IMF),* World Economic Outlook, *April 2000*

What factors affect growth rates?

If countries knew precisely which were the important factors affecting economic growth then remedial action could be taken and we would notice a large number of countries with extremely high and similar growth rates. The factors that are believed to influence growth may have an individual country dimension, or constraints to growth might involve policies at a wider level, such as that of the trading bloc (for example, the North American Free Trade Association) or economic bloc (the European Union).

Cook (1996) has suggested a range of factors which can be growth-enhancing or growth-suppressing. The growth-enhancing factors are:

- schooling and education investment;
- capital savings and investment;
- equipment investment;
- the level of human capital.

The growth-suppressing factors are:

- the level of government expenditure;
- political and social instability;
- trade barriers;
- the political nature of the ruling party.

More specifically, reasons cited for slower UK growth performance are:

- the short-termism of UK industry – industry favouring projects which give large short-term returns rather than investing for the long term;

- poor labour relations between unions and management;

- its less skilled and less qualified workforce;

- rising exchange rates during the early 1980s making its exports less competitive and imports more attractive to purchase;

- its poor record on non-defence research and development.

Porter (2003) in a recent study of UK competitiveness notes that the UK appears to have halted its relative decline against its major competitors by becoming more efficient within the constraints of the UK economy but now these efficiency improvements are almost exhausted and the UK needs to look elsewhere to achieve further catch up. There are still problems with the UK's transport infrastructure, issues with skills and education and although its science base is adequate its private sector and commercial R&D appears to be disappointing. Porter suggests that if the UK is to become more efficient it should:

- move to a higher-value, innovation-driven level where it can create leading-edge products and services;

- change management behaviour;

- target investment in the business environment;

- strengthen areas such as education, industrial clusters and regions.

Minicase 3.1 shows the situation policy-makers may face.

Structural change

By structural change we mean how the sectors in an economy have changed. It is useful to give some broad definitions of these sectors:

- The primary sector includes activities directly related to natural resources, for example farming, mining and oil extraction.

- The secondary sector covers production industries in the economy such as manufacturing, the processing of materials produced in the primary sector and construction.

- The tertiary sector includes all private sector services, for example banking, finance, computing services and tourism as well as public sector services such as health and defence.

Table 3.3 above shows that in the 1950s and 1960s growth rates of the industrialised economies were at historically high levels. There was an abundant supply of labour,

Minicase 3.1   Getting out of the growth doldrums: only a disaster can save Japan and Germany

Much has recently been made of the similar nature of the economic problems that afflict Germany and Japan. Both countries have weak banking systems and Germany now appears vulnerable to the deflationary disease that already plagues Japan. Both have made serious economic policy mistakes over the past decade. And both will have to struggle against a powerful demographic tide to generate economic growth in future decades, when a dwindling workforce will have to maintain a growing mass of retired people.

No less important than this economic diagnosis is the broader political question. Why is it that these hitherto highly successful countries have found it so hard to confront their respective difficulties? For in both cases governments have signally failed to measure up to the challenges they face.

Despite presenting a reformist agenda to the Japanese electorate, the government of Junichiro Koizumi has achieved precious little in its economic policies. Germany, meantime, suffers from what Thomas Mayer, Deutsche Bank's chief European economist, calls a complacent electorate and weak political leadership. Under Gerhard Schroder, the chancellor, the ruling coalition has failed adequately to tackle a creaking tax and benefit system or to deregulate markets that are palpably sclerotic.

Part of the problem is that these countries suffer from what might be termed the paralysis of the rich. In order to persuade electorates of the need for radical change it is necessary to generate a sense of crisis. In Japan, despite all the economic difficulties of the past decade, per capita gross domestic product stood at $37 600 (£24 100) in 2000, while the comparable figure for Germany, inevitably lower because of unification, was $22 530.

These, then, are prosperous countries. And because their political processes are rooted in consensualism it can take large shocks to bring about change. Yet they also manage to be remarkably shock-resistant. In Germany, unemployment is high but the generous social security system reduces the incentive for the unemployed to look for work. A reduced participation rate in turn exacerbates the demographic problem. And demographic problems, of their nature, do not induce crises because they grow worse at a snail's pace.

In Japan the more obvious source of a shock is a debt crisis. Since the bursting of the stock market bubble, the government has sought to compensate for the decline in corporate investment by running ever-larger fiscal deficits. So public sector debt has risen to unprecedented levels. Yet it is virtually impossible to have a fiscal crisis in Japan when short-term interest rates are near-zero and the yield on long-term government bonds is a mere 1.5 per cent.

So, too, in the private sector, where over-indebted 'zombie' companies go on for ever because debt servicing costs are low. Deflation and bad policy have substantially removed the discipline of bankruptcy from Japanese capitalism.

Meanwhile, the historical experience of very high or hyper-inflation in Germany and Japan means that policy-makers are highly orthodox. At German behest the European Central Bank was given a constitution stricter than that of the Bundesbank. Its interest rates, even if suitable for the eurozone as a whole, are now too tight for the Germans.

For their part, policy-makers at the Bank of Japan have been reluctant to contemplate the unorthodox moves that may be needed in a period of deflation, when nominal short-term interest rates are zero but real rates are rising because of a falling price level. It could be sensible, for example, to increase money supply by having the central bank or the commercial banks finance the budget deficit. Conventional bankers demur.

Many of these constraints on policy reflect the characteristic of consensually managed economies noted by the economist Mancur Olsen – namely, that they are often hostage to the stultifying influence of interest groups. In Germany and also Italy, which faces many similar problems, the unions have been particularly effective in slowing labour market and pensions reform. In Japan vested interests in the Liberal Democratic party, with their strong money links to sectors such as construction, have prevented much radical change.

It is easier to cut through such vested interests in a predominantly two-party political system with a first-past-the-post electoral set-up than in countries where coalition government is the norm. The key to the Thatcherite reforms of the 1980s in the UK, for example, was that a government elected by a minority of the voters was able to impose its will on the reluctant majority, on the principle that Lord Hailsham dubbed elective dictatorship.

New Zealand provides another recent example. Its 1980s experiment in liberal economics under David Lange and Roger Douglas was certainly non-consensual and the electorate's distaste for such harsh (and not noticeably effective) medicine ensured an early change in the system to proportional representation.

Part of the dilemma faced by consensually managed countries is that things often have to become a great deal worse before they start getting better. This poses a challenge for the capital markets, where the lion's share of the money is managed by impatient Anglophones. Yet, interestingly, perceptions about Japan and Germany have been at odds.

In the Japanese stock market foreigners have been the marginal buyers of stock as the market has fallen over the past 12 years. Foreign fund managers have continued to absorb equities as members of keiretsu, or loose-knit conglomerates, have sold their cross-holdings in response to financial pressure.

With Germany, capital has been less forgiving. For a period before the introduction of the euro, it became excited about the prospects for restructuring in continental Europe generally and Germany in particular. Then, as the pace of change proved slow, disillusionment set in. Hence the euro's weakness until recently.

Why capital has been more kind to Japan, given that its problems are much deeper-seated than Germany's, is moot. Maybe its economic performance until the 1990s had been so spectacular that it retained an additional residue of goodwill with fund managers. Maybe some of them were still buying into the world's second-largest economy on the basis of the weights in a global index.

What is clear is that a succession of shocks has not been enough to turn round these two huge economies. History tells us that when a big enough shock comes along, these countries can change astonishingly fast. The question is whether the Germans and Japanese will have to become poor again, to be shocked out of their affluent paralysis and back into respectable economic growth.

Source: John Plender, *Financial Times*, 27 December 2002, p. 15

Questions

1. Why have Germany and Japan had such poor growth performances during the twenty-first century?

2. How have Germany and Japan attempted to improve the growth performances of their economies?

moving from agriculture into other sectors of the economy. Oil discoveries in the Middle East ensured cheap oil supplies, particularly as oil production was in the hands of a few major Western European companies. Further, technology transfer from the United States enabled the relatively backward industries of post-war Europe to make rapid improvements in productivity. Increasing real incomes improved market sizes and coupled with the removal of trade barriers through the development of the European Free Trade Area (EFTA), the development of the European Community (EC) and the successes of the General Agreements on Tariffs and Trade (GATT), conditions were ripe for high levels of sustained growth.

By the early 1970s conditions were beginning to change. The movement of labour from agriculture to manufacturing had begun to decline; labour relations deteriorated. The 1973/74 oil price rise led to a period of more expensive and less secure energy, and exchange rate movements led to European commodities losing some of their competitiveness. In addition, there was increasing competition from Japan and the newly industrialised countries (NICs) – Singapore, Hong Kong, South Korea and Taiwan – in shipbuilding, steel and car manufacture – areas in which the Europeans had regarded themselves as pre-eminent.

At the same time Japan, in particular, had begun to adopt different working practices which implied that the old labour rules needed adjusting, a feature which was heavily resisted by the trade unions in Europe. In other words, inadequate adjustment of its industry had reduced Europe's ability to compete in global markets. Free marketeers believe that the weakness of governments and the strength of trade unions allowed real wage rates (the amount that take-home pay will purchase) to soar. Thus, products became more expensive within Europe and government policy only served to safeguard jobs rather than improve output. The much more laissez-faire approach adopted by the UK government since the early 1980s has attempted to address the problem of the high price of labour through legislation designed to limit the power of trade unions and encourage private sector involvement through its privatisation policy.

Generally there has been a convergence of economic activity in structural terms. That is, the developed economies have become more orientated towards the service sector whilst developing economies are more concentrated in producing primary products. As Table 3.5 indicates, in many developed countries, 60 per cent or more of economic activity is in the service sector. For example, in Luxembourg, the United Kingdom and the United States it accounts for around 70 per cent of economic activity. In other European countries, such as Portugal and Greece, agriculture plays a bigger part in the economy.

The United Kingdom has seen a fall in its share of world manufacturing exports and a fall in manufacturing employment. For other countries, like Japan, the picture is somewhat different. In fact, between 1964 and 1999 Japan continued to see its manufacturing employment grow, whilst at the same time the United Kingdom lost over 43 per cent of manufacturing employment (OECD, 2000).

Not only has the overall structure of economies changed, but within the various economic sectors, countries have tended to specialise in producing certain products. The United Kingdom is more specialised in extractive industries, chemicals and financial services, France in food products, Germany in engineering and chemicals, and Italy in clothing, textiles and footwear.

Table 3.5 Sectoral contribution to GDP and employment, 2001, percentages

	Agriculture		Industry		Services	
	GDP	Employment	GDP	Employment	GDP	Employment
Greece	10.1	17.7	22.8	23.0	67.1	59.2
Luxembourg	1.0	3.0	24.0	24.9	77.0	72.0
Portugal	3.6	13.6	28.5	36.0	67.9	48.4
United Kingdom	1.5	1.7	25.1	26.5	73.1	71.8
USA	1.6	2.7	27.4	23.6	71.0	73.7
Japan	2.0	3.0	39.0	32.2	59.0	62.5

Source: OECD economic surveys, 2002, various countries

Consideration of the sectors overall may hide important changes within sectors. Within the secondary sector it is manufacturing which has felt the full force of any structural change, though the impact has been different within manufacturing (the high technology/skill areas have remained very competitive, though the reverse is true for low technology/skill areas). Once again there are differences by country, as Table 3.5 indicates.

The costs of growth

Firstly, it may be assumed that growth brings only benefits. However, there is a view that growth has a number of negative aspects in terms of environmental damage and that the process of achieving higher growth may not be worth the effort. Growth may cause negative externalities, where the actions of producers or consumers affect not only themselves but also third parties, other than through the normal workings of the price mechanism. It is the developed countries which produce the greatest amount of pollution, including 45 per cent of greenhouse gases, and consume around 70 per cent of all resources; see Chapter 6 for a discussion of environmental costs. Many of these costs are likely to be understated, since precise measurements are not available. If, as Meadows *et al.* (1992) suggest, the costs of growth are included in the estimates of real national income then the benefits of economic growth may be overstated.

Secondly, to achieve a higher growth rate some consumption expenditure may have to be foregone today and resources switched to investment goods so that future consumption may be higher.

Thirdly, growth also has an impact on resources, particularly non-renewable ones. If growth is stimulated today we are just bringing the day forward when non-renewable resources will disappear. Growth also brings technical progress, which may create jobs but, at the same time, destroy others by making skills redundant. People may be forced to take low-paid, unskilled work or migrate. The results of this process can be seen in the structural changes outlined earlier.

Whether governments should pursue the goal of growth depends, therefore, on the costs and benefits of growth and how much weight individual groups in society attach to them. Perhaps constrained growth is the solution, where growth is sought, but subject to, for example, levels of environmental protection, minimum wages, and maximum rates of resource depletion.

There are individuals who suggest that we do not have to worry about using up finite resources. It is their view that as the resource is depleted so its price will rise and consumers will purchase less of it. It is possible too that resources which were not profitable at the old price will come into use, as was the case in the development of North Sea oil and gas reserves. These marginal resources may be used efficiently if technology can provide a means of increasing the capacity usage. Suppose, however, that there comes a point when technology cannot make marginal resources as effective as those that have been depleted. It follows that the prices of materials would rise; this would feed through to inflation, and a wage price spiral would ensue, reducing everyone's standard of living. Alternatively, resources could be rationed.

Although these arguments seem a little improbable on first viewing, the notion of resource depletion did receive support at the Earth Summit in Rio de Janeiro in May 1992 and was considered further at the environmental conferences at Montreal (1996), Tokyo (1998), and Johannesburg (2002). The call was for controlled growth. A constrained growth rate is easier to bear for the developed countries, but for many less developed countries (LDCs) or newly industrialised countries (NICs) the development of indigenous natural resources is seen as a prerequisite for escape from low levels of GDP per capita. The acceptability of this constrained growth scenario to those countries depends upon whether the developed nations provide increased aid to finance any difference between sustainable growth and their 'normal' level of growth. Even without consideration of the environmental impact of growth, on a macroeconomic level growth can have an important impact on prices. High levels of growth which are coupled with resource constraints can lead to inflation. The Johannesburg conference also called for the diversification of energy supply with a move towards cleaner and renewable technologies. Sustainable development was high on the agenda with the notion of minimising waste, maximising use and recycling. However, the commitment to the reduction in greenhouse gases and sustainability was not considered a high priority for some countries, notably the United States.

Inflation

Inflation may be defined as a persistent increase in prices over time, in other words, the rate of inflation measures the change in the purchasing power of money.

There are a number of ways in which inflation can be measured. One method is by measuring changes in the Retail Price Index (RPI) (sometimes called the headline rate). The RPI measures the change in prices from month to month in a representative 'basket' of commodities bought by the average consumer. The commodities in the basket are weighted differently to indicate the proportion of expenditure made by the average consumer on various items. As Table 3.6 indicates, the weights change over time as goods change in relative importance in the average basket of commodities purchased by consumers. Thus in the United Kingdom since 1987, food, fuel and light (due to privatisation and the growth in competition) and clothing and footwear account for smaller proportions of the average expenditure of consumers, whilst housing costs, motoring expenditure and to some extent leisure services have increased.

In the UK, mortgage interest payments are included in the RPI. This means that higher rates of interest will push up mortgage rates and increase the rate of inflation. So if it is the government's intention to reduce inflation by increasing interest rates and thereby reducing consumer expenditure, the opposite effect will occur. Since the RPI was the index usually used as a basis for wage claims, workers and trade unions could be encouraged to pursue higher wage claims if the RPI increased through increased mortgage rates. These would then increase the costs of industry, causing further price rises.

Table 3.6 General index of retail prices: group weights

Category	1987	1994	1998	2002
Catering	46	45	48	52
Food	167	142	130	114
Alcoholic drinks	76	76	71	68
Tobacco	38	35	34	31
Housing	157	158	197	199
Fuel and light	61	45	36	31
Household goods	73	76	72	73
Household services	44	47	54	60
Clothing and footwear	74	58	55	51
Personal goods and services	38	37	40	43
Motoring expenditure	127	142	136	141
Fares and other travel costs	22	20	20	20
Leisure goods	47	48	46	48
Leisure services	30	71	61	69
	1000	1000	1000	1000

Source: Labour Market Trends *(1988, 1994, 1998),* Monthly Digest of Statistics, *Dec. 2002*

Other European countries, for example France and Italy, exclude owner-occupation from their consumer price index, whilst other countries, because of the small size of their home ownership sector compared with their rental sector, will exhibit different changes in their retail price index for an equivalent change in interest rates.

In the United Kingdom a measure of inflation has been developed which does not include the costs of mortgages, RPIX, now called the underlying rate of inflation. A further method for measuring inflation has also been developed, called RPIY. This measure of inflation excludes both mortgage interest rate payments and indirect taxes such as VAT and excise duty. This is a measure, therefore, of the true underlying rate of inflation.

Why the concern about inflation?

From 1950 to 1970 prices were fairly stable in Western nations. The first oil price rise in 1973/74 changed this. The increase in the price of oil pushed up energy prices and transportation costs, and increased the prices of goods which were oil-related. The

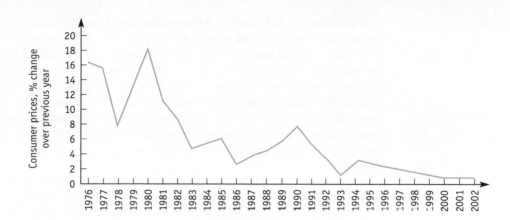

Figure 3.1 Inflation in the UK (percentage change over previous year)

response of the Western nations was to try to squeeze inflation out of the system. Figure 3.1 shows how inflation has changed in the United Kingdom over the years since 1976, and indicates the price rises following the 1979 oil shock and the further rise in inflation towards the end of the 1980s.

Inflation is said to have redistribution effects. If money wages rise at the same rate as inflation, then real wages remain constant. However, if tax bands and tax thresholds do not rise in line with inflation a greater proportion of income is subject to tax. Inflation also reduces the real value of the debt to the government, thus redistributing income from the people to the state.

The redistribution effects of inflation not only take place from individuals to governments but also affect individuals and businesses. Inflation favours debtors rather than creditors, as it erodes the value of debt.

Inflation also has external consequences, making domestically produced goods more expensive and less competitive on world markets and imported goods cheaper on the home market. In this case the balance of payments position will worsen and pressure will mount for the exchange rate to fall. As the exchange rate falls it will make imports more expensive and reduce the price of exports, thereby restoring equilibrium in the balance of payments. Governments, however, may pursue a policy of managed exchange rates which prevents the market from restoring equilibrium in the balance of payments. In these cases, controlling the effect of inflation by other means rather than letting the exchange rate do the correction may be a better approach.

During the 1980s, government policies throughout Europe shifted from reducing unemployment to controlling the rate of inflation. Policy-makers argue that this is the correct approach since, once inflation is beaten, unemployment will fall. The arguments are stated as follows. High and variable inflation makes future income from investment projects uncertain. Thus firms may reduce investment or may only consider undertaking investment projects which yield a high rate of return in the short term. However, the positive link between inflation and unemployment is somewhat tenuous; Friedman (1977) supports the relationship, while Higham and Tomlinson (1982) find no general evidence.

High inflation may lead to governments imposing wage and price controls which inhibit the working of the market mechanism. Some firms, which may be relatively more efficient or in markets where the demand for their products is rising, may be prevented from offering their employees better rewards because of the controls put in place by government. In addition, the more efficient firms may be unable to offer rewards high enough to entice staff from other sectors of the economy. High inflation may also lead to industrial unrest as unions seek money wage increases in order to prevent a deterioration in their real wages. It may also be expected that high inflation depresses saving, as consumers purchase products from organisations before the prices increase once again.

Inflationary expectations also take time to adjust downwards. A reduction in current inflation may not lead to an improvement in the amount invested since it is possible that investors may feel that the inflation rate will increase again in the future.

Given the problems that can arise from inflation it would be easy to suggest that countries which have relatively higher rates of inflation perform less well than countries with lower levels of inflation. However, this is not always the case. For example before joining the Euro bloc Spain had relatively high inflation but high growth. Conversely Germany had relatively high growth and low inflation.

The causes of inflation

Inflation can be damaging both internally and externally and it is not surprising that governments have used a variety of means to control inflationary pressures. The more traditional view was that inflation could be due either to 'cost–push' or 'demand–pull' factors. In the former it may be due to:

- increases in costs of labour that are not linked to increases in labour productivity;

- increases in the costs of raw materials which could come about in buoyant stages of the economic cycle, where the demand for raw materials may outstrip supply in the short term;

- a deterioration in exchange rates, which tends to cause import prices to rise.

In the demand–pull scenario, it is the excess demand for goods that pulls up prices. If aggregate demand increases, the increased demand for labour would push up real wage rates. If unions in other sectors of the economy attempted to keep their members' wages in parallel, then it is possible that, even with an excess labour supply in these other sectors, unions would be able to force up wage rates. The overall general increase in wage rates then feeds through into the costs of industry and is subsequently passed on in price increases. This causes real wages to fall, with the possibility that further wage demands could follow. In such circumstances a damaging wage–price inflationary cycle is likely to be established.

Inflation can also be caused by governments 'accommodating' price increases. In this instance, whenever aggregate demand falls, leading to higher levels of unemployment, governments step into the economy directly through changes in either government expenditure or taxation to stimulate the economy. This increase in economic activity would increase national income but can also cause the price level to rise.

Monetarists saw the excessive role of governments during the 1960s and 1970s as being directly responsible for the rise in inflation and argued that this type of intervention would have no long-term impact on output and unemployment. They suggested that the economy would return to some natural level of economic activity, but at a higher level of inflation. Does this mean that government activity in the economy may not be worthwhile since it cannot increase output or employment in the long term? From a governmental perspective the long term may extend beyond the lifetime of an elected government; it still might be possible, therefore, to increase employment during the government's term of office! See Figure 3.2(a).

Monetarists argue that if real output and employment is to be increased then governments should intervene not in the demand side but in the supply side of the market. As Figure 3.2(b) indicates, the level of output can be increased not only by shifting the aggregate demand curve to the right from AD_1 to AD_2 but also by shifting the aggregate supply curve to the right from $SRAS_1$ to $SRAS_2$. Thus the monetarists advocated the use of policies to shift the supply curve to the right, so-called 'supply-side measures'. These policies are designed to reduce government involvement and so reduce the frictions they perceive exist in markets (see also Chapter 2).

In addition monetarists see the need to control the amount of money in the economy, so would suggest that governments control either the quantity of money (the money supply) or the price of money (the interest rate).

Since government expenditure often exceeds the revenue from taxation, the consequent deficit, the Public Sector Borrowing Requirement (PSBR), was often financed via government printing the extra money. Seigniorage – the printing of money to finance government expenditure – alleviates the government's need to borrow. However, this growth in the money supply increases the amount of money in circulation and could have inflationary consequences. Monetarists suggested that governments seek to reduce the amount of borrowing they undertake. If the monetarists are to be believed then all governments need to do is control the money supply and introduce a

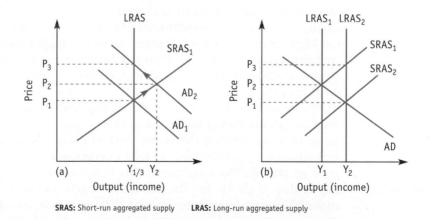

SRAS: Short-run aggregated supply   LRAS: Long-run aggregated supply

Figure 3.2 Prices/output in the aggregate demand/aggregate supply framework

series of supply-side measures – policies aimed at improving the quantity and quality of supply – as a means to reduce the level of inflation.

It has been notoriously difficulty to control the money supply. This is for two main reasons. First, we need to define what we mean by the money supply. Is it notes and coins in circulation (this is defined as M_0), is it notes and coins in circulation plus bank deposits (this is known as M_1) or is it some other definition? The Federal Reserve Bank, in the United States, has over 20 definitions of the money supply.

Second, it was found that, when the UK government targeted a particular measure of the money supply during the 1980s, it had the habit of going out of control, that is exceeding its target rate of growth.

The monetarist approach of using higher interest rates to control inflation can damage business confidence and increase the costs to industry. In addition, if government expenditure is controlled then this subsequently affects consumer expenditure and business sales. The difficulties experienced by the UK government encouraged it to abandon direct controls over money supply in 1985.

Non-monetarist views of inflation

It has been argued that monetarist approaches to inflation have not been responsible for bringing inflation under control, and that other forces have played a more dominant role.

As Table 3.7 indicates, the United Kingdom's anti-inflation strategy appeared to be succeeding during the early and middle parts of the 1980s and in the middle-to-latter 1990s, but was less satisfactory at other times. Beckerman (1985) suggests that much of the fall in inflation in the early 1980s can be attributed to the fall in commodity prices that followed from the world recession. The very tight fiscal stance taken by the government also had an influence. Soteri and Westaway (1993) suggest that, for the UK, world inflation, and the exchange rate and its effect on import prices have both played an important part in explaining the changes in its inflation record.

We should also consider the UK's 'temporary' membership of the Exchange Rate Mechanism (ERM). Under fixed exchange rates organisations cannot rely on the exchange rate to restore competitiveness in their prices if their relative inflation rates are too high. In the short term, if labour seeks too high a wage claim, then the loss of competitiveness that follows from any increases in prices would lead to job losses. Thus, the ERM was seen as providing discipline for the labour market. From the middle part of the 1990s we have seen inflation at low levels once again. Some consider that inflation is now very much under control and is not the major concern of the developed nations. Part of the reason as to why governments attach less significance to inflation in the 1990s is that many Western developed nations have been following anti-inflationary policies and the level of economic activity has not been allowed to grow so rapidly. The outcome of this policy approach is to have unemployment higher than it should be. The pursuit of targets for entry into the European single currency, where low inflation was one of those targets, has also led to lower inflation. At the same time the UK government has given control of its interest rates to the Bank

Table 3.7 The UK and European economies since 1986

	Inflation (% rate)		Unemployment (% level)		Real GDP (% growth rate)	
	UK	Euro area	UK	Euro area	UK	Euro area
1986	3.6	2.5	11.7	9.4	4.2	2.4
1987	3.7	2.6	10.2	9.2	4.2	2.5
1988	4.6	2.7	7.8	8.8	5.2	4.1
1989	5.9	3.8	6.1	8.1	2.2	4.0
1990	8.1	5.8	5.9	7.4	0.8	3.6
1991	6.8	4.3	8.2	7.6	−1.4	2.5
1992	4.7	3.8	10.2	8.4	0.2	1.4
1993	3.0	3.4	10.3	10.0	2.5	−0.8
1994	2.4	2.8	9.4	10.7	4.7	2.3
1995	2.8	2.6	8.6	10.5	2.9	2.2
1996	2.9	1.3	8.0	10.7	2.6	1.4
1997	2.8	1.7	6.5	10.8	3.4	2.3
1998	2.7	1.2	6.3	10.2	2.9	2.9
1999	2.3	1.2	5.9	9.4	2.4	2.8
2000	2.1	2.4	5.4	8.4	3.1	3.6
2001	2.1	2.5	5.1	8.0	2.0	1.5

Source: OECD Economic Outlook, *December 2002*

of England, which may have adopted a stronger grip on squeezing inflation out of the system.

For some countries, notably a number of those in South America which have had historically high levels of inflation, the approach adopted to reduce inflation was to fix their exchange rates against the US dollar, and this has successfully reduced their inflationary spiral. It is also worth noting that while inflation has been reduced within Europe, the UK still has a higher inflation rate than many of its major trading partners.

The link between inflation and unemployment may also have changed. The UK, during the opening part of the twenty-first century, has experienced low inflation and low unemployment. This can be partly explained by its highly flexible labour market when compared with continental Europe. Similarly the United States has experienced low inflation and low unemployment. Again its flexible labour market plus its higher level of entrepreneurship and business start-ups when compared with Europe may explain this.

At this stage let us consider the arguments. Inflation is costly both domestically and internationally. Many reasons have been put forward to explain why inflation occurs, and almost as many remedies. For the latter there does not appear to be any consensus. However, in seeking to bring down inflation countries have often deflated their economies and in doing so worsened the conditions for business. For Eastern European countries the scenario is somewhat different. By Western standards, inflation has remained high in most parts of the region, as Table 3.8 indicates. However, for those countries that have adopted a more market-orientated approach to economic management and are seeking entry into the EU in the first wave in 2004 (see later in this chapter), inflation appears to have come under control remarkably well.

Part of the explanation for the relatively poor inflation performance of many Eastern European countries has been the introduction of market forces into many sectors and the reduction in state management of prices. Nonetheless, there are signs that inflation is being controlled, especially in Slovakia, the Czech Republic and Poland,

Table 3.8 Consumer price inflation (% per annum) in selected Eastern European countries

Year	Bulgaria	Czech Republic	Hungary	Poland	Romania	Slorakia
1989	5.6	1.4	17.0	251.1	1.1	1.3
1990	23.8	9.7	28.9	585.8	5.1	10.4
1991	338.5	56.6	35.0	70.3	174.5	61.2
1992	79.4	11.1	23.0	43.0	210.9	10.0
1993	59.1	25.2	22.5	35.3	256.1	23.2
1994	121.9	10.0	16.8	30.7	62.0	15.5
1995	32.9	9.1	28.3	26.8	28.0	7.2
1996	311	8.8	23.5	20.2	57.0	5.0
1997	1089	8.4	18.3	15.9	150.0	6.0
1998	18.8	10.7	14.3	11.8	59.1	6.7
1999	2.6	2.1	10.0	7.3	45.8	10.7
2000	10.4	3.9	9.8	10.1	45.7	12.0
2001	7.5	4.7	9.7	5.4	34.5	7.3

Sources: Employment Observatory, Central and Eastern Europe, *No. 6, 1994, European Commission; Barclays Bank Country Reports*, World Economic Outlook, *April 2002*

although high levels of inflation probably have affected business formation and development.

Dealing with deflation

Whereas the 1970s and parts of the 1980s were associated with relatively high levels of inflation, the 1990s have been denoted as a period of not only low levels of inflation but also with negative price increases (deflation). For example, Japan experienced deflation in 1995 and again from 1999 to 2002. Although for many consumers the RPI is still positive, the reason for it being that way is that the prices of some heavily weighted commodities in the average consumer's basket are still rising but the prices of many other commodities, less heavily weighted, are falling. For some countries such as Germany and Japan, even the more heavily weighted goods whose prices are rising cannot outweigh the falls in other commodities, thus at the end of the 1990s they are actually showing negative inflation figures.

Deflation sounds like a consumer paradise. Even in the United Kingdom we have seen mortgage rates falling and prices of goods considered as luxuries, such as television sets, video recorders and hi-fi systems, falling to just over half the 1987 level. Computers continue to fall in price and there is a similar scenario in clothing with many shops having continuous sales. The fall in these prices can be explained by:

- the fall in commodity prices as the global economy slows;
- the opening up of markets such as telecoms and electricity to competition;
- the role of technology increasing productivity;
- the behaviour of organisations which are being threatened by investigation into their pricing practices (supermarkets, over-the-counter medicines, etc.).

Living in more deflationary times may be good for consumers but it is not easy for businesses. If consumers believe that prices will fall in the future then they may wait longer to make purchases. This reduces current demand and this in turn drives down prices. The economic crisis in South-East Asia in the late 1990s has resulted in lower prices for UK imports, both through absolute price falls in commodities/goods and through the devaluations that have taken place in South-East Asian currencies. Both these factors are leading to increased competition for domestic producers. Exporters too are facing similar problems. In order to sell products abroad in markets in which there is competition from South-East Asian companies, businesses in the developed world are having to reduce their prices too.

For some industries deflation is not bad – industries with rapidly improving technologies and productivity, such as computers. It is the mature industries which have more problems, as they face reduced demand and overcapacity due to lower competitor prices. Lower demand leads to price reductions and lower levels of investment. This, through the circular flow, leads to further demand falls and so the cycle continues. So long as global demand remains relatively sluggish, we may have to get used to living with deflation for some time to come (see Minicase 3.2).

Minicase 3.2   Deflation – stubborn deflation challenges Tokyo to break with orthodoxy

Hayao Kawai, Japan's commissioner of cultural affairs, is a spry 74-year-old psychologist who has spent most of his career treating clinical depression. That, he says, is the perfect qualification for enticing the Japanese people to spend their way out of their decade-long economic malaise.

Mr Kawai is intent on injecting a 'feelgood' factor into the Japanese economy by encouraging people to spend more time and money on cultural activities. Not only will that pump more money into the economy, it will also help free up people's thinking, he says:

> Unless the Japanese people move towards challenging conformity, we will not be able to keep up with the international community.

Some of Japan's economic partners certainly wish the country would break with conformity when it comes to dealing with the problem of deflation. It has been dogging the economy for the past few years and exacerbated the weaknesses in the country's banking system.

This week the Organisation for Economic Co-operation and Development (OECD) urged the Japanese authorities to 'move further into uncharted territories' to address the problem, easing monetary conditions still further by purchasing a wide range of financial assets.

Koichi Hamada, one of Japan's most respected economists, certainly agrees that the Bank of Japan could do more to tackle deflation.

'I take the orthodox view that deflation is a monetary phenomenon. It is very strange that most parties and even some of the bureaucrats cook up anti-deflationary measures without mentioning monetary policy. It is like Hamlet without the Prince of Denmark,' he says.

Mr Hamada argues that fiscal and structural reforms should be pursued simultaneously, while a more expansionary monetary policy would help change consumers' deflationary expectations.

'I still advocate that the Bank of Japan can buy more long-term JGBs (Japanese government bonds). The Bank of Japan claims they cannot cause inflation at all. Their logic is very twisted,' he says.

But a series of interviews with senior Japanese officials has revealed stark divisions about how to tackle deflation. In particular, the institutional clash between the BoJ and the ministry of finance appears as intense as ever. Sharp differences of opinion are apparent, not only between those institutions but also within them. The promises of Junichiro Koizumi, the prime minister, to co-ordinate economic policy more closely have yet to be fulfilled.

Some finance officials argue that Japan has pursued a zero interest rate policy for seven years without stimulating the economy. For the past four years the central bank has also been increasing the money supply on a massive scale, with little impact on price levels.

The trouble is that the banking sector, waterlogged by bad debts, cannot function as an effective monetary transmission mechanism. The government must therefore implement structural reforms before further monetary easing can be effective, they argue.

Heizo Takenaka, the new head of the Financial Services Agency, is now promising to 'fix' that monetary transmission mechanism by straightening out Japan's twisted banking sector. In the face of fierce opposition, he is pushing the banks to accelerate the disposals of their massive non-performing loan portfolios to restore their financial health.

But finance officials claim the Takenaka plan might only worsen deflationary pressures in the economy in the immediate future, as so-called zombie companies are wound up and thousands of workers are laid off. Most of the bad loans are concentrated in the construction, distribution and property sectors, which employ millions of workers.

In such circumstances, some officials argue the only macroeconomic lever left to reflate the economy would be a significant depreciation of the yen. 'But we would need a jump from Y120 (to the US dollar) to Y180 to Y200 to have any effect,' says one official.

Any such drastic shift in the exchange rate would be extremely difficult to implement. Most importantly, it is no longer clear that Washington would tolerate such instability in the world's financial markets.

Source: John Thornhill, *Financial Times*, 21 November 2002, p. 11

Questions

1. Why do other countries want the Japanese economy to come out of its deflationary period?

2. How has the Japanese government attempted to stimulate the economy? Why have these policies failed so far?

The role of the state in the economy

Table 3.9 indicates that government expenditure by European Union governments is, in total, around half of EU GDP. The five top-spending governments are Sweden, Denmark, France, Belgium and Austria, all of which spend between 50 and 55 per cent of GDP. Control of this expenditure has partially come through the Stability Pact of the euro.

Table 3.9 Government expenditure 2002

Country	Total Government Expenditure as Percentage of Nominal GDP
Belgium	50.2
Denmark	55.3
France	54.0
Germany	48.6
Greece	46.3
Ireland	34.4
Italy	47.7
Netherlands	47.3
Portugal	46.1
Spain	39.8
United Kingdom	40.9
Austria	51.9
Finland	49.2
Norway	46.7
Sweden	58.3
EU-15	47.7
Japan	38.6
USA	35.6
Korea	24.6

Source: OECD National Accounts

Government spending by nearly all European Union governments exceeds that of the United States (35 per cent of GDP), Korea (25 per cent of GDP) and Japan (38 per cent of GDP). There is no single reason to explain why some countries have higher proportions of GDP devoted to government expenditure than others.

These different levels of government activity occur for a variety of reasons. Part of the spending represents a redistribution of income amongst citizens. Governments may also play an active role in macroeconomic stabilisation of the economy, using government spending to prevent excessive fluctuations in income and unemployment, thus smoothing out business cycles.

Government expenditure is a very important part of total expenditure in most economies. Governments are big consumers, spending around a third of the total that all households spend on goods and services. Like many households they are prone to over-expenditure and are forced to borrow money from the private sector or from abroad. The level of this debt can reach almost unmanageable amounts and, as Table 3.10 indicates, for

Table 3.10 Government debt as a percentage of nominal GDP (Maastricht definition)

Country	1988	1993	1996	1998	2002
Belgium	132	139	136.4	118.4	105.4
Denmark	61	80	68.4	57.3	45.2
France	34	46	60.9	58.9	59.5
Germany	44	48	62.5	60.7	60.8
Greece	80	115	120.2	108.2	104.9
Ireland	118	96	79.1	57.0	33.5
Italy	93	119	120.5	118.5	106.7
Luxembourg	10	8	6	6.3	5.8
Netherlands	79	81	79.5	99.5	52.5
Portugal	75	67	64.0	63.4	58.1
Spain	42	60	68.7	68.5	54.0
United Kingdom	50	48	52.8	52.1	38.4
Austria	58	57	61.4	64.8	67.6
Finland	17	62	71.4	53.4	42.7
Norway	43	45	46.5	—	—
Sweden	54	84	86.3	74.5	52.4

Sources: European Economy, Supplement A, *11/12 November 1998; European Commission, OECD,* Economic Outlook, *various years*

some countries, such as Greece, Italy and Belgium, this burden of debt can be in excess of a full year's domestic product. What is noticeable is that government debt has decreased in many countries. This is partly explained by the need to adhere to the growth and stability pact of the single currency, but it also indicates the strength of some economies, notably Ireland (the 'Celtic' tiger economy), and of the windfall gains that have come the way of some governments by having lower levels of unemployment (hence higher tax receipts and lower benefit payments) and through the sale of state assets and 3G telephone licences, the money from which was used to reduce some countries' government debts.

Interest payment on these debts is an important problem for countries, particularly those with debts in excess of 100 per cent of GDP. In these countries higher taxes, both on the business sector and on consumers, may have to be levied, for a long period, to finance the interest payments and to repay the debt.

Another way to hold down the rise in government debt is to curtail government expenditure. However, this may be difficult, since as unemployment rises there is often a concomitant rise in state benefits and reduction in tax revenue. It may, of course, be possible to reduce the deficit through increasing tax revenues. Figure 3.3 shows the main sources of revenues for governments in the European Union, the tax on labour, and social security contributions of employers and employees.

The proportion of revenues obtained from the various sources differs from country to country. The average tax as a percent of labour costs is higher in Belgium, Germany, Sweden, France, Finland, Italy, Austria and the Netherlands compared the European Union as a whole. Only the United States, Great Britain, Ireland and Japan have an average tax rate on labour costs below the OECD average. In the UK, Portugal, Greece and France, indirect taxes are a more important source of revenue, while in Belgium, Denmark, Finland, Italy and the Netherlands the reverse is true. Contributions by employers and employees on social security are also higher than the EU average in the Netherlands, Austria, Greece, France, Germany and Belgium. These differences between the burdens of the various forms of taxation can have an impact on company location, level of profits, consumer behaviour and the incentive to work harder.

Economic cycles

It could be argued that one role of government is to reduce the fluctuations that occur in the economy. Often these fluctuations are not random but follow a cyclical pattern. There are long and short cycles in the economy. The long cycle (Kondratief cycle) is estimated to have a period of 50 years and to be associated with technological breakthroughs. Other cycles are observable, such as the business cycle (trade cycle), a seven- to ten-year economic cycle, and political cycles, cycles of four or five years coinciding with elections. We would expect to find that in the boom periods of the cycle economic activity is buoyant and organisations find it much easier to sell their goods and services. At the same time there may be pent-up pressures beginning to appear which serve to drive up prices. At this stage the government may seek to dampen economic activity. Conversely, at the bottom of a cycle, economic activity is subdued; there may be high levels of unemployment and less pressure on prices, and the government may perceive a need to step into the economy more directly and stimulate the level of economic activity.

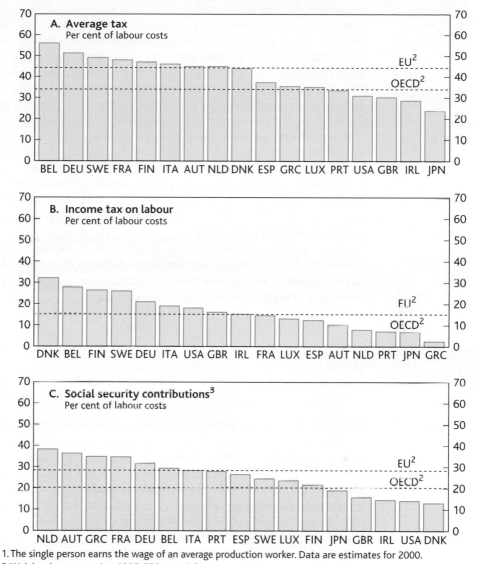

1. The single person earns the wage of an average production worker. Data are estimates for 2000.
2. Weighted average using 1995 GDP as weights.
3. Contributions of employers and employees, calculated as average tax minus income tax on labour.

Figure 3.3 Average tax on labour: an international comparison for a single person with no children, 2000[1]
Source: OECD, Taxing Wages 2000 Edition

Over time markets have become more internationalised and countries have increasingly been involved in closer trading groups so that the phases of their cycles are more concurrent. Thus, when one trading bloc or area goes into recession, it may cause other trading blocs to do the same. One national government cannot, on its own, stimulate its economy whilst others in its trading bloc do nothing. It is now necessary for groups of countries to co-ordinate economic intervention. For example, the bursting of the dot.com bubble in the United States led to a loss in confidence by investors in the United States and the American economy began to slow. This subsequently reduced confidence in the European economy as their dot.com bubble also imploded. The result of this combined with the September 11th problems and the uncertainties leading up to the war in Iraq resulted in much slower growth rates in the global economies in 2002/3. This had further repercussions on the global stock markets, which also suffered downturns during this period. Co-ordination also takes place on an international level. For example, the global community moved together to stimulate the global economy following the financial crashes in South-East Asia, and the Federal Reserve Bank in the United States, the Bank of England and the European Central Bank have lowered interest rates to stimulate the global economy during 2002/3.

We should recognise that governments sometimes attempt to drive their economy out of its normal business cycle for political reasons, such as re-election. Alesina (1989) suggests that it is politically risky for governments to approach an election with deteriorating economic conditions.

It is relatively easy to see the impacts of economic cycles on international economies, but explaining why they occur is much more difficult. The political cycle can be explained, though not fully, by the behaviour of domestic governments, but the trade cycle is much more difficult to interpret.

Employment

From the end of the second World War until the 1970s control of unemployment was the main goal of most European governments. During the 1970s and 1980s control of inflation assumed greater importance. Phillips (1958) argued that low inflation is not compatible with low unemployment. Nonetheless, a number of governments saw that low relative inflation could lead to higher competitiveness and provide the conditions for improvements in employment, a feature that has appeared once more to be in place during the early part of the twenty-first century. Minicase 3.3 illustrates the problems faced by the Slovak government.

Although unemployment has fluctuated with the general level of economic activity there has been a slow upward trend in the natural level of unemployment until the 1990s – the level of unemployment which is consistent with overall equilibrium in the labour market – since the second World War. Since the end of the 1990s the UK and United States have experienced almost unprecedented low levels of unemployment (in the UK around 5 per cent) and this is much lower than the OECD's estimate for the natural rate of unemployment in the UK of 8 per cent in 1996. This suggests that some progress on supply-side measures in the labour market has been made (Cook and Healey, 2001). At the same time, 5 per cent unemployment does suggest that the UK economy is getting dangerously close to full employment.

Why has there been a general rise in the natural rates of unemployment in Europe since the 1960s, particularly when compared with the United States? Burda and

| Minicase 3.3 | Unemployment – threat to high growth posed by rising value of the crown |

Hopes are high finally that the Slovak economy is poised to take off. But old problems still threaten to hold it back.

Economic growth this year should be the highest in central Europe at close to 4 per cent. The government forecasts it will fall back slightly to 3.7 per cent next year before exceeding 4 per cent in 2004. But strong domestic growth is widening the current account deficit again, while the budget deficit and the unemployment rate remain stubbornly large. Moreover, optimism about the economy is fuelling a surge in the Slovak crown, which has appreciated by almost 4 per cent since the beginning of September against the euro.

This threatens to make Slovak industry uncompetitive and worsen the current account deficit. The central bank has had to intervene repeatedly against the rising crown, and last month cut its benchmark two-week repo rate by a massive 1.5 percentage points to 6.5 per cent. The central bank now fears that if it cuts rates again this could overstimulate the domestic economy and widen the current account deficit.

'The appreciating crown is a danger as the deficit in the current account is higher than we would wish,' says Marian Jusko, central bank governor.

The current account deficit has become a problem again because buoyant consumer and government spending are sucking in imports, while exports are struggling because of the western European slowdown. The current account deficit is expected to reach 8.5 per cent of gross domestic product (GDP) again this year, close to the level bequeathed by the last Meciar government. This deficit is currently being covered by privatisation revenue inflows – but it is unsustainable in the long term.

However, the government forecasts the current account deficit will subside to 6.3 per cent next year as economic revival in western Europe stimulates Slovak exports. Import demand should also moderate as public spending is cut and sharp increases in regulated prices stem the private consumption boom.

Reducing the budget deficit remains central to controlling the current account deficit and creating space for the central bank to make further cuts in interest rates. The general government deficit overshot to an estimated 7.5 per cent of GDP in this election year, though this is swelled by around 1.5 percentage points by interest payments on bailing out the insolvent state-owned banks before their privatisation. Next year, the government plans to bring the deficit down to 5 per cent, with a target of meeting the Maastricht criterion of 3 per cent at the end of its term in 2006. This would allow for adoption of the euro in 2008, ahead of the neighbouring Czech Republic.

The International Monetary Fund recently called for swifter cuts and Ivan Miklos, finance minister, believes the government should be more ambitious.

'We can go further,' says Mr Miklos. 'It may be possible to complete this sooner.'

In the 2003 budget the deficit will be narrowed by raising indirect taxes and restricting public sector wage increases. From 2004 onwards, Mr Miklos wants to make deep structural changes to public spending. This will involve introducing more private contributions into the health and education systems, establishment of a funded pension system and radical reform of the welfare system to reduce abuse and target real need.

Welfare reform will help bring down what is one of the highest unemployment rates in Europe. Next year unemployment is forecast to average 18 per cent. In parts of eastern Slovakia it is double this rate, and in the medieval-looking settlements of the large Roma (gipsy) minority it can be close to 100 per cent.

Foreign investment provides the only real solution for the country's unemployment problem. Foreign investment will also improve the country's export performance, narrow the current account gap, and generate stronger sustainable growth. Slovakia's efforts to attract foreign direct investment (FDI) have had only limited success. Per capita, it received $1050 in FDI between 1989–2001 compared with $2570 for the Czech Republic.

The country's performance has improved since 1999, the first year of Mr Dzurinda's government, but most FDI has been devoted to privatisation or retail development, rather than brownfield or greenfield industrial investment. This year FDI is estimated at $3.7bn, but $2.7bn came from the privatisation of SPP, the gas monopoly.

But with the government's re-election and the invitation to join Nato, the government believes FDI should boom. 'Nato membership was the only significant difference from our neighbours in the past,' says Mr Miklos. 'This is changed now.'

'There has been a considerable amount of investment activity since the elections,' confirms John Goodish, chief executive of US Steel Kosice, 'not only new foreign investors but also investors already here are expanding their operations.'

Source: Robert Anderson, *Financial Times*, 12 December 2002, p. 2

Questions

1. How does an appreciation in the value of the Slovak crown impact on employment in the Slovak economy?

2. How might the structural changes to public sector spending by Mr Miklos affect unemployment?

Wyplosz (2001) present some evidence:

- Where the safety provisions, such as benefits, for the unemployed are more extensive then unemployment levels are higher. Benefits may allow some people to stay out of the labour market.

- Their skills become inappropriate for the needs of the labour market and they become part of the long-term unemployed.

- Trade unions have been more militant in Europe.

- Labour costs consist of more than wages; they include labour taxes (social security and retirement contributions), and these too have risen steeply.

- Regulation of the use of labour, for example length of the working week and dismissal procedures, is also of importance.

- Productivity – output per person – must also be examined. As labour becomes more productive fewer employees are required to produce a given quantity of output.

- Sectoral changes have taken place in a number of European economies as they have moved from labour-intensive manufacturing based industries to service-orientated ones (see above).

- Minimum wage levels may be set higher than the clearing wage in some European countries.

- The European economy is less dynamic than that of the United States, hence fewer jobs are provided.

Job creation in the United Kingdom is possible. This is unlikely to come from a simple boost in demand but rather from a longer-term emphasis on investment in infrastructure, training and education (Begg, 1995). Indeed, evidence suggests that there has been a decline in the natural rate of unemployment in the UK since the mid- to late 1990s. This is due to:

- improved labour market skills and a better educated workforce;

- the introduction of back to work schemes for the long-term unemployed;

- the continued weakness of trade unions;

- flexibility of the workforce;

- the success of supply-side measures introduced in the previous decade.

For more than a decade the UK government has been acutely aware of the lack of training taking place, a shortage of skills and a general failure to keep pace with the rapidly changing world of work. The world of education has seen the development of a new National Curriculum and vocationally-orientated qualifications. The government's response to the skill shortages that have appeared in UK industry, even though unemployment has been relatively high, includes, for example, NVQs, Investors in People, Modern Apprenticeships and the New Deal.

Nonetheless, Campbell *et al.* (2001) indicate a number of deficiencies that still exist within the UK labour force. There are still skill imbalances in many sectors the result of which is driving up wages with the fastest increases in the managerial, professional and associate professional occupations. There is an over-supply of people with no qualifications. Around 4 per cent of employers are reporting skill shortages and these are more acute in small establishments. Moreover, the skills shortages are sector-specific, affecting manufacturing, construction, wholesale/retail, health and social care and more particularly business services. Skill gaps (the difference between the current skill levels of the workforce and the skills needed to meet the objectives of the organisation) affect around 7 per cent of establishments. Skill shortages are also regionalised affecting more establishments in the South-East of England. There is also evidence of latent skills gaps – gaps that are likely to emerge if the establishment were to improve its performance relative to its competitors.

In terms of international comparisons the UK is around the OECD average for the proportion of its workforce qualified to NVQ 2 and 3 or its equivalent. However, it is older workers who are more likely to have these qualifications and younger workers have below-average levels. The UK does have the highest rate of university graduation amongst the OECD countries, though both in the case of degrees and NVQs other OECD growth rates exceed that of the UK.

Perhaps more of a problem is in the area of literacy and numeracy. The UK is just below the OECD average for both, yet it is the older workforce where the shortfall is the greatest. In fact 20 per cent of the adult population are proficient at only level one – the sixth worst in the OECD, though at the same time in terms of higher levels of education the UK is ranked highly. Therefore there is a polarisation of skills and education within the UK workforce.

International trade

Since the second World War, markets have become increasingly internationalised, and it follows that economies have become more 'open', that is, more heavily involved in international trade. But why do countries trade? Clearly, much trade takes place because one country is better able to produce particular products and services than its trading partners. For example, a country situated closer to the equator than the United Kingdom is better able to produce tropical fruit, whilst it is possible that, because of its manufacturing base, the UK is better able to produce some manufactured goods. Countries, by specialising in the products in which they are more efficient, can gain by trading these products for other products produced more efficiently elsewhere. These concepts of efficiency and specialisation lie behind two of the oldest theories of international trade, those of Absolute Advantage (Adam Smith) and Comparative Advantage (David Ricardo).

These two theories tell us why trade takes place but perhaps do not provide us with the complete picture as to why there has been a growth in international trade. The role of mutual benefit is certainly one driving force. Businesses and governments are unlikely to engage, voluntarily, in international trade if they do not expect either to improve their economic situation or to achieve any material gain in return. Variations in the costs of production constitute another incentive for international trade to occur. In particular, international trade may lead to domestic firms achieving economies of scale which were not available in their domestic markets alone. Another factor is the globalisation of business through the ability to develop global brands such as Nike, Coca-Cola, etc., and the desire by organisations to dominate not only their domestic markets but also global markets.

Changes that have taken place in international markets are of great importance. Many markets have recently become deregulated with reductions in the barriers to trade, and this has enhanced trading opportunities. New patterns of organisation and business location have emerged, including using foreign suppliers, foreign direct investments, joint ventures, and international co-operation. These have arisen to obtain better access to markets and to enhance competitiveness by exploiting specific local production factors such as favourable labour costs, labour skills and tax situations.

If trade is encouraged, the world may be better off in terms of total production of goods and services and in terms of the efficiency with which resources are used. However, countries taking this 'specialisation' route could end up being dependent upon a small range of products or services. For example, many developing countries are dependent upon minerals, natural resources and/or agricultural products not only as their main item of production but also as their main export item. In this case, if another country is able to produce one of these items more cheaply or erects sufficiently strong trade barriers then the first country may see a large reduction in demand for its product or service. This could lead to balance of trade problems, reductions in sales and increases in unemployment. Countries may therefore consider producing items which they are less efficient at providing by using trade barriers.

Before we consider barriers to trade and the attempts made to reduce trade restrictions, let us appraise the importance of trade in the international arena.

Exports by country

The importance of international trade continues to increase, though there are differences between regions in the value of their intra-trade (trade between the members that make up a region trading bloc) and extra-trade (trade between the members of the bloc and other countries outside of the trading bloc). There is evidence that intra-trade is becoming more important than extra-trade as Table 3.11 indicates.

The main target markets for European Union exporters and importers are other European Union markets and, in particular, those of neighbouring countries. This is especially true for the relatively smaller countries within the European Union such as the Netherlands and Portugal. Larger EU members are more likely to possess a greater number of large-scale enterprises which can address global markets, thus their proportion of intra-EU trade tends to be lower. Other smaller EU countries such as Denmark, by being on the periphery of the EU, will have a greater proportion of their trade

Table 3.11 Merchandised trade of selected regional integration arrangements, 2001 – share in total exports/imports

Region	1990	1995	2001
EU			
Intra-exports	64.9	64.01	61.85
Extra-exports	35.1	35.99	38.15
Intra-imports	63.0	65.23	60.89
Extra-imports	37.0	34.77	39.11
NAFTA			
Intra-exports	42.6	46.06	55.46
Extra-exports	57.4	53.94	44.54
Intra-imports	34.4	37.72	39.55
Extra-imports	65.6	62.28	60.45
ASEAN			
Intra-exports	20.1	25.52	23.46
Extra-exports	79.9	74.48	76.54
Intra-imports	16.2	18.89	22.77
Extra-imports	83.8	81.11	77.23

Source: WTO statistics, 2002

directed to countries fringing the EU. A similar picture emerges for the North American Free Trade Area (NAFTA) and ASEAN.

On a regional basis, Europe has seen its percentage share of world merchandise exports fall since the early 1990s, though it is still the dominant region in 2001 (see Table 3.12). The share of world merchandise exports for the United States, Latin America, Central and Eastern Europe, Asia and more especially China has grown over the past decade. Japan, Africa and the Middle East, like Europe, have seen reductions in their percentage share, though not necessarily in absolute amounts of exports of manufactures.

In contrast to merchandise exports, Table 3.13 indicates the importance of commercial services for the developed economies. The percentage share of world commercial services has increased over the period since 1990 for the United States, Latin America, Central and Eastern Europe, the Middle East and Asia. Although the EU (15)'s share of world commercial services has fallen slightly since 1990, The UK has increased its share. The reverse is true for Japan within Asia's share of world commercial services.

Table 3.12 World merchandise exports by region, 2001
(percentage share)

Country/Region	1990	2001
United States	11.6	12.2
Latin America	4.3	5.8
Western Europe	48.2	41.5
EU (15)	44.4	38.3
Central/Eastern Europe	1.4	2.2
Africa	3.1	2.4
Middle East	4.1	4.0
Japan	8.5	6.7
China	1.8	4.4
Asia	21.8	25.0

Source: WTO 2002

Trade barriers

The evidence indicates that:

* there has been a growth in trade, especially over the last five decades;

* trade has become increasingly focused on particular trading blocs;

* there should be specialisation through trade;

* some countries may lose from trade as their particular historic advantages are eroded.

With regard to the last factor in particular, and because of the costs of economic change, countries have sought to protect their industries, using such devices as:

* subsidies – payments to reduce domestic prices down to, and sometimes below, world competitive levels;

* tariffs – taxes placed on imports to raise prices up to, and above, domestic prices;

* quotas – limits on the supply of imports into the domestic market;

* Voluntary Export Restraints (VERs) – agreements by an exporter to limit exports into a foreign market.

Table 3.13 World exports of commercial services by selected region, 2001 (percentage share)

Country/Region	1990	2001
United States	17.0	18.1
Latin America	3.8	4.0
Western Europe	53.1	46.5
EU(15)	47.2	41.9
UK	6.9	7.4
France	8.8	5.5
Germany	6.6	5.5
Central and Eastern Europe	2.6	3.8
Africa	2.4	2.1
Middle East	2.0	2.2
Japan	5.3	4.4
Hong Kong, China	2.3	2.9
China	0.7	2.3
Singapore	1.6	1.8

Source: WTO 2002

All prevent the free flow of goods between countries. These types of measures may appear to protect a country's domestic firms but may not bring long-term advantage as other countries may respond. For example, the UK does well in terms of high-technology exports being above the EU average; however, import penetration has grown appreciably in the UK market. Japanese market import penetration is low. This could imply that the Japanese do not wish to buy foreign imports, but it could suggest that there are various barriers to entry into the Japanese market. Trade barriers also proliferate when the global economy slows and international trade tensions rise. Minicase 3.4 shows how trade tensions can rise.

The growth of tariffs leads to economic inefficiency, companies find it difficult to export their products and world activity levels fall. The General Agreement on Tariffs and Trade (GATT) was set up in 1946 in an attempt to reduce tariffs which had been ratcheted upwards between the two world wars.

There have been eight rounds of GATT trade talks; the first five concentrated solely on reducing tariffs on manufactured goods. However, since the Geneva (Kennedy) Round in 1964 they have become increasingly complex. Table 3.14 shows the subjects

Minicase 3.4   Trade disputes – Daewoo must charge more for six ships

Daewoo Shipbuilding has accused the South Korean government of 'meddling' after it was forced to increase the price of its ships in a bizarre twist to the country's bitter trade dispute with the European Union. South Korea's commerce ministry has told Daewoo, the world's second-largest shipbuilder, to raise the price of six container ships ordered by a German marine company from $55m to $58m each.

Seoul's unusual step appeared designed to combat accusations by the EU that South Korean shipbuilders are guilty of dumping ships at below cost price. The EU lodged a complaint against South Korea with the World Trade Organization last month after talks aimed at resolving the dispute broke down.

Brussels has accused South Korean shipbuilders of receiving government subsidies through state-controlled banks. Seoul has argued that its shipbuilders are simply more efficient. However, South Korea's intervention in Daewoo's deal with Hamburg-Sud appeared tantamount to an admission that the shipbuilder was selling at an unfair price. The commerce ministry said it had ordered Daewoo to charge its customers more to prevent a damaging price war between South Korean shipbuilders.

However, Daewoo said the government had no right to interfere in the market. 'We need [to know] the government's logic behind this meddling; it has set an undesirable precedent and we are considering legal complaints against the government,' it said on Friday.

Seoul acted after Samsung Heavy Industries, a rival South Korean shipbuilder that competed for the German deal, complained that Daewoo's price was unfair.

Daewoo said Hamburg-Sud had accepted the new price but was disappointed by the government's interference.

The EU decided in September to restore state aid to shipbuilders to protect them against allegedly unfair competition from South Korea. Daewoo is one of the South Korean shipbuilders pinpointed by Brussels because of the bail-out it received from government-controlled banks after the collapse of Daewoo Group, its parent, two years ago.

However, South Korean shipbuilders have accused the EU of using them as an excuse to rescue struggling European shipbuilders. The conflict over ships is one of several ongoing trade disputes between the EU and South Korea. Brussels is also investigating whether South Korea's memory chip manufacturers, such as Hynix Semiconductor, have received state support.

Source: Andrew Ward, *Financial Times*, 11 November 2002

Questions

1. Why has Daewoo pushed up the price of its container ships?

2. How might the EU respond to South Korea's protection of its shipbuilding industry?

covered in the later GATT rounds. Whilst GATT has been successful in reducing tariffs generally, countries have still sought to limit the free flow of trade via other means. In particular, barriers such as quotas, voluntary export restraints and non-tariff barriers – the use of red tape, government legislation, and health and safety factors – have come increasingly into play.

A final conclusion to the Uruguay Round was agreed in December 1993 and involved 28 separate accords devised to extend fair trade rules to agriculture, services, textiles, intellectual property rights and foreign investment. Tariffs on industrial products were cut by more than a third and were eliminated entirely in eleven sectors. Non-tariff barriers were to be converted into tariff barriers and these would subsequently be removed.

GATT was replaced by the World Trade Organization (WTO) on 1 January 1995. The WTO differs from the GATT in a number of respects:

- The WTO has a greater global membership, comprising over 146 member countries (April 2003).

- It has a far wider scope than GATT, considering, for the first time, trade in services, intellectual property protection and investment.

Table 3.14 The later GATT trade rounds

Year	Place/Name	Subjects Covered	Countries
1964–7	Geneva (Kennedy Round)	Tariffs and anti-dumping measures	62
1973–9	Geneva (Tokyo Round)	Tariffs, non-tariff measures, plurilateral agreements	102
1986–93	Geneva (Uruguay Round)	Tariffs, non-tariff measures, rules, services, intellectual property, dispute settlement, textiles, agriculture, creation of the WTO, etc.	123

- It is a fully-fledged international organisation in its own right, while GATT was basically a provisional treaty by an ad hoc Secretariat.

- It includes a package of instruments and measures to which all members are agreed, whilst GATT included a number of policy measures agreed to by a limited range of countries.

- It contains a much improved version of the original GATT rules.

- It reverses policies of protection in certain sensitive areas such as textiles and clothing and voluntary export restraints which had been tolerated under GATT.

- It is to be the guardian of international trade, making sure that the agreements at the Uruguay Round are adhered to. It will also examine on a regular basis the trade regimes of individual member countries and try to reduce the level of trade disputes.

Members of the WTO are also required to supply a range of trade statistics. Perhaps more importantly, it has a speedier trades dispute settlement mechanism, encouraging parties to go for arbitration rather than resorting to their own domestic trade policies.

A new range of trade talks are now under way, begun at Doha in Qatar in November 2001 with the idea that negotiation on the various provisions will be completed by 1 January 2005. Part of the reason for this deadline was that many of the Uruguay Round agreements will finish around this time. Moreover, the new trade talks will consider issues that have arisen since the agreements and accords were signed in the last trade round (Uruguay Round). Furthermore, the Doha trade talks give the global community an opportunity to enhance trade flows during a period of global economic uncertainty at the start of the new millennium.

The main areas under discussion at the Doha Round include:

- Agriculture – market access issues, export subsidies, domestic support for agriculture.

- Services – liberalisation of the trade in services.

- Market access for non-agricultural products – reduction of tariffs, reduction in tariff peaks, and tariff escalation.

- Trade-related aspects of intellectual property rights (TRIPS) – issues about generic drugs and the protection of medical discoveries.

- WTO rules on anti-dumping and subsidies.

- WTO rules on regional trade agreements.

Trading blocs

The GATT rounds were a series of multilateral trading agreements – trade agreements between different countries at the same time but in different geographical areas of the global community – and these have been paralleled by a process of regional trade agreements. These trading agreements can be of various types such as:

- those that involve reducing tariffs between member countries;

- those that involve reducing tariffs among member countries together with a common external tariff against non-members;

- those that are similar to the second but promote much more commonality than trading arrangements and can cover other rules and regulations, such as common currencies and defence/social policies.

In the period 1948–94 the GATT received 124 notifications of regional trading agreements relating to the trade in goods. Since the creation of the WTO in 1995, there have been over 130 additional arrangements covering both the trade in goods and services.

The European Union is one of the oldest and best known trading blocs. More recently the United States has become increasingly focused on the issue with the development of the North American Free Trade Agreement (NAFTA), signed in 1993, which includes the United States, Canada and Mexico. Chile has also opened negotiations with the United States and by the year 2010 it is forecast that a free trade area will exist which will cover the whole of the Americas. Table 3.15 indicates those regional trading agreements operating as at May 2003.

A further, ambitious project is under way to create an Asia–Pacific Economic Cooperation Forum (APEC) to include America, Japan, China, Taiwan, Malaysia, Australia and other countries with Pacific coastlines. The European Union is looking for closer ties with its Eastern European neighbours and there is even talk of a free trade area being set up between the European Union and North America.

To what extent do free trade areas affect companies? We need to consider the concepts of trade creation and trade diversion. When a free trade area is set up it encourages trade between member countries. This is trade creation, and it occurs because previous

Table 3.15 Reciprocal regional integration agreements notified to the WTO and in force as of May 2003

Europe

- European Community (EC): Austria, Germany, Netherlands, Belgium, Greece, Portugal, Denmark, Ireland, Spain, Finland, Italy, Sweden, France, Luxembourg, United Kingdom

- EC Free Trade Agreements with Estonia, Latvia, Norway, Iceland, Liechtenstein, Switzerland, Israel, Lithuania

- EC Association Agreements with Bulgaria, Hungary, Romania, Cyprus, Malta, Slovakia, Czech Republic, Poland, Turkey

- European Free Trade Association (EFTA): Iceland, Norway, Switzerland, Liechtenstein

- EFTA Free Trade Agreements with Bulgaria, Israel, Slovakia, Czech Republic, Poland, Turkey, Hungary, Romania

- Norway Free Trade Agreements with Estonia, Latvia, Lithuania

- Switzerland Free Trade Agreements with Estonia, Latvia, Lithuania

- Czech Republic and Slovakia Customs Union

- Central European Free Trade Area: Czech Republic, Poland, Slovakia, Hungary
- Czech Republic and Slovenia Free Trade Agreement
- Slovakia and Slovenia Free Trade Agreement
- BAFTA – Baltic Free Trade Area – Estonia, Latvia, Lithuania

North America

- Canada–United States Free Trade Agreement (CUFTA)
- North American Free Trade Agreement (NAFTA)

Latin America and The Caribbean

- Caribbean Community and Common Market (CARICOM)
- Central American Common Market (CACM)
- Latin American Integration Association (LAIA)
- Andean Pact
- Southern Common Market (MERCOSUR)

Middle East

- Economic Co-operation Organisation (ECO)
- Gulf Co-operation Council (GCC)

Asia

- Australia–New Zealand Close Economic Relations Trade Agreement (CER)
- Bangkok Agreement
- Common Effective Preferential Scheme for the ASEAN Free Trade Area
- Lao People's Democratic Republic and Thailand Trade Agreement
- AFTA – ASEAN free Trade Area

Africa

- COMESA – Common Market for Eastern and Southern Africa – Angola, Burundi, Comoros Democratic Republic, Djibouti, Egypt, Eritrea, Ethiopia, Kenya, Madagascar, Mauritius, Namibia, Rwanda, Seychelles, Sudan, Uganda, Zambia, Zimbabwe
- CEMAC – Economic and Monetary Community of Central Africa – Cameroon, Central African Republic, Chad, Congo, Equitorial Guinea, Gabon

Other

- Israel–United States Free Trade Agreement

Source: WTO, June 2003

barriers to trade will be reduced, giving each of the countries' industrial sectors reduced costs and therefore encouraging inter-country trade within the free trade area. Countries now outside the free trade area may find it more difficult to sell their products to countries which used to be outside the free trade area but are now inside the free trade area, since they often face external tariff barriers. Thus trade is diverted away from the countries outside the free trade area because the price of their products will increase as they face external tariffs, and countries inside the free trade area which do not face any of these external tariffs are more likely to trade between themselves.

There are also problems with rules of origin. Is a Japanese car made in Europe Japanese or European? The definition may depend on the proportion of parts that are provided by the European country. If it is European then it can be exported within the free trade area subject to no additional tariffs.

What appears to be happening gradually is the development of trading areas or zones. These might lead to significant reductions in trade barriers within the trading area that then get transmitted throughout the rest of the world in a kind of domino effect. The result of which is that many firms are likely to be winners. On the other hand trading blocs can lead to some firms being excluded from markets thereby damaging exports. The WTO rules say that trade agreements have to meet certain conditions, but the interpretation of these has proved to be controversial. The Regional Trade Agreements Committee of the WTO has, since 1995, failed to complete all its assessments of whether individual trade agreements conform to WTO provisions. Therefore it is still possible that some trading blocs have damaged the growth in world trade.

Exchange rate systems

Within the context of the growth in trade we should consider how different exchange rate regimes affect business behaviour.

Fixed exchange rate

A fixed exchange rate is one which fixes the value of one country's currency against another. The are two key advantages of a fixed exchange rate system:

- The stability that it provides for businesses encourages long-term contractual arrangements between businesses.

- Since the exchange rate cannot be altered to restore a country's competitiveness, if it runs a balance of payments deficit, it imposes a disciplined fiscal and monetary policy, which means a tight grip on inflation.

Floating exchange rate

Alternatively it is possible to have a floating exchange rate – an exchange rate which responds to the market demand and supply of the currency. If there are differences between the demand for and supply of the domestic currency, the price of the currency, the exchange rate, should automatically adjust. Thus one of the great advantages of this type of exchange rate is that it does not require any government intervention; market forces undertake the adjustment (see Chapter 6). The problems with floating exchange rates are:

- Increased uncertainties for traders which may lead to a greater proportion of short-term contracts.

- Import prices rise then the balance of payments deteriorates, leading to a depreciation in the value of a currency. This restores the competitiveness of exports but further raises the price of imports, and these increased import costs can feed through into domestic inflation levels.

Evidence suggests that fluctuations in the exchange rate are more likely to have harmful effects on business investment. That is, both international investment and domestic investment may be reduced, with concomitant effects on exports, in general, and output in particular. It follows that any move to a fixed exchange rate system within Europe reduces this uncertainty and improves businesses expectations. With regard to whether flexible exchange rates lead to more imported inflation it was notable that when both Italy and the United Kingdom left the European Exchange Rate Mechanism (ERM – a fixed exchange rate system operated by the European Union since 1980) in 1993, the depreciation in the value of their currencies did not lead to higher inflation and higher interest rates as might have been believed. In fact it had quite the reverse effect.

The decision, therefore, to adopt one exchange rate system in preference to another may not be taken purely on economic grounds, but may be the result of the need for closer political ties. It is to this area of closer integration and commonality of policy within Europe that we turn next.

Europe as one

The establishment of the European Economic Community in the 1950s was a major step towards helping trade within the European 'six' at the time. The widening of membership to the twelve member states by the early 1980s, the further reductions in trade barriers and the setting up and development of pan-European forums appeared to move the major Western European countries to a stronger economic position. In the 1980s there were, however, signs to suggest that the EU twelve were experiencing some difficulties. First, their growth rates had begun to slow and, second, unemployment levels had begun to rise. There was also a distinct lack of co-operation between Community members and a weakness of common policies. Since a number of countries appeared to be pulling in different directions, the European Community appeared to be paralysed. In addition, the massive technological changes that had taken place in the world had, to some extent, left Europe behind. It was importing increasing amounts of high-technology products. The Community's external position, to some extent, was weakening and it was becoming increasingly dependent on foreign suppliers. The fragmented home market in the Community was seen as a main reason for this development and there was a desire to speed up integration between the various member countries. It was argued that a Single European Market (SEM) would stimulate the scale of production, marketing and R&D, and also strengthen competition, enhancing the efficiency and competitiveness of European industry. However, to get to this stage the European Union needed to tackle the various barriers that existed within the EU market. These included:

- physical barriers such as form-filling and the cost of keeping frontier posts to govern goods and people;

- fiscal barriers – differences in VAT and excise duties distorted trade patterns;

- technical barriers – obstacles to the free movement of goods, services, labour and capital; throwing open to competition the bidding for local or national government contracts (public procurement).

Once the shackles on markets within the European Union had been reduced this could lead to increased social problems as organisations switched their production to cheaper sites. Therefore, to deal with the social element of the SEM programme, a social charter was drawn up. This was approved in December 1989 by eleven of the European Union states – without the United Kingdom. The Social Chapter of the social charter was originally set to cover a range of social issues including:

- employment rights;

- minimum wages;

- the right to training;

- collective bargaining;

- freedom of association;

- health and safety.

Because of the controversy this raised the final proposal was much watered down, leaving many of the social issues to be decided by the individual nation states, rather than the Commission. In 1998 the United Kingdom signed up to the Social Chapter.

A further condition deemed as necessary for the successful creation of the 'internal market' was a change in the Community decision-making procedures, which until then required unanimous decisions in the Council of Ministers. This condition was met by the adoption of the Single European Act (SEA) in 1987 whereby in matters concerning the internal market qualified majority voting was permitted. The SEA included the provision that the internal market should be completed before the end of 1992 (see Chapter 7).

Impact of the Single European Market

Assessing the impact of the Single European Act is difficult, since, as Kay (1993) and Swann (1992) note, it is likely to have effects in the long term as well as in the short term. The removal of barriers between markets was expected to encourage competition.

The European Commission made an evaluation of the SEM in their report, *The Impact and Effectiveness of the Single Market*, in October 1996. It should be noted when considering the results from this report that a number of the pieces of legislation pertaining to the Single Market did not come into force until 1994 or 1995. The report, however, noted the following effects:

- Both intra-EU trade (trade between EU countries) and extra-EU trade (trade between the European Union and the rest of the world) have been boosted. Despite predictions that the SEM would lead to 'fortress Europe', this does not appear to have taken place. In addition the SEM appears to have accentuated intra-industry trade.

- There has been an increase in both domestic and cross-border mergers and acquisitions. There is some indication of increasing concentration ratios across Europe, but on a national level the growth in some European countries' industries appears to be much greater relative to other countries. This is particularly the case in Germany and France compared with the UK. Thus the SEM appears to have reinforced different industry structures in some countries rather than equalising it between member countries.

- There has been a growth of FDI into the European Union, rising from 28.2 per cent of world FDI in the mid 1980s to over 44 per cent in 2001.

- On a macroeconomic level, investment appears to have risen by 1 per cent more than it would have done without the SEM, inflation is 1 per cent to 1.5 per cent less, and income between 1.1 per cent and 1.5 per cent higher. Employment is estimated to have grown by somewhere between 300 000 and 900 000.

- For businesses, the view was that the SEM had removed a number of obstacles to cross-border transactions and that greater opportunities were apparent. This level of approval was stronger for manufacturers than services, and larger companies compared with smaller ones.

The SEM did appear to lead to a major restructuring of European industry through an upsurge in merger and takeover activity. This is particularly the case for cross-border mergers between EU companies. Between 1986 and 2001 the number of mergers and takeovers increased from around 1500 to over 12 000. However, over 60 per cent of these mergers and acquisitions were between domestic companies up to 1995 and this has only marginally fallen back to 54 per cent in 2001. This suggests that the SEM has also led to restructuring in national markets due to the greater level of competition. The restructuring of European industry appears to have continued well into the decade as Table 3.16 indicates, but is now not only driven by the impact of the SEM but also by:

- the deregulation of markets in the EU;
- the growth in privatisation;
- the fall in the relative prices of some companies;
- the impact of the single currency within the euro-zone.

In the case of the latter it appears that increased integration of financial markets may have made it easier for euro-zone companies to make acquisitions. However, it does not appear that EMU has made euro-zone companies more attractive as targets of cross-border acquisitions. The mix of cross-border merger and acquisition behaviour has also changed with transactions in services on an upward trend whilst those for industrial firms have shown a slight downward trend. The share of domestic and cross-border mergers also varies by country. In 2001 over 50 per cent of the merger activity of Greece, Spain, Italy, Portugal, Finland and the UK involved domestic organisations whilst for Belgium, Ireland, Luxembourg and the Netherlands cross-border operations accounted for the largest part of merger and acquisition behaviour.

Although the SEM has removed a number of barriers, a number still exist through culture, tradition and consumption patterns. At the same time there are still gaps in

Table 3.16 Evolution of merger and acquisition behaviour involving EU firms

Year	Number	Percentage Change
1991	10 657	
1992	10 074	−5.5
1993	8 759	−13.1
1994	9 050	3.3
1995	9 854	8.9
1996	8 975	−8.9
1997	9 784	9.0
1998	11 300	15.5
1999	14 335	26.9
2000	16 750	16.8
2001	12 557	−25.0

Source: European economy, *Supplement A, December 2001*

the legislation, such as the issue of European company law and the harmonisation of taxation. In addition, some of the legislation has still to be enforced, adopted or implemented. To complete the SEM also requires liberalisation and deregulation of markets such as those for airlines, transport in general, telecommunications and utilities. Whilst governments control these sectors or limit competition with domestic firms then the effects of the SEM may be limited. A further obstacle to a single market is that of different national currencies and it is to this issue that we now turn.

Maastricht and beyond

The Single European Act can be viewed as a major step towards an economically united Europe, but it is not the ultimate step. If Europe is to be truly united then some argue that there is a need for both political and economic union. The move towards economic union was further developed through the proposal for a Europe-wide single currency. The move towards monetary union (EMU) sought to co-ordinate both monetary and economic policies. Monetary policy, which was under the jurisdiction of each country, has now been transferred to the European central bank based in Frankfurt and national currencies for the twelve member states have been replaced by a single currency – the euro. Fiscal policy is still in the hands of national governments, but is now subject to common policies and restrictions – the so-called 'Stability Pact'. Because of the development of a single currency for the twelve member countries, each national government has lost the ability to use its exchange rates as a competitive tool. The Treaty of European Unity also included a number of other important issues, see Chapter 7.

1 January 2002 ('E-Day') was the date on which the circulation of euro banknotes and coins began. On 1 July 2002 national currencies were completely replaced and the legal status of national banknotes and coins cancelled.

Twelve countries joined the euro in January 2002. Although Sweden, Denmark and the United Kingdom met most, if not all, of the criteria, they chose not to be members of the first wave. There are a number of consequences arising from the adoption of the single currency.

Impact of EMU on policy

Monetary policy has become the concern of the European Central Bank (ECB) rather than being the responsibility of each nation's monetary authority. This means that an individual country will not have the ability to use interest rates for any other economic requirement such as to reduce domestic unemployment or control domestic inflation. Conversely, to what extent would a country which is not within the single currency have the ability to set interest rates which diverge greatly from those set by the single currency bloc? It was notable that during the ERM crisis in the early 1990s UK interest rates were forced to respond to those being set at that time in Germany. Thus even if a member of the European Union stays out of a single currency its interest rates may need to respond to those being set by the ECB.

Although monetary policy would be lost as a management tool, for each of the individual monetary authorities this would leave fiscal policy as the only form of discretionary economic policy available. The Maastricht Agreement set out targets for fiscal policy expenditure as a prerequisite for joining the single currency and the worry about fiscal mismanagement resulted in 1996 in a proposal to establish a new European Union 'Stability Council' – a council set up to monitor individual nations' fiscal policy expenditure after entry into a single currency – to make sure that fiscal policy guidelines were not breached. If these fiscal policy guidelines were breached then the Stability Council would have the power to impose fines on any individual country if it takes more than a year to address its fiscal policy difficulties. Without such a stability pact it is possible that excessive borrowing by one or more of the members of EMU could force up interest rates for all other members.

A third problem with a single currency is that a member country faces a loss of discretionary exchange rate policy – the ability of a country to set its own competitive exchange rate. Before a single currency came into existence a country could use its exchange rate as a 'safety valve' if its economy became uncompetitive, say, due to some internal shock, such as a rapid decline in competitiveness of one sector of its economy. Under a single currency an internal shock of this type could only be solved by the use of massive European Union fiscal transfers (regional policy).

Impact of EMU on business

The impact on business can be looked at from a number of perspectives: first, from the point of view of businesses in countries within EMU; second, from the perspective of businesses in European countries which stay outside of EMU; third, it can be considered from the position of businesses from countries which are non-European but which are active in European markets.

Impact on businesses inside

From a purely economic standpoint, a single currency appears to be attractive for at least some of the larger countries within the European Union. It is anticipated that there would be low inflation and interest rates, participation in setting of these interest rates and belonging to a currency area which may have more equal power with those of Japan and the United States.

In addition, a single currency removes transaction costs (the costs of converting one currency into another), which are estimated to average at 0.4 per cent of EU GDP. This may be especially important for small and medium-sized businesses.

Competitive pressures will increase due to price transparency. This will also lead to organisations reviewing their business strategy and could encourage innovation as companies try to stave off competition. Moreover, price transparency will force companies to put an end to differential pricing across the European Union. For the airline industry and travel firms there will also be greater price transparency of air fares and hotel rates. At present the same airline often charges more for flying from, say, Frankfurt to London than in the opposite direction. It may also charge different fares on two routes of similar length. The travel industry will see some elements of price instability reduced with the development of the euro. Tour operators who book hotel rooms without knowing the conversion rate of the local currency and therefore the impact on package holiday prices will have this problem diminished.

Almost certainly there will be more bids and mergers both within and between countries in the euro bloc.

One of the main benefits from a single currency comes through the greater development of intra-EU trade and through its greater certainty this could boost investment (FDI and domestic), growth and jobs. In the case of FDI a single currency should lead to greater market size/potential and this should encourage larger amounts of FDI.

Set against the benefits outlined above are a number of potential costs following from the establishment of a single currency. First there are the costs of transition. Costs of doing business could rise. ECTAA (European Association of Travel Agents and Tour Operators) puts the changeover costs from investment in new technology and finance at between 1.8 and 3 per cent of a travel company's turnover. This is a significant cost for a low-margin industry.

Machines and other appliances (such as cashpoints and parking meters) which take money will have to be adapted to take the euro. Staff need to be trained and customers educated. During this transition period 'double bookkeeping' or dual currency price tags and invoices will be required. This could be administratively expensive. For example, in Germany more than half the accounting software cannot deal with more than one currency (DIHT, 1995).

The euro could also alter things such as the basic design and size of a product. A marketing price of say, £45.99, when changed into, say, €55.73, may make the product unattractive psychologically. Should the product price be rounded up or rounded down? To achieve an acceptable price point, retailers may have to ask suppliers to alter the way the product is manufactured.

Along with price transparency there will also be wage transparency. Therefore, employees will know whether companies in the same sector but in different countries are offering higher wages.

Impact on businesses outside

In terms of merger and acquisition behaviour, because the UK is not in the first wave of countries entering monetary union there may be important consequences for foreign acquisition activity in the UK. Marsh (1997) suggests that while many US executives express concern about Britain's lack of entry in the first wave, they expect the UK to join eventually and therefore this has not affected their acquisition behaviour for UK firms. However, for some investors the greater costs of being outside the euro bloc could lead to some FDI being switched to countries within the euro bloc. During the last two years the proportion of EU FDI coming to the UK has fallen. This has been mooted as being one of the factors which has led to Toyota undertaking new investment in France rather than expanding its activities in the UK. On the other hand Wachman (2003) reported on suspicions that an agreement had been reached between Ghosn (Nissan's chief executive) and Tony Blair that the new Micra would be built in Sunderland so long as the UK joined the euro eventually. British companies will also face exchange rate risks not experienced by those in countries with the euro area. In fact it is possible that the pound may become more volatile.

Even though the UK is not in the first wave, some foreign companies, notably Siemens and Daimler-Benz, have arranged for their UK suppliers to price and charge for things in euros. The euro has also been pushed through the supply chain in many other organisations. Marks & Spencer will even accept the euro at its cash desks, as will many other major retail stores in most of the popular tourist sites. Thus non-participation will not shield the UK from the effect of EMU. So companies will prepare irrespective of the UK government's strategy – in terms of their technical systems, financial systems and even corporate strategy. Moreover, UK companies will be affected by the way in which their European competitors change their strategy. For example, if Ford Europe or BMW change their pricing strategy so that cars carry a single pre-tax price tag in euros, this will have major effects on the UK car market.

The single currency is meant to provide lower interest rates, thus companies in countries outside the euro bloc may face a competitive disadvantage in the cost of borrowing. The euro is also meant to encourage better integration of national markets and in some industries this will mean restructuring.

The operation of the euro has already led to further co-ordination of economic policies. Nonetheless in the areas of tax harmonisation the bringing into line of the different tax rates operated by the European Union countries is becoming more of a possibility. This may not result in unified rates of tax, but is likely to lead to common tax bands and rules. Thus the UK would be expected to adopt whatever the prevailing rules are among the euro-12.

The development of a single currency for Europe, therefore, poses many opportunities and threats for businesses, the outcome of which will not be equally borne by all sectors of the business community. For countries such as the UK, Sweden and Denmark, the costs to industry of remaining outside the single currency may dent competitiveness.

Finally, major concerns have been expressed regarding the whole process of moving towards EMU. Concern has been voiced that the financial and monetary elements of the economy have been prioritised and very little emphasis has been given to unemployment. In fact, as mentioned above, in an attempt to hit the targets set out at Maastricht, the European economies have been operating tight fiscal policies which have resulted in growing levels of unemployment and labour unrest. For example, the series of strikes in France and Italy in 2002/3 concerning the financing of pensions can be partly explained by the difficulty both governments are facing through not being able to increase their government expenditure due to the growth and stability pact. In addition, for some countries the role of privatisation has taken on a higher profile as they seek to balance their government accounts. If countries need to be more convergent in their performances as expressed through the Maastricht criteria then any fudging of the criteria for entry will make the member countries of a single currency less convergent and thereby weaken the strength of the euro. As Desai (1997) notes, the euro could be a severely deflationary currency. Countries may have to continue tight fiscal stances and if entry is too broad in the first instance then the euro will be seen as a weak currency. This did appear to be the case until 2002 making UK exporters less competitive within the euro-zone. However, since 2002 the euro has strengthened both against the US dollar and against sterling making UK exports more competitive in Europe.

The UK and Monetary Union

Like Sweden and Denmark the UK also decided not to become part of the euro-zone in January 1999. In fact the UK under its chancellor Gordon Brown set up a further 'five economic tests' which the UK was to pass before entry into the euro would be considered. The results of the five tests were given in June 2003 and are shown in Table 3.17 below.

The UK Treasury considered that the UK had only passed one of the tests (Treasury, 2003). However, the pro-Europeans in the country have been bolstered by the fact that the government's position has switched from 'if the UK should join the euro' to 'when they can join the euro'.

Further enlargement of the European Union

Although the European Union has agreed that enlargement will not be considered until economic and monetary union has been securely established, the European Union sees its expansion to include a number of the Central and Eastern European countries (CEECs) as being a natural progression. In the light of this, the European Union set out, in Agenda 2000 in July 1997, the criteria for future membership. The criteria included a number of political and economic 'hurdles':

- political issues: the stability of democratic institutions, the rule of law, the respect of human rights and the protection of minorities;
- economic issues: the Copenhagen European Council suggested that these economic issues required the existence of a functioning market economy as well as the capacity

Table 3.17 The UK's five economic tests for entry into the euro

Convergence: Are business cycles and economic structures compatible so that the UK could live with euro interest rates on a permanent basis?	Test – failed
Flexibility: If problems emerge in Europe is there sufficient flexibility in the UK economy to deal with these?	Test – failed
Investment: Would joining EMU create better conditions for firms making long-term decisions to invest in Britain?	Test – failed
City: Would entry into EMU damage the competitiveness of the UK's financial industry?	Test – passed
Investment: Will joining the euro promote higher growth, stability and a lasting increase in jobs?	Test – failed

to cope with competitive pressures and market forces within the Union. Included here was that significant barriers to market entry and exit should be absent, that there should be adequate price stability and sustainable public finances and external accounts, and that the finance sector should be sufficiently well developed so that savings could be channelled towards productive investment;

- the ability to take on the obligations of membership (the *acquis communitaire*), including adherence to the aims of political, economic and monetary union.

Chapter 7 identifies the countries comprising the enlarged EU in 2004 with Bulgaria and Romania following in 2007.

These new entrants bring a number of costs and benefits to the European Union. The CEECs' economies are at present twice as agricultural as the EU15 and two and a half times poorer in terms of GDP per head. The combined GDP of the 10 is less than that of the Netherlands and it will take up to 30 years for the newcomers to bridge the economic gap between themselves and the poorest member of the current EU.

East–West integration should expand the CEECs' opportunities much more than those for the EU15. Trade with the CEECs is dominated by Germany from the European Union, but overall export trade with the CEECs accounts for around 5 per cent of total EU15 exports. Of total exports from the CEECs, the EU15 account for approximately 60 per cent of export trade.

Further costs to the EU15 can been seen in terms of the level of agricultural and regional support which the CEECs hope to gain from the current members. However, proposals put forward by the EU15 in March 1999 and in June 2003 are seen as, firstly, a way to reduce agricultural expenditure as part of the total European Union budget and, secondly, a way to cope with the costs the new entrants will bring with their large agricultural sectors.

The CEECs will also require large amounts of regional funding given that many, if not all, of their regions have GDPs per head lower than 75 per cent of the EU average. There will be, therefore, many problems to overcome in the further expansion of the European Union, but if all proceeds to plan, by the year 2007, the European Union will be seen to cover a region from the Arctic to the Mediterranean and from the Atlantic to the Baltic. The costs of this expansion may be high for the big four countries of the EU15 but this may be a price worth undertaking to reduce the political risks of having the CEECs outside of the European Union.

The advantages for business may be great. With the accession of the first ten countries there will be 450 million consumers in the EU single market and with the entry of Romania and Bulgaria that figure increases to 500 million. Europe will be the world's biggest unified market in trade, services and investment – larger than the US and Japan combined. However, lower production costs in the new member states could place pressures on manufacturers in the UK, France and Germany. In addition, because it has not always been easy to develop policy agreements for the current fifteen countries of the EU, the added problems of an EU with 25 could mean a move away from the need to get total agreement on policy decisions to one where majority decision making occurs in a much wider range of areas than currently operates. Minicase 3.5 outlines the impact of enlargement on migration patterns.

| Minicase 3.5 | Migration and EU enlargement – fears of big move west may be unfounded |

Politicians like to use the word 'historic' to describe the European Union's eastward expansion, but the popular mood in the current fifteen member states is more often one of sullen indifference, even hostility. While the cost of admitting ten countries, mainly from the former communist bloc, is one issue, much of the angst in the west stems from the perceived likelihood of massive east–west migration.

In recent years nationalist, xenophobic parties of the far-right have been stoking these fears in countries such as Austria, Italy, Belgium, Denmark and France, warning of an impending tide of cheap foreign labour and social unrest.

The EU's mainstream politicians have responded with a mixture of silence – few have shown any relish for engaging in a debate about the consequences of enlargement – and by bowing to the pressure of the nationalists.

Although EU membership confers the right of free movement, that right will not apply immediately to the ten countries expected to join the EU in 2004. Free movement will not be available for up to seven years after accession, with Germany and Austria particularly determined to impose a lengthy transition period.

'We need to give these countries time to catch up, and for their economies to feel the benefit of EU membership,' says one Austrian diplomat.

But research and previous experience suggest the fears of uncontrolled migration to the west may turn out to be unfounded. Such are the imperfections of Europe's internal market – language, cultural and structural barriers abound – the EU enjoys little of the labour market mobility of the US.

Take the last big EU enlargement in 1986, when the poor Mediterranean countries of Spain and Portugal joined the rich club and were also forced to wait seven years for full freedom of movement.

Rapid economic advances in both countries, largely attributable to EU membership, meant that by 1995 there were 100 000 fewer Spaniards living in other member states than before enlargement and 110 000 fewer Portuguese.

'On top of that there was a net inflow of Germans and British in particular, which far surpassed the number of people leaving Spain,' says a Spanish diplomat who remembers the migration fears of 1986.

Most of the former communist bloc countries do not enjoy the climatic advantages of Spain and Portugal, but they are experiencing much more rapid economic growth than the sclerotic economies, particularly Germany, farther west. Germany insists it still needs the transition period to allow its new neighbours to benefit from EU membership before it fully opens its borders, although that country's 4m unemployment rate is hardly enticing to incomers.

The European Commission's own research suggests 'there will be no dramatic increases in migration, and that the impact on the EU labour market should be limited'.

The Commission's work suggests the long-run migration potential from the candidate countries at roughly 1 per cent of the current EU population, but that is likely only after many decades of steadily declining flows. In the early years, it estimates that between 70 000 and 150 000 from the former Soviet bloc might head west every year, although many of the workers would be on temporary, particularly agricultural, contracts. The figures do not include any eastward migration from the current EU member states.

That may come as a blow to more dynamic economies looking for new, low-cost sources of labour to plug gaps in their labour market, but most of the academic research shows that most Europeans would prefer to stay at home.

Source: George Parker, *Financial Times*, 10 December 2002, p. 10

Questions

1. Why is labour relatively immobile in the EU?

2. Why do France, Germany and the UK fear the consequences of labour migration from the Central and Eastern European countries after 2004?

Conclusion

Business has always been aware of the impact of the economic environment on its performance and behaviour, but whereas businesses would have paid heed to changes in their own domestic economy, the post-war years have seen markets becoming increasingly internationalised so that it is now changes in the international economic environment which may have more impact. Some of these changes, such as alterations in environmental legislation, agreements about the provisions for labour and corporate tax changes, have a direct impact on organisations; other changes alter the environment in which the firm exists and, although not aimed at organisations directly, potentially have greater influence on their behaviour. Here we would include on an international level the Single European Market legislation, the South-East Asian crisis, monetary union and external trade policies.

Over the last two decades closer co-operation between countries in pursuing macro-economic policies and the internationalisation of markets has been evident. Such moves require co-ordinated actions amongst countries. Of course, not all industries are uniformly affected by international macro policy changes – companies which undertake much of their business in the domestic market are perhaps less affected by exchange rate changes than those which are exporting a proportion of their output abroad. In addition, as discussed in other chapters, the impacts of technology are not equally borne by the different sectors in our society. Nonetheless, businesses cannot ignore the changes that are taking place in their domestic, European and international environment. If they do so it is highly likely that in the longer term their position in the market will be weakened to such an extent that their businesses are placed at a competitive disadvantage.

Summary of main points

We have seen that organisations are influenced by the many forces at play in the wide economic environment and therefore need to be aware of these forces and to be able to react to any changes. The main points made are that:

- GDP can be used as a measure of economic growth and it can be used to compare the performance of countries.

- Governments have four main economic goals: a high level of growth, a strong balance of payments, a low level of inflation and low unemployment.

- The goals of the government may conflict.

- Governments may steer the economy and smooth economic cycles through the use of fiscal and monetary policy.

- The industrial structure of an economy is not static but open to continual change.

- Generally, Western industrial economies are seeing a shift to the tertiary sector.

- Growth can bring with it improvements in real incomes and a greater choice of goods and services.

- Economic growth in the European Union has been relatively disappointing for the past decade.

- Growth also brings with it costs to society.

- Inflation can be caused in a number of ways – through excess demand in the product market, through increased costs of the factors of production, and through slack monetary policy.

- Inflation causes both internal and external problems. It may make exports less competitive and therefore imported goods more competitive with domestically produced goods. Internally to the economy it harms those groups on fixed incomes, can cause disruption in the labour market, can lead to even higher levels of expected inflation and favours debtors rather than creditors.

- Government expenditure plays a key role in the functioning of all countries. In the pursuit of the targets for monetary union, unemployment is higher than it would have been in the twelve single currency countries.

- The UK economy still has a number of skill gaps which prevents the economy operating efficiently.

- Countries have become more open, and this has stimulated international trade.

- Evidence suggests an increasing Europeanisation of trade and the establishment of trade blocs which could both create and divert trade.

- Exchange rates affect trade and competitiveness.

- The Single European Market provides opportunities to and costs for businesses.

- The process of integration arising from the TEU is likely to continue and gather pace.

- The European Union will seek to expand its membership during the next four years to encompass a number of Central and Eastern European countries.

Discussion Questions

1. What can governments do to stimulate growth in their economies?

2. Why has there been a general upward trend in average unemployment levels within Europe over the last fifteen years?

3. Should the UK be worried about its relatively poorly skilled workforce?

4. What are the implications of the growth in trading blocs for export-orientated businesses?

5. What could be the advantages, to organisations, of a country joining a single currency? What may be the costs for those countries which join and those which opt to stay out?

6. What are the implications for organisations in the current EU15 from widening the membership of the European Union?

Web Links

http://europa.eu.int/comm/economy_finance
This website is one of many at the European Commission. Although not always that easy to navigate it provides a range of important financial statistics.

http://www.imf.org

The International Monetary Fund website provides a range of economic reports and up-to-date economic statistics on the global economy.

http://www.open.gov.uk

This is the UK government's website. It enables you to search both for economic reports and links to their other websites that provide good quality data on the UK economy and sometimes a comparison with other major trading partners.

http://www.wto.org/

This the website of the World Trade Organization. It contains reports on trade disputes, regional trade relations and a wide range of good quality data on trade statistics.

http://www.oecd.org/

The OECD website covers the main industrialised countries. It provides a wide range of economic statistics and forecasts on these economies. It is good for most aspects of country data.

http://www.ilo.org/

The site of the International Labour Organization. It contains good data on all aspects of the labour market for a wide range of countries. The ILO also produce some good economic analysis of labour market issues.

Further Reading

Griffiths, A. and Wall, S. (2001) *Applied Economics*, 9th edn, Prentice Hall.
A text that covers a wide range of economics areas from a national, regional and international perspective.

European Economy, Supplement A – Economic Trends (various years)
Produced by the European Commission both in hard copy and online, usually addressing a theme appropriate to the European economies, such as mergers and acquisitions. Supplement C covers issues to do with enlargement.

Piggott, J. and Cook, M. (2001) *International Business Economics: A European Perspective*, 2nd edn, Addison-Wesley-Longman.
A book that covers not only the main policy issues in the EU but covers both European and international business.

El-Agraa, A.M. (2001) *The European Union: Economics and Policies*, 6th edn, Prentice Hall.
One of the best texts if you are interested in the European Union. It has some use statistical tables but on the whole concentrates on policy changes. The book is large but worth the effort.

Sloman, J. (2003) *Economics*, 5th edn, Prentice Hall.
A good introduction to economics. Wide range of short cases but a book that covers a lot more than just the internal macro economy.

References

Alesina, A. (1989) 'Politics and business cycles in industrial democracies', *Economic Policy*, 8.

Beckerman, W. (1985) 'How the battle against inflation was really won', *Lloyds Bank Review*, 15 January.

Begg, D. (1995) 'The anatomy of a recovery: the UK since 1992', *The Begg Update*, McGraw-Hill, No. 5, Summer.

Burda, M. and Wyplosz, C. (2001) *Macroeconomics: A European Text*, 3rd edn, Oxford: Oxford University Press.

Campbell, M., Baldwin, S., Johnson, S., Chapman, R., Upton, A. and Walton, F. (2001) *Skills in England 2001*, Policy Research Institute, Leeds Metropolitan University.

Cook, M. (1996) 'Economic growth and the UK economy', *Economics and Business Education*, Summer.

Cook, M. and Healey, N. (2001) *Supply Side Policies*, 4th edn, Oxford: Prentice Hall.

Desai, M. (1997) 'Better late than never: strong enough to cope', *Observer*, 17 August, p. 2.

DIHT (1995) Survey among 733 German Companies, September.

European Commission (1996) *The Impact and Effectiveness of the Single Market*, Communication to the European Commission, EU.

Friedman, M. (1977) 'Inflation and unemployment', *Journal of Political Economy*, 85 (3).

Higham, D. and Tomlinson, J. (1982) 'Why do governments worry about inflation?', *National Westminster Bank Review*, May.

Kay, N. (1993) 'Mergers, acquisitions and the completion of the internal market', in Hughes, K.S. (ed.) *European Competitiveness*, Cambridge: Cambridge University Press.

Marsh, P. (1997) 'US engineers invest in EMU', *Financial Times*, 31 December.

Meadows, D. Meadows, D. and Randers, J. (1992) *Beyond the Limits*, London: Chelsea Green Publishing.

OECD (2000) *Economics Statistics*, Paris: OECD.

Phillips, A.W. (1958) 'The relationship between unemployment and the rate of change of money wages in the United Kingdom', *Economica*, 25, November.

Porter, M.E. (2003) *UK Competitiveness: Moving to the Next Stage*, DTI Economics Paper No. 3, May.

Schneider, F. and Enste, D. (2000) 'Shadow economies: size, causes and consequences', *Journal of Economic Literature*, 38, 77–114.

Soteri, S. and Westaway, P. (1993) 'Explaining price inflation in the UK: 1971–92', *National Institute Economic Review*, 144, May.

Swann, D. (1992) *The Single European Market and Beyond: A Study of the Wider Implications of the Single European Act*, London: Routledge.

Treasury (2003) *The Five Tests Framework*, London: HMSO.

Wachman, R. (2003) 'Nissan closure fear haunts Blair', *Observer*, Business, 11 May, p. 4.

The Technological Environment

Stephen Swailes

On completion of this chapter you should be able to:

- explain the importance of technology and innovation;
- explain some of the generic technologies that are affecting organisations;
- outline how different countries support research and development;
- discuss how technology affects organisations, people and jobs;
- identify reasons why organisations do not always benefit from technology investments;
- discuss ethical problems arising from technological change.

Key Concepts

- knowledge, technology and innovation
- research and development
- technological change and technology indicators
- technological change and competitiveness
- technological change and labour
- technology, society and ethics

Introduction

Making sense of the business environment is a constant challenge for managers and employees and this book introduces the main effects of macro environmental forces on organisations. Economic forces impact upon organisations through factors like exchange rates, interest rates and consumer spending. Social changes affect public attitudes, the availability of labour and skills and the demand for products. Political forces set a broad framework for all organisations to operate in and have a particularly strong influence upon public sector organisations.

This chapter introduces what is arguably the biggest story of the twentieth century – the proliferation of technology and its effects on organisations. Unlike political, economic and social forces, which are mostly beyond the influence of organisations, managers have much more control and influence over technological forces. After all, technology is developed by organisations for use by organisations but, as we will see, the pace of technological change can pose some difficult problems for society.

The use, or lack of use, of technology has a strong influence upon the competitiveness of firms, sectors and nations. The extent that technology is adopted can be affected by the attitudes and behaviour of employees and some organisations fail because they are unable to respond to technological shifts quickly. Technology growth and adoption are linked to other macroenvironmental forces such as the health of the economy which influences the funds that organisations have to invest in using knowledge and developing and implementing new technology. Political decisions have a strong bearing upon the amount and direction of government-sponsored research and upon assistance programmes for industry. Furthermore, governments have to respond to the changes that new technologies bring to society. Politicians have to cope with the near instantaneous spread of news and information in an era of satellite communications and powerful media. Politicians also have to wrestle with the ethical problems that some new technologies, like genetic science, create.

While all the primary macroenvironmental forces discussed in this book wax and wane in their intensity and impact over time, the technological environment is currently witnessing a 'new wave' of information-based change. Recent trends towards deregulation in Western markets and intense cost-centred competition have highlighted the central role of technology in helping to maintain and build competitive advantage.

Why is technology important?

What is technology?

We need a definition of technology to understand the relationship between organisations and their technological environment and to understand the differences between knowledge, technology and innovation. Knowledge is a theoretical or practical understanding of a subject such as chemistry, mathematics, sociology or language. Our stock of knowledge and understanding about a subject usually increases in very small amounts following research studies and leads to improvements to procedures, products and manufacturing processes.

Technology is the application of knowledge into some practical form, typically applied to industrial and commercial use.

There can be long delays between the early development of technologies and their evolution into widely usable formats. Galbraith (1967) defines technology as 'The systematic application of scientific or other organized knowledge to practical tasks'. Monck *et al.* (1988) saw technology as 'both a body of knowledge concerned with the solution of practical problems, what we might term know-how, and also the tools and artefacts which are used to achieve those solutions: it is both software and hardware'. Gillespie and Mileti (1977) define technology as 'the types and patterns of activity, equipment and material, and knowledge or experience to perform tasks'. This latter definition suggests that all organisations use a technology and that only the intensity varies. A useful summary of some of the definitions of technology can be found in Berry and Taggart (1994).

Innovation is the spread and diffusion of technology into society and organisations.

Freeman (1982) saw technical innovation as the introduction and spread of new and improved products and processes in the economy. This definition includes the design, manufacturing, and management activities involved in the marketing of a new or improved product. Examples of the links between knowledge, technology and innovation are shown in Table 4.1. Knowledge of genetics, for example, has led to the development of

Table 4.1 Examples of knowledge, technology and innovation

Knowledge discovery	Radioactivity (nineteenth century)	Hydrocarbon chemistry (early twentieth century)	Discovery of the structure of DNA in 1953 and identifying particular genes (1980s and 1990s)	Storing and processing information in electronic form (mid-twentieth century)
Technology based on the knowlege	X-ray images on photographic plates	Petrol, oils and the internal combustion engine	Tests for specific genes, gene-sensitive compounds	Microprocessor and permanent storage devices (disks)
Innovation from the technology	Improved medical diagnoses and treatment	Automobiles, aircraft	Gene-modifying drugs and genetically modified foods	Personal computers

tests for specific genes and, possibly, will lead to the widespread use of gene-modifying drugs.

A different view of innovation sees it as more than the spread of technology such that innovation includes changes to existing systems or any new thing or old thing that is used in a new context and may not be scientific or technical. This wider view is based on the ideas of Joseph Schumpeter (1883–1950) who argued that technological and organisational innovations were behind business cycles and thus fluctuations in the state of an economy. Schumpeter observed, 'innovation is the outstanding fact in the economic history of capitalist society'.

A historical perspective

Technology has been both attractive and problematic to entrepreneurs and managers for at least the past two hundred years. Throughout the nineteenth century businessmen and workers did not see science as being applicable to their world and treated new machinery simply as labour-saving devices (Coleman and MacLeod, 1986). The British synthetic dye and electronics sectors declined in the face of German and American competition because British attitudes to management stood in the way of businesses responding to technological innovation from competitors (Shiman, 1991).

In the nineteenth century the British cotton textile industry had no international competitors although domestic competition was intense. When economies such as America and Japan became serious threats, British cotton textile companies were unable to respond with appropriate technologies because of the particular industry structure that had evolved (Lazonick, 1981, 1983). This example highlights a link between industry structure and technological change. Structure can impede change, yet we will see later that technology can be a driver of structural change.

From 1929 to 1984 the Japanese economy shifted from mining and light industries to heavy and chemical industries and (after the second World War) to automotive and electronics industries. Companies able to absorb Western technology into efficient production systems quickly established market dominance (Yamazaki, 1988). This shows that technology can help create industries but can also be instrumental in their decline.

Technology and modern organisations

While some technologies are associated with harmful effects such as pollution and exploitation of the earth's resources, the overall benefits of technological change to mankind are well documented. Indeed, technologies, e.g. solar power, are sought to break the link between economic growth and pollution. Governments are anxious to raise national competitiveness and living standards which, in turn, requires a sound economy in terms of job availability, working conditions and public spending. Technology impacts on these factors. It has a large influence on productivity and, in the same way that products pass through a life cycle, so do companies and industries. Sometimes technology accelerates the decline of an industry, as word processors signalled the end for mechanical typewriters. Technology also adds new sectors – all those employed in the development of information technologies and software for example.

Faced with intense competition from low-cost countries, some sectors decline in terms of output and employment levels although often a core of efficient producers remains. Leather manufacture is an example where, faced with intense competition from southern Europe and South America, output in North America and northern Europe fell steadily during the 1970s–1990s. In this example, leather manufacturers in high-cost countries have access to manufacturing technologies that improve both the efficiency of the company and working conditions. The long-term problem, however, is that they will also be able to install the same technologies when the manufacturing infrastructure (a network of machinery and component suppliers and distributors) of low-cost producers is more developed. A cycle occurs in which developed countries attempt to stay ahead of developing nations through continual renewal of their technological base and in which the less technologically advanced organisations can catch up through investment.

Thus technology can help to extend the lifetime of certain industries facing strong competition from less developed producers. It also contributes to economic development through new sector growth, which may arise because technology contributes to achieving competitive prices in world markets, for example in the telecommunications sector. This could arise from technologies that allow quick response to orders, consistent quality and cost reduction, but to support regeneration, growth and competitiveness companies need to invest and a large slice of all capital spending is on technology.

One of the biggest trends affecting business organisations is globalisation – the convergence of consumer tastes and product designs on a worldwide scale and the formation of organisations with global or multinational scale operations. Consider, for example, the world automobile market, where manufacturers seek scale economies by marketing the same designs, albeit with local variations, across many countries. This reduces costs and so makes good business sense. As newly industrialised countries (NICs) such as Thailand and Indonesia develop their economic and social infrastructures, technology greatly assists the process. Technology is a major change agent in world markets and the pace of technological change is rising.

It is widely believed that investment levels have a strong influence on productivity levels and, in turn, the ability to be competitive in world markets. Arguably, one of the most successful business products, the photocopier first introduced by Rank Xerox, was the foundation for that company's domination of the copier market for around twenty years, until patent protection expired. Investment by Canon in copier technology later allowed them to develop their own strong position in the copier market.

We can start to build a picture of technological development underpinning national growth and consumer living standards. However, some emerging technologies present some thorny problems for society as illustrated by the case of genetic science in Minicase 4.1.

Minicase 4.1   Genetic science

Recent advances in the knowledge of human genetics mean that it will soon become possible to develop self-administered screening tests for faulty genes, in the way that pregnancy or blood cholesterol levels can now be tested with over-the-counter kits. These tests will be applicable to unborn babies and to adults to see if there is a gene defect or an increased likelihood of developing a particular condition such as Alzheimer's disease. Furthermore, our improved understanding of genetics will accelerate the production of new drugs to treat conditions such as cystic fibrosis.

Genetic technologies pose some fundamental questions for certain types of businesses, as well as society in general. When each person's genetic fingerprint is identifiable to the extent that their health and even personality can be predicted then how much of this information will be available to employers? How might insurance companies react to the widespread availability of gene testing? Would persons identified as having an increased risk of developing a particular condition in life be able to get insurance? Under present arrangements they may not, so insurers will need to re-evaluate long-held views about personal eligibility for policies with inevitable consequences for the portfolio of policies offered.

The spread and use of genetic information will need tight control by responsible agencies such as the police and government. At the moment, scientists are ahead of society in the understanding and use of genetics as the political and media interest in genetically modified foods illustrates. Despite assurances from the scientific community there can be a long lag between society's acceptance of technology and state-of-the-art science. Society needs to catch up so that restraints and restrictions are enforced and acceptable uses of genetic science become clear.

Questions

1. How could health service providers be affected if a person's tendency towards medical conditions could be predicted by simple tests?

2. How might insurance companies react to technology that allowed simple and quick estimation of a person's future chance of developing a serious medical condition?

Funding of research and development in industrial countries

National differences

New technologies do not evolve by accident: they are the fruits of targeted research and development projects. In our look at the technological environment we need, therefore, to examine how nations organise research and development (R&D). Research spending in the European Union was €171 billion in 2001 and a large slice of this was funded by government. Countries publish details of the research they want undertaken to meet particular social and technical objectives and organisations are free to bid for contracts. At national level, individual governments operate a structure for managing and funding R&D. The Department of Trade and Industry in the UK manages the funding of government-held research laboratories and non-profit-making research and technology organisations. Funding for projects is also provided through Research Councils such as the National Environmental Research Council and the Economic and Social Research Council. The main types of research activity are indicated in Table 4.2.

The main sources of R&D funding are business enterprises and government although universities and non-profit organisations also carry out some of the work. Expenditure on R&D changes with the general state of the economy. When an economy is buoyant, government revenues from taxation support public spending, a small part of which goes towards R&D. In a buoyant economy, business enterprises enjoy relatively higher profits which can be invested in R&D. Table 4.3 shows gross expenditure on R&D in the UK in 2000 at £17.5 billion having grown steadily since the early 1990s when the UK economy was coming out of recession.

In 2000, UK universities provided 0.9 per cent of funding for research and development but performed 20.7 per cent of the work (by value) because of the funding they get from the government and business enterprise. Business enterprises funded 49 per cent of R&D but carried out 66 per cent of the work because they receive funding from

Table 4.2 Types of research and development

- *Basic* or *fundamental research* is experimental or theoretical work undertaken mainly to acquire new knowledge. Such work would be undertaken without a particular end use in mind. An example would be the synthesis of new chemical compounds but without any notion of what use they might have.

- *Applied research* is undertaken with some application in mind, for example investigating the usefulness of innovations to medicine or materials technology.

- *Experimental development* is the use of both basic and applied research in the development of materials, processes and synthesis and would typically extend to the prototype or pilot stage.

Source: adapted from Morgan (2002)

Table 4.3 Gross expenditure on R&D in the UK

Performed by	1992	1994	1996	1998	1999	2000
Business enterprise	9939	10364	10271	10565	11510	11510
Higher education	2592	3074	3085	3170	3385	3633
Government	2247	2404	2286	2167	2110	2137
Non-profit	273	197	196	212	235	253

Note: Figures show expenditure by the sector performing the research, and are given in £m, at 2000 price levels. Government spending includes spending by Research Councils.
Source: Economic Trends, *585, August 2002 (Crown Copyright 2002; reproduced by permission of the Controller of HMSO and the Central Statistical Office)*

governments and from private sponsors such as charities and medical foundations. Government funding of British enterprise R&D fell from 23 per cent in 1986 to 8.8 per cent in 2000, caused partly by cutbacks in expenditure on defence-related R&D. Companies have compensated for the fall by attracting funding from abroad, which now represents about 21 per cent of funding.

Table 4.4 shows gross expenditure on R&D from 1988 to 2000 for several countries expressed as a percentage of each country's gross domestic product (GDP). The UK spent 1.83 per cent of GDP on R&D in 2000 compared to 2.2 per cent for France, 2.5 per cent for Germany and 2.7 per cent in the USA. The UK has decreased the proportion of GDP

Table 4.4 Gross expenditure on R&D as a percentage of GDP

	UK	Germany	Japan	USA	France
1988	2.2	2.9	2.7	2.8	—
1990	2.2	2.8	2.9	2.7	—
1992	2.0	2.4	2.8	2.7	2.4
1994	2.0	2.3	2.6	2.4	2.3
1996	1.9	2.3	—	2.6	2.3
1997	1.8	2.3	—	2.6	2.2
1998	1.8	2.3	—	2.6	2.2
1999	1.9	2.4	—	2.7	2.2
2000	1.8	2.5	2.9	2.7	2.1

Source: Economic Trends, *585, August 2002 (Crown Copyright 2002; reproduced by permission of the Controller of HMSO and the Central Statistical Office)*

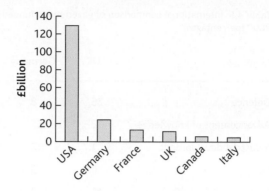

Figure 4.1 R&D performed by business enterprises, 2000

given over to R&D since the late 1980s although it levelled out at around 1.8 per cent in the late 1990s. The share of GDP given over to R&D in Germany and the United States has increased, in France it has decreased slightly and in Italy (not shown in the table) it has remained steady at about 1 per cent.

At first glance, the percentages appear very similar, but it is important to recall that gross national product values are huge, e.g. £6348 billion for the United States in 2000 compared to £1377 billion for Germany and £956 billion for the UK. Small changes to the percentage of gross national product spent on R&D represent very large large sums of money in absolute terms. For instance, 0.01 per cent of the USA's GDP is around £635 million. Figure 4.1 shows international differences in R&D spending by business enterprises in 2000.

Despite overall reductions in defence-related R&D spending, the US, British and French governments still spend heavily on defence, see Table 4.5. In 2000, 54 per cent of US government-funded R&D was allocated to defence compared to 36 per cent in the UK and 23 per cent in France. Germany and Japan spent less than 10 per cent. It may be argued that high levels of spending on defence research hinder industrial competitiveness. Though defence spending does secure many jobs in aerospace, for example, the alternative uses for such large amounts of money may bring wider benefits.

Differences in R&D spending by socio-economic objective shed more light on this point, see Table 4.5. While some allowance should be made for the difficulty of categorising R&D projects to particular socio-economic objectives, Japan, Germany and Italy allocate around 50 per cent of government-funded R&D to the advancement of knowledge, i.e. without necessarily having clear practical applications for the research in mind. The US government, in particular, seems less comfortable with the notion of 'blue sky' research given that 36 per cent is for knowledge advancement. This might reflect political and cultural norms that look to fund projects where clear intended applications for the fruits of research are required before funding is awarded as well as projects with commercial short-term objectives. This short-term outlook prevails in the US and the UK but the US capital market is more willing to invest in technology companies. In the United States, about two-thirds of venture capital is channelled into growth based on new technology compared to less than a quarter of European investment (Galley, 1998). There are big differences in the amount of R&D directed at energy, which

Table 4.5 International comparison of government-funded R&D by socio-economic objective, 2000 (percentages)

Objective	UK	Germany	France	Italy	Japan	USA
Defence	36	8	23	0.8	4	54
Advancement of knowledge	32	55	40	56	49	6
Industrial development	1.7	12	6	14	7	0.5
Energy	0.5	3.5	5	4	18	1.3
Health	15	3	6	7	4	24
Other (agriculture, environment)	14.8	18.5	20	18.2	18	14.2

Source: Economic Trends, *585, August 2002 (Crown Copyright 2002; reproduced by permission of the Controller of HMSO and the Central Statistical Office)*

is interesting in the context of concerns about renewable energy sources and depletion of the natural environment. Britain directs 0.5 per cent of government R&D into energy compared to 18 per cent in Japan.

Another factor to consider is the cost of borrowing money. In the United Kingdom the cost of borrowing has often been high, compared to Germany and Japan, and business-people are pushed towards a short-term outlook on investment and risk-taking (Rassam, 1993). Cheaper borrowing is thought to encourage longer-term planning horizons. Another difference is that UK companies have traditionally paid out higher percentages of net earnings to shareholders than German and Japanese businesses (Foster, 1993).

Indicators of scientific and technological progress

National differences in scientific and technological innovation can be tracked in a number of ways that are summarised below. They include patent applications, spending on R&D and employment in technology-dependent sectors. A patent is a 'legal title of industrial property granting its owner the exclusive right to exploit an invention for a limited area and time' (Frank, 2003a, p. 7). To qualify for a grant of a patent an invention is evaluated for novelty, usefulness and inventiveness.

The total number of applications to the European Patent Office was around 60 000 each year from 1990–4 but has risen steadily since then to total over 130 000 in 2001 (see Figure 4.2 and Table 4.6). The largest contributor was the USA at 47 200 applications that were, in decreasing order, mainly in the areas of physics, electronics, chemistry and human necessities. Japan applied for 22 200 patents in electronics, physics, chemistry and performing operations. EU countries (EU15) applied for 61 000 patents mainly for performing operations, electronics, physics and human necessities. To

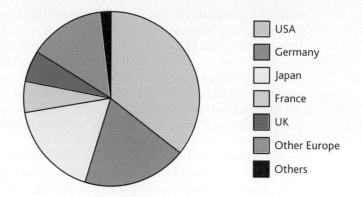

- ☐ USA
- ☐ Germany
- ☐ Japan
- ☐ France
- ☐ UK
- ☐ Other Europe
- ■ Others

Figure 4.2 Patent applications to the European Patent Office, 2000

compare nations the number of applications per million inhabitants is used and this was highest for Sweden (3200 applications equivalent to 367 per million inhabitants), then Finland (1750 at 378 per million). Russia, in contrast, made 477 applications equivalent to 3 per million people.

In high technology areas, the countries with the highest ratio per million people were the USA (57), Japan (45) compared to the EU average of 32. In Europe, Finland

Table 4.6 Indicators of scientific and technological development for selected countries

Country	Patents Applied for at EPO	Number per million Inhabitants	% High Tech Patents	%GDP Spent on R&D	R&D Personnel	% High Tech Employment	% KIS Employment
USA	47 200	170	34	2.70	—	—	—
Japan	22 000	175	26	2.98	920 000	—	—
Germany	25 000	310	16	2.52	488 000	11.2	31
France	8 600	145	21	2.13	307 000	7.2	35
UK	8 000	133	27	1.86	278 000	7.2	40.3
Holland	3 900	75	28	2.02	87 000	4.3	40
Sweden	3 200	367	28	3.78	67 000	7.9	45.7
Finland	1 800	338	40	3.67	53 000	7.4	39.1
Norway	1 300	289	17	1.65	25 000	—	—
Spain	100	24	15	0.97	134 000	5.5	24.9
EU15	61 000	161	20	1.94	1 730 000	7.6	32.9

Sources: based on information contained in Frank (2003a, 2003b), Laafia (2002)

had the highest ratio of 136 per million people and Sweden 101. The UK had 36 high-technology applications per million and the lowest ratio came from Greece (2.1) and Portugal (0.7). The EU15 in total applied for 12 000 high-technology patents of which about half were for communication technology, a quarter for computer and automated equipment and a tenth for engineering. This data shows wide variations in the level of scientific and technological development of nations. Scandinavia and Germany show the highest levels of innovation per capita. Belgium and France are around the EU average and Spain, Portugal and Greece have the lowest rates. These differences reflect different sectoral make-up in these countries.

The average spending on R&D by EU countries was 1.94 per cent of GDP in 2001, up very slightly but considerably less than 2.98 per cent by Japan and 2.70 per cent by the USA. Actual spending was €171 billion in the EU, €287 billion in the USA and €154 billion by Japan. Over 1.7 million people are employed in the EU on R&D, which is defined as creative work undertaken on a systematic basis to increase the stock of knowledge relating to mankind, society and the development of new uses for such knowledge (Franck, 2003b). Scandinavian countries have the highest proportions of R&D personnel in the working population. Most research staff are employed in business organisations (i.e. providing goods/services for sale to markets) although in the USA about 80 per cent are employed by business organisations compared to 65 per cent in Japan and 50 per cent in the EU. The EU had about 35 per cent of researchers employed in higher education (mostly universities) compared to 28 per cent of Japanese researchers and 12 per cent in the USA.

Across the fifteen countries of the EU in 2001, about 67 per cent of the 160 million employees worked in services and 20 per cent in manufacturing. While employment in manufacturing has been falling for some time, the population employed in high- and medium-technology sectors has been steady at about 7.6 per cent of total employment. Employment in knowledge-intensive services (KIS) continued to increase in 2001 to account for 33 per cent of total employment of which 3.6 per cent were employed in high-technology services. Employment in both high-technology manufacturing and services is growing at a much faster rate than manufacturing and services overall (Laafia, 2002).

High-technology manufacturing includes computing equipment, other electronic goods and medical instruments. Medium-technology manufacturing takes in chemicals, machinery and vehicles. KIS include air transport, telecommunications, financial services, research and development, education and health services. Germany has the highest proportion of its labour force in high- and medium-technology sectors (11.2 per cent) with Sweden, Finland, UK, Italy, Ireland, France and Denmark all having between 7–8 per cent and Greece the lowest in Europe at 2.2 per cent. Sweden has the highest employment in KIS (45.7 per cent) followed by Denmark (42.7 per cent), UK (40.3 per cent) with Portugal the lowest at 19 per cent. Ireland and Spain have provided the highest annual average growth rates in high- and medium-technology sectors for 1996–2001 at about 7 and 5 per cent respectively (Laafia, 2002).

Other indicators

Comparing countries by percentage of gross national product spent on R&D is a useful measure but to give a clearer comparison we need to take into account the nature of industry in a country, the extent to which it is labour or capital intensive, and the average size of companies. Some industrial sectors are less research intensive than others and in a labour-intensive business the main source of value added is labour. In a capital-intensive business, plant and machinery are the main sources of value added. Labour-intensive sectors such as footwear and clothing manufacture tend to have low fixed costs and high variable costs. Capital-intensive sectors like electronics and chemicals have, in comparison, high fixed costs and low variable costs and spend proportionally more on research and development than labour-intensive sectors. Average company size could also play a part in explaining the differences in national spending patterns as large companies spend more on research than small companies.

Research on sector differences suggests that large UK companies perform adequately and in some cases above average when compared to other countries in terms of the proportion of sales turnover allocated to R&D but less well when R&D per employee is compared (Small and Swann, 1993). However, ratios based on employee numbers do not make the best indicators with which to compare companies or countries. In reporting the size of their workforce, organisations may or may not include part-time employees, and they may not include persons employed in subsidiary organisations. Comparison on a per capita basis also does not account for the differing skill levels that may exist between organisations.

Value-based ratios are much better indicators of performance but are still vulnerable. Since sales revenues from an organisation's many business units are aggregated into a single group turnover figure it would be problematic to compare a single-product organisation, where all R&D supports all sales, with a multi-product company where R&D might only support some of the product lines. Furthermore, some sectors, e.g. the labour-intensive footwear and clothing industries, find it more efficient to channel much of their R&D activity through one or two research and technology organisations that serve the whole sector rather than conduct it in-company.

One of the best figures to use when different companies and different sectors are to be compared is added value rather than sales. This is a better measure of an organisation's performance because it concentrates on the value created by the organisation's activities and can be related to R&D spending to get a good measure of R&D productivity. Added value is more complex to calculate, however.

Table 4.7 shows the top ten international companies according to research spending and the top ten British companies. The international companies are mostly in the automotive and computing sectors in comparison to the British companies, which mainly serve the pharmaceutical, food, defence, telecommunications and oil sectors.

Expenditure by business enterprises on research has increased overall for the past two decades and there are three explanations for this (Dussauge et al., 1994):

1. The Crisis hypothesis suggests that major technologies, such as petrochemicals, have life cycles. The oil crises of 1974 and 1979 when oil prices increased dramatically signalled the beginning of the end for oil-based major technologies. Increased R&D spending by petrochemicals companies could be a search for cost reductions in the face of rising cost of oil-based products, or searches for replacement technologies.

2. The Sustained Progress hypothesis suggests that as societies accumulate more scientific knowledge it becomes increasingly possible to integrate this knowledge into new technologies. The time lag between discovery of new knowledge and commercial

Table 4.7 Leading firms by R&D spending

Top Ten International R&D Companies	Top Ten UK-Owned R&D Companies
Ford, automotive (£5.1 billion)	GlaxoSmithKline, pharmaceutical (£2.65 bn)
General Motors, automotive	AstraZeneca, pharmaceutical
Siemens, electronics	BAE Systems, aerospace
DaimlerChrysler, automotive	Unilever, foods
Pfizer, pharmaceuticals	Marconi, electronics, defence
IBM, information technology	BT, telecommunications
Ericsson, telecommunications	Rolls Royce, engineering
Microsoft, software	Reuters, media
Motorola, electronics	Shell, oil
Matsushita Electric	BP, oil

Source: adapted from the Research and Development Scoreboard 2002, *Department of Trade and Industry*

application is shortening but the funding to sustain the rate of new discoveries is increasing disproportionately.

3. The Global Competition hypothesis suggests that, since newly industrialising countries (NICs) compete strongly in low-technology industries such as textiles and clothing, the more advanced nations concentrate their efforts on creating new technologies in order to retain their competitiveness.

Sectoral differences

Not all business sectors use technology to the same extent, and technology is not equally important to all sectors. Small local service providers or providers of care services, for example, may use little or no technology in meeting their customers' needs although such organisations require considerable know-how to underpin their business operations, for example the know-how needed to care for people with special needs.

Table 4.8 shows the research intensity (research and development expenditure as a percentage of turnover) for leading international business sectors. The five leading sectors in terms of the amount they spend on R&D are pharmaceuticals and biotechnology, IT hardware, software and IT services, electronics and electrical goods, and health care. The USA dominates in four of these sectors with the Japanese leading the field in electronic and electrical goods. The UK is above the international average in funding R&D in pharmaceuticals and biotechnology, aerospace, defence and health care, and government policy is likely to try to sustain this position (Tubbs, 2002). These sectors

Table 4.8 Average research intensity for international sectors, 2000

Pharmaceuticals	13.0
Computer software	10.2
IT hardware	9.4
Electronics and electrical	5.3
Health care	4.9
Aerospace and defence	4.3
Chemicals	4.2
Vehicle manufacture and engineering	4.0
Engineering	2.6
Telecommunications	1.9
Food manufacture	1.7
Oil exploration and refining	0.4

Note: Research intensity represents R&D spending divided by sector turnover
Source: adapted from The Research and Development Scoreboard 2002, *Department of Trade and Industry*

allocate over 5 per cent of their turnover to R&D whereas other sectors, such as food production and oil exploration, invest about 1 per cent. It is worth noting, however, that this is sometimes offset by the very large spends needed on capital expenditure – land, buildings, plant and machinery. Consider, for instance, the different demands that oil companies and clothing manufacturers would have for capital expenditure.

The textiles and clothing sectors invest relatively small amounts of turnover in research, and that particular sector accounts for about 0.3 per cent of R&D undertaken by businesses. This is not to say that they are somehow worse off than sectors with higher spending levels. Labour-intensive sectors are characterised by small companies that individually are not large enough to justify their own research and development department. They have tended to centralise their R&D efforts in industry research centres as this has been the most efficient way of conducting research and development for the sector. Developments then transfer from the research centre to individual companies. Technology remains important to labour-intensive sectors but on a different scale. Technology tends to be used for incremental process improvements such as combining two or more manufacturing operations so that labour can be released from the production process, automating some processes such as cutting garment sections and cutting multiple layers of fabric, and developing new fabrics or polymers that can be cut and moulded to give enhancements to the manufacturing process or the final product.

It is partly because of the difficulty of achieving radical technological breakthroughs that some sectors remain labour intensive. In sectors such as clothing and footwear manufacture, some of the manufacturing operations needed to assemble the products require manual manipulation and joining of parts. Until solutions are found to the immensely complex problems of manipulating irregularly shaped components in three-dimensional space and joining them to very high accuracy, such sectors will continue to await breakthrough technologies that will alter the cost structure of the industry.

By contrast, in pharmaceutical manufacture, it is through the discovery of new drugs or new ways of making them that companies can gain a distinct advantage over their competitors. Developments of this complexity require dedicated in-house research, for two reasons. First, to keep control over very complex projects so that research spending is managed effectively; second, to keep industrial secrets (intellectual property) within the organisation to retain a competitive advantage.

However, collaboration with other organisations is an important way of supplementing in-company activities. About 25 per cent of spending on R&D by UK businesses takes place in the pharmaceutical sector and 9 per cent in aerospace and communication equipment (Morgan, 2002). Pharmaceutical research has a large appetite for new molecules with medical applications because success is strongly linked to new products. Finding these molecules among the millions of potential molecular structures is costly. Even when drugs have been trialled and approved for use, damaging side effects can be identified. Boots Pharmaceuticals had to withdraw their Manoplax treatment for heart conditions for this reason.

An emerging technology to identify the likely properties of different compounds is known as combinatorial chemistry. The UK pharmaceutical company, Glaxo Wellcome, purchased a US company specialising in this technique for $533 million in 1995 as a way of rapidly integrating the new technology into its operations (Cookson, 1995). Mergers and acquisitions are widely used ways of acquiring technology. Glaxo Wellcome itself was formed in 1995 from the merger of Glaxo and Wellcome and has since merged again to form GlaxoSmithKline. Part of the rationale for the mergers was a drive for greater economies of scale in R&D in an increasingly competitive sector.

Some general technologies

To explain individual technologies in detail is beyond the scope of this chapter. However, some technologies are having a big impact on many business sectors and these are highlighted below along with examples of some specific technologies in different sectors.

Information and communication technologies

Information and communication technologies (ICT) have had a tremendous impact upon financial services such as banking, insurance and mortgage services. This technology is applied to the capture, storage, manipulation and retrieval of information.

Much of the impact of technology in this sector has been to accelerate processing times, to replace labour and to change the nature of work that employees need to do and its impact has been revolutionary when compared to the more incremental impact seen in other sectors. Job losses have been severe and the technology has de-skilled decision processes such that junior staff can be trained quickly to take responsibility for complex customer enquiries. An interesting question about these relatively recent changes, however, is to what extent extensive labour cutbacks cause a loss of organisational knowledge that will have negative effects? In the short term, there are dangers that the quality of decision making can fall, staff loyalty and trust will stay low and customers will be unable to differentiate between providers (see Dopson *et al.*, 1998).

In addition to labour substitution, ICTs have blurred the boundaries between formerly distinct sectors (Porter and Miller, 1985). Developments in information technology, coupled with deregulation of financial markets in the 1980s, allowed building societies to enter the market for insurance services and high street banks to offer mortgage products. Because of trends towards longer working hours and busier social lives many banking services now offer 24-hour telephone banking. In sum, ICT altered the structure of the financial services industry and hence the fundamental competitive forces – ICT changed the nature of competition.

Decision making in organisations is another broad area bolstered by ICT. Corporate databases allow storage of data about sales, costs and customers on a massive scale, leading to data 'warehouses' and data 'mining' (Gooding, 1995). An example would be to identify the demographic profile of a retailer's customer base and the way different products appeal to customers according to their position in the profile. Trends in the data archive are explored to help managers decide, for example, whether to withdraw a product or to extend a product into new outlets. This will help with long-term decisions, for example about the best location of a new supermarket or the optimum timing and content for a forthcoming promotion or campaign.

Information technologies allow much closer scrutiny of individual products in retail outlets. Traditionally, profit margins were thought of in terms of the difference between sales price and purchase price. But products come in different sizes, weights and pack quantities. These variables, and others, affect the actual cost of ordering, transporting and stocking products and thus actual profit margins can be less or more than simple selling price and purchase price would suggest. This concept, Direct Product Profitability, is brought to life with database software and is now important to retailers selling many different lines in a wide range of weights and sizes.

Advanced manufacturing technology

Historically, a manufacturing production line contained a sequence of processes arranged so that each separate process added to a product as it passed down the line. Machines were often not connected to each other or integrated and often performed one process or, at best, only a few processes. Work-in-progress was carried from one machine to another manually or by a conveyor belt. When a new product passed down the line, each machine might have required substantial time to change settings. For example, changing the die (mould) in a sheet metal press to stamp out body parts for cars (doors, wings) might have taken up to a day.

Manufacturers have always preferred long production runs of the same product since the unit cost of producing the product falls as volume rises. This occurs through:

- buying materials and supplies in bulk at lower unit costs;

- gaining experience of making a single product so that problems and breakdowns can be quickly overcome;

- operators becoming more skilled and efficient at making the product.

Collectively, these factors combine to produce an experience curve, on which unit costs continually fall as volume output rises. This experience curve effect (see Chapter 2) lies behind some decisions made by organisations when they take over or merge with another organisation. By integrating with another organisation's experience, the total experience of making a product is increased and, in theory, unit production costs will fall.

The desire to change product designs in response to changing market needs traditionally conflicted with the production department's desire for long runs of the same product. Product innovation and renewal are key parts of an organisation's marketing strategy but they do have big implications for production systems. Companies that rely on long production runs to minimise costs may find their cost structures under threat from consumer demand for product innovation. Shorter production runs are required and some organisations are unable to respond to the challenge. Flexible manufacturing systems have helped manufacturers adapt quickly to market demand by allowing them to produce smaller quantities of a product at economic prices. Shorter production runs have become more cost-effective because technology has helped to reduce the costs of setting up a machine to carry out a particular process and the time taken to switch a machine from performing one process to another. Decision-making and tooling-up times are also reduced. For example, to tool up for a new product traditionally involved manual design drawing, making patterns for new components or tools, manufacture of tools to cut or mould a new component, and re-tooling of machines to cope with new products or components.

Advanced Manufacturing Technology (AMT), which in simple terms means computer-controlled machines, has opened up new possibilities for manufacturers:

1. Machines can be easily re-programmed so that a single machine can cope with changes to processing requirements of different components as they pass through a production line. For example, on a car production line, different fittings are tightened to different levels (torque) by the same machine depending on the model of car being worked upon.

2. Machine re-setting is faster.

3. Machines can share and exchange information about the specification and processing needs of different products so that a machine informs the next process in the sequence.

4. Many different processes can be combined and undertaken by one machine.

AMT typically involves computer-aided design (CAD) and computer-aided manufacturing (CAM). CAD allows clothing or engineering patterns, for example, to be designed on a computer screen and stored for easy alteration and reuse. CAM systems receive and interpret CAD data to co-ordinate the production process.

When computerised designs are confirmed, the digital information is passed on to the next stage so that components are generated from the computerised design and the information used to engineer, for example, new tools or moulds. Designs can be transmitted from European or North American headquarters to offices and factories in low labour cost countries where the products are manufactured. Processes that once took several weeks have been reduced to a few days.

Supply chain management and just-in-time

Installation of AMT has also coincided with a major remodelling of the manuacturing supply chain. Traditionally, buyers dealt with many suppliers of materials who tended to be treated in an adversarial way. Suppliers were often switched to enable the buyer to obtain the lowest cost for components. This relationship evolved in the time of long production runs and relatively long product life cycles. When market changes pushed in the other direction, retail and industrial buyers pushed manufacturers to find ways of making smaller quantities of more items and to deliver them much more quickly. This was made possible with AMT and ICT. Point-of-sale data capture in retailers is analysed to identify the quantity of stock items to reorder. This data is transmitted to manufacturers who are able to tool up rapidly to make the products.

Manufacturers have similar links with suppliers so that the materials needed to make a product can be ordered and delivered. Thus time has been eliminated from the total supply chain. Meeting customer needs in a just-in-time (JIT) environment has also altered the relationship between organisations in the chain. One of the many important things that manufacturers have to manage is stock control. This includes stocks of raw materials, partly made products and finished products. Holding stock ties up cash, while a basic aim of manufacturers is to minimise the amount of cash involved.

Historically, many factories had high stock levels and the advent of ICT supporting a JIT production philosophy has allowed cash to be released from the manufacturing processes. JIT, which originated in the Japanese automotive sector in the 1950s and 1960s, aims to eliminate all activities that do not add value to a product and to cut materials usage to a minimum. To achieve this, JIT focuses on several areas:

1. Designing products to eliminate any features that do not add value. This requires careful attention to market needs while not over-specifying a design.

2. Employees are required to be flexible and participate in actively seeking continuous improvements to processes. Workers often work in small groups or cells to help achieve this.

3. Set-up times for machines, while necessary, do not add value and so need to be minimised.

4. Communication systems are used to ensure that nothing is produced before it is needed. This helps to cut the costs of stocking materials and finished goods.

5. The number of suppliers is minimised and they are involved in processes to boost quality and efficiency. They are seen as part of a production system, not simply as detached suppliers of components at the lowest price. Suppliers may need to locate very near to their customers and work closely with them to raise quality and respond rapidly to problems.

Because of the need to share information and better understand the customer's needs (customers are all those in the supply chain, not just the final consumer), organisations have tended to be much more careful about how they select suppliers. Supplier selection is a much more rigorous procedure with customers seeking assurances that suppliers can consistently meet price, quality and delivery targets. However, once selected, the relationship between suppliers and customer is more secure, organisations work for mutual benefit and long-term relationships are sought. This is in stark contrast to the adversarial and exploitative relationships that commonly existed. The automotive sector is a good illustration of where supply partnerships have been forged.

Business use of the World Wide Web

A survey of business use of the web (Ng *et al.*, 1998) shows that 50 to 60 million people use the Internet, and the number is growing fast. Airlines make reservation systems open to passengers who book their flights and purchase tickets online. Companies put their entire product catalogue on the Net and create a virtual showroom. Universities can place teaching modules on the Net and make distance learning more accessible. Communities of people who share common interests, for example doctors specialising in a particular medical condition, can quickly share new knowledge and information among themselves. The benefits to organisations of maintaining websites include:

- helping to establish a presence, e.g. a small company's website could be more attractive and efficient than that of a well-known large competitor;

- the Internet acts as a distribution channel for electronic products (software, music, images) and thus lowers the cost of transactions;

- as transactions are one-to-one, the Net is suited to the advertising and sale of 'embarrassing' or personal products;

- business-to-business transactions are simplified;

- electronic business with small companies becomes viable.

The current limitations of web use include

- insecurity of financial transactions and the need for new forms of electronic payment to be developed (despite this, the value of e-commerce is growing fast);

- unacceptable connection times;

- the demographic profile of current web users restricts the potential for using it as a marketing medium;

- vulnerability of servers to hacking;

- virtually unrestricted and uncensored access to materials that much of society finds unacceptable, which might, in the long run, alter society's attitudes to such materials.

Other types of communication between organisations are also boosted by the Internet. International and global companies require extensive communications between decision-makers in various countries. Travelling to meetings is costly and yet alternatives such as video conferencing have achieved only limited use. The Internet offers an alternative through posting information on a website. People in global businesses, for example marketing or design, can communicate ideas, concepts and drawings quickly. Technical and scientific conferences can be held on the Internet if authors post their papers on a website for others to see. While this is an important breakthrough, travel to face-to-face meetings will not stop. Humans are social animals after all.

The Internet is revolutionising shopping habits by enabling customers to compare and scan a store's product range and order for home delivery. This seems likely to appeal to professional and managerial classes more than to other groups who might have lower motivation to shop electronically and who, conversely, could be motivated to adhere to more social shopping habits. We should take a cautious view of such possibilities, however, as our desire to rationalise the future often fails to foresee other trends that have a bearing on the issue. When computers began to proliferate in business there was much talk of the paperless office. In fact, the opposite happened because computers made editing and printing much easier and because business trends moved towards greater documentation to support business objectives, for example in quality management systems.

A look into future technologies is revealed in Table 4.9. As the EU continues to expand and develop, five main areas for science and technology research can be identified.

Technology and organisations

While technology, particularly ICT, is often seen as a solution to organisational problems, it is becoming clear that ICT requires good and careful management to bring about the expected benefits. Managers need to be clear about the total impact that will come from investment in technologies. Understanding the impact is a complex task because cost–benefit analysis needs to account for much more than changes to incomes and expenditure, yet the non-financial costs and benefits are difficult to estimate. A key problem in managing large technology projects is their vast size and the high numbers of people and organisations involved. Adcock *et al.* (1993) noted that managers can have expectations of ICT that exceed its capabilities. Technology installations need to

Table 4.9 Priorities for scientific and technical research

Key Priority Area	Example Applications
A knowledge society based on ICT	Remote healthcare systems
	Decision systems for agriculture and manufacturing
	Modelling human behaviour in complex systems
Risk and sustainability	Monitoring of natural resources by satellite observation
	Breaking the link between economic growth and environmental destruction – sustaining resources
	Causes and cures of diseases, understanding how economic systems affect health risks
Sustainable energy and transport	Reducing carbon gas emissions
	Expansion of energy from nuclear sources
Health	Development of preventative medicines
	Improved health and safety from a better understanding of health risks
International integration in light of continuing EU enlargement	Greater integration of national databases on health, security and defence

Source: based on Gavigan et al. (2001)

be backed up by strategies for other critical factors, such as customer service and product delivery.

Information technology in particular has been linked to workplace stress levels (Cooper and Payne, 1990) caused by job and workstation redesign, worries about job losses or worries about retraining needs. As well as directly affecting individual jobs, changes caused by the introduction of new technology can indirectly affect other employees. Managers and supervisors, for example, have to plan and implement change and deal with the human issues arising, including their own fears about loss of control. Because improvement policies are ongoing in organisations, they lead to continuous change and the pressure on employers and managers can seem never-ending. Simons (1986) identifies several human resource issues that need reviewing as a result of technological change:

- job evaluation and grading;

- career development and training;

- remuneration policies and working conditions;

- personnel planning;

- labour relations.

Technology and organisation structure

Much research has looked at the ways that technology affects the structure of organisations. Up to about 1950 there was a belief in 'one best way' of managing and organising. This is summed up in Henri Fayol's early twentieth century approach of planning, organising and structuring, commanding through instructions and assistance, co-ordinating and controlling work activities.

In the 1950s an English academic, Joan Woodward, undertook a study to see why British manufacturers varied in structure and how structure affected performance. Her study became a classic of industrial sociology. One of her questions was, how can organisation structure be measured and described, i.e. what makes one structure different from another? She looked at many different variables, e.g. the ratio of direct to indirect workers and the number of layers of management, and from examining about 100 companies, the initial results were unclear:

- wages accounted for anything from 3 to 50 per cent of total costs;

- the ratio of clerical to direct staff ranged from 3:1 to 1:14;

- the number of levels of management from top to bottom ranged from 2 to 12;

- supervisors' span of control went from 7 to 90.

How could these and other differences be explained? Some of the differences could be explained just through the individual preferences of managers but most variance could not be explained in this way. She then focused on the type of work undertaken and realised that a firm that was into mass production could not organise in the same way as a firm building one-off items to order. In sum, organisation structure has to help further the objectives of the organisation rather than conform to some pre-set management ideal. There is no 'one best way' of organising. The 100 firms were then sorted into three broad technical process types: small batch production, large batch and mass production, and process or continuous production.

Firms using similar technical methods had similar organisational structures – the different types of technology employed seemed to dictate the types of structure required to manage it efficiently. Some generalisations were possible from this study. In particular, as technical complexity increased then:

- labour costs as a percentage of total costs decreased;

- the ratio of indirect to direct labour increased;

- the span of control of top managers increased;

- the ratio of management staff to the total number of staff increased.

The more successful firms had a good fit between their technology level and their structure, the poorer performers showed some departures from the structure that their technology type suggested they should have. Woodward's study sounded the death-knell for the 'one best way' theory of management and opened up a new management approach called *contingency theory* in which structure, management style and organisational success are contingent upon factors like an organisation's production technology.

However, contingency theory can be criticised on the grounds that technology alone cannot be the only determinant of organisational structure – surely other factors have a role to play. For instance, contingency theory gives insufficient weight to the importance of managerial choice in decisions about how to manage technology and overlooks the tensions between management and employees that might otherwise influence structure. In other words, contingency theory requires that technology is neutral and uncontentious to employees. The size of an organisation also has a strong bearing on how it is structured. Woodward's work is very important because it showed how structure, technology and performance can be related and marked the start of many more studies into this area.

ICT is associated with moves away from bureaucratic ways of organising to looser, networked organisations where the boundary between one organisation and another is fuzzy. This arises because ICT allows multiple organisations to work around the same database(s) at high speed to create new ways of offering value to customers. Technological changes are seen as a driving force behind internal restructuring, e.g. changes to the number, size and type of departments in an organisation and the reporting relationships among employees. External structuring is also affected, e.g. supply chains and partnership agreements. Partnerships may arise in attempts to spread the costs and risks of business ventures and to pull together areas of different technical and commercial expertise.

Souder (1991) argued that classical management philosophies, in which managers plan, organise and control the work of others through a hierarchical chain of command that oversees employees organised into specialist, separate departments, are not conducive to innovation. He further argued that the organisation of business enterprises 'has not kept pace with demands of modern technology'.

An assumption of the classical approach is that organisational efficiencies are best achieved through specialisation of tasks and subdivision into specialist units. This notion extended to individual jobs being clearly defined and distinct. Many people might have done the same job, but there was little overlap between jobs. By the early 1960s this form of organisational structure was recognised as being a significant barrier to the innovation process. Burns and Stalker (1961), in another classic study, called the traditional organisational structure 'mechanistic' and argued that a different, 'organic' organisational structure was much more conducive to innovation. The main differences between mechanistic and organic structures are shown in Table 4.10.

In essence, organic structures are less burdened by rules and restraints upon employees, tasks are less rigidly defined and creativity is assumed to come from co-operation and exchange of ideas and information, facilitated by a less hierarchical chain of command. Managerial control is present, of course, but the climate is one of involvement, participation and sharing, rather than close supervision and demarcation. Horizontal co-operation across an organisation, rather than vertical authority relationships, is stressed.

Burns and Stalker (1961), however, also related organisation structures to the organisation's environment. Where environments were essentially stable – that is, the past tended to repeat itself, and predictions could be made with high degrees of confidence – the

Table 4.10 Characteristics of organic and mechanistic organisations

Organic	Mechanistic
No rigid rules	Many rules/low individual freedom
Participative/informal	Bureaucratic/formal
Views aired openly	
Face-to-face communication	Written communication
Interdisciplinary teams	Functional separation
Creative iteration	Long decision chains
Outward-looking	Slow decision making
Flexible adaptor	
Non-hierarchical	Hierarchical
Information flows up and down the organisation	Information flows up the organisation Directives come down the organisation

Source: adapted from Rothwell (1992)

mechanistic form of organisation could be successful. Confectionery and insurance companies, at the time, fitted this category. Where environments were more dynamic – that is, less easy to understand and harder to predict – organic structures were more successful at supporting innovation processes.

The finding that mechanistic organisation structures could be successful in stable environments is probably still true today. However, far fewer sectors still enjoy a stable business environment. The first oil shock of 1974 signalled the vulnerability of Western oil-based product markets, including transport, energy and plastics. Higher energy costs resulted thereafter and the search for non-oil-based energy sources began in earnest.

Political deregulation of the financial services market in the United Kingdom in the early 1980s had major impacts upon the stability of business environments for banks and insurance companies. Privatisation of the UK water, gas and electricity utilities has dramatically increased the rate of change and degree of uncertainty in those sectors.

The increasing complexity of markets evidenced through continuing cost pressures and pressure for internationalisation or globalisation of products and activities has affected once stable professional partnerships. Accounting and legal partnerships, for instance, which formerly operated in a stable environment have seen their clients' environments become more complex. KPMG, one of the world's largest financial consultants, found that it could no longer function with a structure based on historic lines, for example separate audit and tax divisions. Clients' business affairs were becoming more complex through mergers, acquisitions and internationalisation, and so 'complete' consulting packages for business growth were sought. These complete solutions required integration of previously distinct business areas and in general a shift towards the organic organisation (Johnson, 1993).

We might now begin to expect that organisation structure needs to change with the business environment, to continually evolve to cope with fresh demands upon it. This idea of constant metamorphosis has been advocated by Greiner (1972). Whether environmental change is driven by new technology or not, Greiner's notion is worth remembering. Over short periods (up to a few years) organisational restructuring may be small and incremental in nature. During this time there will be periods when structure will not change at all. Every few years, however, a major transformational change is needed to realign the organisation with its fast-moving environment.

Technology, jobs and skills

It is true that technological change leads to loss (or displacement) of jobs although it is better to see a bigger picture of how change affects jobs. Job loss does occur but, simultaneously, new jobs can be created that require the skills to work with new technologies as well as jobs in companies making and supplying them. We saw above how technology influences structure and another main focus for research on technological change looks at the implications for the skills that organisations need, pay levels, types of working contract and gender issues such as the link between gender and job type in addition to job displacement. One overall effect of technological change is that the nature of work has shifted from physical to mental (intellectual) labour (McLoughlin and Clark, 1994). Of course much manual work is still needed, but the overall amount is less.

Studies of the impact of ICT on organisations point to very little job displacement in manufacturing caused by innovation in production processes (Campbell, 1993). Job losses from organisational change have much more impact across all occupations than losses from technological change. Production and professional workers have mostly not been badly affected, although clerical staff have proved more vulnerable. These findings have been supported by Matzner and Wagner (1990), who found that diffusion of new technology favours better quality labour, although there is a small net negative loss when considering jobs in both technology providers and adopters. It seems likely that there are several variables that can intervene between technological change itself and job change. The attitude of management to the job security of the workforce is one, the ability of workers to negotiate protection from job loss another.

In general, the skills that are linked to increased use of flexible technologies include problem solving, interpersonal skills such as team working, computer skills, reading and mathematics (Gale *et al.*, 2002). Other generalisations are that the impact of technological change at the level of the firm, e.g. on competitiveness, is much larger than at national level and wage increases for people working with advanced technologies are higher at the national level than the firm level (Brown and Campbell, 2002). Suppose an organisation has an urgent need to adopt new technologies then it has an increased demand for higher skilled workers. If it needs these workers in greater proportion to their availability in the labour market then wages for higher skills will increase relative to lower skills. The level of impact on wages depends upon how quickly the supply of skilled workers increases, e.g. through education and training. In simple terms, skills can be seen as something that organisations buy through wages. Basic laws of supply and demand (see Chapter 6) would suggest that high demand for scarce skills, e.g. certain types of ICT professionals, will raise the wages paid and reducing demand for a skill in plentiful supply, e.g. factory production workers, will lower wages.

Technology and productivity

Conventional wisdom holds that technological change is a driver of productivity improvements although it is not the only one. The USA is usually placed at the top of international productivity leagues, with the UK some distance behind. Such global comparisons, however, obscure the fact that in certain sectors, such as pharmaceuticals and agriculture, the UK has competitive advantages. Overall, however, the UK has some embedded features of its business environment that appear to impede progress (Lorenz and Smith, 1998), including:

- a naturally smaller market than the United States and Japan, which both enjoy large domestic markets that make capital investment more attractive;

- a national culture which is thought to devalue manufacturing and production in favour of services, and which inhibits the training and development of engineers who can compete internationally;

- relatively poor management skills that fail to capitalise on creativity and productivity of employees;

- insufficient development of companies operating in high-growth sectors, such as electronics and electronic engineering, and reluctance to cast off declining and low-growth sectors, such as brewing and textiles.

Even when technology is available to a sector, organisations may not enjoy fully all the potential benefits from it. A study of the UK footwear manufacturing industry found that while technological change was a source of productivity growth, the industry had been slow to exploit the gains available to it and technology had not diffused fast enough (Guy, 1984). Footwear is historically a low-profit industry, and a brief consideration of the sector using Porter's (1979) five forces model (see Chapter 2) shows why. Barriers to entry are small, scale economies occur at low volume, and there are many competitors who use price as the basis of competition. Much of the output is purchased by large retail chains with high power. In contrast, supplier power is weak and there is no substitute for footwear. The continuing low profit levels that this position brings to most footwear manufacturers act as a brake on investment which tends to be sporadic, following relatively good profit years, rather than part of a long-term investment strategy. The returns on investment in these circumstances are limited (Guy, 1985).

Technological change has been a major agent of productivity growth in the food and drink sector although other causes are returns to scale and an excess of workers in the short term (Clark, 1984). In chemicals, a highly research-intensive sector, both technology and the state of demand for chemicals are major productivity drivers (Clark, 1985). A study of paper manufacturing found three main ways of raising labour productivity – technological change, rationalisation and the reorganisation of workers into more efficient arrangements.

Investment in ICT by the financial services sector (e.g. banks) has been extensive although studies show that ICT investment has often not delivered the expected benefits (Harris, 2001). In the context of the banking sector, the main reasons put forward for this are:

- ICT is available to other organisations, e.g. large food retailers, who have entered the market in efforts to offer new services to their large customer bases.

- Banks had a poor grasp of how to measure the effectiveness of the ICT projects that they had implemented.

- Banks had not learned from unsuccessful ICT projects in ways that helped reduce the chance of repeating the mistakes made.

- Responsibility for project management was sometimes 'fuzzy' and so it was difficult to hold people accountable for a lack of success.

- There was a tendency to try to integrate ICT into existing structures and processes rather than 'focus upon innovation and business transformation'. Organisations tended to let old knowledge influence the extent of new knowledge that projects generated.

These, and other, factors are used by Harris to explain an 'IT productivity paradox' in which the predicted benefits of technology investments do not always come to fruition.

Technological change and job stress

Stress is not an easy concept to define but does relate to the physiological reactions (e.g. tiredness, headaches) and psychological reactions (e.g. irritability, fear of failure) that people have to the situations that they get into. Research on stress often makes the distinction between things that provoke stress (stressors) and the responses to them (strains) (Arnold et al., 1998; Ganster and Murphy, 2000). Workplace stressors include high workloads and pressure to meet deadlines. It was not too long ago, 25 years perhaps, when most jobs were, relative to today, fairly predictable in the way they were carried out. Since then and due to political, competitive and technological changes, expectations put upon employees have changed. Although different people have different capacities to cope with job stressors there seems little doubt that levels of workplace stress are much higher than they were. Reasons for this include:

- Regular change to work systems requiring new learning and adaptation.

- Many organisations operate continually such that the pressure to perform and deliver is ever present.

- The amount of information that employees have to process has increased and this is closely linked to ICT.

- There is greater pressure on employees to manage their own careers rather than rely upon a benevolent organisation to provide life-long work.

- There is greater regulation of working methods from political insistence and technological systems, such that employees have less control over what they do and how they do it.

An eighteenth century proverb said that, 'it's not work that kills, but worry' and herein lies the problem. Recent information-based technological changes have coincided with rising stress levels although they are by no means the only cause.

Teleworking and working from home

Teleworking (telecommuting) is a system in which employees use ICT to perform work some distance away from the organisation for which it is carried out. The simplest form is where teleworkers work from their own homes for an employer or client. Teleworking is applicable to many sectors and the type of work undertaken includes information analysis, data processing, financial services, sales, journalism and publishing. Basically, teleworking represents a trend towards remote working (e.g. at home) that is enabled through ICT in which information is exchanged between teleworkers and another organisation.

As a result of the recessionary times of the early 1980s and early 1990s, organisations began to look very closely at the cost of overheads like personnel services and data-processing departments. There was a general trend to eliminate these functions from corporate structures and to buy in the services as needed. Often, displaced employees would set up a bureau and sell their services back to their former employer. Having made some savings on overheads, organisations turned their attention to the remaining employees. Organisation structures were 'flattened' by moving away from pyramid-like structures containing several layers of management. Layers were eliminated, remaining managers had larger spans of control, and there were fewer grades of employees. Job security declined as the number of fixed-term and part-time contracts grew. Organisation structures moved towards a core of decision-making managers and a platform of flexible employees. A continuing focus for cost cutting is the cost of occupancy, that is, building costs, rents, rates and maintenance, lately called space management. Where employees are able to telework, the need for permanent office space is reduced. An organisation of 400 employees could exist with space for 100, knowing that 300 will be working at home, with customers or travelling.

Prior to the industrial revolution, most people worked at or near their home but the rise of the factories meant that large numbers travelled to organised workplaces. This became, and remains, the normal working pattern but teleworking is perhaps the beginning of a reversal to the patterns of past times. It is important to note that not all homeworkers are teleworkers. Furthermore, some people work where they live, often performing manual, low-technology work, and others have the option to regularly work from home even though they are normally working elsewhere. One difference between these groups is that those who have the option to work from home tend to be well educated and well paid, in higher status occupations and satisfied with their jobs. In a way, choosing to work from home, say one day a week, is a job perk to those already in good positions (Felstead *et al.*, 2002).

The main drivers for teleworking include:

- cost reductions for employers arising from lower overheads (savings on space, facilities and employment costs);

- potential access to a larger and more flexible workforce that helps employers cope with sudden rises and falls in demand;

- teleworkers may prefer the flexibility and freedom relative to regular attendance at a remote site;

- employers perceive that teleworkers deliver greater productivity.

While teleworking seems to offer advantages to both employers and teleworkers, it does bring about changes to the relationship between teleworkers and organisations that need careful management (Chapman *et al.*, 1995; Teo *et al.*, 1998). These include:

- reduced promotion prospects caused by the 'marginalisation' of teleworkers, i.e. falling victim to the 'out of sight, out of mind' problem;

- reduced opportunity for peer interaction and professional development;

- reduced job security;

- confusion over the boundaries between home and work that influence social relationships;

- greater feelings of social isolation that can lead to low motivation;

- the need for a particular management style which is task-focused and relies on trust and shared responsibility.

These and other issues need to be managed if teleworking is to spread. Managers will have to learn how to manage without close control and supervision and this will require a revolution in the mindset of many managers. Employees will need to take responsibility for their own careers and act as if self-employed, looking after their own pension and sickness arrangements, as there will be little likelihood of reliable employment with a single organisation for more than a few years. The extent of teleworking seems likely to grow and it is a reasonable supposition that many more employees could carry out some of their work from home, even if not by teleworking.

Managing technology

Technology development

Before the industrial revolution and the growth of the large organisation, important developments in, for example, metalworking and milling evolved over many hundreds of years and some came about by chance. People of independent means pursued life-long interests which gradually advanced understanding and occasionally led to a new exploitable technology. Several people worked independently, but simultaneously, on the steam engine, yet it is Stephenson's *Rocket*, of 1829, that is remembered. Accidental or random discoveries of important new knowledge such as Alexander Fleming's discovery of antibiotic behaviour are now very much the exception. In the main, discoveries and the innovations resulting from them are not random processes. Scientific and engineering know-how are usually deliberately focused on a problem in response to societal pressures or needs (Ayres, 1991). This is certainly the case today when business and government research funding is clearly targeted on, for example, specific social, industrial or agricultural problems.

Yet we should not expect technological progress to be in simple proportion to the amount of R&D invested. Barriers exist to advances which can prove particularly troublesome to overcome. Nuclear fission reactors were developed soon after the first fission (atom) bomb was exploded in 1945. The controlled nuclear fusion reactor once thought to be imminent after the invention of the fusion H-bomb in the early 1950s is still thought to be at least several decades ahead (Ayres, 1991).

The state of related and supporting technologies also affects the rate of progress in an area. Consider for instance the growth in computerised travel booking systems and the increase in demand for air travel. This simple example shows how progress in one area can accelerate progress in another. Recently motor manufacturers have used advances in electronics to produce engine management systems to help maximise fuel economy. Catalysts are now commonly used to detoxify exhaust gases. But we may consider that the limits of efficiency and cleanliness from the internal combustion engine are being approached. Breakthroughs in vehicle technology await possible advances in fuel systems or radically new engine designs. Arguably, advances to automotive engines have held back the development of alternative drive units like electric motors.

Thus significant technological breakthroughs are not random happenings, nor are they purely dependent upon the amount of research and development by companies and nations. Ayres (1991) suggests that important innovations occur in clusters after a scientific breakthrough that opens up new territories for process and product development. Researchers can be imagined pushing on a particular door until it begins to open. They may need to push for years, even decades, until the breakthrough emerges. If this simple vision of the technical environment is representative, then it raises some important questions for managers of research-dependent organisations:

- How do we determine how much money to invest in an area?

- What is the best organisation structure to get results?

- What collaborative or co-operative research is needed?
- How do we measure progress with particular research projects?
- When should we stop supporting a project?

The clustering of innovations was one of five causes of innovation identified by Rothwell and Wisseman (1991). They noted the connections between social, economic and technological developments as follows:

- There is a need for technological change – simply stated this says that technologies are developed when there is a need for them, as with the development of radar in the late 1930s to respond to the obvious role of air power in war.

- Very often, major inventions are not single advances, but rely upon clusters of related technologies to make them work. There may be a time lag between one breakthrough and a breakthrough in an important related area.

- Social resistance to change is well known, though it varies between nations and between age groups. America is associated with entrepreneurship and risk-taking and is open to change more so than other countries. Satellite TV receiver dishes were prohibited in Iran to stop the spread of Western ideas and images (Temourian, 1995).

- In addition to technical capability (including expertise, finance, and organisation), driving force and dogged perseverance are needed to see projects through to marketable ends, such as new processes or products. The few years between President Kennedy's announcement of a space programme and Neil Armstrong's lunar walk testifies to a national driving force.

- Social objectives are important. At any point in time, a society will have objectives for its development. These objectives in turn influence the direction of technology development. Volvo's pioneering work with semi-autonomous work teams in the 1970s may well reflect a general Scandinavian preference for group decision making (see Chapter 5).

Rothwell and Wisseman (1991) argue that there is a reciprocal relationship between technology and culture; technology follows culture and culture follows technology. Both statements seem to be true.

Integrating technology in the organisation

When business environments were mostly stable and the rate of technological progress was slow, technology could be integrated into production processes with minimum disruption to an organisation. That said, adopting new technology has never been easy. Think of the English Luddite movement of 1811–13, when organised gangs smashed machinery in cotton mills in reaction to the threat posed to jobs in a time of general economic depression.

Environments are no longer stable; they are turbulent, dynamic arenas. While technology, for some organisations, represents small incremental improvements to tools and equipment, it increasingly involves complex interactions between people and information-based systems. Complex systems cannot easily be integrated into organisations. In technology-intensive sectors, managers can no longer devise a strategy and a structure for an organisation and then seek technologies to make the strategy work. Advanced technologies need careful management if they are to make maximum contribution to organisations. They should not be seen as obedient servants to their masters. Technology choice needs to evolve at the same time as decisions are made about strategy and structure, not afterwards (Parthasarthy and Sethi, 1992).

The organisation of research and development

There are several ways of organising successful R&D. The simplest and traditional approach is to manage in-house facilities under the control of an R&D director. It gives full control over projects, and sensitive information is relatively secure. Problems with this approach have surfaced, however, as it can be slow and inward-looking. Given the trend towards shorter product life cycles and expanding legislation covering products, working conditions and the environment, shorter development times are needed. For instance, the technology behind more than 70 per cent of products sold by German electronics company Siemens is less than five years old (Wood, 1998). To accelerate idea generation and development, organisations actively seek collaborative projects, spin-offs, joint ventures, mergers and acquisitions to supplement in-house research (see Minicase 4.2).

When large-scale development takes place, as with, for example, building a major industrial complex, the client, possibly a government department, may want a turnkey project, that is, one where contractors supply and install all the necessary technology. In turnkey projects, one supplier might be unable to provide all the expertise needed and so alliances with other organisations are essential to win contracts and for project completion. Alliances could also be necessary to begin trading with a particular country. For example, a company with no experience of trading with a country might need to form an alliance with another company already established in that country.

Sometimes an organisation comes unstuck in a product area. This happened to Mercedes (see Minicase 4.3) and Boots Pharmaceuticals in 1993 when clinical trials of their heart drug Manoplax indicated that people taking it had a higher chance of returning to hospital or dying than people not taking it. Boots' drug portfolio was small by comparison to other pharmaceutical companies and the failure of Manoplax, which had attracted hopes of boosting Boots into a more dominant market position, was instrumental in bringing about the division's sell-off. Boots' pharmaceutical division was later sold to the German chemical company BASF. This suited BASF since Boots' portfolio was largely in the UK, the USA and Commonwealth countries while BASF mostly focused on continental Europe (Jackson, 1993).

Minicase 4.2   Managing technology – collaboration

Leading nations agreed through the Montreal Protocol to end the production of harmful chlorofluorocarbons (CFCs) by the end of 1995. CFCs are thought to interact with ozone in the upper atmosphere causing a depletion in the ozone layer which protects us from the extremes of the sun's radiation.

CFC producers were already seeking replacements for CFCs following research that pointed to their harmful ecological role. To accelerate commercialisation of alternatives, the chemicals group ICI and pharmaceutical company Glaxo signed a joint venture. Under the venture, Glaxo provided funds to build a new plant to produce CFC alternatives on one of ICI's sites and took all the production for use in its inhalable asthma drugs. ICI earned a 'generous management fee' reflecting the value of its proprietary technology.

ICI held about a third of the world market for CFC replacements and was determined to 'capitalise on its technology as the market expands'. Expansion was assured by the Montreal Protocol and the continuing need for industrial-grade CFC replacements for use in factories as well as purer pharmaceutical grades.

Source: 'ICI & Glaxo join forces to replace CFCs', *The Times*, 16 January 1995

Questions

1. Given the rate of economic development across the world, how realistic are prospects for reductions in pollution from industrial processes?

2. What are the main barriers to major cutbacks in pollution?

Technological change and society

Ethical aspects of technological change

The subject of ethics deals with the moral issues arising from decisions open to individuals and groups, including business enterprises. In the simplest terms, ethics deals with the rights and wrongs of things. Throughout history, technology has changed human society – from the first use of flint axes as weapons, through the discovery of farming practices and the working of metal into art, tools and weapons. Modern society is more alert to the ethical issues of technology such as ICT, the science of cloning and the

Minicase 4.3   Managing technology – the elk test

German car producer Mercedes unveiled its new A-class small car to expectant journalists in October 1997. The car was a much-heralded move by Mercedes into the small-car market and included radical design aspects. With an engine slung underneath the car, instead of the usual front or back, the space inside the car would comfortably hold four people. This was the most advanced small car since the Mini was introduced forty years earlier.

Now, in Sweden, the docile elk causes thousands of motor accidents a year and motor testers use an 'elk test' on all new cars. This involves swerving sharply from side to side as if to simulate sudden elk avoidance. Unfortunately for Mercedes, the A-class flipped over when attempting the elk test and in front of the assembled media. Mercedes were faced with an immediate public relations crisis given their reputation for vehicle safety and engineering excellence.

The car's launch was delayed to give time to modify the chassis and Daimler's share price was affected for a short time, but in the long run Mercedes' reputation was not harmed and the car was successfully introduced. The story highlights the highly unpredictable and costly nature of new product development.

Questions

1. What technologies are used to increase driver and passenger safety?

2. What aspects of motoring are currently out of reach of safety improvements?

science of genetically modified (GM) foods. These developments raise ethical questions, for instance, about the working conditions in call centres, the amount of information that organisations hold on people and the effects on the natural environment.

One big area of concern relates to approaches to risk. In the 1950s and 1960s when nuclear power was a focus of government policy, there were, and still are, serious questions about the health and safety risks to people living in the vicinity of power stations and about the best ways of dealing with highly radioactive wastes. A more recent example concerns the supposed risks to regular users of mobile phones of brain damage from frequent exposure to radio waves. The key question surrounding technology boils down to whether the benefits arising from using a new technology outweigh the known or presumed disadvantages. A common approach to resolving this question examines whether a majority of people will benefit from a technology even though some will be disadvantaged, perhaps seriously. This idea of greatest benefit for the greatest number is called a utilitarian approach to decision making.

A current and future ethical problem concerns the issue of privacy in light of the near limitless capacity of ICT to store information about individuals from their internet usage, motor insurance and credit card transactions among others. Government departments such as the Inland Revenue, Vehicle Licensing Authority, the police and social services hold information on individuals, and questions have been raised about whether the type and amount of information held goes beyond what is needed for the operation of government in a free society.

The Vehicle Licensing Authority holds records of registered vehicles and it is easy to identify vehicles that are not taxed. Number plate recognition software installed in police cars and on the roadside checks the numbers of passing vehicles and where unlicensed vehicles are observed this provides irrefutable evidence for a court that an unlicensed vehicle was used on a public road. At a very simple level of analysis it seems reasonable that technology should be used to identify offenders. For serious crimes few would disagree with this principle but for less serious offences, how much should the routine activities of people be monitored in order to identify breaches of the law?

For decades, the police have stored items, e.g. clothing, from serious crime scenes. The recent technology of DNA profiling which produces a person's unique 'DNA fingerprint' has allowed DNA samples from old crime scenes to be matched against fresh DNA samples taken by the police. Presently, the police take DNA samples (a mouth swab usually) from people charged with serious offences and these are routinely compared to all DNA profiles obtained from unsolved crimes – some 30 years old. Several people have been convicted of murder using this evidencing technique but lesser crimes also. Proposals exist, in 2003, that would allow the police to take DNA samples from anyone arrested and these 'fingerprints' will be compared against databases of DNA from crime scenes.

Undoubtedly, since criminals tend to re-offend, this will lead to some convictions that might not otherwise occur. At a simple, rational level of analysis one could argue that society would benefit from such a policy. But look more closely. A proportion of people charged with offences may later be found innocent and a proportion of people arrested are not even charged. Is it right that people who have not broken the law should have a DNA sample, taken by force if they refuse, on permanent file and have it compared to databases of DNA samples from scenes of crime? Is it right that people arrested for minor offences should be evaluated as potential rapists, burglars or murderers?

If the proposal to DNA-sample anyone arrested becomes law, how long will it be before the government deems it in society's interest that a DNA sample be taken from all people on reaching the age of 16? The rationale that the innocent have nothing to fear is seductive but can be used as a licence for security services to monitor people without limit, in the name of safety and justice, such that the freedom of the individual is seriously curtailed (see Minicase 4.4). It is arguable that issues of privacy and freedom are fundamental concerns in a society that feeds on information storage and exchange. The way our attitudes to the collection and use of information about people change in the future has the potential to alter the relationship between individual and state.

Another technology presenting serious ethical problems concerns GM foods given the uncertain effects upon humans who consume them and upon plant and animal

Minicase 4.4   The surveillance society

Listed below are some of the actual, emerging and potential mechanisms for monitoring your movements and activities.

- Credit card details show exactly what you purchased, where and when. Your supermarket loyalty card does the same.

- A mobile phone acts as a tracking device that pinpoints where it, and you, are. Your location when you make a call is known and mobile calls and text messages can easily be recorded.

- E-mail traffic is probably being intercepted and read, for security reasons, on a sampling basis. Past connection, albeit innocent, to a person or organisation deemed by security services to be of interest could put your e-mail traffic under scrutiny – just in case. Your employer can monitor your e-mail and web usage.

- Your personal computer records all the websites that you have visited plus deleted files.

- On your shopping trips, you are filmed in most shops that you enter and some CCTV cameras in public places can compare faces with facial recognition software against databases of people of 'interest' to the authorities. Facial recognition software needs to be more accurate than it is now if it is to be more widely used – but those times will come.

- On your drive to work, cameras can record registration numbers fixing a vehicle in place and time and, potentially, run the number against databases such as motor insurers.

Questions

1. To what extent does routine surveillance of normal, law-abiding activities represent an invasion of privacy?

2. How will society benefit from routine surveillance and database checking of people going about their everyday life?

species that interact with them in their natural environments. Ethical problems are also raised by the technologies that support cloning. For instance, research upon human embryos which, while appearing distasteful to many, may have the potential to lead to breakthroughs in medical sciences and hence produce benefits to mankind.

Technology and safety

The UK's industrial revolution (about 1760 to 1830) led to large numbers of people working in factories as well as an improved transportation system involving canals and railways. At that time, and in the decades that followed, safety hazards were largely seen as an accepted part of working life. Working conditions were poor and hazards were ever-present. In the UK, about 4750 people were killed in industrial accidents in 1900 compared to about 200 in 2000. Hazards came from crude production processes, e.g. in mining and heavy industry, and others came from a lack of knowledge about the effects of materials, such as lead, mercury, gases, solvents and fibres, on the human body, leading to many industrial diseases (see Minicase 4.5). The first Act of Parliament (Factory Act) relating to health and safety at work was passed in 1802 and gave some protection to children working in cotton mills. Other Acts in the 1800s specified working hours, working times and minimum ages of employees and extended to include other industries and the mines. In the UK, worker safety was brought under a comprehensive system of law through the Health and Safety at Work Act of 1974. This imposes duties on employers and employees to uphold safe practices.

Accident rates are inevitably linked to the extent of exposure to hazards and the potential consequences of those hazards. Trawler fishing is far more dangerous than writing software. While technology-intensive sectors seem less hazardous, when high-technology systems go wrong the effects can be disastrous.

An example of the widespread use of a technology to improve safety stems from the UK government's targets for reductions in casualties from road traffic accidents. One of the tactics used to achieve the targets involves speed (safety) cameras that use accurate speed measurement and vehicle recognition technologies to identify vehicles exceeding set limits. We are approaching the time when it will be possible to fit cars with devices that, via satellite positioning, 'know' a road's speed limit and control the engine so that speeds cannot be exceeded. There are concerns, however, that this technique could itself be dangerous because a driver would lose control of the vehicle until the speed dropped to within the limit. Alternatively, vehicles could be fitted with devices that log vehicle speeds in excess of limits and which can be checked later by the authorities.

Technological change and vulnerability

Although human societies have been adopting new technologies for thousands of years, communities remained largely self-sufficient until recently. If some disaster befell a community, the impact was contained and the bulk of society carried on unaffected.

Minicase 4.5   Technology catastrophes

Thalidomide – a drug marketed in the 1960s to treat morning sickness. Unknown to its developers, Thalidomide has a horrible side effect if taken during a short period in early pregnancy. If taken when the limbs of a foetus are forming the drug interferes with normal limb development. Thousands of babies were born with missing or deformed limbs. It was taken out of use when its effects were discovered. Very recently, new uses for Thalidomide have been found but its use must be very strictly controlled to prevent use by pregnant women.

Three Mile Island – a nuclear power plant in the USA where, in 1979, a small amount of radioactive material was released into the atmosphere when safety systems failed. Although a major radiation incident was avoided, the US authorities were sufficiently concerned about what might have happened that government policy on nuclear power was re-evaluated.

Chernobyl – in 1986 this nuclear power plant in the Ukraine was the site of a major (non-nuclear) explosion that released radioactive material into the atmosphere. There was an immediate effect whereby hundreds died of radiation poisoning. People living in the region are still affected as long-lasting radiation entered the food chain.

Bhopal – the site in India of a chemicals plant that, due to failures of safety procedures, released deadly methyl isocyanate gas killing thousands of people living around the plant (see Minicase 6.4 in Chapter 6).

Dow Corning and breast Implants – Dow made silicone breast implants in the 1970s and 1980s and most implant operations were done for cosmetic rather than medical reasons. There was strong evidence that, for some women, the implants had led to major medical problems including inflammation, excessive scarring and problems with the immune system. Legal proceedings rumbled on into the 1990s with concerns that information showing that implants could lead to health problems had been suppressed alongside medical opinion that the link between implants and the observed symptoms was inconclusive.

Exxon Valdez – in 1989 this loaded oil tanker ran aground in one of the world's unspoilt natural environments in Alaska. Major damage to marine and shore life occurred plus disruption to the livelihoods of a working community based on the sea. Tanker spills are all too common, and while they are not directly caused by technological failures (more likely bad weather, incompetence, mistakes) oil is an indispensible part of energy and transport systems.

Questions

1. How should an organisation react to a crisis arising from its own operations or products?

2. What systems and procedures should organisations have to deal with major crises caused by their own activities?

Recent technologies based on oil and electronics have led to extensive integration of communities such that they (we) are highly dependent upon others. Indeed, we are highly dependent upon a small number of providers of essential services. Imagine, for instance, the effects of a large-scale shutdown of electricity generation. All ICT-based work would cease. Financial systems would be thrown into chaos given the volume of electronic transactions. Air and rail transport would stop, emergency services would be paralysed and factories and hospitals would stop functioning. The effects would be virtually instantaneous.

While leading to great advances, these same technologies have made the developed (and developing) countries very vulnerable to industrial action (see Minicase 4.6) and to terrorist acts. It has been argued that part of the explanation for America's attacks on Afghanistan and Iraq lies in eliminating threats to vital technologies.

Minicase 4.6   The UK petrol crisis of September 2000

One week in September 2000 showed how vulnerable an advanced society can be. Fuel prices had risen substantially above the general price index due to government tax policies. Farmers and hauliers, for whom fuel costs are important, protested against continuing rises by picketing fuel refineries. The normal flow of tankers to petrol stations was affected. Many stations quickly ran dry as consumers fearful of long-term shortages filled up. The sudden rise in demand for fuel made the supply situation worse. Supermarkets reported 'panic' buying of foods. The government was suspicious that the oil companies were not doing all they could to get tankers out in the hope that the government might cave in and reduce taxes, something it pledged not to do. Oil company executives were summoned to Number 10 and the Cabinet's emergency committee met regularly. Troops were on standby to move fuel supplies. After about a week the protestors gave up their peaceful picketing and normality resumed. The Home Secretary was quoted as as saying, 'as a consequence of these protests, essential services, the basic fabric of our society and national life, was brought to the brink'.

Questions

1. How far do you agree with the notion that society could be paralysed by industrial action or terrorist attacks?

2. How might governments deal with increasing vulnerability from technological integration?

Conclusion

Technology represents an environmental force so strong that it can affect the competitive advantage of nations and shape the attitudes of whole societies. The days of R&D departments pushing their ideas sequentially through design, development, production and into markets have gone. Technology management today involves scientists and engineers working with suppliers and early adopters of products and processes to learn from each other. Managers must understand how emerging technologies could affect their organisation so that it responds to threats and opportunities in the best way. Information technologies are affecting organisations and whole economies in a revolutionary way. Managing technology into the organisation is a difficult skill to acquire as there are many examples of project failure. This calls for a sound understanding of the benefits technology can offer and of the people management issues created inside the organisation. ICT and genetic science are posing complex ethical problems.

Summary of main points

This chapter introduces key aspects of technological change that relate to business organisations. Specifically:

- Knowledge and technology evolve, usually in small steps but occasionally in large jumps. We are experiencing such a jump in information-based technologies at present.

- Innovation is a key feature of business organisations and has been for 200 years.

- ICT is having a revolutionary impact upon governments, business organisations and individuals.

- For optimum performance, organisations need to find the best fit between technology available to them, the socio-economic environment and their choice of strategy.

- Where technology is a major factor in determining organisational performance (in some organisations and sectors it is a minor factor) it must be seen as central to organisational decision making.

- Technological change affects jobs, skills and productivity.

- Technological change offers the only prospect of sustainable economic growth on a world scale.

- Technological change is creating controversial decisions about personal privacy and interference with plant and human biology.

Discussion Questions

1. To what extent do you agree with the statement that British scientists and engineers are not as effective at exploiting new technology as those in other industrialised countries?

2. How can Europe and North America sustain a technological lead ahead of newly industrialising countries? Will the NICs eventually catch up?

3. Think of a range of goods and services (industrial and retail) – what characteristics of these goods/services support sales over the web? What characteristics impede web sales?

4. What factors might intervene to minimise the impact of technological change on job losses in an organisation? What other factors could cause job losses?

5. How might scientists and engineers differ from unskilled and semi-skilled employees in their attitudes to work, to their managers and to their organisations?

Web Links

http://www.gov.uk

http://www.dti.gov.uk
UK government sites giving information on how the government supports science and technology, UK statistics and science policy.

http://crito.uci.edu
Centre for Research on Information Technology and Organisations. Examples of projects on IT benefits to a range of organisatons.

http://www.oecd.org
Organization for Economic Co-operation and Development. Follow links to science and technology for information on effects on economic development.

http://www.thecarbontrust.org.uk
Information on efforts to reduce carbon emissions, e.g. using alternative fuels.

http://www.sustainabletechnologies.ac.uk/home.htm
Details of research projects aimed at growth without harm to the natural environment.

http://www.innovation.gov.uk/
Contains the UK government's R&D Scoreboard.

Further Reading

Baruch, Y. (2000) 'Teleworking: benefits and pitfalls as perceived by professionals and managers', *New Technology Work and Employment*, 15 (1), 34–49.

This paper considers how teleworking is perceived based upon interviews with teleworkers in five organisations and examines the impact of teleworking on effectiveness, the quality of working life and family life.

Currie, G. and Proctor, S. (2002) 'Impact of MIS/IT on Middle Managers: some evidence from the NHS', *New Technology Work and Employment*, 17 (2), 102–18.

This paper uses research in three hospitals and finds that IS/IT boosts the role of middle managers by providing them with information for top management.

Harris, L. (2001) 'The IT Productivity Paradox – evidence from the UK retail banking industry', *New Technology Work and Employment*, 16 (1), 35–48.

This paper demonstrates why investment in information technology projects may not always lead to the expected improvements to organisational performance.

References

Adcock, H., Helms, M. and Jih, W-J.K. (1993) 'Information Technology: can it provide a sustainable competitive strategy?', *Information Strategy – The Executive's Journal*, 9 (3), 10–15.

Arnold, J., Cooper, C. and Robertson, I.T. (1998) *Work Psychology: Understanding Human Behaviour in the Workplace*, 3rd edn, FT Prentice Hall.

Ayres, R.U. (1991) 'Barriers and breakthroughs: an expanding frontiers model of the technology industry life cycle', in Rosseger, G. (ed.) *Management of Technological Change*, Oxford: Elsevier Science.

Berry, M.M.J. and Taggart, J.H. (1994) 'Managing technology and innovation: a review', *R&D Management*, 24 (4), 341–53.

Brown, C. and Campbell, B.A. (2002) 'The Impact of Technological Change on Work and Wages', *Industrial Relations*, 41 (1), 1–33.

Burns, T. and Stalker, G. (1961) *The Management of Innovation*, London: Tavistock.

Campbell, M. (1993) 'The employment effects of new technology and organizational change: an empirical study', *New Technology, Work and Employment*, 8 (2), 135–40.

Chapman, A.J., Sheehy, N.P., Haywood, S., Dooley, B. and Collins, S.C. (1995) 'The organizational implications of teleworking', in Cooper, C.L. and Robertson, I. (eds) *International Review of Industrial and Organizational Psychology*, Chichester: John Wiley, vol. 10, pp. 29–248.

Clark, J. (1984) 'Food, drink and tobacco', in Guy, K. (ed.) *Trends and Employment, 1: Basic Consumer Goods*, Aldershot: Gower.

Clark, J. (1985) 'Chemicals', in Clark, J. (ed.) *Technological Trends and Employment, 2: Basic Process Industries*, Aldershot: Gower.

Coleman, D.C. and MacLeod, C. (1986) 'Attitudes to new techniques: British businessmen', *Economic History Review*, 39 (4), 588–611.

Cookson, C. (1995) 'Breakthrough in mixing the molecules', *Financial Times Survey*, Chemical Industry, 27 October, p. 1.

Cooper, C.L. and Payne, R. (1990) *Causes, Coping and Consequences of Stress at Work*, Chichester: John Wiley.

Dopson, S., Ruddle, K. and Stewart, R. (1998) 'From downsizing to revitalisation', *Financial Times*, 27 February, p. 12.

Dussauge, P., Hart, S. and Ramanantsoa, B. (1994) *Strategic Technology Management*, Chichester: John Wiley.

Felstead, A., Jewson, N., Phizacklea, A. and Walters, S. (2002) 'The option to work at home: another privilege for the favoured few?' *New Technology, Work and Employment*, 17 (3), 204–223.

Foster, G. (1993) 'The innovation imperative', *Management Today*, April, 60–63.

Frank, S. (2003a) 'Patent applications to the EPO continue on an upward trend 1990 to 2001', *Statistics in Focus*, 4/2003, Eurostat.

Frank, S. (2003b) 'R&D expenditure and personnel in Europe: 1999–2001', *Statistics in Focus*, 3/2003, Eurostat.

Freeman, C. (1982) *The Economics of Industrial Innovation*, London: Frances Pinter.

Galbraith, J.K. (1967) *The New Industrial State*, Harmondsworth: Penguin Books.

Gale, H.F., Wojan, T.R., and Olmsted, J.R. (2002) 'Skills, Flexible Manufacturing Technology and Work Organization', *Industrial Relations*, 41 (1), 41–79.

Galley, C. (1998) 'An investor's perspective', in *The UK R&D Scoreboard 1998*, Department of Trade and Industry, pp. 7–9.

Ganster, D.C. and Murphy, L. (2000) 'Workplace Interventions to Prevent Stress-Related Illness: Lessons from Research and Practice', in Cooper, C.L. and Locke, E.A. (eds) *Industrial and Organizational Psychology*, pp. 34–51, Oxford: Blackwell Publishers.

Gavigan, J. Zappacosta, M., Ducatel, K., Scapolo, F and di Pietrogiacomo, P. (2001) 'Challenges and priorities for European research: a foresight review', *Foresight*, 3 (4), August, 261–71.

Gillespie, D.F. and Mileti, D.S. (1977) 'Technology and the study of organizations: an overview and appraisal', *Academy of Management Review Symposium: Organizations and Technology*, 4 (1), 7–16.

Gooding, C. (1995) 'Boosting sales with the information warehouse', *Financial Times*, 1 March, supplement p. 15.

Greiner, L.E. (1972) 'Evolution and revolution as organizations grow', *Harvard Business Review*, July, 37–46.

Guy, K. (1984) 'Footwear', in Guy, K. (ed.) *Technological Trends and Employment, 1: Basic Consumer Goods*, Aldershot: Gower.

Guy, K. (1985) 'Paper', in Clark, J. (ed.) *Technological Trends and Employment, 2: Basic Process Industries*, Aldershot: Gower.

Harris, L. (2001) 'The IT Productivity Paradox – evidence from the UK retail banking industry', *New Technology Work and Employment*, 16 (1), 35–48.

Jackson, T. (1993) 'Boots withdraws heart drug after 2 year study', *Financial Times*, 20 July.

Johnson, G. (1993) 'A strategy for change at KPMG', in Johnson, G. and Scholes, K., *Exploring Corporate Strategy*, Hemel Hempstead: Prentice Hall.

Laafia, I. (2002) 'Employment in high tech and knowledge intensive sectors in the EU continued to grow in 2001', *Statistics in Focus*, 4/2002, Eurostat.

Lazonick, W. (1981) 'Competition, specialisation and industrial decline', *Journal of Economic History*, 41 (1), 31–8.

Lazonick, W. (1983) 'Industrial organization and technological change: the decline of the British cotton industry', *Business History Review*, 57 (2), 195–236.

Lorenz, A. and Smith, D. (1998) 'Britain fails to close competitiveness gap', *Sunday Times*, 11 October, section 3, pp. 10–11.

Matzner, E. and Wagner, M. (eds) (1990) *The Employment Impact of New Technology*, Avebury: Gower.

McLoughlin, I. and Clark, J. (1994), *Technological Change at work*, Milton Keynes: OU Press.

Monck, C.S.P., Porter, R.B., Quintas, P. and Storey, D.J. with Wynarczyk, P. (1988) *Science Parks and the Growth of High Technology Firms*, London: Routledge.

Morgan, J. (2002) 'Research and experimental statistics 2000', *Economic Trends*, August, pp. 32–56.

Morgan, J. (2002) 'Research and experimental development (R&D) statistics 2000', *Economic Trends*, 585, August.

Ng, H.I., Pan, Y.J. and Wilson, T.D. (1998) 'Business use of the world wide web: report and further investigations', *International Journal of Information Management*, 18 (5), 291–314.

Parthasarthy, R. and Sethi, S.P. (1992) 'The impact of flexible automation on business strategy and organizational structure', *Academy of Management Review*, 17 (1), 86–111.

Porter, M.E. (1979) 'How competitive forces shape strategy', *Harvard Business Review*, March April.

Porter, M.E. and Miller, V.E. (1985) 'How information gives you competitive advantage', *Harvard Business Review*, July–August, 149–60.

Rassam, C. (1993) 'Science in crisis', *Management Today*, June, 60–3.

Rothwell, R. (1992) 'Successful Industrial Innovation: Critical Success Factors for the 1990s', *R&D Management*, 22 (3), pp. 231–39.

Rothwell, R. and Wisseman, H. (1991) 'Technology, culture and public policy', in Rosegger, G. (ed.) *Management of Technological Change*, Oxford: Elsevier Science.

Shiman, D.R. (1991) 'Managerial efficiency and technological decline in Britain 1860–1914', *Business and Economic History*, 20, 89–98.

Simons, G.L. (1986) *Management Guide to Office Automation*, National Computing Centre.

Small, I. and Swann, P. (1993) 'R&D performance of UK companies', *Business Strategy Review*, 4(3), 41–51.

Souder, W.M. (1991) 'Organising for modern technology and innovation: a review and synthesis', in Rosegger, G. (ed.) *Management of Technological Change*, Oxford: Elsevier Science.

Temourian, H. (1995) 'Iran bans Baywatch with purge on Satan's dishes', *Sunday Times*, 23 April, p. 18.

Teo, T., Lim, V. and Wai, S. (1998) 'An empirical study of attitudes towards teleworking among IT personnel', *International Journal of Information Management*, 18 (5), 329–44.

Tubbs, M. (2002) *Research and Development Scoreboard – Analysis*, Department of Trade and Industry.

Wood, A. (1998) 'An industry perspective', in *The UK R&D Scoreboard 1998*, Department of Trade and Industry, pp. 3–5.

Yamazaki, H. (1988) 'The development of large enterprises in Japan: an analysis of the top 50 enterprises in the profit ranking table (1929–1984)', *Japanese Yearbook on Business History*, no. 5, pp. 12–55.

5 The International Cultural, Demographic and Social Environment

Jon Stephens

Learning Outcomes

On completion of this chapter you should be able to:

- understand the concept of national culture and its link with globalisation;
- have increased awareness of differences in national cultures and the reasons for this;
- identify differences in business cultures through the work of Hofstede and Trompenaars;
- appreciate the key factors that determine changes in a country's population;
- understand how demographic changes can be significant for both businesses and governments;
- have a clearer understanding of some of the key social trends in terms of family, lifestyle and crime;
- appreciate how the nature of organised labour has changed.

Key Concepts

- national culture
- the convergence/divergence debate
- Hofstede's five dimensions of national culture
- Trompenaars' dimensions of national culture
- culture shock and culture shift

- national culture and business practices
- the rate of natural population change
- birth rate and death rate
- replacement fertility rate
- population pyramids
- dependency ratios
- international migration
- patterns of family development
- lifestyle trends
- organised labour
- changing work trends

Introduction

This chapter covers some of the wider factors that will influence the business environment facing firms in the increasingly complex environment faced in the twenty-first century. It will start by examining the national cultural environment which is becoming increasingly important as the process of globalisation continues and companies are increasingly faced with operating in different countries. This may be through direct investment or through joint ventures or strategic alliances but it will mean that management styles and practices that are used in the home country may or may not function efficiently in a different cultural environment. If these issues are not addressed by companies it could even lead to the culture shock effect which can have a damaging impact on the companies' performance overseas.

The first section of this chapter will seek to identify some of the issues that determine cultural differences, making use of some key theoretical studies such as Hofstede and Trompenaars, and then will then seek to show how cultural differences can create problems within the business environment before seeking to show how some of these cultural differences can be overcome and even turned into competitive advantage for companies that handle cultural differences effectively.

The second part of the chapter will look at the demographic environment and many of the issues arising from the demographic structures faced by organisations when they are operating internationally. Demographic changes are some of the most predictable changes in the business environment and the first section will look at some of the key components of natural population growth and the factors that influence these with examples drawn from many countries. The issue of international migration has also become more significant in determining population size and both legal and illegal migration will be looked at in this context. Whilst the absolute size and the change in size of population will be very significant, it is also important for organisations to examine the changing structures of populations as this may have important implications for market attractiveness. One way of looking at changing populations is by using population pyramids and these will also be examined in this section. The structure of the population may have very important implications for governments as well as business organisations. One of the major issues facing governments in Western Europe is the impact of ageing populations and particularly the implications of this trend for public pension provision in the future and this issue will be examined in more depth (see Case Study 5).

The final part of the chapter will explore the social environment and again look at some of the implications of these changes for the business environment. There are increasing studies of changing social trends and there is such a wealth of data (see web links) that one can analyse information at local and regional level as well as at national and inter-country levels. One of the factors that links with the previous section is the issue of the changing nature of the modern family both in terms of family size and the changing relationships and lifestyles within families. Within the context of lifestyle changes we will look at changes in trends of consumer behaviour, in smoking and drinking and also in crime trends. The changing nature of work is also explored, especially in terms of the impact of new technologies and the resultant trend to more flexible working practices and some of the implications of these changes for organised labour. Wider social trends such as education and crime trends are also explored as both of these may be of significance for companies and managers who may be operating outside their home country.

The national cultural environment

Definitions of national culture

One of the immediate problems faced when looking at national culture is to find an acceptable definition of what it is. Kroeber and Kluckholm (1985) found over 160 definitions when they were researching this issue. The culture of countries was originally examined from an anthropological or sociological one as opposed to a business one, although the development of globalisation has thrown the national cultural issue much higher up the agenda for business people who are working in countries other than their own. One of the most commonly used definitions is that of Geert Hofstede (1984) who defines national culture as:

> The collective programming of the mind which distinguishes the members of one human group from another . . . . Culture, in this sense, includes systems of values; and values are among the building blocks of culture.

This definition highlights the significance of values and the fundamental taken-for-granted assumptions that are held by a large group of people in the country and which in turn will influence their behaviour. It is often differences in these sets of values that will drive differences in national culture and perceptions of what is acceptable and not acceptable in behaviour in the culture. This can obviously be of great significance for

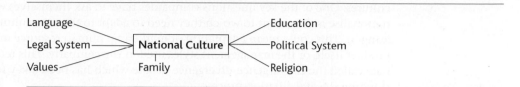

Figure 5.1 Factors influencing national cultural values

business operations in countries other than your own, an issue which will be explored later in the chapter. Development psychologists believe that by the age of ten most children have their basic value system firmly in place and that after this age changes are more difficult to obtain.

Figure 5.1 shows that national cultural values will be influenced by a range of factors and the degree of difference between these factors may well determine the degree of difference between national cultures.

One of the most significant factors is that of language and thus countries which speak the same language tend to be closer culturally than where there are strong linguistic differences. It can also explain why there can often be significant sub-cultures in a country built around different languages. An example in Europe would be Switzerland where citizens might speak either French, German, Italian or Romansch. Sometimes there might be a shift in languages taught in countries which might have some impact on cultural attitudes; an example here would be the shift towards Mandarin Chinese from Cantonese Chinese in Hong Kong since Hong Kong was returned to China in 1997. Sometimes these language changes can be fiercely resisted as has been seen in France where there has been some resistance from the Academie Française to the new 'pop culture' words which are mainly English in origin.

One should not discount the impact of religion upon culture, especially where the political systems and religious systems are closely intertwined, as in many countries in the Middle East where the impact of Islam and Judaism has been very strong and has conditioned cultural attitudes strongly as it directly affects the value systems of individuals which we have seen as a central factor influencing culture. One of the main reasons why Eastern cultures are significantly different to Western ones is the impact of Confucianism on the region.

It should be stressed that whereas country analysis does suggest certain national behavioural patterns there do still remain significant sub-cultures in many countries where the national pattern may be modified. These sub-cultures can be because of historical factors and may be enhanced by different religious or linguistic patterns.

National culture and globalisation

The role of national culture and potential national cultural differences has become an increasingly important part of the business environment as a result of the increase in globalisation, with more and more countries looking to operate outside their home base and thus finding that they are coming into increasing contact with different cultures. One of the key questions companies have to ask themselves when they internationalise is the extent to which they need to adapt to the new culture they are operating in. This could mean adaptation of marketing, human resource management, the product itself, or the management styles used in the company. This reflects a wider debate called the convergence/divergence debate which has been a key feature of understanding the globalisation process.

The convergence perspective (Kerr *et al.*, 1960; Levitt, 1983) suggests that globalisation is inevitably leading to more and more standardisation as consumers become aware of global brands and companies realise the advantages of having standardised products or practices that can be used throughout the company, no matter which country they are operating in. Brands such as Coca-Cola, Nike and Nokia are recognised globally which means the potential global market is enormous and opens up opportunities for economies of scale through global advertising campaigns and standardised manufacturing. Even football clubs are seeking global identities with Manchester United developing links with the New York Yankees for the North American market and setting up several franchises in China and South-East Asia where the Manchester United brand is very strong.

The divergence perspective suggests that in reality it is not always that easy to transfer brands across countries and that companies may face difficulties when transferring management practices because of national cultural differences. This may be especially so where the company has an ethnocentric perspective in which it assumes that the practices used in its home country will work in any other country (the opposite is a polycentric perspective where different strategies may be adopted if significant local differences occur). As can be seen, the degree of national cultural differences may well determine whether practices can be easily transferred from the home company to its overseas business units. A close cultural fit (for example the USA and the UK) would probably suggest that little adaptation is needed and therefore the convergence perspective might be a valid one to follow, whereas if there were significant cultural differences then adopting an ethnocentric approach might be a high risk strategy.

One of the most famous examples of this was the early stages of the operation of the Eurodisney theme park in France, just outside Paris. The early stages of the project were fraught with problems both in terms of customer retention (the French were not happy about wine being unavailable in the Park) and in keeping staff (in the early days there was a very high rate of staff turnover) with the result that the project nearly failed. It has been argued that one of the main problems here was misunderstanding between managers (mainly American and Canadian) and staff (predominantly French). It was only with the appointment of a French CEO that things began to turn around to the point that the park is now well established. Similar issues might be significant in the new Disney theme park which will open in Hong Kong in the future.

Identifying differences in national culture

As can be seen from the convergence/divergence debate, a critical factor will be whether there is a close cultural fit between two countries or whether there are significant cultural differences. Whilst we can make various generalisations arising out of historical, linguistic, religious and other factors, we need some more precise criteria to evaluate the differences in national culture from a business perspective. Here we would turn to two of the most significant writers about national culture who both provided frameworks against which we could test a country's national culture in order to see how closely it fits with other countries' patterns.

One of the most significant writers on national culture is Geert Hofstede who wrote 'Culture's Consequences' in 1984. This provided a useful framework by which we can measure national cultures. A key weakness of Hofstede's work is that it was based only on the responses of IBM staff around the world. This meant that it might have been influenced by the corporate culture of IBM and also that it was limited in its scope, because in 1984 IBM did not have offices in certain countries such as China and Russia. However, it was important because it identified certain dimensions around which one can examine cultures and which have remained valid.

In Hofstede's original work (1984) he identified four variables or dimensions around which one could begin to evaluate differences in national culture and some of these are identified in Table 5.1.

Table 5.1 Selected examples of Hofstede's Cultural Dimensions (1984)

Country	Individualism (IND)	Power Distance (PD)	Uncertainty Avoidance (UA)	Masculinity (MA)
Denmark	74	18	23	16
Sweden	71	31	29	5
Japan	46	54	92	95
Malaysia	26	104	36	50
Singapore	20	74	8	48
UK	09	35	35	66
France	71	68	86	43
Germany	67	35	65	66
Italy	76	50	75	70
Spain	51	57	86	42
Greece	35	60	112	57
Brazil	38	69	76	49
Australia	90	36	51	61
USA	91	40	46	62

Note: when comparing countries along these criteria, the key is to see how close the figures are – the closer they are then the closer the cultural fit. As a rough guide, if the gap rises above twenty then it suggests a significant cultural difference.

The first of these dimensions is power distance which represents the social distance between people of different rank. If we look at a country with a high power distance score (Malaysia for example), this would suggest that there is a clear gap between superiors and subordinates in this country. This would be reflected in the way that superiors are addressed (formal or informal) and the willingness or unwillingness to question any decision made by a superior, i.e. in a high power-distance country superiors' decisions would be accepted without discussion and they would carry great respect. This is very common in Asian cultures where this is underpinned by the Confucian philosophy which encourages respect for superiors and elders. Low power-distance countries would suggest cultures where managers may be challenged more openly and where respect may draw more from ability than seniority.

The second dimension identified by Hofstede is individualism which reflects the extent to which an individual relies on a group or collectivist approach to issues (a low individualism score) or the extent to which the individual takes individual initiatives to solve problems or make decisions (a high individualism score). Table 5.1 shows the high score for the USA, one of the most individualistic cultures in the world, whereas Singapore reflects a much more collectivist approach (hence a low individualism score), which again is quite common in Asian cultures.

The third dimension identified by Hofstede is uncertainty avoidance, which essentially reflects people's attitudes towards ambiguity in a society or country. When there is a high score for uncertainty avoidance it suggests a culture where people are unhappy with ambiguous situations and prefer more direction. It also suggests that in these countries it will be hard to undertake rapid changes in the organisation because this would probably cause anxiety and stress, as the nature of rapid change is that it does lead to uncertainty. According to the Hofstede data Greece has a high level of uncertainty avoidance whereas in a country like Sweden uncertainty would be much more tolerated and thus change programmes might be likely to receive less resistance.

The final dimension identified by Hofstede was that of masculinity, which is probably one of the more complex of his variables. It reflects values which are widely considered to be more 'masculine', such as assertiveness, competitiveness and the need to achieve results. A low masculinity figure suggests a higher degree of co-operation and more caring approaches to dealing with people in the organisation. This value can also reflect the level of discrimination against women in the organisation, i.e. it might be hard for a woman manager to progress in a high-masculinity culture or to have the same degree of respect as a male manager. A good example in this context is Japan which has the highest masculinity index in Hofstede's survey and where it is seen as very difficult for female managers to progress up the corporate ladder.

Although there were only four dimensions of culture in his original work Hofstede identified a fifth dimension through work carried out with Bond and the Chinese Culture Connection Group (1987) which was evaluating the Asian context of national culture. The main outcome of Bond and Hofstede's later work was evidence that most Asian cultures seemed to have a long-term perspective about work and relationships as opposed to a much shorter-term perspective found primarily in Western cultures. This might explain why Asian companies prefer to build relationships with Western companies through joint ventures and strategic alliances rather than attempting mergers.

A further development from Hofstede's work is the idea that you can place countries in clusters of those showing similar patterns of the dimensions just described. If, for example, we look at the two variables of power distance and uncertainty avoidance we could end up with a pattern as suggested in Figure 5.2.

It is interesting to note here that although countries may be geographically close (e.g. France and the UK) they may have very different cultural characteristics which might be significant when managers of these two countries are working together. Figure 5.2 suggests that Spanish managers would be much more at ease with their French counterparts than with, say, Swedish managers because of the different perceptions about how to deal with subordinates and how much direction to give to other managers.

The second key writer on cultural differences is Fons Trompenaars, who drew on the work of Hofstede and others such as Kluckhohn and Strodtbeck (1961). Following a questionnaire survey of 15 000 respondents, he identified seven areas where cultural differences could occur. The seven areas identified were:

- universalism vs. particularism;

- affective vs. neutral;

- collectivism vs. individualism;

- specific vs. diffuse relationships;

- achieving vs. ascribing status;

- time as sequence vs. time as synchronisation;

- inner directed vs. outer directed.

The first of these, universalism vs. particularism, is where a universalist approach suggests that culture should be driven by rules and that there are universal rules that should

Denmark	UA:23 PD:18		
Sweden	UA:29 PD:31		
UK	UA:35 PD:35		
USA	UA:46 PD:40		
		Italy	UA:75 PD:50
		France	UA:86 PD:68
		Greece	UA:112 PD:60
		Japan	UA:92 PD:54
		Spain	UA:86 PD:57

Figure 5.2 Cultural clusters

be respected, whereas a particularist culture tends to have a more flexible interpretation of rules and draws more on people relationships. Universalist cultures tend to be found more in the UK and the USA whereas particularist cultures are more common in Asia. This may cause problems in negotiating between these countries as managers may have different conceptions as to what rules of business behaviour will apply.

Affective vs. neutral cultures relates to the extent to which emotion is used and is acceptable in a culture. In some countries people keep emotions under check (the 'stiff upper lip' approach) whereas in others emotional behaviour would be expected and condoned within a working environment. The implications for the successful operation of international teams are self-evident.

Collectivism vs. individualism reproduces the dimension previously identified by Hofstede, whereas specific vs. diffuse relationships relate to the extent to which managers separate their work relationships from other relationships. In a specific culture the manager–subordinate relationship may be observed at work but is not necessarily replicated in their relationship outside work, whereas in a diffuse culture (as is often found in Asia) the relationship at work influences all other relationships.

The issue of status is also identified in terms of achieving vs. ascribing status. In a culture with an achieving status, status is seen very much as something that is achieved by the individual through their own actions. In an ascribing culture status might be ascribed to an individual through factors like age or gender. You would find achievement status cultures in Scandinavia; ascribing status cultures are found in Asian countries as well as Argentina and Egypt.

Another dimension identified by Trompenaars was how time is perceived in a culture and he identified time as sequence vs. time as synchronisation. Time as sequence suggests a rational linear approach to issues where one issue is dealt with before another begins (one step at a time approach). Time as synchronisation suggests that time is seen as circular in the sense that a number of parallel activities can continue at the same time. A sequential time approach is found in Germany. The French tend to have a more synchronic approach which again may have implications for joint projects or teamworking between these two cultures.

The final dimension is inner directed vs. outer directed. This contrasts those countries like the USA and Switzerland where there is a belief that the individual can determine events and control situations (inner directed) with those countries where the belief is that the individual's actions are determined by other forces such as the need for harmony with nature. This belief is central to both Confucianism and Buddhism and thus colours attitudes in Asian cultures (outer directed).

Through looking at the frameworks provided by Hofstede and Trompenaars it can be seen that there are a number of dimensions against which differences of national culture can be measured. We have also seen how some cultures have a relatively close fit with each other, whereas others have significant cultural differences where the divergence theory becomes more significant. Sometimes the differences in culture can lead to the phenomenon of culture shock where the businessperson operating in a different culture may suddenly find themselves disorientated as they realise they are having problems adapting to the local culture. Torbiorn (1982) suggests that businesspeople working overseas usually have an initial 'honeymoon period' where the excitement of working in a different country outweighs any initial problems encountered. It is only later as cultural misunderstandings and confusion occur that this initial positive dimension fades. There might also be the problem of language, which means that communications do not run smoothly, which again leads to confusion and stress. This is where the culture shock begins as the manager realises that cultural misunderstandings are undermining their effectiveness and their confidence.

Much will depend upon the ability of the individual manager to overcome this and the support given by the manager's organisation through cross-cultural training and support. Without this there is the danger that the manager will reject the culture they are operating in and turn very negative against it. Sometimes they may seek other expatriates and create an expatriate 'bubble' in terms of seeking to surround themselves with other people from their own culture and thus restrict contact with the local culture. The other extreme is that they will completely adapt to the local culture and 'go native' which has advantages but might affect their loyalties when difficult decisions have to be made on a corporate basis. In the twenty-first century the demand is for managers who are culturally aware and who can operate in a range of cultures, as opposed to the traditional expatriate who might work for many years in one base overseas.

The impact of national culture on business practices

If one accepts that national cultural differences can be significant in terms of affecting the international business environment then the question arises as to identifying some of the key areas of business practice where some cultural adaptation may be necessary (especially when there is a significant gap in the cultures of the countries concerned). This idea can be explored further in the Minicase 5.1.

With increased globalisation there has been a significant increase in international mergers, alliances and joint ventures where the successful adaptation to national cultural differences may be an important factor in determining their effectiveness. Any such venture would require a number of meetings where negotiations would take place. This is where issues such as effective communication between the prospective partners would be significant and where cultural factors could come into play, e.g. in a German business culture humour is not usually used in business discussion whereas it is much more common in British business culture and therefore the use of jokes by the British managers may be misunderstood by German managers. Humour is also acceptable in Chinese business cultures although Chinese humour may differ from British humour. The issue of power distance would also come into communications in terms of how people are addressed, i.e. formally or informally, and certain forms of non-verbal communication might be frowned upon in different cultures. In Malaysia the smile can mean many things. A smile and a nod may suggest that your opinion is respected but it does not mean that the person agrees with you, or a smile may be a cover for extreme embarrassment when the person wants to avoid losing face.

One consequence of international mergers, joint ventures and alliances is the increased use of international teams and again issues of how the team works together might be significant, e.g. when there are different perspectives on time (sequential vs synchronic), attitudes to hierarchy in the group (power distance) and the way the group handles ambiguity (uncertainty avoidance).

Minicase 5.1   American investment in China: some cultural dimensions

By 2001 the People's Republic of China (PRC) had become the primary location for global foreign direct investment with over US$47 billion being invested, with a large amount of that figure coming from corporate investors in the United States, which remains the base for a majority of the world's largest multinational corporations. Although there is some direct investment in China, the preferred method of market entry is by forming a joint venture with a Chinese company. This has the advantages for the investing firm that the Chinese company will have useful contacts and an existing distribution system whereas the Chinese company can benefit from using improved management techniques and technology transfer. Given the significant increase of Chinese–US joint ventures, there will be increased pressure on managers from the two countries to work together in order to make the joint ventures or direct investment work effectively.

This is where the issue of national culture comes increasingly important as it will be necessary for managers to identify and adapt to national cultural differences if they are to work together effectively. A starting point is to use the data from Hofstede (1984) and Trompenaars (1997) to have a look at cultural characteristics of China, Hong Kong and the United States.

Table 1 Cultural characteristics

	PRC	Hong Kong	USA
Hofstede (1984) ranking			
Power Distance	20	15	38
Uncertainty Avoidance	1	49	43
Individualism	23	37	1
Masculinity	54	18	15
Trompenaars (1993) Ranking			
Achievement	32	20	2
Universalism	39	38	7
Internal Control	19	8	7
Specificity	34	16	17
Affectivity	41	38	20

From the table above we can immediately see that there are significant cultural differences in some of the above areas between the PRC and the USA. The Americans are extremely individualistic whereas the managers in the PRC will be much more comfortable when working on a group basis and we can also see that the Chinese would not be happy with uncertainty whereas this would not be a problem for the American managers. Similar differences occur with many of Trompenaars' dimensions. It is interesting to note the position of Hong Kong in this respect as it is close to the PRC in some respects and close to the USA in others. This reflects the phenomenon of culture shift in that Hong Kong, whilst part of the PRC since its handover from the UK, has been exposed to other business cultures over a period of time and so its cultural behaviour may have changed in some respects. Thus our American company would probably find less of a culture clash if setting up in Hong Kong than in mainland PRC.

We can look at these cultural differences in more depth by comparing American and Chinese management styles. We have already seen that the American management style is very individualistic in nature and there is relatively low uncertainty avoidance – individuals will be expected to make decisions and to react to change effectively. It is certainly a hard-working culture where excessive working will be encouraged and where the practice of the business breakfast is well established. Americans like decisive leaders and new ideas are generally welcomed. Communication is generally informal in nature with the use of first names between senior managers and their subordinates. The American manager will tend to be short-termist in nature and will be looking for instant results from a meeting and status in the organisation is more likely to be based on salary size than age.

If we contrast this with the Chinese management style we might notice a few differences. The Chinese manager will be influenced by the Confucian influence that pervades many aspects of Chinese life. Thus there will be great respect for more senior people in the organisation (linked to high power distance), respect for elder people and especially the need for politeness and harmony in their working life. The Chinese manager will also be a hard worker and a lot of time will be spent on developing relationships (*guanxi*) with people both inside and outside the organisation. Communication will usually be very formal and often top-down and great effort will be made that no one loses 'face' in discussions or negotiations, although the Chinese manager may not be expecting an instant decision from the meeting – it may be more about building up the *guanxi* with new partners. The Chinese manager might also be more comfortable about working in groups rather than on an individual level, although less happy about close physical contact with other people and they would not be happy about any personal disclosures, preferring to talk solely about the business in hand. Meals will be an important part of negotiations and humour is very acceptable in these situations.

It can be seen that there are significant differences in management styles, reflecting some of the cultural differences and so the ability of managers to adapt to each other's cultures will appear to be a significant factor in the potential success of American–Chinese joint ventures.

Questions

1. Imagine an initial meeting taking place between Chinese and American managers concerning a new joint venture. Using material from the case, try and imagine potential problems that might arise in this meeting through cultural misunderstanding – look at it from the perspective of both the American and the Chinese manager.

2. You have been asked to lead the American delegation in the negotiations above. How would you brief them in terms of the management style to be adopted with the Chinese? Should you adapt or not?

There will also be functional areas of business that will be affected by cultural differences, most notably in Marketing and Human Resource Management (HRM). From the marketing perspective there will be the discussion of whether to go with global marketing campaigns (the convergence perspective) or whether there is a need to adapt the product for the particular cultural needs of the country concerned. The attractions of following the convergence approach would be in terms of economies of scale in that the same advert could be used on a global basis, thus reducing costs and also developing a global brand image. The divergence approach might be needed if the product needs adapting for particular markets. For example, the British tend to use a lot of humour in their advertising but this humour might not be seen as humour in other countries and thus there is a need to adapt the campaign according to local demands. Although McDonald's in many respects follows a convergence perspective in terms of common approaches to layout, design and a common brand, it still adapts its product range in different countries, especially in countries where certain foods may be banned for religious reasons, for example cows are sacred to Hindus in India and elsewhere, so lamb is served as an alternative.

From the HRM perspective, national culture may be very significant when looking at areas like training, appraisal and recruitment. In terms of training, it may be dangerous to use direct training approaches such as direct discussion/questions or role-play situations when you are working in an environment where there is a high power distance and people prefer to be told what to do rather than discussing it with the trainer. It may also be difficult to get responses in Eastern cultures where there is the fear of loss of face. Performance Appraisal might also have to be adapted as it suggests an appraisal of a subordinate by a superior whereas modern styles of appraisal such as 360-degree appraisal would also include assessment by fellow workers and subordinates as well as your line manager. This might be difficult to translate into a culture where there is traditionally a high power distance. The issue of recruitment might also be significant in terms of whether you employ expatriate managers (from your home country) or local managers (who will know local conditions but may be less familiar with the corporate culture of the company). It is clear (Daniels and Radebaugh, 2001) that it is getting harder to find managers willing to spend long periods abroad. The trend is clearly towards managers spending shorter periods abroad, but in a variety of countries, and many of these managers will become more culturally sensitive through training and experience.

The demographic environment

Demography concerns the study of population and population change and can be seen as another important factor that will affect the business environment. Whereas many of the environmental indicators such as social and technology trends are hard to forecast, the impact of demographic changes can be more confidently predicted, i.e. if we know the number of five-year-olds in the UK in 2003 we will have a pretty clear idea of the number of fifteen-year-olds there will be in 2013 and this may be useful when predicting potential markets.

This section will examine some of the key drivers of population change and draw out some of the main trends that are affecting population change worldwide and then look at some of the implications of population change for individuals, businesses and government.

Key drivers of population change

The two main indicators of natural population change are birth rate and death rate. Birth rate can be defined as:

the number of live births per thousand of the population

The death rate can be defined as:

the number of deaths per thousand of the population

When these two figures are put together you will get the natural increase or decrease of the population, again measured per thousand of the population.

However, there is another factor that has to be taken into account when looking at population change. This is the net migration per thousand of the population, which reflects the difference between immigration (into a country) and emigration (out of a country). If we add this figure to the natural change in population we will see the overall increase or decrease in the population.

Information on population change in Europe in 2001 for selected countries is shown in Table 5.2.

From the information in Table 5.2 we can see that there are some significant differences in population patterns in Europe. Ireland has a birth rate which is far in excess of

Table 5.2 Population change in Europe, 2001

	BR	DR	NC	NM	TC
EU15	10.6	9.5	1.1	2.8	3.9
Germany	9.0	10.0	−1.0	2.2	1.2
France	13.1	8.9	4.1	1.0	5.1
Greece	10.1	9.5	0.6	2.4	3.0
Italy	9.4	9.3	0.1	2.9	3.0
UK	11.2	10.2	1.0	2.6	3.6
Ireland	14.6	7.5	7.1	5.2	12.3
Portugal	11.2	10.2	1.0	4.8	5.8
Sweden	10.2	10.6	−0.4	3.4	3.0
Czech Republic	8.8	10.4	−1.6	−0.4	−2.0
Bulgaria	8.4	13.6	−5.2	0.0	−5.2
Poland	9.4	9.4	0.0	−0.4	−0.4
Romania	9.5	11.2	−1.7	0.0	−1.7

Key: BR = birth rate/thousand
   DR = death rate/thousand
   NC = natural population change (BR − DR)/thousand
   NM = net migration/thousand
   TC = total rate of population change/thousand
Source: United Nations

its death rate and also has a lot of inward migration which means that its population is increasing at a healthy rate. This could be contrasted with the figures from Germany where the death rate exceeds the birth rate, meaning that the population is declining. This decline is only offset by inward migration, meaning that population growth in Germany is extremely slow and is in fact forecast to decline in the future. A further example can be seen with the case of the Czech Republic where not only does the death rate exceed the birth rate but there is also a net outflow in migration, all leading to a decline in the population. The European Union has carried out forecasts of population change by 2050 based on current trends and whereas strong population growth is expected in Ireland (increasing 31 per cent), the UK (increasing 13 per cent) and France (increasing 10 per cent), population decline is anticipated in other countries such as Germany (declining 4 per cent), Spain (declining 8 per cent), Italy (declining 22 per cent) and Russia (declining 30 per cent). These trends obviously have significance for businesses which will be exploring potentially high-growth markets against those where demand is likely to fall as a result of population decline.

To understand why these changes are taking place we need to understand why birth rates, death rates and migration rates are changing.

Birth rate factors

Birth rates tend to be more volatile than the death rates and thus may have more short-run impact on population changes. Birth rate may be affected by many factors such as attitudes towards family size. The trend seen in most of Europe is a decline in family size (see Chapter 9). The usual litmus test in this respect is to look at your family size and then compare it to your parents' family size and grandparents' family size and so on. One undoubted factor here is the fact that more women wish to follow their own careers before having children and so delay the age at which they have them. The cost of having children might also be taken into account as well as the degree of flexibility in the labour market which determines the extent to which women (or men) can follow more flexible work patterns in order to look after children whilst continuing in a work pattern. Other determinant factors could be the values of the country or the impact of religion on attitudes towards children or the availability and use of contraception in a country.

A critical indicator which will reflect all these factors is the fertility rate which reflects the average number of children per female. Even more significant is the replacement fertility rate, the fertility rate needed if a population is to replace itself. The recognised replacement rate needed for this is 2.1 children.

If we look at Table 5.3 we can see some of the current predicted figures for replacement fertility rates as suggested by the UN.

From the table we can see that Sri Lanka has a figure which fits the desired replacement rate exactly, while the United States is not far behind. France and the UK have relatively good rates, which is reflected in their higher birth rates and their predicted population growth. The lowest figures seem to come from either Eastern European countries where the recent economic dislocation may be a factor in smaller family size, or the Mediterranean countries (such as Italy, Spain and Greece) where the cause is less

Table 5.3 Replacement fertility rates, 2000

Sri Lanka	2.10	USA	1.99
China	1.80	France	1.89
UK	1.60	Sweden	1.64
Germany	1.35	Greece	1.27
Italy	1.23	Spain	1.15
Russia	1.14	Bulgaria	1.10

Source: United Nations

easy to define but may be linked to inflexible labour markets and changing attitudes amongst women. Certainly this decline in the number of children in these areas may be having a significant impact not only on the future population size of these countries but also on the future age structure, as this trend will (other factors remaining equal) lead to a rapid ageing of the population with all the implications that has for businesses and government (see later).

Death rate factors

As has been previously suggested, the death rate tends to be more stable than the birth rate and it usually reflects the changing age structure of the population. A higher concentration of older people will tend to lead to a gradual increase in the death rate. Death rates have come down in many parts of the world as a result of better medicines and improved sanitation and health care, although there are still significant discrepancies between the developed and the developing world. In many parts of the developing world people generally have very basic diets which might make them more vulnerable to epidemics or illnesses, such as those illnesses linked to poor drinking water. These factors help explain the higher death rates and lower life expectancies in these countries.

There is also the impact of armed conflict which may have an impact on the death rate if there is a prolonged civil war, as has been seen in several countries in Central Africa. With globalisation and improvements in transport, diseases can travel much more quickly as can be seen with the recent (2003) SARS outbreak which quickly spread from Guandong province in China to Hong Kong and thence to several places, most notably Toronto in Canada.

A much more significant epidemic in terms of its impact has been the spread of the HIV/AIDS virus. Whilst this virus has spread throughout the world, its most serious effects are being felt in sub-Saharan Africa as Minicase 5.2 illustrates.

Migration factors

Migration of people across borders has long been a feature of history and in the modern globalised economy it seems that migration is seen as a global issue rather than a regional one. An economic migrant from Afghanistan would now look as much at emigrating to Western Europe as to moving to the countries adjacent to Afghanistan. Historically there have been many great shifts of population. In the nineteenth century there was great movement from Western Europe to the USA, Canada, Australia and Argentina where there were new prospects for economic development and there were more opportunities. People migrating in search of new opportunities for work are seen as economic migrants whereas those migrating to escape oppression and persecution in their home country could be seen as political migrants. Usually the people who migrate are younger and more ambitious. They can enrich the economy into which they move in terms of providing new skills and filling gaps in the labour market.

Minicase 5.2	Life chances in the UK and Malawi

When looking at population change it is usually considered that birth rate is more volatile than death rates and that changes in population are primarily driven by changes in birth rates and replacement fertility rates. Sometimes, however, the key driver affecting a country's rate of population change can be a dramatic change in the death rate. A region that has been devastated by an epidemic is sub-Saharan Africa where the HIV/AIDS virus has spread alarmingly in some countries and has led to severe changes in mortality rates.

We can highlight these changes by contrasting life chances between Malawi and the United Kingdom. Malawi is a much smaller country in population terms than the UK (10.7 million in Malawi compared to 59.7 million in the UK) and is also a much poorer one with an average annual income per head of £106, compared to £14 150 in the UK. This lack of wealth has meant that the country's medical resources are much more thinly spread with only one doctor per 45 000 people (the UK rate is one doctor per 480 people).

All these factors have meant that Malawi is poorly positioned to deal with the HIV/AIDS virus. If we look at the UK we can see that HIV incidence is about 0.1 per cent of the population which meant that in 2001 there were about 34 000 people with HIV. AIDS deaths in that year were 460. Whilst these figures are significant, they have not had a major impact on mortality rates in the UK; in fact life expectancy in the UK is gradually rising and was estimated in 2001 as being 75 for men and 80 for women.

The impact of HIV/AIDS has been much more devastating in Malawi with over 15 per cent of the population being affected by the illness and with AIDS deaths in 2001 being estimated at 80 000. The effect of the epidemic has been to leave many children orphaned (360 000 in 2001) and many of those, in turn, may carry the virus. This is having a significant effect on infant mortality rates with the one-year infant mortality rate at 138 per thousand and the five-year infant mortality rate at 215 per thousand – in effect meaning that one in five children in Malawi will not make it past their fifth year. The corresponding figure in the UK is 7 children per thousand who do not make it past their fifth year.

The frightening thing about the epidemic in Malawi is that life expectancy is now **falling**, with the current life expectancy for men now down to 39 years and for women down to 40 years.

Questions

1. What can Malawi do to control and eradicate the HIV/AIDS epidemic in the country? Has it the resources to do so?

2. Do you feel that the ease with which viruses spread (SARS and HIV/AIDS) is linked to increased globalisation or can they be controlled locally?

The Republic of Ireland has for a long time experienced significant outward migration, predominantly to the United States, the United Kingdom and Australia. It is said that there are more people of Irish descent in New York than there are in Ireland – it is believed that there are 44 million Americans of Irish descent. The horrific potato famine in 1845/46 was a significant spur to migration, primarily to the 'New World', and continual waves of outward migration occurred as younger people looked for new opportunities away from the depressed economy. This is obviously a loss for the country as the younger people are the most flexible in terms of taking up new job opportunities and in learning new skills. Irish migrants were seen as an asset to the United Kingdom where many worked in the construction trade. What is interesting now is that the economic resurgence in the Irish economy, sometimes described as the 'tiger economy' of Europe, has led to greater opportunities for young Irish people within Ireland and this has considerably reduced the flow of young Irish people abroad. Indeed, we can see from Table 5.2 that there was a strong inflow of migrants to Ireland in 2001, suggesting that the traditional outward flow has reversed itself.

If we look at the same table we can see the case of Germany where the inward migration is offsetting the decline in natural population growth, although the longer-term projections still forecast a decline in the population by 2050. Germany has traditionally been a magnet to economic migrants because of its successful economic growth record, which has encouraged inflows of migrants, predominantly from Turkey and Eastern Europe. However, the result has often been political and social tensions which have been manifest by racial attacks and have encouraged the growth of far-right political parties, a feature found across Europe. Migrants also face other problems with some of them finding themselves in areas characterised by low-quality and poorly maintained housing with all the resulting social problems that follow from that. So, whereas the influx of migrants can be a boost for a country's labour supply and can improve mobility of labour, it can result in some of the tensions identified above.

One of the biggest challenges faced by the EU in the twenty-first century is that of illegal migration, which constitutes mainly economic migrants looking for new opportunities and deriving mainly from developing countries. An example of this is the influx of Albanians coming illegally into Italy with some moving on to other countries and some staying in the 'hidden economy' of Italy where they don't have to declare their earnings. It often poses a quandary for governments as to how tight their restrictions should be. One could look at Italy with its predicted 22 per cent fall in natural population by 2050 and question whether in fact inward migration might be necessary for the country to maintain its current economic structure.

Another migration issue that can be seen throughout Europe is the shift from rural locations to urban locations, leaving many villages in the more remote regions populated mainly by older people. However, this in turn causes problems in cities with uncontrolled urban sprawl and increased congestion. Some major urban areas continue to suffer from poor housing and education, overstretched services, increasing crime and general social and economic hardship. The better-off tend to move to the affluent suburbs leaving the very old, the unskilled and certain ethnic minority groups concentrated in inner-city areas. This leads to a range of social problems allied to high crime rates which pose additional problems for governments.

Patterns of population change

The impact of population growth

Table 5.4 shows how the world's population has changed together with the predicted population figure for 2050.

From the table we can see that it took 123 years for the world's population to increase from one billion to two billion but only another 33 years to increase from two billion to three billion, with the last landmark of six billion being passed in October 1999, a mere twelve years after reaching five billion. This does reflect a quickening of population growth, driven primarily by population growth in developing countries where high birth rates have been accompanied by falling death rates (through improved medicine and sanitation), thus creating population growth. This high rate of growth, if unchecked, will continue to put extreme pressures on the world's resources unless they could be developed at a commensurate rate (e.g. increasing agricultural production through more use of genetically modified crops).

In some countries high population growth could be seen as a real inhibitor to economic growth and development. In Bangladesh, for example, the population was 123 million in 1998 and is predicted to grow to 210 million by 2020. It is characterised by a high birth rate and low death rate and 45 per cent of the population are currently under 15 (compared to only 13 per cent of the EU's population being under 15 in 1998). Bangladesh has some fertile countryside but is prone to flooding and there is limited room for further agricultural expansion with the result that the increasing population is putting tremendous pressure on existing resources. The country needs to double agricultural output by 2020 to stand still and already 50 per cent of the population are below the poverty line, so the need for more control on population growth is very clear in order to reduce the existing pressure on resources. One country that has managed

Table 5.4   World population growth

1804	1 Billion
1927	2 Billion
1960	3 Billion
1974	4 Billion
1987	5 Billion
1999	6 Billion
2050 (pred)	8.9 Billion

Source: United Nations

this very well is China with its 'one-child policy' where significant social pressure is brought on couples to have just one child with the result that the recent surge in economic growth in China is not being held back by too rapid a population growth.

However, Table 5.4 shows that world population, though still increasing, is growing at a slower rate (only rising by about three billion between 2000–2050). This is because of the effect noticed earlier (in Table 5.2) of many countries (especially European ones) where population growth is practically static or is even declining through the very low fertility rates identified in Table 5.3. This does suggest in the future something of a redistribution of world population away from areas like Europe towards areas like South-East Asia and this may have implications for businesses' long-term investment plans and development strategies.

The distribution of population

Whilst it is interesting to look at actual population changes it is also important to look at the structure of the population in terms of the relevant age structures as this will also give us clues as to how the population is evolving and some of the implications of this for both businesses and governments. The distribution of population can be looked at both within a country and between countries.

An example of differences within a country can be seen by taking two different parts of the UK and using material from the 2001 census.

The age structure of a country or region can best be illustrated by a population pyramid and an example of such a pyramid is shown in Figure 5.3, which shows how the age structure of the EU will change between 1990 and 2020.

This population pyramid clearly shows that the population of the EU is ageing. At all ages greater than 45 the numbers (as a percentage of the population) will increase by 2020 whereas at all ages below that they will decrease. We will see more and more older people and relatively fewer younger people than at present. We have already seen the very low replacement fertility rates in many European countries and this is a prime causal factor for this change, allied to the fact that older people are living for longer. If we look at the global picture we see that in 1950, 27 per cent of the world's population was under 15 and only 12 per cent above 60. By 1998 the figures were nearly level with 19.1 per cent of the world's population under 15 and 18.8 per cent over 60 and by 2050 the predicted figures are much more dramatic with 15 per cent of the world's population predicted to be under 15 and 33 per cent over 60. It is perhaps these figures that are more significant than the figures for overall population growth as they show a relatively rapid ageing of the world's population. The predicted figures for Europe in 2050 are even more extreme with only 13 per cent of the population predicted to be 15 or less compared to 39 per cent being over 60. This will also be reflected in changes in the average age of the population. The average age in the UK in 150 was 35 which had risen to 38 in 2000 and is predicted to rise to 44 by 2050. In rapidly ageing countries such as Italy it will rise even higher to 52 in 2050.

These rapidly ageing populations (unless they are changed by significant influxes of young migrants) may pose problems for companies who operate in these markets and

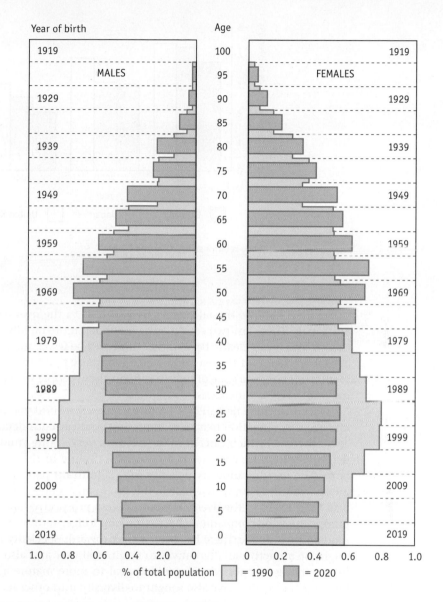

Figure 5.3 EU population pyramids 1990 and 2020

for governments faced with a significant increase in older people. One critical ratio that is affected by these changes is the Dependency Ratio, which reflects the number of 15-64-year-olds to the rest of the population as it is from this group that the taxes will be raised which will support the schools, hospitals and other support services that are needed for groups outside that age range.

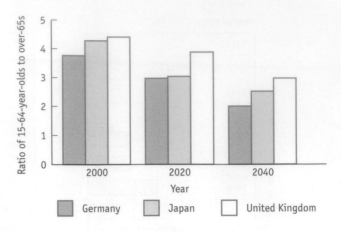

Figure 5.4 Dependency relationships 2000 and 2040
Source: Eurostat, 1991

Figure 5.4 shows the ratio of 15-64-year-olds to the over-65s in the UK, Germany and Japan. These last two countries have a much more rapidly ageing population than the UK and it can clearly be seen that there will be fewer and fewer numbers of people available to support the over-65s, which has many significant implications for governments, not least the issue of how to support these people with pensions without resorting to massive tax increases.

In sectors where demand for products is based around younger age groups, the rapidly ageing population may have important strategic considerations. A company, such as Mothercare, which catered to the needs of very young children, extended its product ranges to older children as a result of a decline in the number of children being born. The brewing industry depends for a significant part of its sales on the male age group from 18 to 30, with a male in this group on average consuming 70 per cent more beer than males in the over-40s group. With a prospective fall in this age group across Europe, brewing companies have to think up longer-term strategies which can accommodate this. Hence, there has been a shift towards speciality beers and drinks which might be attractive as alternatives to traditional beer and also the shift by companies into catering in pubs which would appeal to more mature adults and families. The brewing companies have also sought to diversify into other sectors such as hotel ownership and recreation facilities.

On the other hand the growth in the proportion of older people throws up opportunities for businesses which seek to target this group (see Minicase 5.3). Examples of this would be travel firms which seek to cater to the needs of the older consumer or the potential for pharmaceutical companies producing drugs which are much more likely to be used by this age group. Numerous financial services groups target this sector offering products at those who are retired or are about to retire. There has also been a significant increase in the number of registered nursing and retirement homes which cater for the older citizen and which provide more sheltered housing for older people.

Minicase 5.3   Saga holidays

In the mid 1950s, entrepreneur Sidney De Haan decided to offer cheap holidays to retired people at off-peak times. He took advantage of the low prices offered by hoteliers who were only too willing to see their poor occupancy rates rise. Forty years on, the Saga group, with a turnover in excess of £150 million, offers holidays, financial services and magazines to the over-50s. Saga recognised that the special needs of older customers represented a market opportunity.

Retired people have grown progressively wealthier and Saga now offers holidays trekking in the Himalayas and round-the-world cruises costing up to £30 000 per head. They have expanded in the lucrative US market. They have also developed their 'product' portfolio to include financial services such as insurance brokering. They can negotiate many preferential rates for their low-risk customers, since, for example, older people tend not to drive great distances hence reducing the probability of being involved in a car accident. They also spend more of their time in their houses, so reducing the opportunity for burglars to strike.

About half of Saga's 750 staff employed in Folkestone, Kent, now work on the financial services side of the business. What is more, they find their business is virtually recession-proof as a decline in a national economic cycle has little influence on the income of retired people. What is damaging, however, is a decline in interest rates which does adversely influence the incomes of their clients.

Questions

1. Saga has been one of the most successful companies in terms of catering to the needs of the older population. What other companies and industries have responded to the increased demand from this group?

2. Which types of companies have suffered from the ageing of the population and what strategies can they follow to counteract these problems?

Wider implications of population change

As has been previously suggested, population change is slower moving and is the most predictable aspect about the business environment. At the same time it will have important wider implications, which can be seen at individual, corporate and governmental levels.

At the individual level the changes we have looked at will be reflected in the sort of life people can expect to live in the twenty-first century. One of the key indicators will be that of life expectancy as that reflects the changes of lifestyle and medical improvements,

Table 5.5 Selected examples of life expectancies, 2001

Country	Men	Women
France	74	82
Germany	74	80
Greece	76	81
Italy	75	81
Switzerland	75	82
UK	75	80
Bulgaria	68	75
Poland	68	77
Russia	61	73
Czech Republic	70	77
China	68	72
India	62	63
Singapore	75	79
USA	73	80
South Africa	52	58
Zimbabwe	44	45
Brazil	63	71

which means that people can generally expect longer lives than in previous times. Table 5.5 shows some examples of life expectancy in 2001.

From this it can be seen that women usually outlive men by some years, which explains the relatively high number of women found in the older age ranges of the population pyramid (see Figure 5.3). However, the trends of life expectancy have seen a gradual increase to the extent that there are increasing numbers of people reaching one hundred years of age. Against this generally positive picture one should not forget that average life expectancies can also decrease as in sub-Saharan Africa (see Minicase 5.2). Another indicator of improvements in living standards is the decline of the infant mortality rate which shows that children have a much stronger chance of survival in their first year as a result of medical and sanitary improvements, particularly in developing countries. However, one should not forget that there are still serious global discrepancies in this respect as in 2003 approximately one-sixth of the world's population does not have access to safe water and approximately three-fifths of the world's population do not have adequate sanitation.

At the corporate level we have already seen how businesses in markets with ageing populations may have to refocus their selling strategies. This is particularly relevant when the older age groups have more spending than previously, which has led to the concept of 'grey power'. In developing countries where there is still a high birth rate and a significantly higher proportion of younger people, companies may find substantial markets for products which are wanted by this age range – this could apply to certain global products with strong brand images that are associated with younger people and may sometimes be seen as essential fashion accessories. An example here would be the effect that satellite television has had on the merchandising of football clothing linked to well-known global clubs such as Manchester United and Real Madrid, especially in South-East Asia.

Another factor that might be significant for companies when considering overseas investment decisions might be the geographical mobility of labour, which reflects the ease with which labour can move around the country in search of employment, and also the occupational mobility of labour, which reflects the ease with which labour can move between jobs and how quickly they can be retrained. It is usually the case that younger people are more mobile both in terms of geographical and occupational mobility and so a younger age-profile might be attractive to some companies, especially those who invest in labour-intensive industries. It has been noticeable that many large organisations have been moving their labour-intensive call centres to developing countries where there is an established pool of young, educated people who are available for work.

Perhaps the most challenging dimension of demographic change is that faced by governments. When there is high population growth (as we saw in the case of Bangladesh), there are enormous pressures on governments to provide adequate resources for the growing population. Whilst the prime requirement is for food and water, there will also be requirements for educational and medical facilities which will be very difficult to fulfil without help from other sources. In the situation of Europe and Japan, where the trend is essentially that of an ageing population, the governments will face other issues. One factor will be a gradual decline in the number of younger people. This might mean that in some cases schools have to be closed down, especially in areas where natural population decline has been exacerbated by migration. On the other hand, with a significant increase in the number of older people there will be a significant increase in the demand for medical services, especially as older people generally require significantly more medical support than younger people. Thus the demand for hospitals and medical support provided by the government will grow and governments will have to become increasingly aware of the needs of older people when determining their political programmes.

Social dynamics

The final part of this chapter will examine some of the social trends that have occurred over the last years and assess some of the implications of these for the way we live and how they might be significant for the business environment.

Social dynamics will be looked at from three perspectives with current trends identified in each case. The first dynamic of social change relates to changes in the changing family. The family is the basic building block of society and yet it has been influenced by many factors over the last twenty years. We have already seen how the falling birth rates might be significant for family size, although we will also examine changes in family structure and changes in the patterns of relationships. A very good source to identify such trends is the National Census in the UK which first took place in 1801 and has taken place every ten years since that date with the census material from 2001 now being available. An additional source is the General Household Survey which began in 1971 and which is carried out each year based on a sample of 9000 households. The second social dynamic we will examine will be the change in lifestyles. This will reflect some different aspects of how we live and how we spend our leisure time and what we spend our money on. It will also reflect how healthy our lifestyle is and our educational needs as well as looking at trends in crime in our society. The third social dynamic to be examined will be the change in work and the extent to which the nature of work is changing in the twenty-first century and will also cover other work-related issues such as the minimum wage and changes in organised labour.

The changing family

We have already identified that falling birth rates have tended to lead to a reduction in family size. Household size has declined in a fairly consistent pattern from a figure of 2.91 persons in 1971 to a figure of 2.48 in 1991 and then again to 2.33 in 2001. Many of the reasons this have been discussed above; also more people are living alone than at any previous time. One-person households have increased from 17 per cent of all households in 1971 to 30 per cent in the census of 2001 (a total of 6.5 million households). There are always a number of older people who live alone, but the figure for this group has remained stable, with the big increase in single households occurring in the 25–44 age group. This may be significant for companies who might target this age group and might be one of the factors behind the significant increase in demand for satellite television in the UK. The 'traditional' family pattern where there exists a married or cohabiting couple with dependent children has declined from 31 per cent of all households in 1979 to 22 per cent of all households in 2001 (General Household Survey), so companies might have to start thinking about non-traditional targets when they target their markets.

Another area of change in the family is that of changing family relationships. One key issue here is that of marital status. The 2001 census found that the majority of people were married (54 per cent of men and 52 per cent of women). It appears that more people are cohabiting rather than marrying (10 per cent of men and 9 per cent of women) and this trend appeared to be stronger in the younger age ranges. This is reflected by the fact that people seem to be marrying at a later age as they seek to develop their careers or move through the cohabiting phase previously identified.

A factor influencing this is the changing role of women in society and the increased career expectations of women. Women are increasingly seeking to develop their own careers before having children and the development of flexible working is meaning that they can return to work on a full-or part-time basis much more easily than in the past. One consequence of this is the massive increase in demand for child-caring facilities, such as nurseries where the demand has mushroomed, despite there being a gradual decline in the birth rate.

There are also some changes in traditional family roles, where the roles may be shared more between the household members. There are increasing cases where the female partner or wife may earn a higher income than her husband/partner and so we see the development of the 'househusband'.

Another factor that has contributed to the increase in single households (especially in the 25–44 age group) is the increase in divorce in the UK. The latest figures suggest that about one-third of marriages end in divorce in the UK, although many divorced people will re-marry. There are significant differences in divorce rates across Europe which reflect different religious, social, legal and cultural factors, with the countries in Northern and Western Europe typically having higher divorce rates than Southern Europe. In 2001 the EU average for divorce was 1.9 per thousand people and the highest rate was found in Belgium (2.9 per thousand) with the UK also above the EU average (2.6 per thousand). Not surprisingly the lowest rates in 2001 were found in Ireland and Italy where the rate was 0.7/1000.

The role of the family in society also varies across Europe. Vogel (1998) suggests that there are three clusters of European Society:

- the Nordic countries, comprising Denmark, Sweden, Norway and Finland;

- the Southern European countries of Greece, Italy, Spain and Portugal (although Ireland could also be included in many respects);

- most of the continental countries in between, which show characteristics of the first two clusters but not as strongly – this group would include France, Germany and the Netherlands.

The differences between these clusters would be determined by religious, social, political and cultural factors but might also be linked to the labour market and the role of the state. The Nordic cluster operates in a climate of large government spending on social programmes and high rates of labour market participation (through full-time and part-time work). There is less financial dependence on the traditional family unit and more opportunities for people to follow their own course and live independently (another factor contributing to the increase in single households).

The Southern European countries tend to have less comprehensive social programmes and more rigid labour markets with less opportunity for flexible working. There tends to be a higher financial dependence on the traditional extended family that is familiar in Italy for example. Whilst the traditional extended family undoubtedly has many benefits such as emotional security and personal identity, it might also account for fewer younger people leaving home until a much later age and having some degree of social control and psychological constraints being placed upon them. It might be particularly difficult for women in these cultures to enter the labour market and reduce their financial reliance on the family. This will certainly create different lifestyle experiences within these countries and might also be significant for companies planning European marketing campaigns. In Southern Europe, advertisements would be much more likely to revolve around the 'traditional family' than in Northern Europe.

Changing lifestyles

Whereas the earlier population censuses focused on demographic factors, more recent ones have begun to explore much more about lifestyle in order to measure how lifestyle may have changed over time. One aspect of this might be to look at how our use of consumer durables has changed over time. In the 1950s televisions were extremely rare and seen as a luxury item whereas a television is now seen as almost as a necessity by many people and there is practically 100 per cent saturation in the UK. In the UK in 1972 only 37 per cent of households had central heating and 42 per cent a telephone. The figures in the 2001 General Household Survey were 92 per cent for central heating and 98 per cent for telephones. Companies operating in such saturated markets may find it difficult to achieve high rates of growth unless they can convince consumers to upgrade their products (possibly as a result of new technological break-throughs). An example here would be in the saturated television market where there is a move to flat-screen and digital technology.

What the General Household Survey of 2001 did show was that there was still con-siderable market growth potential in new products, particularly in new technology and home entertainment. In terms of new technology there had been a significant increase in the use of mobile phones (from 58 per cent of households in 2000 to 70 per cent of households by 2001), there were more home computers (50 per cent of households in 2001) and 40 per cent of households had Internet access. The increase in home enter-tainment had been equally rapid with sharp increases in the number of satellite, cable and digital television receivers (up from 29 per cent of households in 1998 to 42 per cent of households) and 88 per cent of households had a video recorder (18 per cent in 1983).

We also appear to be much more mobile than 30 years ago. In 1972, 48 per cent of households had no car whereas the figure in 2001 is 28 per cent, which may reflect im-proved income levels stimulating the demand for cars. Interestingly, the number of one-car households has hardly changed (43 per cent in 1972 to 44 per cent in 2001) but the most significant change is in households with two or more cars, which has in-creased from 9 per cent in 1972 to 28 per cent in 2001. This might be a reflection of more dual-income households where two cars are needed for work purposes or it might reflect greater affluence. What it certainly shows is a greater concentration of cars which has boosted the car market but it also implies that there is a likelihood of in-creased pollution and overcrowding on the road system as a result of this trend.

These changes in spending are obviously of great significance for companies oper-ating in these sectors but they also can suggest a picture of how lifestyle has changed in the twenty-first century from previous decades with the wider implications of that.

Another aspect of lifestyle is the issue of health and how healthy our lifestyle has be-come. One way of looking at this is to look at healthcare systems. The amount spent on healthcare systems varies considerably with high rates of spending in the United States and Germany contrasting with much lower rates of spending in countries like Ireland, the UK and Turkey. There are also some contradictory trends occurring which reflect differing attitudes towards having a healthy lifestyle and some of these issues are covered in Minicase 5.4 which contrasts the increasing evidence of obesity in Europe with the massive explosion of health and fitness clubs.

Minicase 5.4   Calorie wars: couch potatoes or fitness fanatics?

An article in *The Observer* in June 2003 (Revill, 2003) identified the potential problems of increased obesity in the UK population and the potential health risks that the population faced as a result of this. The UK health and fitness industry is witnessing dynamic growth with about 8.3 per cent of the UK's population expected to belong to a fitness club by December 2004. So it appears that one part of the population is getting increasingly unhealthy in terms of their eating and fitness habits and adding on the calories whereas another part is rushing off to the gym to burn some calories. These 'calorie wars' seem to reflect changing social trends in our society.

If we look at the obesity issue first, it is hard to find comparative European studies in this area but a World Health Organization Study of Europe in 1998 suggested that between 27 per cent and 35 per cent of adults in the EU are overweight and between 7 and 12 per cent are obese. However, the figures are higher in the UK where one in five adults is classified as obese and also one in nine children. The reasons usually quoted are to do with changing lifestyles in terms of increased consumption of 'junk' foods and a lack of physical exercise for many people with people staying at home more for their entertainment (the couch-potato lifestyle). The main concern is with children with 9 per cent of boys and 13 per cent of girls classified as obese, a figure that quadrupled between 1984 and 1994. When children become overweight it vastly increases the risk of them developing diabetes – and the rate of diabetes has increased considerably. There have been government initiatives to try and counter this trend such as encouraging families to eat five portions of fruit and vegetables a day and to make it easier for people to walk to work, although one could question how effective this will be when addressed to the socio-economic groups which are most obese.

At the same time we see more and more people joining health clubs with a significant expansion in this area. The drivers for this are obviously health-linked but it has also become a lifestyle trend, even to the extent of individuals having personal trainers. When surveyed on why they had joined health clubs, the majority had joined to get fit although 30 per cent had also joined to lose weight and 31 per cent had joined to relax and relieve stress with 10 per cent joining for social purposes. It certainly seems a thriving sector with the fitness chain operators (such as Fitness First and David Lloyd Leisure) expected to grow at a rate of 11 per cent per annum to December 2004 (from June 2003), despite the relatively high cost of some of these clubs.

Questions

1. How can you explain the fact that we have a trend towards increasing obesity and a trend towards increased use of health clubs at the same time?

2. Should the government tackle the problem of increased obesity? How could they do this?

Two key areas which link both health and consumer spending are the trends in drinking and smoking. Both of these areas reflect lifestyle decisions made by people and they are also both multi-million pound industries and yet at the same time there is a health dimension involved because of the specific diseases linked with these two products.

In the UK, the trend in the 1990s was for a slight increase in overall alcohol consumption for men, but a much more marked increase for women, especially younger women. UK consumption is still relatively low by European comparisons (see Table 5.6). The reason for this is that many Central and Southern European countries are wine producers and it is much more normal to drink with a meal than is the case in Northern Europe. There are signs of changing drinking habits, however, with a decline of beer drinking in Northern European countries as many people have switched to wine and other beverages. In the traditional wine-growing countries the reverse effect has been noticed with less consumption of wine, especially amongst younger people. This has implications for beer and wine producers who may diversify into new areas.

There are also significant differences in the pattern of alcohol consumption across Europe. In Southern Europe daily drinking will be most common and yet the quantity consumed per drinking occasion is much higher in Northern Europe. This has been linked to the concept of 'binge drinking' (Institute of Alcohol Studies, 2002), which is defined as 'the consumption of five or more standard drinks in a single drinking occasion'. This has been found to be particularly prevalent in Northern Europe, especially Finland, Sweden and the UK and even more prevalent in teenagers and young adults where British, Irish and Danish teenagers have been identified as the heaviest drinkers in Europe and are more likely to get drunk and to report problems associated with drinking compared with their counterparts in other European countries. This raises ethical questions about drinks companies who target this age group in these countries.

When looking at the trends in smoking it can be seen through the General Household Survey results that the prevalence of cigarette smoking fell substantially in the UK in the 1970s and 1980s and, to a lesser extent, in the 1990s. The decline has been strongest in men, from 51 per cent of men smoking in 1974 to 28 per cent in 2001, although it has also declined amongst women with 26 per cent of women smoking in 2001. The highest rates of smoking were traditionally found in the 20–24 age group, although the 2001 figures suggested that the 25–34 age group were also high smokers.

When looking at the European picture on smoking the decline observed in the UK is not so common and there is increasing debate about the effectiveness of tobacco

Table 5.6 Alcohol consumption by country (1997–2000)

Country	1997	1999	2000
Luxembourg	11.4	12.2	12.3
Romania	9.8	12.2	12.1
Portugal	11.3	10.3	11.7
Republic of Ireland	9.7	11.0	10.8
Czech Republic	10.5	10.5	10.6
France	10.9	10.7	10.5
Germany	10.8	10.6	10.5
Spain	10.2	9.9	10.0
Denmark	9.9	9.5	9.5
United Kingdom	8.2	8.4	8.4
Greece	8.3	8.2	8.0
Latvia	6.9	7.7	7.4
USA	6.6	6.7	6.7
Japan	6.4	6.6	6.5

Note: Measured in litres of pure alcohol per capita consumption
Source: IAS (2001)

control systems in Europe. Ashraf (2002) comments on the disappointing results from the World Health Organization (WHO) for its third action plan, which covered the period 1997 to 2001 and was aimed at reducing the level of smoking within Europe through stronger anti-smoking measures. The WHO report identified that 30 per cent of adult Europeans are smokers (38 per cent of men and 24 per cent of women), although it noticed an increasing gap between Western and Eastern Europe with regards to cigarette consumption in that 34 per cent of men in Western Europe smoked compared to 47 per cent of men in Eastern Europe. This might reflect response of the tobacco companies who, faced with stronger anti-smoking legislation in Western Europe, are targeting the new high-growth markets of Eastern Europe. The prevalence of smoking amongst young people was 30 per cent and the report noted that there had been no decrease in cigarette consumption for this age group over the period of the report. The health dimension linked to smoking is the occurrence of lung cancer and here the death rate for men in Western Europe has stabilised at a rate of 73 per 100 000. Another trend identified by the report was the massive increase in cigarette smuggling in order to avoid paying government duty on cigarettes. It is now estimated that one-third of cigarettes traded worldwide are smuggled, although the figures are slightly lower in Europe where the UK government has estimated that about 20 per cent of the cigarettes consumed in the country are smuggled. There is undoubtedly a move towards more tobacco controls through taxation, advertising bans and protection of the rights of non-smokers but this is only leading to different strategies from the big tobacco companies.

Another area of changing lifestyle is the issue of crime. Heidensohn (1991) suggests that the quite dramatic change that continues to affect family life and gender roles may have an impact on crime. She points out that a growing number of children are being raised in one-parent households, often poorly housed in the worst areas. It seems that these children may be more likely to be 'pushed' into criminal activity.

On the other hand, UK government statistics from the British Crime Survey (BCS), which is an annual survey based on a sample of 40 000 people and which began in 1995, have shown a gradual decrease in crime in the UK and they suggest that there has been a 22 per cent fall in crime measured by the BCS for the period 1997 to 2001/2. This is born out by Barclay *et al.* (2001) who carried out an international comparison of criminal justice statistics for the Home Office. This covered the period 1995–99 and showed that recorded crime fell by 10 per cent in the UK compared with the EU average of a 1 per cent decline.

In terms of different types of crime, the highest levels of homicide in Europe during this period were found in Northern Ireland with a rate of 3.1 per 100 000 followed by Finland and Spain on 2.6 and in fact the UK rate of 1.5 was below the average figure. Some of the highest figures came from the USA (6.3), Estonia (12.2) and South Africa (56.5). They also researched the homicide rates in some of the leading cities. These figures might be significant as high levels of violence and homicide may be a factor influencing the willingness of executives to live in these cities and could be a deterrent to inward investment.

A new area of crime is computer crime, which seems to be on the increase and which is becoming a major concern to governments and business corporations. A 1995 study of 1200 American companies by the management consultants Ernst and Young showed that over half the companies in their survey had suffered financial losses related to computer security. The theft of computers and computer parts, rather than the theft of information, seems to be one of the major problems facing small businesses. No one is exempt from the risks associated with computer crime. The 2002 Computer Crime and Security Survey conducted by the Computer Security Institute and the FBI confirms that the threat of computer crime is rising at a drastic rate in the USA and 80 per cent of the respondents in the survey acknowledged financial losses due to computer breaches although, interestingly, only 34 per cent of the respondents had reported these crimes to the authorities. An example of such crime was how criminals stole the authorisation code from Ford Motor Credit to obtain credit reports on 13 000 individuals. With the rapid growth in electronic commerce the attractiveness of such crime is growing, which contributes to concerns about the security of e-commerce transactions and thus inhibits growth in the sector.

The final social dynamic we shall look at is the changing work trends which will affect people in society, although many of these themes are developed in more depth in Chapter 9. One of the trends we have already identified is the increased possibility of part-time working in countries with more flexible working practices where there are opportunities for part-time working, teleworking, job-sharing and outsourcing of labour to specialist agencies. This throws up new opportunities for part-time work, especially for women. It is interesting here to compare data for part-time and full-time working for women with the society clusters suggested earlier by Vogel (1998). In the Northern cluster of countries such as Scandinavia and the UK, female employment is approaching the level of male employment as more opportunities through flexible working, better childcare facilities and greater independence have seen more opportunities for working women, although much of the growth has been in part-time jobs. At the lower end of the scale we see again the cluster of Southern European countries and Ireland, all of which have large proportions of traditional families with full-time housewives. This may be a problem when companies try to introduce more flexible working patterns in certain countries and can lead to rigidities in the labour market.

Another aspect of labour is the extent of organised labour in countries, usually reflected by membership of Trade Unions. The general trend in Trade Union membership has been for a steady decline in numbers. Metcalfe (1990) argues that the decline in union membership is the result of an interaction of five factors:

- the macroeconomic environment;
- the composition of jobs and the workforce including the relative decline in manufacturing industry;
- the policy of the state;
- the attitudes and conduct of employers;
- the stance taken by employers.

For example, in the UK one of the main factors was the big increase in legislation during the Thatcher government which significantly changed the behaviour and practices of Trade Unions. The trend can clearly be seen in the UK where Trade Union membership fell from 13.3 million in 1979 to 7.9 million in 2001. In Germany and Belgium there are Works Councils which have the right to be consulted over closures or prospective merger activities, and European legislation has also seen the introduction of minimum wage levels to protect the lowest-paid sectors of the community. The minimum wage was finally introduced in the UK in April 1999 when it was set at a basic level of £3.60 an hour. This compared with Portugal's £1.65 an hour and Belgium's £4.56 an hour. This may be a factor that would need to be taken on board in industries which depend on low-paid and largely unskilled labour.

Hillman (1996) has examined the wider trends in the working environment and how we will work in the twenty-first century and he suggests that there will be a transformation in social life and the way we work. He suggests that the key trends in the twenty-first century will be:

- increasingly footloose economic activity;
- fierce global competition, fuelled by advances in information and communication technologies;

- shifts in occupational patterns in favour of managerial, professional and technical jobs in the service sector and a shift to knowledge workers;

- a growth in the importance of small and medium-sized enterprises, reflecting changes in the nature and organisation of work as many large organisations are forced to restructure;

- more flexible labour markets in many countries, with part-time and temporary work, weaker relationships between employers and employees and the threat of recurrent unemployment and underemployment;

- fractured career patterns and work/leisure boundaries, with training increasingly the responsibility of individuals themselves;

- increasing dangers of exclusion for socially and economically disadvantaged groups.

Many of these trends are already becoming clearer in the years since Hillman (1996) wrote about these issues and make the way we will work in the future much more complex than in the past. The likelihood of staying with one employer for the bulk of your working life is becoming increasingly remote with more emphasis being placed on the individual to develop their skill base to cope with more flexible working environments of the future. One could argue that this is making the working environment much more stressful than in the past but also more challenging and potentially rewarding.

Conclusion

This chapter has covered a number of cultural, demographic and social aspects of the business environment which may have significance for companies. We have seen that when companies have an international dimension then they are much more likely to be influenced by exposure to other cultures and it may well be the success with which the company handles these differences that will determine its success in any overseas activities, although the extent of the problem may be determined by the closeness or otherwise of the cultural fit between countries.

We have also seen that companies and governments are having to pay increasing attention to changes in the demographic structure within the business environment. Population changes may be gradual, compared to other areas such as technological change, but their significance is becoming increasingly recognised and nowhere more than in those countries who are facing rapidly ageing populations, as we have seen in Europe and Japan.

Finally we have examined a number of social changes in terms of family changes, changing lifestyles and the changing nature of work, all of which may be very significant for businesses in certain sectors in terms of identifying developing or declining markets and developing strategies to deal with these.

Summary of main points

- When businesses operate internationally, they will need a clearer understanding of national cultural differences.

- Hofstede and Trompenaars give us frameworks for understanding differences in national business cultures.

- The extent of cultural adaptation will depend upon the closeness of the cultural fit between countries.

- Businesses may have to alter their management styles, their marketing policies and their HRM policies to take cultural differences into account.

- Demographic changes can be easily identified and easily predicted.

- The pattern of falling fertility rates is leading to a rapid ageing of the population in Europe and Japan.

- The increased pressure on the working population to support the retired population will put severe pressures on governments.

- The nature of the family and family relationships is changing rapidly in the UK.

- The role of the family varies across Europe.

- Changing lifestyles are leading to changing consumption of tobacco and alcohol, although there clear evidence of increased obesity – especially amongst younger people.

- The level of criminal activity may influence international investment decisions.

- Trade Union membership has continued to decline against a background of more flexible working patterns in the country.

Discussion Questions

1. By using data from Hofstede in the text, compare the national culture of France and the United States. How might the differences you identify have affected the relationship between American managers and French workers in the early days of Eurodisney?

2. Imagine that there is a proposed merger between your Italian company and a British company and you have been appointed to lead a team made up of managers from both countries to examine any cultural problems linked to the proposed merger.

How close would the cultural fit be and how might you seek to improve cultural understanding between the two groups of managers?

3. Critically assess the extent to which some companies would benefit and some face a crisis through the ageing of the population. Look for examples in your own country of companies who will be affected by this trend and suggest strategies they could follow in response to this.

4. To what extent do you agree with Vogel's (1998) views about the three clusters of European society? To what extent does your own country fit into the family behaviour suggested in this analysis?

5. To what extent do you feel that the level of crime is becoming a bigger factor in the social environment? To what extent will it influence investment decisions by companies?

6. Assess the extent to which the decline in Trade Union membership is likely to continue into the twenty-first century. Are there any factors that might reverse the current trend of decline?

Web Links

The following links are some that have been found useful when researching this chapter:

http://www.statistics.gov.uk/census
This page will give you information about the recently completed national census of 2001 – you can even get the data for your local region.

http://www.statistics.gov.uk/datasets.asp
Using the same site, this will give you a mass of datasets covering a massive range of social and demographic areas.

http://europa.eu.int/eurostat
This is the EU's database, which will give you a range of materials on the European Union.

http://www.executiveplanet.com/index2.jsp
This website will give you an absolute mass of information on different business cultures from how to greet people to behaviour in business situations.

http://www.un.org/csa/population/unpop.htm
The home page of the United Nations Population division which will give you any material you need on population as well as special reports.

http://upmystreet.com
This website will give you any local information you need.

Further Reading

United Nations (2003) *State of the World Population 2002*, United Nations Publications.
Gives you all the information you need about population change.
Halsey, A.H. and Webb, J. (2000) *Twentieth Century Social Trends*, 3rd edn, Macmillan.
Covers all the main social changes that occurred in the twentieth century, although it is a lengthy book.
Gatley, S., Lessem, R. and Altman, Y. (1996) *Comparative Management: A Transcultural Odyssey*, McGraw-Hill.
An excellent book which gives innovative insights into differences in national culture.
Stephens, J. in Brooks, I. (2003) *Organisational Behaviour: Individuals, Groups and Organisations*, 2nd edn, FT/Prentice Hall.
The chapter on National Culture (ch 10, pp. 263–94) will give a good general overview of the main theories and issues concerned with national culture.
Tayeb, M. (2003) *International Management: Theories and Practice*, FT/Prentice Hall.
A recent book which is very good on the management implications of national culture.

References

Ashraf, H. (2003) 'European Tobacco Control reaches a critical phase', *The Lancet*, Vol. 359.
Barclay, G., Tavares, C. and Siddique, A. (2001) *International Comparisons of Criminal Justice Statistics 1999*, Home Office Statistical Bulletin, Issue 6/01.
Daniels, J.D. and Radebaugh, L.H. (2001) *International Business: Environments and Operations*, 9th edn, Prentice-Hall.
Heidensohn, M. (1991) *Crime and Society: Sociology for a Changing World*, Basingstoke: Macmillan.
Hillman, J. (1996) *University for Industry: Creating a National Learning Framework*, London: Institute for Public Policy Research.
Hofstede, G. (1984) *Cultures Consequences: International Differences in Work-Related Values*, abridged edn, Beverley Hills: Sage.
Hofstede, G. and Bond, M.H. (1988) 'Confucius and Economic Growth: New Trends in Culture's Consequences', *Organisational Dynamics*, 16, pp. 4–21.
Kerr, C., Dunlop, J.T., Harbison F. and Myers C.A. (1960) *Industrialism and Industrial Man*: The *Problems of Labour and the Management of Economic Growth*, Cambridge MA: Harvard University Press.
Kluckhohn, F. and Strodtbeck, F. (1961) *Variations in Value Orientations*, New York: Peterson.
Kroeber, A. and Kluckhohn, C. (1985) *Culture: a Critical Review of Concepts and Definitions*, New York: Random House.
Levitt, T. in Kantrow, A.M. (1985) *Challenging the Myth of Industrial Obsolescence*, New York: John Wiley and Sons, pp. 53–68.

Metcalfe, D. (1990) 'Union presence and labour productivity in British manufacturing industry: a reply to Nolan and Marginson', *British Journal of Industrial Relations*, 28.

Revill, J. (2003) 'Fat Chance', *The Observer*, 8 June.

Torbiorn (1982) *Living Abroad: Personal Adjustment and Personnel Policy in an Overseas Setting*, New York: Wiley.

Trompenaars, F. (1997) *Riding the Waves of Culture*, London: Nicholas Brealey.

Vogel, J. (1998) *Three Types of European Society*, available at http://www.nnn.se/n-model/europe3/europe3.htm.

The Ecological Environment

Jamie Weatherston

On completion of this chapter you should be able to:

- understand some of the ecological and ethical effects that arise because of business activity;

- appreciate the basic economic arguments which underlie the operation of the marketplace (including the law of demand and supply and the concept of externalities) and which underpin any analysis of how business organisations are able to pollute the environment;

- outline the range of actions which can be taken by governments to monitor and regulate the output of pollutants from economic activity;

- appreciate the range of organisational responses to ecological issues in general and to environmental legislation in particular;

- recognise the impact of economic activity, and of different regulatory regimes, on consumers, and appreciate the extent of consumer power in respect of ecological issues;

- set the above outcomes in the context of actions taken at global, national and local scales.

- environmental pollution
- climate change
- theory of demand and supply

- price determination
- equilibrium
- market failure
- externalities
- the principle that the polluter pays
- sustainable development
- BATNEEC
- environmental impact assessment
- environmental contexts
- environmental options
- the consumer and the environment
- ethics

Introduction

We are all aware of a range of environmental problems facing the planet. In this chapter we look at some of the most serious ecological and ethical concerns and the extent of their impact, investigate the economic arguments which help us analyse how organisations are able to pollute the environment and explore the range of actions which can be taken by governments to monitor and regulate the outputs from economic activity.

Over recent years the basis of much environmental regulation has been via market-based mechanisms. Therefore, the introductory part of this chapter examines the economic arguments which underpin the operation of market-based economies. The areas covered include the laws of demand and supply and the price mechanism. This section also has a wider purpose: it links to the coverage of competition in Chapter 2, as demand theory underpins much of the work related to market structure (please note that this section features general, rather than environment-related, examples to explain the ideas).

The chapter moves on to consider externalities and different approaches to regulation. We end the chapter by examining the different approaches adopted by organisations towards environmental issues, discussing the impact of these upon consumers and noting the extent of consumer power in respect of ecological issues. This analysis is set in the context of actions taken at a global, national and local scale.

Environmental pollution has an impact on a number of areas which affect us all. In order to assess the nature of this impact we need to distinguish between renewable and non-renewable resources. Renewable resources can be replaced, but non-renewable resources when used are lost forever.

There has been considerable concern about the effects of acid rain, loss of biodiversity, sea pollution, depletion of natural resources such as tropical rainforests, and the destruction of the ozone layer. In Stockholm in 1972 the international community met for the first time to consider global environment and development needs. Since this

UN Conference on Human Environment the concept of sustainable development has been on the agenda.

The twentieth anniversary of Stockholm was in Rio de Janeiro in 1992. The UN Conference on Environment and Development, the 'Earth Summit', agreed Agenda 21 and the Rio Declaration. Since then a further ten conferences have been held, including Berlin in 1995, Kyoto in 1997 and Johannesburg in 2002. This chapter explains the impact of these on organisations and government. Agenda 21 elements and issues are shown in Table 6.1.

Without naturally occurring greenhouse gases like carbon dioxide, methane, nitrous oxide and water vapour, human life would not exist. However, industrial development has necessitated the burning of significant amounts of coal, oil and methane and the felling of more and more forests resulting in excessive carbon dioxide (CO_2) emissions. Carbon dioxide and chlorofluorocarbon (CFC) gases are said to contribute to the greenhouse effect. The greenhouse effect brings a rise in global temperatures. CFCs are being steadily banned due to their adverse effects on the earth's protective ozone layer.

The increase in the earth's temperature has, in turn, caused sea levels to rise. It has been predicted that, at current rates of increase, sea levels could rise by another 50 cm by the year 2100 (Radford, 1997). This would have a serious impact on coastlines, particularly those in East Anglia, Holland, Egypt, India and Bangladesh, as well as imperilling many small low-lying islands such as the Maldives in the Indian Ocean and

Table 6.1 Elements of Agenda 21

Elements	Issues
Social and economic dimensions to development	Poverty, production and consumption, health, human settlement, integrated decision-making
Conservation and management of natural resources	Atmosphere, oceans and seas, land, forests, mountains, biological diversity, ecosystems, biotechnology, freshwater resources, toxic chemicals, hazardous radioactive and solid wastes
Strengthening role of major groups	Youth, women, indigenous peoples, non-government organisations, local authorities, trade unions, business, scientific and technical communities, farmers
Means of implementation	Finance, technology transfer, information, public awareness, capacity building, education, legal instruments, institutional frameworks

Source: http://www.earthsummit2002.org/Es2002.PDF [accessed 5 February 2003]

the Marshall Islands in the Pacific Ocean (Brown, 1995). Effects would clearly be felt in communities near the coast and have severe consequences for agricultural areas such as the Ganges Delta, an area already prone to flooding.

Whatever one's view of the seriousness of the problems of global warming and destruction of the ozone layer, it is clear that environmental problems result from economic activity. The growth of business activity is often at the expense of the environment.

The balance of power between business organisations, particularly large multinationals, on the one hand, and individuals and environmental groups on the other, is grossly unequal. Government has a role to play regarding the potentially polluting activities of organisations. Regulation proceeds, essentially, from a knowledge of how markets operate. It is therefore appropriate to examine the theory of demand and supply and of externalities in order to appreciate the debate on environmental regulation and the role of government intervention. For the global economy to become ecologically sustainable, it may be necessary to organise business and industry along ecologically sound principles. This will require the transformation of corporations, their products, production systems and management practices (Shrivastava, 1995). In this chapter we will explore the role and activities of each of these actors and their effect, both positive and negative, on the environment.

The impact of the marketplace on the ecological environment: an economic perspective

The two extremes of economic management, the free market (see Chapter 2) and the command economy, are not evident in their purest form within any country. For example Hong Kong, which used to closely resemble a pure market economy, now has to follow the diktat of the Communist government in China to some extent. The recent past has seen the demise of command economies in, for example, Poland, the Czech Republic, Bulgaria and the former Soviet Union. Market forces have been allowed to become more active in these economies to alleviate the worst excesses of state control.

Within all Western-style market economies government influences the allocation of goods and services. It does this for a number of reasons:

- to moderate the trade cycle by demand management and supply-side policies to promote such things as employment, investment and direct structural change (see Chapter 3);

- to restrain unfair use of economic power by, for example, monopolies (see Chapter 2);

- to correct inequalities through the redistribution of wealth via taxation or regional policy to support industry (see Chapter 3);

- to manage price levels, employment, balance of payments and growth rate in accordance with social objectives (see Chapter 3);

- to provide public goods, such as defence, law and order, roads and parks; such things are socially desirable, but unprofitable, and it is generally not possible to directly charge for them;

and, of specific relevance to the subject of this chapter,

- to remove socially undesirable consequences of commercial activity. The private profit motive does not always ensure that public wealth will be maximised; it can create environmental problems, such as pollution and resource depletion.

Society has to find a way of resolving the primary economic issues of what to produce, and how, and for whom, to produce it. In many economies we have seen that these questions are now more commonly being answered by market forces (see Chapter 2). In this chapter we will explore the problems that industrial activity causes to the environment. However, in order to understand how market forces can result in environmental problems and to appreciate the viability of potential solutions it is necessary to understand the foundations of the market system, that is, the concepts of demand and supply.

The theory of demand

Demand is the quantity of a commodity which will be demanded at a given price over a certain period of time. By 'demand' we mean demand backed by money, or effective demand. Common sense says for most goods (normal goods) a lower price will mean that more will be purchased (even if this increase in consumption leads to an increase in pollution or environmental damage) and at a higher price less will be purchased. This is the law of downward sloping demand. For any commodity it is possible to use market data to construct a demand schedule, showing how many units of the commodity would be demanded at various prices. In reality this is difficult to do. However, King (1972) did try to estimate the demand relationship for beer in 1960's America, based on the wholesale price of beer and it did show an inverse relationship between price and quantity demanded.

However, it is easier for our purposes to work with hypothetical data. Table 6.2 shows how the demand schedule for cinema tickets may look.

The data in Table 6.2 can be presented in the form of a graph. Price is plotted on the vertical axis and quantity on the horizontal axis. This is the demand curve as shown in Figure 6.1.

The demand curve tells us the quantities which would be demanded at each price. From the area of the rectangle $OXYZ$ we can calculate the total revenue at the given price, as the area of the rectangle is equal to price multiplied by quantity ($P \times Q$). As the price of tickets (P_x) changes there will be extensions or contractions of demand (changes in the quantity demanded) as shown in Figure 6.2.

As the price of cinema tickets decreases from £5.00 to £4.50, demand extends along the demand curve to three tickets. The opposite effect is evident, as can seen from Figure 6.2: as price rises there is a contraction of demand. In this example we see the

Table 6.2 Demand schedule for cinema tickets

Price/Unit (£)	Quantity Demanded/Week (000s)
6	0
5.5	1
5.0	2
4.5	3
4.0	4
3.5	5
3.0	6
2.5	7

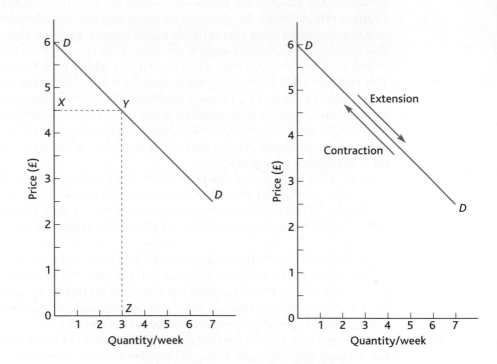

Figure 6.1 Demand curve for cinema tickets

Figure 6.2 Extensions and contractions in demand

effect of a price change only. However, it is not only price that determines or influences the demand for a product. The other determinants or conditions of demand are:

1. *Price of other related goods* (P_r) – changes in the price of other goods will affect the demand for cinema tickets, whether the goods are substitutes, such as film rental or concerts, or complements, such as a carton of popcorn. Substitute goods are competitively demanded. If the price of film rental rises then demand for that product will fall. Some consumers will switch to the substitute product; in this case demand for cinema tickets will rise. Complementary goods, in comparison, are jointly demanded: if the price of food and extras at the cinema falls, for example, then more people may be encouraged to go to the cinema. The demand for CDs trebled between 1988 and 1993, largely as a result of the lower price of compact disc players, a complementary good.

2. *Income* (Y) – a rise in income will result in more goods demanded, whatever the price. Your spending on cinema tickets is likely to increase when you begin to earn more money. A reduction in income will obviously have the reverse effect. However, in the case of inferior goods, an increase in income will result in a fall in demand. For example, your spending on baked beans is likely to fall as you earn more money and are able to buy higher quality items.

3. *Taste* (T) – a change in taste or fashion (perhaps influenced by advertising) will alter the demand for that product.

4. *Other factors* (Z) – these include seasonal factors, government influences such as legislation limiting the sale of firearms, the availability of credit and changes in population size or structure, see Minicase 6.1 below.

Minicase 6.1   Cinemas in 2002

Data for 2001 shows that cinemas in the United Kingdom and the United States proved hugely successful, giving the cinema industry a significant boost. *Harry Potter and the Philosopher's Stone* and *The Lord of the Rings: The Fellowship of the Ring* became the second and third, respectively, most successful films at the UK box office of all time (behind *Titanic* in 1998). The UK enjoyed buoyant attendances in 2002, with tickets sales growing by 10 per cent. This is in contrast to France, Germany and Italy, who all saw attendances fall. UK sales are reported to have reached 176m in 2002, up from 156m the previous year. Blockbuster movies such as *Star Wars Episode II: Attack of the Clones, Minority Report, Spider-Man, Lord of the Rings: The Two Towers* and *Harry Potter and the Chamber of*

Secrets helped to bring in the crowds. Overall UK gross sales were put at £750m, making it Europe's biggest cinema market. The second instalments of *Harry Potter* and *The Lord of the Rings* sustained high admissions well into the first quarter of 2003. It is an amazing comeback for UK cinema visits, which had slumped in the 1980s.

The key demographic group for the cinema industry is the 15–24 age bracket. People in this group are visiting the cinema more often than ever before and have more money available with which to do so. Personal Disposable Income (PDI) has risen in the UK with young people now contributing more expenditure to the 'leisure pound'.

Multiplex cinemas have a hold on the market and this seems to have resulted in higher average ticket prices. In September 2000, Mintel showed that the average admission price was £4. By December 2001, this had risen to £4.15. However, in the survey 27 per cent of the respondents agreed with the statement that 'cinema tickets are too expensive'. However, compared to other leisure activities, the cinema, arguably, constitutes value for money.

Improved marketing of cinemas and the advent of out-of-town multiplexes have helped to drive consumer demand. Many of the cinema chains, be they large multinational or smaller, regional concerns, are looking at ways to encourage people into the cinema other than the attractiveness of the films on release. Examples of initiatives and designs undertaken include UCI's Gallery package (which includes larger, more comfortable seating and free drinks).

Source: adapted from BBC News Online, 16/01/2003, 'UK cinemas had a buoyant 2002', and 'UK Cinema Market May 2002', available from: http://reports.mintel.com/ [accessed 17 February 2003]

Questions

1. Using the theory of demand identify and explain the possible reasons why cinema attendances in France and Germany fell. Show this on a diagram.

2. Identify five complementary goods to a cinema show. How does a change in the price of these goods affect the demand for cinema tickets?

Demand for a good can be influenced by all of these factors. We can express this by the demand function:

$$D_X = f(P_X, P_R, Y, T, Z)$$

If any one of these determinants of demand changes then the demand curve will shift to the right or the left. For example, if there is a rise in disposable income (a change of

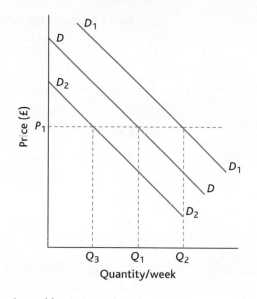

Figure 6.3 Changes in the demand for cinema tickets

Y in the equation) we have seen that demand for cinema tickets will increase and the demand curve moves to the right. If income falls in the future, other factors remaining constant, fewer tickets will be demanded so the demand curve will move to the left (see Figure 6.3). Note that we need to qualify this by stating that we expect this to happen *ceteris paribus* – other things being equal.

To summarise, it is important to distinguish between movement *along* the demand curve, due to change in price of a good, and movements *of* the demand curve, due to change in one of the other determinants of demand.

The theory of supply

The market for goods and services is determined not only by demand. The demand which consumers express, through their willingness to buy, needs to be met by the willingness of producers to supply goods. Supply is the propensity of producers to sell the commodity at a given price over a certain period of time.

More goods will be supplied at a higher than at a lower price. This law of the upward sloping supply curve can be explained by the aim of producers to maximise their income. We know from our earlier discussion of the demand side that the data can be presented either in the form of a schedule or graphically, as shown in Table 6.3 and Figure 6.4.

As price changes there will be extensions or contractions along the supply curve (changes in the quantity supplied). For example, if the price of cinema tickets moves from £4.50 to £4.00 the quantity supplied falls from five tickets to four tickets per week, as shown in Figure 6.5.

Table 6.3 Supply schedule for cinema tickets

Price/Unit (£)	Quantity Supplied/Week (000s)
6.0	8
5.5	7
5.0	6
4.5	5
4.0	4
3.5	3
3.0	2
2.5	1

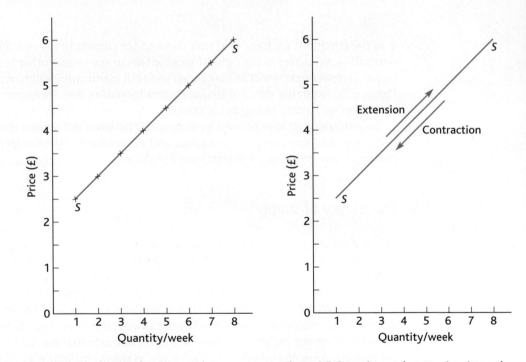

Figure 6.4 Supply curve for cinema tickets

Figure 6.5 Extensions and contractions in supply

In this example we see the effect of a price change only. However, as with demand it is not only price that determines or influences the supply of a product. The other determinants or conditions of supply are:

1. *The objectives of the firm* (B) – a firm aiming to achieve maximum profits will have a different level of output (lower) from one which is aiming to maximise sales.

2. *The price of certain other goods* (P_g) – where goods are jointly supplied, they are said to be complements in production, like beef and leather; a decrease in the price of one good will lead to a decrease in the quantity of the other good which will be supplied. If the price of beef falls then farmers are less likely to supply it to the market. The result may be a reduction in the supply of leather. Goods that are substitutes, such as beers at a brewery, are said to be competitively supplied. A brewer could probably switch production from one brew to another, for example from bottled beer to draught if the price of draught beer were to rise while the price of bottled beer was unchanged.

3. *Price of the factors of production* (P_f) – the cost of production will rise if the price of a factor of production increases. For example, if raw materials were more expensive and the price of a good remains unchanged then its output becomes less profitable, and less will be produced. In this scenario it may be better to look for an alternative source of supply. Other costs, such as labour costs and the cost of capital, are also important to companies and influence their output decisions.

4. *The state of technology* (T) – technology can be used to improve productivity and so increase supply. However, the widespread use of the Internet and downloading of music has created serious problems for the music industry worldwide. Profits for the six major companies have tumbled.

5. *Other factors* (Z) – although this heading acts as a 'catch-all' it is important in its own right. An organisation can be influenced by its expectations of what is likely to happen in the future or the number of new companies entering the market. Changes in government practices with regard to taxation, subsidies or regional policies have a substantial impact.

Supply of a product can be influenced by all of these factors. We can express this by the supply function:

$$S_x = f(P_x, B, P_g, P_f, T, Z)$$

The rules that apply to the demand curve also apply here. If there is a change in one of the conditions influencing supply, assuming other factors are held constant (*ceteris paribus*), then the supply curve may be shifted to the right or left. For example, a business organisation may seek to supply more to the market by investing in new technology. As a result the supply curve will move to the right because the firm has increased its output. The reverse situation will also be true (see Figure 6.6).

To summarise, it is important to distinguish between movement *along* a supply curve, due to change in price of a goods, and movements *of* the supply curve, due to change in one of the other determinants of supply.

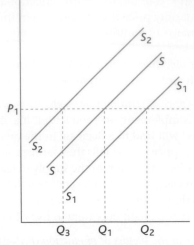

The original supply curve is SS, quantity supplied at price P_1 is Q_1. As output rises, assuming price remains fixed SS shifts to the right S_1S_1, quantity supplied rises to Q_2. If the firm cuts back supply shifts the other way to S_2S_2 and quantity facts to Q_3.

Figure 6.6 The impact of changes of supply conditions

Price determination

Economists use the term 'equilibrium' to describe a state in which internal forces, or variables, are in balance and there is no tendency to change. Market price is determined by the price at which consumers are willing to buy and producers are willing to sell. This is called the equilibrium price. The corresponding quantity is called the equilibrium quantity. In the case of the market for cinema tickets, in our example, the equilibrium price is £4.00 and the equilibrium quantity is four tickets per week. The point of intersection is called the equilibrium point in the market (see Figure 6.7).

If there are changes in demand the demand curve moves and changes in supply result in the movement of the supply curve. Both market price and quantity will change. The extent of the changes depends on the price-elasticity of supply and elasticity of demand, that is, the extent to which demand and supply are sensitive to changes in price. However, in general we can state that:

1. An increase in demand causes an increase in the equilibrium price and quantity.

2. A decrease in demand causes a decrease in the equilibrium price and quantity.

3. An increase in supply causes a decrease in the equilibrium price and a rise in the equilibrium quantity.

4. A decrease in supply causes an increase in the equilibrium price and a fall in the equilibrium quantity.

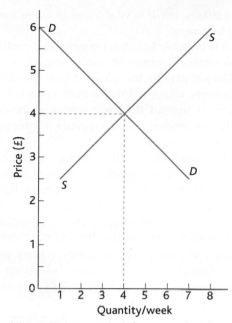

The equilibrium price is k4 and the equilibrium quantity is four per week: at any other price there would be an excess demand or supply.

Figure 6.7 Equilibrium price of cinema tickets

Market forces and the environment

When every person's standard of living is maximised, market forces can be said to be an efficient mechanism for the allocation of resources. In this case the market can operate free from any regulatory control. This scenario is unrealistic; it is unlikely that a market can ever achieve such an allocation and so be completely free from intervention. The release of CFCs from, for example, aerosol containers, was thought to be having a serious impact on the ozone layer (see above). Resources, in this case, were being used to the detriment of society in general. The market did not act to reduce the impact of CFCs and adopt less-polluting propellants until put under substantial consumer and political pressure (e.g. the Montreal Protocol). Even so, many refrigeration systems and car air-conditioning units still use CFCs. This example shows that, although the market may act to reduce the harmful impact that it has on the environment, it is often in response to stakeholder pressure, discussed later in the chapter, and frequently an incomplete response. Finally, governments had to play a role in reducing the use of CFCs; on 1 January 1995 the production and import of CFCs was banned in the European Union.

It is likely that market forces will not bring about the best or optimum allocation of resources. It is beyond the scope of this book to look in detail at all aspects of the failure of markets, but it is vital for us to assess how this failure can result in damage to the environment.

It is not only in market systems that high levels of pollution have been experienced. The former Communist states have also suffered. In east-central Europe considerable pollution may be the result of four decades of central planning by Communist governmants, which failed to adhere to declared priorities for sound environmental management; instead, there was serious ecological damage of the sort previously attributed only to Western capitalist regimes (Carter and Turnock, 1993). The same scenario can also be seen in parts of China.

The production and consumption of goods and services can generate spillover effects that indirectly affect persons other than those who produce or consume them. These effects are known as externalities. Pollution may result from economic activity. An organisation producing chemicals may discharge waste into a river, causing fish to die. In this case the producer, while undertaking its normal business, has harmed third parties such as the marine life and the fishing industry. It has created an external cost known as a negative externality (Lipsey and Harbury, 1992). Alternatively, positive externalities are created when there is an external benefit from economic activity. Education provides spillover benefits to business organisations by them having access to better quality staff.

Nomille (2003) introduces the related idea of multifunctionality, an issue that has arisen in the WTO agriculture negotiations. Multifunctionality refers to the concept that, besides producing food and fibre, agriculture creates nonfood spillover – multifunctional – benefits such as:

- open space;

- wildlife habitat;

- biodiversity;

- flood prevention;

- cultural heritage;

- viable rural communities;

- and food security.

Organisations do not, generally, fully consider the wider social costs or benefits of their business activities. For example, a company may argue that it is not in its economic interest to invest in anti-pollution systems and so may economise on the provision of anti-pollution controls (this will be discussed later in the chapter). In this case 'private costs' and shareholder returns are of uppermost concern to the organisation. This judgement may lead to higher levels of noxious emissions into the environment.

However, if the organisation were to take stock of all of the costs involved in its activities it would have to include external costs, that is, the cost to society of the externalities caused. Adding external cost to private cost gives us the social cost and shifts the supply curve to the left. Price would rise and quantity demanded would fall.

The resulting lower output should reduce the externalities. This new level of output is the socially efficient level of output with no welfare loss to society.

It is clear that negative (and positive) externalities arise under specific circumstances. Companies do affect individuals and vice versa. We can examine this situation under four main headings:

- actions by companies which affect other companies;

- actions by companies which affect individuals;

- actions by individuals which affect companies;

- actions by individuals which affect other individuals.

Actions by companies which affect other companies

Industrial waste from production processes can enter the sea and so impact on commercial fisheries. The gradual pollution of Japan's inland sea, between Honshu and Shikoku, in the 1950s and 1960s severely damaged fish stocks. A similar situation can be seen in the North Sea and in many of Europe's rivers. In these cases private costs have predominated as it is not in the economic interests of those industries producing the waste to reduce pollution caused by their activities. In these cases a negative externality has arisen.

Positive externalities can be of great benefit. The success of some football clubs, especially the large Public Limited Companies, can enhance business activity in a town or city. With over 40 000 spectators at some games the knock-on effect on shops, restaurants and pubs is substantial. The 'feel good' factor is also felt by supporters, who, as employees, may even bring benefits to their employing organisations. It has even been suggested that sporting success can help to attract inward investment.

Action by companies which affects individuals

A common example is the case of a firm polluting an air or water source as a by-product of production. Examples here include the production of refrigerators using CFCs, a coal-burning electricity plant with nitrous oxide and sulphur oxide by-products, or a paper mill, which dumps chlorine bleach into a river as a by-product of producing white office paper. In the Far East of Russia, a huge health issue has been created by gold mining. The mine owners used magnesium to separate gold ore from quartz, but did not recycle the magnesium. Instead they washed it into the river, the source of drinking water for cities in Eastern Russia, such as Vladivostok and Khaborovsk. Partly as a result of poor water quality, the life expectancy of citizens in the Russian Far East has dramatically decreased (Zilberman, 2002). A further dramatic illustration of producers affecting individuals was illustrated by the Union Carbide disaster in Bhopal, India in 1984 (see Minicase 6.4).

However, actions by companies can have a positive impact on individuals. International experience confirms that education and training is a positive externality. In

2000 Brooke Bond Kenya (BBK), a Unilever subsidiary, began a tree-planting project, Trees 2000. The project has involved local people to extend awareness. Books on trees have been given to primary schools. The aim was to increase biodiversity, complement existing conservation and environmental protection programmes, and provide an amenity for staff and the neighbouring community. After a year the project had planted over 30 000 indigenous trees and produced 50 000 seedlings for later planting. They provide beneficial habitats for birds and insects, shade for animals and medicines and recreation areas for local people. They also improve the efficiency of water catchments – a direct business benefit to rain-dependent crops such as tea (Unilever, 2003a).

Action by individuals which affects companies

Road traffic has been growing substantially and is likely to continue for the foreseeable future. Minicase 6.2 shows the situation facing Bangkok in Thailand. The example of traffic congestion illustrates how individuals do not consider their full impact on road conditions. This increasing congestion raises transportation costs for firms and has direct repercussions on the price of goods in the shops.

There is a clear positive benefit to industry of a better trained and more highly qualified workforce. However, it is increasingly difficult for organisations, particularly in times of recession, to fund in-house training. This training gap is now being filled by individuals taking the initiative for their own training. Student numbers have grown substantially in many European Union countries since 1976, and there are more than 16 million higher education students in 30 European countries. Table 6.4 shows that

Table 6.4 Rate of expansion of student enrolment across Europe 1975/6 to 1999/2000

Country	Growth Rate	Country	Growth Rate
Portugal	4.2	Norway	2.1
Greece	3.6	Belgium	2.0
Ireland	3.5	Denmark	2.0
Spain	3.3	France	1.9
Iceland	3.2	Sweden	1.9
Finland	3.0	Italy	1.8
United Kingdom	2.8	Netherlands	1.7
Austria	2.7	Germany	1.5
EU average	2.2	Luxembourg	1.2

Source: Times Higher Education Supplement, *7 March, 2003*

Minicase 6.2   Bangkok to combat traffic congestion

Thailand's capital has adopted pedestrianised streets in parts of the city in an attempt to improve the city's appalling traffic congestion and pollution levels. More than 2.6m vehicles drive through the streets of Bangkok every day. The resulting air and noise pollution has proved a constant headache for the city's population and the Thai government. Every day the number of cars on the city's streets increases by 481, and Bangkok drivers spend the equivalent of 22 days a year in their vehicles.

In December 2001 a two-month pilot scheme was launched in Silom Road, in the heart of the city's commercial district. An 800m part of the road was closed every Sunday, an action which led to thousands of rural Thais flocking to the region to see the area, which had previously been flooded with traffic. Figures, quoted by the AFP news agency, indicated that about 70 per cent of Bangkok residents approved of the closures, saying they hoped it would improve air quality.

Thailand's tourism authority praised the scheme as one where people could finally walk around 'in an atmosphere of clean air and total comfort'. Following the success authorities were planning to halt weekend traffic along four more roads, including the infamous Khao San strip where backpackers congregate.

Bangkok has two main problems. Firstly, there is a severe shortage of roads – a mere 8 per cent of its surface is covered with roads compared with 16 per cent in Tokyo and 20 per cent in the majority of other major cities. Secondly, there is a lack of viable alternatives for Thais wishing to travel. Bangkok has little in terms of mass transport for its citizens. Bangkok possesses no underground rail system, and its much-vaunted Skytrain, an elevated system, has been criticised for its high prices and limited network.

However, an underground system is due to be completed by 2003 and the government is considering an extension to the Skytrain, which would extend its track by 280 km.

Thailand's government has also introduced several other measures aimed at improving traffic congestion. These include stiff fines handed out by Thai police to speeders and jaywalkers and the threat of increased insurance premiums for repeat traffic offenders.

Source: adapted from 'Bangkok to combat traffic congestion', Friday, 21 December, 2001, 22:17 GMT, available from http://news.bbc.co.uk/2/hi/asia-pacific/1723804.stm [accessed 24 February 2003]

Questions

1. Using the four headings in the section 'Measures available to limit externalities' below, categorise the measures that the Thai government has put in place and identify and evaluate other measures to help reduce congestion.

2. Identify the negative externalities that may result if the situation is not improved.

numbers have increased 1.5 times in Germany, 3.3 times in Spain and by more than 4 times in Portugal over the period (Jobbins, 2003).

Action by individuals which affects other individuals

Concerns have long been raised by communities across the world arising from higher volumes of tourism which can have an impact on the environment and culture. This is clearly an example of a negative externality where the activity of individuals affects other individuals. On the other hand, a positive externality is created when individuals improve their driving habits or maintain the area in which they live. Immunisation is also an example of a positive externality. Not only are those who have been immunised protected from the disease, but others in the wider community, who have not received the treatment, also benefit as there will be fewer carriers of the disease overall.

Summary

Negative externalities are a direct consequence of economic activity. If private producers exclude the costs imposed on other people from their output calculations they will produce more of the good than is socially desirable. The direct result will be negative externalities, as outlined earlier, and a welfare loss to society. Some pollution, however, is socially acceptable because the enormous cost of reducing many types of pollution to zero may pose even more limits on society.

It has been suggested that it is in the economic interests of individuals and companies to accept the consequences of these externalities. This view, which encourages negative externalities, may be blinkered. Short-term benefits of having more and cheaper products to consume may not be in the wider long-term interests of the community and the environment. However, organisations in some parts of the world are often encouraged to take this short-term view by their shareholders as they strive for greater returns. Having considered the difference between the private and social optimum output, we now need to examine the role of the government.

Measures available to limit externalities

There is a disincentive for organisations to develop or install new, more environmentally friendly equipment, because the cost of so doing is likely to be a reduction in their competitiveness. The shoe industry in Europe, for example, has a dilemma regarding the harmful effects that can result from the extensive use of adhesives in the manufacture of shoes. The excessive cost of pollution control equipment will increase costs overall and, perhaps, result in an inability to compete with cheaper, less environmentally conscious, competitors from the developing world. However, taking no action may mean that stricter legislation is imposed on the industry.

Governments do not have to let all negative externalities persist. They can intervene in the market through a range of means, including adopting policies that use, or improve, the price mechanism, or by employing extra-market policies. Cost is a key consideration for government and the organisations when deciding upon the appropriate type and timing of intervention. In this section we discuss limiting externalities under four headings:

- property rights;

- market solutions;

- tradeable permits;

- regulation and legislation.

The principle is designed to encourage businesses to improve processes and is achieved by setting standards and controls which companies have to comply with in order to avoid incurring any extra costs through taxes or fines.

Organisations will usually try to pass on their increased costs to the consumer. Some consumers will refuse to pay the increased price and consumption of the good will fall. As was noted earlier in the chapter, this will reduce the level of externalities, for example pollution, and result in a more socially efficient level of production.

Property rights

For some negative externalities, such as pollution, if somebody had ownership rights to the air, sea, etc., then they could take the polluters to court and sue for compensation. If it is possible to identify the legal rights of the parties involved then bargaining may be viable. For example, a paper mill producing pulp may be willing to compensate a sailing club that owns a stretch of water if the latter accepts a certain amount of pollution. In return the mill will save money on its waste treatment.

Four problems arising from the use of bargaining are evident:

- it is difficult to establish the legal rights involved;

- it would be impossible to list everyone who is affected by noxious emissions from a particular factory for the purpose of compensation;

- there may be no bargaining machinery in place;

- the costs to an organisation of administering such a system, even if agreements were reached, could be enormous.

Because of these problems bargaining is unlikely to be successful. As the market finds it very difficult to respond to the problem, many argue that there is a need for government intervention.

Market solutions

The aim here is to change the costs of the activity to account for the negative externality. This usually involves the use of charges, taxes or subsidies.

The tax mechanism can be used to impose extra costs on both producers and consumers. The increased use of financial instruments, such as regulatory charges, landfill levies and fines, are all manifestations of the 'polluter pays' principle (Welford and Gouldson, 1993).

The Swedish government has indicated that tax is 'one of the few efficient tools for reducing CO_2 emissions because when it comes to economy and industry, this task requires the market's own tools' (Boulton, 1995). A firm could be forced to pay an indirect tax, such as the carbon taxes imposed by the Danish and Swedish governments, on each unit of its polluting emissions. The effect of the tax is to increase the costs of production for manufacturers and reduce the output of pollutants. In Singapore car buying permits are necessary before anyone can purchase a car. Additionally, high import duties, which increase the purchase price of a car, high road tax and road pricing in the central business district all serve to reduce demand for cars. Allied to this is a very efficient public transport system.

If a tax reflects the full external environmental cost then the externality has been fully internalised. This is a very big 'if', since the issue is whether the tax can ever accurately reflect the external cost. The aim is to impose a tax that will result in the socially efficient level of output. In such situations organisations have a choice: they can continue to pollute and pay for it or invest in anti-pollution measures which will, in the short term, reduce their tax liability and, possibly, save them money and/or offer competitive advantages in the long term.

Grants can be provided to polluters as an incentive to reduce the amount of discharge and encourage environmentally friendly forms of behaviour. Farmers can obtain subsidies under the Common Agricultural Policy (CAP) for land improvement schemes that enhance the environment. One key reservation is that the use of grants or subsidies flies in the face of the 'polluter pays' principle.

Tradeable permits

A more recent development in the area of controlling negative externalities has been the use of tradeable pollution permits. These can be used to control the degree of structural change and focus on tackling the worst culprits.

Under a tradeable permit system, a government issues a fixed quantity of permits giving authorisation to discharge a certain level of waste. In America, for example, clean air legislation sets a cap on emissions of nitrous oxide and sulphur dioxide from power stations. Companies are given annual permits to emit a certain amount of the gases.

These permits are tradeable, allowing those companies which find the cost of pollution control to be relatively low to sell their rights for a fee or allow those which have invested in long-term 'clean-up' measures to sell their permits to those whose emissions exceed their permit.

Organisations will buy rights to discharge, as long as the cost of the permit is below the cost of the pollution control measures they would otherwise have to undertake.

Having such a market means that resources are used more efficiently to control the overall level of pollution.

Regulation and legislation

A common method of intervening in the market to force organisations to address negative externalities is by regulation, usually by imposing a set of legal obligations upon organisations or individuals. Regulations are commonly used to impose external costs on producers. Regulations can take many forms which include (Lee, 1994):

- prohibiting the abstraction, use or disposal of particular substances, products and processes which are considered to be environmentally damaging (e.g. CFCs have been banned because of the damage they cause to the ozone layer);

- setting maximum limits for the abstraction of particular natural resources (e.g. water from rivers);

- setting maximum limits for discharges of pollutants to air, water or land (e.g. exhaust emission standards must be met by all cars taking an MOT test in the UK);

- prescribing the technology which may be used for particular processes of production or the materials which may be used in particular processes (e.g. catalytic converters must be used on cars to cut emissions);

- establishing ambient quality standards.

Regulations are used because they are easier than other types of intervention to administer. Taxation of, for example, CO_2 discharge into the atmosphere such as that discussed above requires sophisticated and costly monitoring. Regulations may not require this level of monitoring as spot checks may be enough. Through regulation, such as the placing of a legal maximum on the amount of pollution that a business organisation can produce, an organisation could be prohibited from producing more than the socially efficient level of output.

Regulation at all levels takes the lead from European Union environmental legislation which is grouped into seven fields. Regulations can be applied that relate to all these areas:

- general environmental policy regulations;

- air;

- chemical, industrial risks and biotechnology;

- nature conservation;

- noise;

- waste;

- water.

For example, the Council directive 99/31/EC of 26 April 1999 on the landfill of waste entered into force on 16 July 1999. The deadline for implementation of the legislation in the Member States was 16 July 2001. The objective of the Directive was to prevent or reduce, as far as possible, negative effects on the environment from landfill, in particular on surface water, groundwater, soil, air and human health, by introducing stringent technical requirements for waste and landfills (European Commission, 2003a).

The amount of materials that are recycled is increasing, partly due to this legislation. Some European countries are much better placed than others. Recycling rates in Germany and Denmark are around 80 per cent. In Germany, for example, householders sort waste into separate containers to facilitate recycling.

However, regulations do cause problems. Because the legislation is often uniformly applied it tends to be costly for the industries affected to keep up with the changes. This may mean that the government will 'tone down' legislation under pressure from powerful lobbyists or that there is no incentive to improve performance beyond compliance with the regulation. For the eight years of the Clinton/Gore administration in the US all efforts to reduce carbon dioxide in air or arsenic in water were resisted (Moore, 2002). It has even been suggested that trying to make industry cleaner, by applying tighter standards, may protect old, dirty technology already in place and discourage cleaner innovation.

Regulations, however, may also be able to promote business activity. Opportunities will flourish in the waste clean-up industry, giving export opportunities as other countries adopt similar regulations that tend to minimise waste. Porter (1990) argued that environmental regulations can create new jobs. It is possible that the imposition of strict regulations can actually improve the ability of a firm to compete. Stringent standards for product performance, product safety, and environmental impact can stimulate companies to improve quality, upgrade technology and provide features that respond to consumer and social demands. Easing standards, however tempting, is counterproductive (Porter, 1990). The environmental technologies industry could be losing as much as £2 billion in annual sales due to the weak regulation and enforcement of legislation requiring these safer processes on the rest of industry (Environmental Industries Commission, 1996).

Environmental standards can also act as a barrier to entry (see Chapter 2): those car manufacturers which had already fitted catalytic converters on cars for sale in the United States lobbied in favour of their adoption in the European market.

Organisations that are based in countries with substantial regulations, such as Sweden, may be in a position to gain competitive advantage over organisations operating under a more lax regime. As legislation changes and converges throughout Europe and the world, those organisations that have worked under the strictest regimes will have a distinct competitive advantage. Scania, the multinational truck manufacturer, has used the strict legal environment in Sweden to compete successfully in the truck industry (see Minicase 6.3). Murray and Fahy (1994) suggest that the advantage to the early movers is most likely to arise from:

- positive consumer perceptions and attitudes which become attached to companies and their brands;

- the accumulated experience of dealing with new materials, technologies and processes;

- the ownership of proprietary design, recovery and recycling technologies and processes.

It may be difficult for organisations that are left behind to catch up.

| Minicase 6.3 | Environment and competition: the case of Scania |

Scania is a Swedish manufacturer and distributor of trucks, buses, coaches and marine engines. Their lorries, or trucks as they are referred to in the industry, are manufactured and assembled in Sodertalue in Sweden, Zwolle in Holland, Angers in France and a number of sites in Latin America. Scania trucks have been referred to as the Rolls-Royce of the truck industry.

Their prime business comprises the sale of new and used trucks, servicing and repair.

Environmental concerns

Until the mid 1960s there were few environmental issues at stake for commercial vehicle manufacturers. Legislation was limited, there was no significant body of opinion voicing concern and few facts were available to demonstrate that a problem existed. In those circumstances manufacturers' prime concern was to build trucks that would prove competitive in their marketplaces. In the late 1960s West Coast (USA) laws were established which began to regulate pollution from commercial vehicles.

Progress was slow in Europe during the 1970s and the 1980s; it was hampered by the lack of clear-cut evidence and adequate methods of measurement. This has now changed, and while we are still a long way from the harmonised legislation many standards for the present and future have been established. Environmental legislation in Sweden, the home of Scania (and of its major rival Volvo), is amongst the strictest in the world.

To a large extent these standards drive change, although some 'environmentally friendly' activity also improves competitiveness. Leif Ostling, the President and CEO, argues that technological improvements linked to emissions will have competitive pay-offs. Methods are being developed to improve the efficiency of engines; non-engine-related improvements can also reduce emissions and fuel consumption by increasing aerodynamic qualities. Improvements in aerodynamics and rolling resistance and reductions in weight have reduced energy consumption by up to 50 per cent in a little over two decades. Scania's designers have achieved a steady reduction in fuel requirements from the application of aerodynamic technologies.

Scania regards the integration of environmental work into all of its processes as a key competitive factor. Nearly half of Scania's product development work occurs in fields related to the environment. These include materials selection, exhaust emissions, noise, fuel consumption, alternative fuels and recycling of components and materials.

Scania's environmental policy

A growing number of national and international organisations have developed an environmental policy which sets out their ecological position. Scania have long recognised that industrial production and ecological concerns often conflict. When an industry is primarily concerned with the manufacture of vehicles which burn fossil fuels and contribute to traffic flows, the environmentalist lobby is particularly watchful and active. However, partly perhaps due to their liberal and sensitive Swedish cultural origin, Scania are renowned within the truck industry for the attention they pay to ecological concerns. Scania's environmental (meaning, here, ecological) policy is enshrined in its mission statement and explicitly stated thus:

- Scania shall achieve and maintain leadership within its field of competence in order to provide a better environment;

- Scania shall by foresighted research and development continuously reduce the environmental impact coming from its production, products and services;

- Scania shall actively promote internationally harmonised and effective environmental legislation – for Scania current legislation is the minimum standard;

- Scania shall increase the confidence in its environmental work through openness and regular environmental reporting.

Scania also publishes an annual Environmental Report which sets out its annual environmental goals and evaluates progress against previous goals. Scania claims to match or improve upon all statutory environmental standards despite the inevitable cost of following such a policy. However, of equal certainty are the competitive benefits that ensue from the application of technology to forge a bridge between ecological concerns and competitive pressures.

Questions

1. How can concern for the environment act as a source of competitive advantage to Scania? How might that concern, if it were taken to greater extremes, prove to be a liability?

2. Why do you think that companies like Scania are concerned to achieve a harmonisation of environmental legislation across the globe?

Anti-monopoly legislation may be necessary to prevent the abuse of monopoly power which could include infringement of environmental regulations. Firms may be taken into public ownership and their output controlled to take into account both public and private costs. How ineffective this may be can be judged by reference to the high levels of pollution in the former Soviet Union. One of the key foundations of environmental policies adopted by the Conservative government in the United Kingdom from 1979 was that effective regulation did not require legal ownership of industries.

Government regulation at different geo-political scales

Government at various geo-political scales, from international to local, oversees the marketplace. Increasingly, much of the development of policy relating to environmental issues is taking place at global and regional scales. Nation states, which will have participated in the formulation of policy, will then often have to give domestic effect to such things as international treaties or European directives via legislation and appropriate executive action. Various global and regional institutions monitor activities in different nation states.

Regulation at global level

At the global level regulation is primarily concerned with nations agreeing to environmental protection initiatives via international summit meetings. The United Nations Framework Convention Climate Change (UNFCCC) shows how progress at this global scale is slow.

On 9 May 1992, the world's governments adopted the UNFCCC. The Convention entered into force on 21 March 1994. As of 17 February 2003 188 countries had ratified the convention.

The Convention divides countries into two main groups. A total of 41 industrialized countries are currently listed in the Convention's Annex I, including the relatively wealthy industrialised countries that were members of the Organisation for Economic Co-operation and Development (OECD) in 1992, plus countries with economies in transition (the EITs), including the Russian Federation, the Baltic States, and several Central and Eastern European States. The OECD members of Annex I – not the EITs – are also listed in the Convertion's Annex II. There are currently 24 such Annex II parties.

All other countries, mostly the developing countries, are known as non-Annex I countries. They currently number 145.

The text of the Protocol to the UNFCCC was adopted in Kyoto, Japan, on 11 December 1997. The Kyoto Protocol and its rulebook set out in the Marrakesh Accords consist of five main elements (Unfccc, 2003):

- *Commitments* – at the heart of the Kyoto Protocol lies its set of legally binding targets on greenhouse gas emissions for industrialised countries. These amount to a total cut among all Annex I Countries of at least 5 per cent from 1990 levels by 2008–12. All countries are also subject to a set of general commitments.

- *Implementation* – to meet their targets, Annex I countries must put in place domestic policies and measures that cut their greenhouse gas emissions. They may also offset their emissions by increasing the removal of greenhouse gases by carbon sinks. Supplementary to domestic actions, countries may also use the three mechanisms – joint implementation, the clean development mechanism and emissions trading – to gain credit for emissions reduced (or greenhouse gases removed) at lower cost abroad than at home.

- *Minimising impacts on developing countries* – the Protocol and its rulebook include provisions to address the specific needs and concerns of developing countries, especially those most vulnerable to the adverse effects of climate change and to the economic impact of response measures. These include the establishment of a new adaptation fund.

- *Accounting, reporting and review* – rigorous monitoring procedures are in place to safeguard the Kyoto Protocol's integrity, including an accounting system, regular reporting by countries and in-depth review of those reports by expert review teams.

- *Compliance* – a Compliance Committee, consisting of a facilitative and an enforcement branch, will assess and deal with any cases of non-compliance.

The protocol will enter into force on the ninetieth day after the date on which at least 55 countries, incorporating Annex 1 countries that account for at least 55 per cent of the total carbon dioxide emissions in 1990, have ratified, accepted, approved or acceded to the protocol. As of 2 September 2003 116 countries, 32 Annex 1 and 84 non-Annex I, had ratified the Kyoto Protocol. The total of carbon emissions that these Annex 1 countries represent is 44.2 per cent. This means that it has not yet come into force. Table 6.5 shows the carbon dioxide emissions of the main Annex 1 countries (Unfccc, 2003).

The European Union has ratified the Kyoto Protocol. Both the US and Australia have refused to ratify the protocol. Canada did so on 17 February 2002. Russia plans to. If Russia does ratify the convention then that will represent 61.3 per cent of the carbon dioxide emissions, above the 55 per cent threshold. This will mean that the protocol will come into force. At that stage a surcharge of 30 per cent per ton of CO_2 exceeding the target would be enforced.

At this global level the chief guiding concept is sustainable development assuring that, for the sake of generations to come, the amount and quality of what has been called 'natural capital' – for example, atmosphere, water, tropical rainforest and biodiversity – are

Table 6.5 Total carbon dioxide emissions of main Annex I countries, 1990

Country	Emissions (Gg)	Percentage
Australia	288,965	2.1
Canada	457,441	3.3
France	366,536	2.7
Germany	1,012,443	7.4
Italy	428,941	3.1
Japan	1,173,360	8.5
Poland	414,930	3.0
Russian Federation	2,388,720	17.4
Spain	260,654	1.9
United Kingdom	584,078	4.3
United States of America	4,957,022	36.1
Other Annex 1 countries	1,395 216	10.2
Total	13,728,306	100.0

Source: adapted from unfccc, available from http://unfccc.int/resource/guideconvkp-p.pdf [accessed March 18 2003]

not reduced by economic development. From the early 1980s onwards a range of key reports from institutions, such as the World Commission for Environment and Development and the World Bank, made pleas for integrating environmental considerations into policy making on economic development.

Regulation at regional level

We turn now to the regional scale to discuss the role of the European Union in respect of environmental regulation. The signatories to the Treaty of Rome (1957), which created the EEC, were not particularly concerned with environmental issues. This oversight was rectified by the Single European Act (SEA) 1987 which adopted the specific environmental objectives in Article 130R, namely:

- to preserve, protect and improve the quality of the environment;
- to contribute towards protecting human health;
- to ensure a prudent and rational utilisation of natural resources.

These objectives were extended by the Treaty of European Union (1992) (the so-called Maastricht Treaty) to include:

- sustainable and non-inflationary growth respecting the environment;

- promotion of measures to help resolve global environmental problems.

EU policy intentions are set out in its Environmental Action Programme. The first was from 1973 to 1976. The European Commission, through Directorate General (DG) XI, is responsible for the environment. DG XI takes the role of initiating and implementing European Union policies on the environment. EU policy has, over the years, changed in its scope. In the past, European environmental initiatives tended to be reactive and based on regulation; they are now becoming more market-driven and voluntary. The 'polluter pays' principle, discussed above, is now at the centre of much EU legislation.

Towards the end of 1993 it was agreed that a long-planned European Environment Agency (EEA) should be set up in Copenhagen, Denmark. One of the major tasks of the EEA has been to set up a European Information and Observation Network (EIONET) to provide objective, reliable and comprehensive scientific and technical information at a European level. The aim is to provide data to enable the European Union to 'take the steps necessary to protect the environment as well as to assess the results of their actions' (CEC, 1994).

The EEA co-ordinates a system of national networks to enable it to achieve its objectives. Collaborative activity is important in order to avoid duplicating work being carried out by other bodies. It published its first report on the environment in 46 countries in 1995, the Dobris assessment, which uses a wide range of headings to analyse the extent of any progress, including:

- climate change;

- stratospheric ozone depletion;

- acidification;

- tropospheric ozone;

- chemicals;

- waste;

- biodiversity;

- inland waters;

- marine and coastal environment;

- soil degradation;

- urban environment;

- technological and natural hazards.

A second version followed in 1998. Conferences of European environment ministers, such as those in Sofia in 1995 and Aarhus in 1998, aim to use these assessments to help to develop principles and policies designed to bring about environmental improvement and convergence upon a more sustainable pattern of development in Europe. The EEA has an ongoing programme of assessments available from their website.

In Brussels on 24 January 2001 the European Commission put forward its proposals for the next five to ten years outlined in the Sixth Environmental Action Programme 'Environment 2010: our future, our choice'(European Commission, 2003b). The programme identifies four priority areas for urgent action:

- climate change;

- nature and biodiversity;

- environment and health and quality of life;

- natural resources and waste.

The new programme stresses the need for member states to better implement existing environmental laws, and the Commission announced that it will bring increased pressure to bear on member states by making implementation failures better known. Another theme in the new programme is working with business and consumers to achieve more environmentally friendly forms of production and consumption.

As we turn to consider regulation at a national level, it is important to note that the environmental laws of EU member states are increasingly determined by the Union, 'while the mechanisms through which these objectives are to be reached are determined nationally' (Welford and Gouldson, 1993). Furthermore, as industries are becoming increasingly globalised, organisations need to comply with varying environmental legislation and respond to action from cross-border pressure groups which may differ widely from those in their home market.

Regulation at national level

In the United Kingdom, the task of central government in regulating health and environmental issues or providing support for organisations is largely carried out through the Department for the Environment Food and Rural Affairs (DEFRA). Other ministries, such as the Department of Trade and Industry, whose Business Link scheme provides advice on environmental issues for small firms in particular, also provide support.

The main legislation in this field is the Environmental Protection Act 1990 (EPA) and the Environment Act 1995 (EA). Chien (1991) suggests that legislation is based on the 'four Rs':

- reduction of the amount of waste produced;

- reuse of durable items;

- recycling of natural resources;

- regeneration of discarded products for use as new materials or products.

There are a wide variety of means available for the enforcement of environmental law. Criminal prosecution may impose a fine or imprisonment. Injunctions or claims for damages may prevent some harm from occurring or compensate for injury sustained. Licences or contracts may regulate and set standards. Enforcement agencies (such as the Environment Agency) have wide powers to inspect, report and take action over pollution (Hartshorne, 2003).

If organisations produce waste they have a duty of care in respect of that waste under the EPA 1990. Managers in such businesses need to be aware that breach of this duty of care can lead to fines and prison sentences in addition to civil liability for causing damage to environmental or human health by waste. The EPA 1990 can grant authorisation to make emissions from any 'prescribed processes' but the process must satisfy a test known as BATNEEC ('best available technique not entailing excessive cost'). BATNEEC obliges organisations which are polluting to adopt cleaner technologies than those in place, providing they are not 'excessively' costly. However, the definition itself is ambiguous, and subject to a test of 'reasonableness'. Welford and Gouldson (1993) note that organisations which have developed self-regulation schemes such as EN ISO 14001 'will be at a considerable advantage when gathering the information and applying the criteria of BATNEEC'.

Additionally, the EPA 1990 subjects the most polluting processes to an 'integrated' scheme of pollution control. Here, control is integrated in the sense that the impact of an organisation's emissions to air, water or land must be treated in a holistic way, in order to achieve what is known as the 'best practicable environmental option'.

Enforcement notices may be served if an organisation is in breach of the terms of its authorisation to emit. More serious risks which cannot be dealt with in this way will result in the issue of a prohibition notice, which can force the closure of a facility until an organisation complies with its authorisation.

The Environment Agency (EA) was established in England and Wales by the EA 1995 and came into existence in April 1996. It is a key body in respect of enforcement issues in the UK. It is responsible for issuing discharge consents for companies wishing to discharge wastes into rivers. The EA combines all the functions previously undertaken by H.M. Inspectorate of Pollution, the National Rivers Authority and the waste regulation authorities under one umbrella. The EA 1995 established the principal aim of the agency to protect or enhance the environment as a whole and make a contribution towards attaining sustainable development. In an attempt to approach environmental issues from a holistic perspective the EA has identified nine key themes in environmental management:

- addressing climatic change;
- regulating major industries;
- improving air quality;
- managing waste;
- managing water resources;
- delivering integrated river basin management;

- conserving the land;

- managing fresh water fisheries;

- enhancing biodiversity.

All other EU governments are also moving forward on this agenda. To improve environmental performance in 2003 and to incorporate EU directives Ireland is planning to introduce the Protection of the Environment Bill. The Bill covers integrated pollution prevention and control, a licensing system, new waste management measures and amendments to the Litter Pollution Act 1997.

Under the legislation local authorities will be given more powers and tougher laws against those breaching environmental regulations will result in more licences being revoked or suspended and larger fines, up to €3000 for a conviction or a €600 daily fine.

The approach of governments within the EU, as we can see, closely follows EU directives and guidelines. We turn now to examine regulation at the local level.

Regulation at local level

In the UK, local authority environmental health departments have regulatory responsibility for a number of areas, including food hygiene, health and safety (together with the Health and Safety Executive), pest control and air and noise pollution. Local authorities are also responsible for planning, licensing and trading standards.

The issue of planning controls is a crucial one in terms of more localised environmental issues. In England and Wales a series of Town and Country Planning regulations between 1990 and 1995 gave effect to a European directive on Environmental Impact Assessment which required member states 'to consider the environmental effects of new developments before planning consent is given' (Croner Guide, 1998). The regulations require developers to produce an 'environmental impact statement' to help the planning authority make a decision.

The Environment Act 1995 set up an improved network of centres for monitoring air quality. This local authority responsibility is the only area not incorporated into the work of the Environment Agency.

In the spring of 2003 the Scottish Executive announced an allocation of £15 million amongst 32 local authorities for cleaning up Scotland's most polluted land. The funding stemmed from the Contaminated Land (Scotland) Regulations 2000 and was made available over the period 2003/04 to 2005/06. The funding was aimed at helping to bring historically contaminated land, polluted through earlier mining or industrial activities, back into productive use and eradicate threats to human health and the environment. The funds aim to help local authorities to identify and investigate contaminated sites. Responsibility for cleaning up polluted land rests with the polluter. Where local authorities can identify those responsible, necessary enforcement action can be taken (Croner, 2003).

In summary, it is true to say that progress at the global level in taking ecological regulatory action is often slow. However, since most serious ecological concerns tend not to be confined within particular geographical boundaries, the ability to make progress at this global level is critical to the effective tackling of many of the earth's ecological problems. Action at regional, national or local levels often stems from these wider global initiatives.

Organisational agendas

All organisations cause environmental problems and disasters as a direct result of their activities. Taylor *et al.* (1994) identify three categories of company:

- High penetration companies have the greatest impact on the environment. They include agriculture, chemicals and plastics and metals and mining.

- Moderate penetration companies have some impact, and can save money by cutting wasteful practices. They include electronics, leisure and tourism, and packaging and paper.

- Low penetration companies feel that environmental matters do not concern them. These include advertising, education, and local government.

An example of a high penetration incident occurred in March 1989. Exxon faced a $2 billion clean-up operation and fines of a similar amount, resulting from an oil spillage, when the tanker *Exxon Valdez* ran aground in Alaska. The number of cases of this type of violation is still substantial. From 1992–9 fifteen cases were reported in which a ship or cruise line had been fined more than $100 000 for an environmental violation. The biggest fine, $23.5 million, was levied on the Cunard Line for the damage sustained to a coral reef in the Gulf of Aqaba when it was hit by the vessel *Royal Viking Sun*. It is not only the fines that damage organisations. Cannon (1994) has estimated that loss of market share, disruptions to supplies, compliance with new regulations and the effect on share price cost Exxon a further substantial sum – between $8 billion and $15 billion. Rebuilding consumer confidence in such cases may prove very difficult.

Unilever has reported that it has incurred a number of penalties for infringement of environmental regulations. The fines were due to exceeding limits in liquid effluent at three sites (five cases), three incidents where trade effluent was accidentally mixed with storm water discharges, and one case of disposal of prescribed waste at an unlicensed site. Under Taylor et al (see earlier) this may be an example of moderate penetration. However, Unilever has an improving record in environmental management and its aim is to reach 100 per cent compliance (Unilever, 2003b). Its food business has almost 300 sites and in 2001 they attracted only 7 fines. Home and Personal care has almost 200 sites and they only had 2 fines. In total the fines totalled only €19 000 which for a global operator such as Unilever with a multi-million dollar turnover the total in fines is really insignificant.

Even organisations, which may be labelled as low penetration, such as universities, are taking action to reduce the impact that they have on the environment. A number of institutions are taking action to reduce the number of inputs they use and are putting in place effective recycling policies.

It is evident that organisations also have responsibilities. Hutchinson (1996) outlines four responsibilities of business, which are shown in Figure 6.8.

Given the nature of the business environment facing them, it is clear that organisations throughout the world realise that there is a wide range of responses available to meet the changing environmental agenda. More are discovering that they need to be seen to be responding to this changing context. Hamel and Prahalad (1994) suggest that radical change is necessary if lasting solutions are to be found, and government, business and individuals have a role to play. The future is about sustainability. Companies are competing for the future but can only do so if they are farsighted, regenerate their core strategies, innovate and use new ways of thinking to transform their organisations. Of importance to this agenda are changing stakeholder views, which we will explore in the next section.

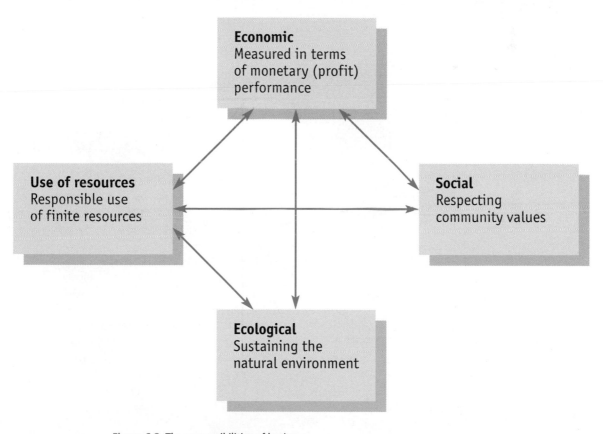

Figure 6.8 The responsibilities of business
Source: adapted from Hutchinson (1996)

The environment and stakeholders

Stakeholders are groups or individuals who have a stake in, or an expectation of, the organisation's performance (see Figure 6.9 and also Chapter 1). The environmental stance of an organisation is influenced by the perceptions of its stakeholders and the relative power which each possesses. Minicase 6.4 demonstrates such a case.

Many organisations, such as The Body Shop and the Co-op Bank believe that 'good ethics' and consideration of wider stakeholder interests will pay in the long term (these two companies could be described as being good performers).

The influence of stakeholder power

In much of our coverage of factors in the business environment we have noted that the way in which organisations perceive changes is dependent upon their unique 'perceptual filters'. Divergent stakeholder interests add another level of complexity. It must be recognised that changing stakeholder views are beginning to have an impact on how organisations perceive the environment, and are likely to have effects on business and profit.

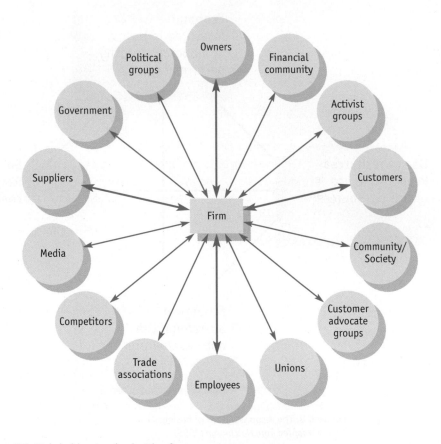

Figure 6.9 Stakeholders involved with a firm

Argenti (1980) identifies three categories of stakeholder:

- those internal to the enterprise, such as employees/management and shareholders;
- those immediately external to the enterprise, for example suppliers and customers;
- other external stakeholders, such as the community and pressure groups.

The expectations and aspirations of stakeholder groups differ. The short-term profits desired by shareholders are often given priority over the interests of other stakeholders. Company managers, particularly in the UK and the USA, have traditionally managed shareholder value, at the expense of other stakeholder requirements, by maximising shareholder returns through higher dividends or a better capital return from the sale of shares that have increased in value. This requirement frequently conflicts with the adoption of more socially and environmentally sound policies. This policy is not as visible in Europe and Asia.

The expectations of the local community may substantially differ from that of a company, resulting in a conflict of interests. How do these wider social needs for more jobs, improvements in local amenities and minimum pollution correspond to the aims of a company? A major problem for the external stakeholders, such as the local community, is that they have insufficient power to influence company strategy because of their fragmented nature (see Minicase 6.4). Ansoff (1984) suggested that the dominant coalition, those in positions of power, such as the board of directors, can bias strategy toward their own preferred course of action. In this way senior management can initiate strategies to support shareholders' wishes which may be to the detriment of the environment and the local community. It would be unusual for external stakeholders to be part of the dominant coalition, so their influence is rarely felt.

Pressure in respect of environmental performance can be applied on the organisation by pressure groups, media and insurers (Welford and Gouldson, 1993). Thilo Bode, head of Greenpeace International, stated at the Rio summit in 1992, 'Big corporations today have a responsibility that goes beyond their aim to make a profit. The focus is on social, moral and ethical considerations'.

A survey by Entec in 1996 suggested that green issues were moving up the corporate agenda (Caulkin, 1996). In November 1997 an Institute of Management survey of 423 companies found that 24 per cent said they were fully committed to environmental issues at board level, with a further 34 per cent taking a proactive stance towards environmental issues (Charlesworth, 1998).

Forum for the Future (2003) reported a survey of mainstream fund managers in the UK and US which revealed the increasing importance of social and environmental issues. The majority of fund managers interviewed in the UK and US now see social and environmental performance as part of the 'non-financial' risks facing their investments. They are integrating engagement on these issues with companies into their mainstream corporate governance process, and the number of large institutional investors engaging on these issues has grown substantially.

Evidence, including that from World Resources Institute (2003), is rapidly accumulating that companies who best manage risks and opportunities related to the natural environment gain durable competitive advantages. This fact elevates environmental

Minicase 6.4   What happened in Bhopal?

Between 1977 and 1984, Union Carbide India Limited (UCIL), located within a crowded working class neighbourhood in Bhopal, was licensed by the Madhya Pradesh Government to manufacture phosgene, monomethylamine (MMA), methylisocyanate (MIC) and the pesticide carbaryl, also known as Sevin.

On the night of 2–3 December 1984 one of the world's worst industrial disasters occurred at this Union Carbide plant. Water inadvertently entered the MIC storage tank, where over 40 metric tonnes of MIC were being stored. The addition of water to the tank caused a runaway chemical reaction, resulting in a rapid rise in pressure and temperature. The heat generated by the reaction, the presence of higher than normal concentrations of chloroform, and the presence of an iron catalyst (resulting from corrosion of the stainless steel tank wall), resulted in a reaction of such momentum that the gases formed could not be contained by safety systems. As a result, MIC and other reaction products, in liquid and vapour form, escaped from the plant into the surrounding areas.

There was no warning for people surrounding the plant as the emergency sirens had been switched off. The effect on the people living in the shanty settlements just over the fence was immediate and devastating.

Many died in their beds, others staggered from their homes, blinded and choking, to die in the street. Many more died later after reaching hospitals and emergency aid centres. The early acute effects were vomiting and burning sensations in the eyes, nose and throat, and most deaths have been attributed to respiratory failure. For some, the toxic gas caused such massive internal secretions that their lungs became clogged with fluids, while for others, spasmodic constriction of the bronchial tubes led to suffocation. Many of those who survived the first day were found to have impaired lung function.

Follow-up studies on survivors have also reported neurological symptoms including headaches, disturbed balance, depression, fatigue and irritability. Abnormalities and damage to the gastrointestinal, musculoskeletal, reproductive and immunological systems were also frequently found.

The factory was closed down after the accident. The accident also led, as expected, to intensive experimental and epidemiological research into the toxicity of MIC and the tissue damage it could cause. Prior to the Bhopal accident, practically nothing was known, and therefore since 1984 numerous human health investigations and laboratory toxicity studies have been conducted. However, amongst the controversies regarding blame and accountability, and the research into the toxicity of MIC, the fate of the redundant former UCIL site was largely overlooked.

The survey conducted for the Bhopal Legacy report by Greenpeace International has demonstrated substantial and, in some locations, severe contamination of land and drinking water supplies with heavy metals and persistent organic contaminants both within and surrounding the former UCIL pesticide formulation plant. There is an urgent need for a more detailed and extensive survey if the full extent of ongoing contamination from the plant is to be determined.

Source: Greenpeace, 19 March 2002, available from http://www.greenpeace.org.uk/ [accessed 26 March 2003]

Questions

1. Identify the stakeholders in the Bhopal case and comment on their power to influence decisions.

2. Identify other instances where consumer pressure has forced an organisation to re-think its actions. Comment on the impact on the organisation.

topics from an operational concern handled by engineers, lawyers and specialised environmental staff to a front-line, strategic imperative for all business units of the firm – and their managers. As environmental and sustainable development pressures inexorably intensify, managers in the twenty-first century will need a much thicker, more adaptive 'playbook' than their grey pinstripe-clad predecessors.

It is open to organisations how they respond. In the next section we will examine the range of alternatives.

Environmental options

Roome (1992) sets out a continuum of five possible environmental options for organisations:

- non-compliance;

- compliance;

- compliance plus;

- commercial and environmental excellence;

- leading edge.

The first three options may be taken by businesses whose primary reference point is legislation.

Non-compliance

An organisation that adopts a non-compliance position may, because of lack of resources or managerial inertia, be unable to satisfy legal requirements. It may also be the case that an organisation makes a business decision not to satisfy basic legal requirements. Some may make a policy decision not to comply with the regulations in order to secure lower costs. Either or both of these scenarios can often be found in the small and medium enterprise sector, although not exclusively.

A recent reminder of this came in September 2002. Some of America's biggest retailers, including Gap, Tommy Hilfiger, Calvin Klein and Sears Roebuck, paid out $20 million in an out-of-court settlement to compensate more than 30 000 Asian workers for alleged sweatshop abuses on the island of Saipan. The settlement marked the end of a bitter three-year legal dispute – without any wrongdoing being admitted by the defendants (Lopatin, 2002).

Compliance

The 'compliance' standpoint is clearly a minimal response and focuses efforts upon the action required to satisfy the minimum legal requirements.

These two stances are essentially reactive. By adopting a reactive stance it is possible that a company may fall behind competitors that are developing products and processes to meet the tougher environmental conditions. In fact because of European Union objectives it is becoming evident that organisations cannot take decisions without reference to environmental consequences (see above). It is likely that policies will have to have an environmental dimension at the early stages of formation. This may cause a change in direction for many organisations as business decisions may take on a completely different perspective depending on the applicable environmental legislation.

Compliance plus

During the 1980s a shorthand reference to environmentally concerned organisations – and consumers – was use of the word 'green'. 'Green' organisations, such as the Body Shop, were said to have a positive and proactive stance toward environmental and ethical issues. The 'compliance-plus' option demonstrates that a proactive stance towards legal standards can benefit the organisation. The reduced probability of fines associated with non-compliance and the reduced likelihood of bad publicity leading to a loss of market share are a demonstrable benefit of taking this option (see above).

Nike, Gap, Adidas and Wal-Mart continue to be high-profile targets of non-government organisations (NGOs) and consumer activists seizing on the latest whiff of worker exploitation and environmental scandal. During the 1990s one global consumer brand after another was hit where it really hurts: on its balance sheet. Many were badly hurt and have since learnt that a serious commitment to corporate social responsibility (CSR) is central to improving the bottom line. The clamour for corporate righteousness has led to an explosion of corporate social responsibility literature on websites belonging to Gap, Coke, McDonald's and Nike to name but four (Lopatin, 2002). Internal and external pressures are said to have prompted over 50 per cent of companies to go beyond compliance with existing legislation and 75 per cent have begun developing environmental management systems and so moving toward compliance plus.

Such an organisation might aim to integrate an environmental management system into its overall business strategy via a standard such as EN ISO 14001. By the end of 2002 about 80 of the largest 350 companies in the United Kingdom issued environmental reports in the last year (*Observer*, 2002).

Commercial and environmental excellence and leading edge

Roome's two remaining options incorporate Kleiner's (1991) approach, which identified three key components of green companies:

- They will have developed a mechanism for placing a monetary value on the complete life cycle of their products, from raw materials through production to distribution, consumption and disposal. Such 'cradle-to-grave' or 'life-cycle cost' accounting will assist in the development of products and limit environmental impact.

- They will record and publish environmental data, possibly thereby averting environmental disasters and improving community relations.

- They will be committed to reducing waste at source, for example via some form of Total Quality Management programme.

A business focused on 'commercial and environmental excellence' would ensure that its core corporate and managerial values always take account of environmental management issues; 'leading-edge' businesses set the standard for a particular industry through the adoption of 'state-of-the-art' environmental management systems. This more proactive stance can be illustrated by the systems adopted by 3M in Minicase 6.5.

A brief examination of a range of company Annual Reports suggests that shareholder expectations in respect of a company's environmental record may be increasing. This may be partly due to pressure groups, which have sought to purchase shares in order to gain access to annual general meetings and be in a formal forum to put over their views. There is evidence, also, of the increasing popularity of 'green' investment funds.

A proactive stance may require substantial amounts of initial capital investment and put an organisation at a cost disadvantage in relation to more reactive competitors. However, there are a number of cases of organisations who justify investment in, for example, waste minimisation schemes, as making hard-headed, if long-term, business sense. The increasing cost of landfill dumping may cause more organisations to make such decisions.

The importance of the organisation's environmental context

The environmental context in which an organisation carries out its business may be a major factor influencing the environmental stance that it adopts. Organisations need to respond to the question of how the environment is viewed in the country or market in which they operate.

Minicase 6.5   3M

Some companies have put in place ecological strategies that seek to eliminate emissions, effluents and accidents through preventative action and continuous improvement at every step of the production process (Shrivastava, 1994). This preventative approach is more efficient than controlling discharges at 'end-of-pipe', which involves pollution control to purify air or water before they leave the plant. End-of-pipe control is often viewed by companies as cheaper than pollution prevention; however, there is an argument that an effective pollution prevention strategy is cheaper in the long run. One company that has taken the longer-term view is the multinational 3M (Minnesota Mining and Manufacturing Company).

3M has a diversified portfolio of businesses, based largely on its wide expertise. It has a strong reputation for product innovation, an example being 'Post-it' notes. 3M develops product lines around a series of small, discrete, free-standing products. The company forms new venture units comprising of small, semi-autonomous teams, led by a product champion to develop its new products.

One of the key tasks of this team is to minimise pollution from the first phase of product development. 3M's Pollution Prevention Pays (3P) programme was launched in 1975; the concept was to apply pollution prevention on a company wide basis and document the results. The programme helps prevent pollution at source, in products and manufacturing processes, rather than removing it after it has been created. In 1989 3M introduced Pollution Prevention Plus (3P+), committing itself to stricter environmental controls and increased R&D expenditure. The 3P programme was further updated in 2002 to provide more opportunities for participation by research and development, logistics, transportation, and packaging employees with the addition of new award categories and criteria. 3M employees worldwide have initiated more than 4820 3P projects. The programme is in four stages:

- product reformulation, where the issue is whether products can be made using fewer raw materials or less toxic materials;

- process modification, in order to cut down on waste;

- equipment redesign; and

- resource recovery. Can waste be salvaged, reused or sold?

Each project undertaken by the 3P programme must meet four criteria:

- eliminate or reduce a pollutant;

- benefit the environment through reduced energy use or more efficient use of manufacturing materials and resources;

- save money – through avoidance or deferral of pollution control equipment costs, reduced operating and materials expenses, or increased sales of an existing or new product;

- a special award also recognises projects that demonstrate technical innovation.

As a direct result of the programme, waste per unit of output fell. From 1975 to 2001 the programme prevented 821 344 tons of pollutants and saved $857 million. The target for 2000 was to reduce their rate of waste generation by 50 per cent from 1990.
Environmental Progress between 1990–2001 shows a:

- 91 per cent reduction in volatile organic air emissions;

- 84 per cent reduction in manufacturing releases to water;

- 12 per cent reduction in solid waste;

- 35 per cent reduction in the rate of waste generation;

- 88 per cent reduction in US EPA Toxic Release Inventory (TRI) releases.

Source: adapted from 'Environmental, Social and Economic Sustainability: Sustaining Our Future: 3M's Progress Toward Environmental, Social and Economic Sustainability and More about Pollution Prevention Pays, available from http://www.3m.com/about3m/sustainability/index.jhtml [accessed 3 April, 2003]

Questions

Using Roome's (1992) continuum:

1. Where does a company stand that uses end of pipe pollution control? Explain your answer.

2. Assess and comment on the environmental option 3M follows (visit the 3M website for up-to-date further information).

Multinational companies are key players in the economic development in less developed countries (LDCs) as they are 'footloose' meaning that they are free to choose any location in the world for their business. The proliferation of legislation in Europe and the United States, as well as increasing costs, has caused the development of 'pollution havens' as some organisations have relocated to less regulated developing countries in order to escape tougher environmental legislation in their home markets (Croner Guide, 1996). There is a clear trade-off between business growth and concern for the environment as these companies exploit the less stringent environmental controls of many LDCs. This may be an example of organisations trying to shirk their environmental responsibilities.

We can examine the environmental context facing organisations with reference to the work of Azzone and Bertele (1994), who outline five environmental contexts which relate either to national context or to the situation prevailing in certain product/service markets:

1. *Stable context* – here there may be either slow changes or no changes in environmental legislation. There may be a of lack of public perception of environmental issues or an almost complete lack of consumer power. Organisations in these circumstances will find it easy to ignore legislation and adopt a non-compliance stance. This could be the case in developing countries of Latin America, for example the *maquiladora* zone in Mexico is home to blue-chip American companies such as DuPont, General Electric and General Motors.

2. *Reactive context* – here environmental problems are known by small groups, consumer interest is limited and legislation evolves slowly. In this context, organisations may comply with legislation, responding only slowly when the pressures build up. Many UK firms have opted for this approach to dealing with environmental problems.

3. *Anticipative context* – here the public are more aware and have the ability to move issues onto the political agenda. It is more difficult for firms to influence the political process. Legislation and regulations become more demanding and organisations need to develop a compliance-plus strategy, anticipating changes and using technological developments to ensure that new standards can be met. The regulatory regime in the European Union is increasingly encouraging this approach.

4. *Proactive context* – within this context 'green' consumers are said to have a major impact. Organisations may need to demonstrate more concern for the environment if they are to prosper. Commercial and environmental excellence may provide a competitive advantage in the short term but may be indispensable if an organisation is to compete in this environment in the long term.

5. *Creative context* – here public opinion is extremely aware of environmental problems but there is a lack of accepted technological solutions to problems. A leading-edge company will be at the forefront of the technological push for the optimal solution. The cost of this could be substantial, but the rewards from developing and controlling a proprietary technological development can be enormous.

Clearly organisations need to be aware of the context in which they operate and need to be able to respond to changes. Organisations that adopt a stance which is out of line with the context in which they operate may not survive in the long term.

Organisations with some of the 'greenest' credentials tend to be engaged in self-regulation schemes of one type or another. Clearly, such companies are in the category of 'compliance plus', or beyond, in Roome's (1992) classifications.

Self-regulation

Global, European and national voluntary self-regulation schemes are having a considerable impact. These self-regulation schemes require organisations to 'sign up' to regimes which typically involve making information available to the public, principally via an environmental policy statement, together with clear targets and objectives needed to meet the policy. In such schemes, considerable stress is placed on plans to achieve continual improvements and of integrating environmental issues with those concerns of general management. Environmental audits and further statements on the progress made in respect of environmental objectives tend to be the final pieces of the jigsaw. The concept of environmental audit, in particular, requires organisations to monitor and collect detailed information in order to judge whether improvement has been achieved.

At the global scale there is an extensive range of such self-regulation schemes sponsored by the International Chamber of Commerce (ICC) and the International Standards Organisation (ISO), among others. The ICC's 'Business Charter for Sustainable Development', for example, outlines a range of actions to integrate the management of environmental issues with the general policies and activities of organisations. Perhaps the best known scheme is EN ISO 14001 – introduced in September 1996 as *the* international standard for environmental management.

The Eco-Management and Auditing Scheme (EMAS) is an example of self-regulation at a European level requiring voluntary eco-audits. EMAS came into operation in April 1995. It originally applied principally to industrial sites. EN ISO 14001 is recognised as a step toward achieving EMAS. In 2001 EMAS was revised. Its main elements are (Europa, 2003):

- the extension of the scope of EMAS to all sectors of economic activity including local authorities;

- the integration of EN ISO 14001 as the environmental management system required by EMAS, so that progressing from EN ISO 14001 to EMAS will be smoother and not entail duplication;

- the adoption of a visible and recognisable EMAS logo to allow registered organisations to publicise their participation in EMAS more effectively;

- the involvement of employees in the implementation of EMAS;

- the strengthening of the role of the environmental statement to improve the transparency of communication of environmental performance between registered organisations and their stakeholders and the public;

- a more thorough consideration of indirect effects including capital investments, administrative and planning decisions, procurement procedures, choice and composition of services (e.g. catering).

Table 6.6 Organisational implications of environmental stances

	The context				
	Stable	Reactive	Anticipatory	Proactive	Creative
Environmental problems	None	Problems addressed when defined	Anticipates new legislation	Examines opportunities for products and company	Searches for new technology
Activities involved					
• R & D	No	No	Yes	Yes	Yes
• Production/logistics	Limited	Yes	Yes	Yes	Yes
• Marketing/sales	No	No	No	Yes	Yes
• External relations	No	Limited	Yes	Yes	Yes
• Legal	No	Limited	Yes	Yes	Yes
• Finance	No	No	No	Yes	Yes
• Environmental department	No	No	Usually	Usually	Usually
• Top management	No	No	Sometimes	Yes	Yes

Source: adapted from Azzone and Bertele (1994)

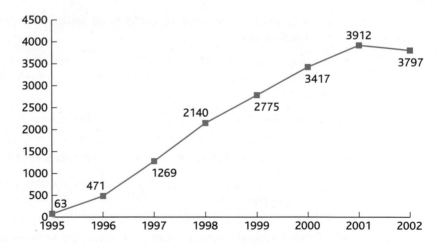

Figure 6.10 Evolution of net EMAS registrations, 1995–2002
Source: European Commission (EMAS), available from http://europa.eu.int/comm/environment/emas [accessed 20 March 2003]

Although schemes are voluntary, in the future customers might place considerable pressure on supplier organisations to 'sign up'. Figure 6.10 shows the take-up of EMAS since 1995. Germany has the largest number of EMAS registered organisations.

Whatever the response to the environment that an organisation adopts, it is likely that an increased level of activity will be necessary as the environmental context moves from stable, at one end of the continuum, to creative, at the other. It is important to recognise the extra costs that will be incurred by an organisation as it moves from one stance to another (see Table 6.6).

To summarise, it is evident that there are many non-legally binding reasons why organisations need to be aware of their impact on the natural environment and, perhaps, to take action to improve the situation. The sort of environmental agenda which an organisation adopts will be influenced by both its environmental context and the extent of stakeholders' power and interest.

The position of the consumer

Environmental issues are becoming increasingly important in consumers' buying decisions. The characteristics of 'green' consumers have been summarised by Elkington and Hailes (1988). These consumers will avoid products likely to:

- endanger health;
- cause significant environmental damage or consume a disproportionate amount of energy during manufacture, use or disposal;
- cause unnecessary waste;
- use materials from threatened species or environments;
- involve unnecessary use of, or cruelty to, animals; or
- adversely affect other countries – particularly those in the developing world.

Research shows that some consumers are ready to reward companies. Creyer and Ross (1997) suggest they may be prepared to pay a higher price or actively seek out those companies which they believe to be ethical. People want reasons to reinforce their relationship with brands, and more ethical standards of operation are one method of encouraging consumer loyalty (Lopatin, 2002). A poll of 25 000 consumers in 23 countries on the issue of corporate social responsibility showed that, in forming impressions of companies, people around the world focus on corporate citizenship ahead of brand, reputation and financial performance. Forty per cent of people surveyed claimed to have either actively punished a company not seen as socially responsible or, at least, to have seriously considered doing so (First & 42nd, 2003).

Alternatively, Malcolm Baker, global director of Research International Qualitatif, estimates that only 5 per cent of consumers actually buy goods on ethical grounds. A November 2002 survey by advertiser WPP of 1500 consumers across 41 countries concluded that consumers were happily married to their brands and would *do anything* to preserve this special material bond (Lopatin, 2002).

Clearly consumers can only act in a 'green' way if they possess reliable information about the relative effects of a range of products on the environment.

Azzone and Bertele (1994) suggest that as eco-labels with third-party certification are developed, such as the Blue Angel in Germany, 'green' qualities of products will become more obvious and 'green' consumers will become more important. It is easier for consumers in Germany to adopt 'green' purchasing habits because they have a comprehensive system of eco-labelling. This provides them with better quality information about products and the effects which their production, use or disposal might have on the environment.

It is interesting to examine the collective power that consumers can exert on businesses and governments in respect of ethical issues. Consumer boycotts can be effective campaigning tools, and can raise people's awareness though the primary effects may be small and many boycotts may be judged not to have succeeded. Trowell (1998) lists a number of boycotts, including those against:

- Nestlé for irresponsible and illegal marketing of breast milk substitutes;

- Barclays Bank for investment in South Africa during the apartheid years;

- meat (vegetarianism);

- South African goods during apartheid;

- French goods over the nuclear testing in the Pacific;

- Lloyds and Midland Banks for irresponsible third world lending;

- Norwegian goods and Icelandic fish for continued opposition to whaling restrictions;

- Shell over the Brent Spar dumping;

- Shell over its involvement in Nigeria;

- British goods during British occupation of India;

- some ferry operators over live animal exports to the European mainland;

- Gillette over animal testing;

- PVC for its long-term effects;

- GEC armaments.

Primary effects may be less than dramatic. Trowell (1998) identifies secondary effects that may be more long term and have a greater impact:

- changes to regulations;

- lasting change in industry practices;

- allowing substantial growth or entrance of ethical players into the market;

- effects on decisions of similar organisations to the target.

The real test for 'green' consumerism is whether consumers will pay premium prices for ethical products. In 2001, the Co-operative Bank and the New Economics Foundation (NEF) published the Ethical Purchasing Index (EPI), which showed spending on green and ethical products in the United Kingdom. The market rose by 18 per cent during 2000, contrasting with growth of 3 per cent in the mainstream economy. Spending on ethical products is said to outstrip growth with 'non-ethical' counterparts by more than six times (Keynote, 2002), although it must be remembered that the combined UK market share of ethical products over seven food and non-food segments is only around 1.5 per cent (Caulker, 2003).

There is some suggestion that consumer power is starting to be influential in respect of products made using child labour. Adverse publicity has caused many companies to amend their sourcing arrangements and to seek assurances about the circumstances of manufacture. A shift to 'ethical consumption' and 'ethical investment' may be the next step from 'green consumption'. Ethical funds such as TSB Environmental, AXA Sun Life Ethical and Standard Life Ethical screen out, for example, companies which produce pollutants, pesticides, or arms, and those which test on animals. The Ethical Investment Research Service provides information on the following (Slavin, 1998):

- positive achievements of companies in respect of products with a positive environmental benefit;

- involvement in the community;

- disclosure of information;

- negative screening.

Of even greater significance is the growing number of organisations 'sleeping with the enemy'. Partnerships between organisations and environmental groups are aimed at promoting organisational goals by adopting 'market-based environmentalism' to reduce costs and create product differentiation. Hartman and Stafford (1997) identify a number of green alliances involving McDonald's, The Body Shop and Friends of the Earth.

To summarise, it is clear that individual consumers have limited influence either upon the environmental stance of organisations or upon government policy but as the environmental context develops more companies are responding in this regard. However, there is increasing evidence to suggest that consumers can, when mobilised by environmental pressure groups, have considerable influence upon organisations, most particularly via the threat of a mass product boycott.

Conclusion

Since it is often difficult to confine environmental and ethical problems within individual countries it is becoming increasingly apparent that 'world solutions' need to be sought. There is also an increasing recognition that in order to address ecological problems it is no longer possible for environmental campaigners and businesses to snipe at each other from entrenched positions. Both sides are recognising the importance of agreeing trade-offs between economic development, which is important in terms of providing people with the means to live, and environmental protection, which seeks to ensure that the natural environment is used sensibly. The essence of this 'trade-off' is encapsulated in the principle of 'sustainable development' – the notion that we need to protect the natural environment for the sake of future generations.

Summary of main points

In this chapter we have identified some of the issues that are important to the well-being of the planet and models that enable us to compare the different stances of organisations with respect to ecological issues. The main points are:

- The Earth is facing a number of serious environmental issues, including the greenhouse effect.

- The operation of the market is based upon the law of supply and demand.

- The concept of externalities describes the situation where an organisation has not fully internalised its costs. Most polluting emissions are, therefore, seen as negative externalities.

- Governments can use a range of actions to monitor and regulate the output of pollutants from economic activity: property rights; market solutions; tradeable permits; regulation and legislation.

- Progress at the global level in ecological regulation action is often slow since it operates via a series of International Summit meetings, such as that at Rio in 1992. However, since most serious ecological concerns tend not to be confined within geo-political boundaries, the ability to make progress at this global level is critical to the effective tackling of many ecological problems.

- The viewpoints which organisations can adopt in respect of ecological regulation range from non-compliance and compliance, through to some more proactive stances, and culminate in the use of state-of-the-art processes by what have been called 'leading-edge' organisations.

- The ecological viewpoint adopted by an organisation is likely to be strongly influenced by the nature of its business environment and by its perceptions of the interest and power of stakeholders.

- The extent of individual consumer power in respect of ecological and wider ethical issues is clearly weak. However, there is an increase in single-issue action taken by environmental pressure groups which is capable of having a serious effect on how organisations view their stakeholders.

- Many companies are taking note of wider ethical considerations.

Discussion Questions

1. Find and examine the figures for the sale of ice cream. Do the figures reveal a particular pattern in demand? What are companies such as Häagen-Dazs trying to do to overcome this pattern of demand?

2. Using appropriate published data examine how major car manufacturers are attempting to reduce the environmental impact of the vehicles they produce.

3. Nomille (2003) suggests a number of benefits arising from agriculture. Find examples of such benefits and assess each. Can this idea be translated to wider business activity?

4. Governments may intervene in order to limit externalities. Identify and assess some recent measures that have been proposed.

5. Do you think that the ethical stance adopted by companies such as the Co-op Bank gives them a sustainable competitive advantage?

6. Taylor et al. (1994) identified three types of company: high, moderate and low penetration. Using appropriate sources identify three high penetration companies and comment on their environmental impact. How has their business performance been affected?

Web Links

The web links below provide the most up-to-date sources. Access to any topic should be possible through the links.

http://www.business-humanrights.org/index.html
Business and human rights resources centre. A collaboration between Amnesty International and a number of academic institutions. Many resources available including access to business sectors, countries, regions and key issues.

http://www.earthsummit2002.org/
Earth summit home. Lots of good references with regard to environmental issues.

http://europa.eu.int/comm/environment/
Home of the EU environment site.

http://www.foe.co.uk
Friends of the Earth website, frequently updated with current issues.

http://www.greenbiz.com/
Site which looks at the business end of the debate. Includes a news centre, business toolbox, reference desk and some good links.

http://www.greenpeace.org
Home page of Greenpeace. Includes a whole host of environmental issues and links with other organisations.

http://www.planetark.org
Home of the Reuters World Environment News. Access to Envirosearch, a search engine dedicated to environmental issues. News is current and software is available.

http://www.webdirectory.com/
This an environmental organisations web directory with search facility.

http://www.wri.org/
Home page of the World Resources Institute of New York. WRI is an environmental research and policy organisation. Provides access to sites covering a variety of environmental issues around the globe.

Further Reading

Hutchinson, A. and Hutchinson, S. (1996) *Environmental Business Management: sustainable development in the new millennium*, London: McGraw Hill.
Provides a useful overview, including a look at ethical and political issues. Parts two and three provide good coverage of the internal and external environment and eco-management. The final part looks at the future and sustainability.

Bansal, P. and Howard, E. (eds) (1997) *Business and the Natural Environment*, Oxford: Butterworth Heinemann.
The text is split into four parts and allows the reader to delve deeper into the subject, covering: philosophical and ethical questions; disciplinary perspectives; regulatory frameworks and management approaches.

Markandya, A. and Halsnaes, K. (eds) (2002) *Climate Change and Sustainable Development Prospects for Developing Countries*, London: Earthscan.
The text develops a framework for evaluating the climate change options faced by any developing country. It includes case studies and assesses present evaluation methods, suggesting ways

in which these might be improved, and proposes ways in which social and developmental aspects can be more fully taken into account.

Earthscan publications provide a wide range of texts on the subject. They can be found at http://www.earthscan.co.uk/

References

Ansoff, I. (1984) *Implementing Strategic Management*, Englewood Cliffs, NJ: Prentice Hall.

Argenti, J. (1980) *Practical Corporate Planning*, London: Allen and Unwin.

Azzone, G. and Bertele, U. (1994) 'Exploiting green strategies for competitive advantage', *Long Range Planning*, 27 (6), 64–81.

Boulton, L. (1995) 'Higher carbon tax heats up debate', *Financial Times*, 14 June, p. 20.

Brown, P. (1995) 'Global warming summit at risk', *Guardian*, 25 March.

Cannon, T. (1994) *Corporate Responsibility: A Textbook on Business Ethics, Governance, Environment: Roles and Responsibilities*, London: Pitman.

Carter, F.W. and Turnock, D. (1993) *Environmental Problems in Eastern Europe*, London: Routledge.

Caulker, S. (2003) 'Fair trade & ethical consumer buying advance in UK', *Observer*, 6 April.

Caulkin, S. (1996) 'Tarmac melts under pressure', *Observer*, 26 May.

Charlesworth, K. (1998) *A Green and Pleasant Land*, Institute of Management

Chien, E. (1991) *Working Towards Environmental Quality in the 21st Century*, Environmental Protection Administration, January.

Commission of the European Communities (1994) *Background Report: The European Environment Agency*, ISEC/B6/94, 11 February, CEC, London.

Creyer, E. and Ross, W. (1997) 'The influence of firm behaviour on purchase intention: do consumers really care about business ethics?', *Journal of Consumer Marketing*, 14 (6), November/December.

Croner Guide (1996) *Environment Management*, Croner Publications.

Croner Guide (1998) *Environmental Management*, Croner Publications.

Croner (2003) *Scottish Councils Get £15 Million for Contaminated Land Clean Up*, available from http://www.environment-centre.net/cgi-bin/croner/jsp/ [accessed 20 March 2003].

Elkington, J. and Hailes, J. (1988) *The Green Consumer Guide*, London: Victor Gollancz.

Environmental Industries Commission (1996) *Croner's Environmental Briefing*, 19 March, no. 62.

Europa (2003) Available from http://europa.eu.int/comm/environment/emas/index_en.htm [accessed 14 January 2003].

European Commission (2003a) 'Landfill of Waste', available from http://europa.eu.int/comm/environment/waste/landfill_index.htm [accessed 17 March 2003].

European Commission (2003b) 'Environment 2010: our future, our choice', available from http://europa.eu.int/comm/environment/newprg/index.htm [accessed 18 March 2003].

First & 42nd (2003) 'The ethical consumer', available from http://www.first42.com/html/notconvinced/ethcon.html [accessed 7 April 2003].

Forum for the Future (2003) 'Ethics go mainstream: Social and environmental performance closely linked to good corporate governance, say fund managers', available from http://www.forumforthefuture.org.uk/aboutus/default.asp?pageid=338 [accessed 1 April 2003].

Hamel, G. and Prahalad, C.K. (1994) *Competing for the Future*, Boston: Harvard Business School Press.

Hartman, C.L. and Stafford, E.R. (1997) 'Green alliances: building new business with environmental groups', *Long Range Planning*, 30 (2), 184–96.

Hartshorne, J. (2003) 'UK law and the environment', available from http://www.naturenet.net/law/envlaw1.html [accessed 26 March 2003].

Hutchinson, C. (1996) 'Integrating environmental policy with business strategy', *Long Range Planning*, 29 (1), 11–23.

Jobbins, D. (2003) 'Euro rivals outpace UK in campus growth', *Times Higher Education Supplement*, 7 March.

Keynote (2002) 'Green and ethical consumer market assessment 2002', available from http://researchandmarkets.com/reportinfo.asp?cat_id=169&report_id=3688 [accessed 7 April 2003].

King, W. (1972) 'Example of the demand relation', available from http://william-king.www.drexel.edu/top/prin/txt/SDch/SD6.html [accessed 18 February 2003].

Kleiner, A. (1991) 'What does it mean to be green?', *Harvard Business Review*, July–August.

Lee, N. (1994) 'Environmental policy', in Artis, M. and Lee, N. (eds) *The Economics of the European Union*, Oxford: Oxford University Press.

Lipsey, R.G. and Harbury, C. (1992) *First Principles of Economics*, London: Weidenfeld & Nicolson.

Lopatin, M. (2002) '"Discredited" labels have most to gain from ethics' *Observer*, 8 December.

Moore, M. (2002) *Stupid White Men*, Penguin, London.

Murray, J.A. and Fahy, J. (1994) 'The marketing environment', in Nugent, N. and O'Donnell, R. (eds) *The European Business Environment*, London: Macmillan.

Nomille, M.A. (2003) 'Multifunctionality: options for agricultural reform', available from http://www.ers.usda.gov/publications/aer802/aer802j.pdf [accessed 19 February 2003].

Observer (2002) 'Corporate accountability: Observer Special', *Observer*, 17 November.

Porter, M.E. (1990) 'The competitive advantage of nations', *Harvard Business Review*, March–April.

Radford, T. (1997) 'Glowing, glowing . . . gone?', *Guardian*, 25 November.

Roome, N. (1992) 'Developing environmental management systems', *Business Strategy and the Environment*, Spring, part 1.

Shrivastava, P. (1994) *Strategic Management: Concepts and Practices*, Cincinnati: South-Western.

Shrivastava, P. (1995) 'Environmental technologies and competitive advantage', *Strategic Management Journal*, 16, 183–200.

Slavin, T. (1998) 'Green – or just cabbage looking', *Observer*, 15 November.

Taylor, B., Hutchinson, C., Pollack, S. and Tapper, R. (1994) *The Environmental Management Handbook*, London: Pitman.

Trowell, J. (1998) 'Secondary effects of consumer boycotts', available from http://www.i-way.co.uk/~jtowell/2bcthome.htm#references [accessed 8 April 2003].

Unfccc (2003) Available from http://unfccc.int/resource/guideconvkp-p.pdf [accessed March 18 2003].

Unilever (2003a) Available from http://www.unilever.com/environmentsociety/community/environment/Kenya_Planting_indigenous_trees.asp [accessed 23 February 2003].

Unilever (2003b) Available from http://www.unilever.com/environmentsociety/environmentalperformance/dataindetail/environmentalfines.asp [accessed 26 March 2003].

Welford, R. and Gouldson, A. (1993) *Environmental Management and Business Strategy*, London: Pitman.

World Resources Institute (2003) Available from http://www.wri.org [accessed 10 February 2003].

Zilberman, D. (2002) 'Negative externalities and policy', available from http://are.berkeley.edu/~sadoulet/PP290/2002/handout/negativeexternalities.pdf [accessed 23 January 2003].

7 The International Political Environment

Graham Wilkinson

Learning Outcomes

On completion of this chapter you should be able to:

- understand the rapidly changing nature of the political environment;
- identify political activity at global, regional, national and local levels;
- understand different systems of government and representation;
- recognise different political viewpoints regarding the role of governments;
- outline the role of key European Union institutions;
- appreciate the role of international institutions;
- consider the issues surrounding the political stability of different states;
- recognise the importance of global political threats.

Key Concepts

- sovereignty
- political economy
- levels of government
- democratic and authoritarian government
- international institutions
- regional co-operation and integration

- political risk and stability
- liberalisation

Introduction

The main aim of this chapter is to examine one of the more complex areas of the environment – political institutions and developments. This area is particularly important because the decisions taken and the policies adopted by institutions at a range of geo-political levels (global, regional, national and local) not only affect many other areas of the business environment but also directly impinge on business activity. We distinguish between each level to ensure that readers are aware of the bodies which exist and appreciate the fundamental role of each body within a specific context. However, the processes involved are very complex with decisions and policies at any one level both being affected by and affecting policies and decisions at the other levels. The situation is made yet more complicated by the fact that the different ideas and views held change over time and from place to place, meaning that the resultant policy decisions are also subject to change.

It is necessary to remember that the ideas discussed in this chapter are closely linked with other elements of the business environment. In particular, political matters are set in the context of culture and demography and are the main source of the decisions affecting economic and legal matters. Political changes are likely to create opportunities or present threats to organisations. In this section we consider a number of such changes in different parts of the world, and look, in general terms, at their impact upon business.

The impact of political decisions at different geo-political scales

Decisions which affect business organisations are made at all geo-political levels. For example, competition policy in the United Kingdom (see Chapter 2) is determined by the European Commission and national government but is also monitored by local authorities through trading standards departments – and all this takes place against a background of global trading rules set by the World Trade Organisation. Political decisions at all these levels, such as those on economic policy, social policy, the control of pollution and support for technology (each of which is examined elsewhere in this book) all have an impact on business activities. The business environment is liable to change as a result of radical political shock, gradual shift, or a combination of the two. The Asian economic crisis in 1998 illustrates such a combination (see Case Study 3).

Organisations will perceive political change differently; some may feel threatened, others may see the changes as offering business opportunities. It is evident that decisions and actions made at the higher geo-political scales can have an impact on organisations, both large and small. This is the context of our analysis of the political environment. The analysis will concentrate on four geo-political scales: global, regional, national and local.

Global scale

The changing international scene, with its powerful interests, has an enormous impact on the operating activities of many organisations. The international agenda is increasingly being set by international protocols and transnational bodies. For example, the World Trade Organisation (WTO) agreement on basic telecommunications services came into force on 5 February 1998. The agreement was signed by 69 countries, and covers 90 per cent of the world's $650 billion telecoms services market, with a turnover of around $1 trillion in 2000. The European Union and Japan have agreed to open competition, though some EU countries were allowed a short delay because of domestic political and technological considerations.

The relationship between politics and business organisations is not a 'one-way street'. Business is not so weak that it always has to pander to politicians. Governments are often keen to encourage multinational companies to invest, and offer financial incentives because of the jobs they may provide. Political parties too can benefit from closer alignments with business, especially media organisations. For example, the *Sun* newspaper, owned by News Corporation, switched support to the Labour party in the run-up to the 1997 general election. After coming to power the Prime Minister, Tony Blair, was alleged to have canvassed the Italian Prime Minister, Romano Prodi, on behalf of News Corporation in a proposed takeover of Mediaset, an Italian television network.

National scale

The national level of political decision making, based on the sovereign rights of the independent nation state (see below), has long been regarded as the most significant level of decision making. Laws passed by national parliaments are thought to reflect the particular priorities of the society they represent. Increasingly, however, the closer integration of economies throughout the world means that the balance of power has, to some extent, shifted away from this level of government. Some commentators, for example Ohmae (1995), claim that this increasing globalisation of markets means that 'Nation states are no longer meaningful units in which to think about economic activity. In a borderless world they consign things to the wrong level of aggregation.' Ohmae lists a number of what he calls 'natural economic zones', which do not recognise geographical or political boundaries. These include: northern Italy (as a separate entity from the rest of Italy); Hong Kong and Southern China; and Singapore and its neighbouring Indonesian islands.

Local scale

The lowest of the levels of government with which we are concerned is local government, that is any authority which is subservient to national governments and whose decision-making power derives from the national government. These vary greatly in both size of population and in the powers they possess. For example, the state of California may be regarded as a local government in as much as the state is just one of the 50 states of the USA and Federal law has priority over local decisions, yet the population of California – around 35 million – is greater than that of many sovereign states. Furthermore, there are other levels of government – city and county – below that of the state.

In the UK local government varies widely in different parts of the country and between urban and rural areas. Scotland now has its own parliament and Wales its own Assembly, even though both still send MPs to the UK's national parliament at Westminster. Below the national level, local government is made up of a patchwork of County Councils, District Councils and unitary authorities, usually large cities or conurbations, each with its own powers and policies. A further tier of government, regional assemblies, may be introduced in England. These would give a regional identity and representation to larger areas; the first three proposed assemblies would be for the north-east of England, the north-west of England and Yorkshire. Other areas may follow.

The nation state

As indicated above, the nation state has traditionally been seen as the most important level of government. This belief is based on several characteristics which states in general possess: sovereignty, territoriality, legitimacy and authority. The political systems adopted within each country vary as a result of independent evolution over hundreds of years. It is important to recognise that these national political systems will have an important impact on the operation of business in a given nation state.

In the modern world each nation state (for example the UK, Russia, Brazil, Spain, Kenya, India) has control over affairs within defined boundaries – and no direct control over affairs beyond its borders. The government of each country is free to pass laws that reflect the priorities and beliefs that reflect its particular culture. Although culture may be hard to define (see Chapter 5), there is no doubt that there are different values and beliefs that distinguish one society from another. The shared values and beliefs within nations also allow the coherence of these societies.

It should, however, be noted that such common beliefs and values are not always reflected in the boundaries of any given state – and that those boundaries can and do change over time. For example, Basque people may be regarded as having a distinctive culture – as being a nation – but politically they are in either France or Spain, the nation states which control the territory where the Basque peoples live. Similarly, the Masai in East Africa are split between the modern territories of Kenya and Tanzania.

This disparity between peoples and nations, coupled with a strong desire on the part of many to control their own society, has led to many conflicts and wars in the past – and seems likely to continue to do so in the future. For example, the state of Yugoslavia as created at the end of the second World War has since fractured into five separate, sovereign states: Slovenia, Croatia, Serbia and Montenegro, Bosnia-Herzogovina and Macedonia. These are, to a large extent, based on cultural groupings, in turn based on factors such as language and religion. In Asia, the people of East Timor have recently won independence from Indonesia after a long and bitter struggle. In other areas independence is still being sought by a variety of means, from political campaigning to war and terrorism.

Nevertheless, despite the changes in boundaries and the apparently transient nature of many states, it is still these countries that form the most powerful political entities. International and supranational bodies such as the United Nations and the World Bank are set up by the nation states and, generally, can only be effective in their work with the consent of nation states. At the other end of the scale, local governments within the territory of a sovereign state are subservient to its national government.

The power of national governments to control affairs within their boundaries is, therefore, based on an acceptance by citizens of their right to do so. In other words, governments can only function effectively when their authority is accepted by those they govern. In such instances government may be regarded as legitimate. If this relationship breaks down, for example if an elected government is forced from office by a military coup (as happened, for example, in Chile in 1973 and Pakistan in 1999), the resultant government may be regarded by many as not possessing any legitimacy; others, however, may simply accept – or even support – the change.

Systems of government

It can be seen that the power of governments can be based on a variety of sources and that citizens participate in government to different degrees. In the industrialised countries of the West, the common belief is that democratic states are the best form of government. Although there are many different forms of democracy, the common theme throughout is that government should represent the will of the people. In general, this is taken to mean that elections should be held periodically. In this way voters may express their desire to return the same individuals to office or to elect a different government to represent their interests. The detailed analysis of the variety of voting systems and ways of representation is beyond the scope of this book but some major systems may be identified. As regards voting: in many countries the 'first past the post' system is employed, whereby the candidate with the largest number of votes wins the election, regardless of how large, or small, a percentage of the votes cast has been received. In other countries, there is a requirement that the winner must receive at least 50 per cent of the votes cast. A further variation is that seats in parliament are allocated to parties in the same proportion as votes cast. This has the advantage of accurately reflecting the voters' preferences, but may well mean that the parliament is made up of a large number of small parties with no one party having anything approaching a majority. Even from this short section it can be seen that there are still considerable differences between systems which share democratic governments. The proportional representation system in Italy has, for example, created a much more volatile environment for business than the system in use in the UK. Italy has had a succession of unstable coalition governments for most of the post-1945 period. In the UK, a 'first past the post' system is used to elect 651 members of parliament (MPs) to serve in the House of Commons and has provided a much greater degree of stability. Although the proportional representation model predominates in Europe, 'first past the post' systems apply to 49 per cent of the world's electors (*The Week*, 1998). The Electoral Reform Society in the UK identifies three main types of voting system, each with sub-categories (Electoral Reform Society, 2003). These are shown in Table 7.1.

However, democracy (of whatever sort) is not to be found in many of the world's nation states. Many governments' power and authority are based not on the consent of citizens as expressed through the ballot box, but rather on the power of the military and other forces the government controls. This was, arguably, particularly evident in the then-Communist countries of the Soviet Union and Central Europe until their governments fell, often without much of a struggle, in the years after 1989. Such governments still hold power in many parts of the world, from the Communist dictatorships in North Korea, China and Cuba to the military governments of Pakistan and Burma, the theocratic governments of some Middle-Eastern countries and the (*de facto*) one-party states of Zimbabwe and Libya.

A further difference is to be found in the relationship between central and local governments. In many countries (such as Ireland, Uganda, Jamaica and New Zealand) there is what is known as a unitary system. This means that the central (national) government retains strong decision-making powers for itself and allows only limited freedom of action to local governments. An alternative is the federal system, in which the central authority is relatively weaker, as much power is devolved to a lower level of

Table 7.1 Voting systems

Type of System	Main Characteristic	Variations Used
Single-member systems	One representative is elected for each seat contested	* First past the post * Supplementary vote * Alternative vote
Multi-member systems	Two (or more) representatives elected for each seat contested	* Single transferable vote * Party list systems
Mixed systems	A combination of the two systems above	* Additional member system * Alternative vote plus

Source: adapted from Electoral Reform Society (2003), www.electoral-reform.org.uk

government often known as states. Examples of federal systems include the United States of America, Australia, Germany and India.

The role of government

It should be noted that there is often – but not always – a close link between the amount of political freedom in a country and the amount of economic freedom. And that there are a variety of political views as to how big a role government should play in economic affairs. Mention has already been made of these philosophies in Chapter 1 of this book, when the difference between interventionist and laissez-faire approaches was highlighted.

The laissez faire approach is customarily favoured by democratic governments that allow oppositions to form and campaign. Such governments are usually also in favour of minimal regulation of business and economic activity. For example, the industrialised countries of North America, Western Europe, Japan and Oceania are among the leaders in liberalising their political and economic systems. This does not mean that they have totally abandoned all regulation of business activities – far from it. But it does mean that there is a belief amongst those governments that political and economic freedom go hand-in-hand to bring benefits of increasing affluence via rapid economic growth to their citizens. For international business this usually means that these governments welcome foreign investment and are happy to create a climate in which business is willing to invest. Indeed, many governments offer incentives to foreign businesses, so keen are they to attract the investment to their country, rather than seeing it go to a rival nation.

On the other hand, many governments that seek to limit individuals' freedom of action politically are also interventionist in nature regarding their economies. In both Cuba and China, for example, business activity is subject to considerable regulation and government involvement. However, even in these countries – and many others with totalitarian systems – attitudes to business are changing. Few countries, North Korea is one, now actively discourage foreign investment, even if many governments, particularly in Africa, Asia and Latin America, remain suspicious of the role of multi-nationals and wary of the power they wield. Indeed, even in the industrialised economies, the increasing power of multinational companies to influence policy is being increasingly questioned.

The impact of government: the UK case

Constitutions and the role of the legislative, judicial and administrative functions of government

This section considers the formal basis of democratic systems of government and looks at the legislative (law-making), judicial (law-applying) and executive or administrative functions which play crucial complementary roles within such systems of government.

British parliamentary democracy has been influential as a model of democratic government in, for example, Germany and Malaysia. However, it is ironic that until the passing of the Human Rights Act 1998 the UK was the only Western European country without either a bill of rights or domestic legislation which gives its citizens the ability to seek redress, in its own courts, for breaches of the European Convention on Human Rights. The Act passed into law in late 1998 and came into force in 1999/2000, finally incorporating the European Convention into UK law; the full text of the Act can be found at http://www.hmso.gov.uk/ acts1998/19980042.htm. The Convention includes such human rights as the right to life, freedom from torture and slavery, and freedoms of thought and expression.

The United States of America has a written constitution and a clear 'separation of powers' in that the legislative, judicial and administrative functions are kept distinct. It is often thought that such checks and balances are important for the effective operation of a democracy. One of the hallmarks of a totalitarian regime (an example being Uzbekistan) is thought to be the lack of a clear separation of the judicial function from the legislative and executive functions.

The UK, however, is not completely fussy in ensuring that there is a rigid separation of powers. The Lord Chancellor, for example, is currently a member of all three of the aforementioned groupings: being a member of the Cabinet (the executive), sitting in the House of Lords (the legislature) and being in charge of all the judges (the judiciary). At the time of writing, the government has announced plans to change this by abolishing the post of Lord Chancellor and reforming the legal system to include a US-style Supreme Court. In the UK, the province of each of the three groups is ever-changing. The role of the judiciary, for example, within the constitution has increasingly come to the fore in recent years. The number of applications for 'judicial review' of administrative actions has increased to 4732 in 2001 from 3604 in 1995. Judicial review is the mechanism by which ministers, government departments, local authorities or public bodies exercise discretion or carry out their duties. Nearly half of the cases involve decisions about homelessness taken by local authorities and immigration decisions by the Home Office. Authorities may be challenged for three broad reasons:

- for illegality in carrying out particular statutory and common law powers and duties;

- for unreasonableness in the reasoning on which decisions were made;

- for not following common law principles of fairness in the way a claim was dealt with.

A recent case decided that the government had unlawfully misused £234 million of foreign aid under the Overseas Development and Co-operation Act 1980 by tying it to a construction contract for the Pergau Dam in Malaysia in 1993. A pressure group, the World Development Movement, successfully challenged the then Home Secretary, Douglas Hurd, in the Pergau Dam case (see *R v Secretary of State for Foreign and Commonwealth Affairs, ex parte* World Development Movement [1995] 1 WCR 386). This case gives an indication of the increasing number of pressure groups who might be able to establish an interest in a government executive decision. It is evident that this kind of intervention may have a wide impact on specific organisations and business in general. Following the Pergau Dam affair the Malaysian Prime Minister, Dr Mahathir Mohammed, banned UK companies from bidding for work with the Malaysian government, because of accusations, mainly in the UK press, of bribery of Malaysian officials by UK government and business. This was at a time of enormous spending on infrastructure projects, such as the new Kuala Lumpur International Airport (KLIA).

The increased willingness on the part of the judiciary to review administrative decisions, particularly those made by ministers, indicates that the interrelationships between the legislative, judicial and administrative functions in the UK are in a state of flux. Many would argue that the willingness of judges to develop the law of judicial review compensates for the lack of a written constitution in the UK. It has also been suggested that judges would not have shown such willingness to extend the boundaries of judicial review if Parliament had proved to be a more effective vehicle for keeping the activities of the administrative branch of government in check.

Judges are also seen to be suitable persons to conduct independent reviews such as those relating to standards in public life (the Nolan Committee) and the Dearing inquiry on student and university finance. By the end of 1998 – little more than eighteen months after it had come into office – the Labour government had established over a hundred inquiries, reviews and task forces. The role of judges in the UK has already been enhanced since the aforementioned Human Rights Act came into effect.

The increased centralisation of government in the UK, implied above, has made Parliament somewhat vulnerable to lobbying activity by individual pressure groups. Such was the level of concern in 1994 that the Prime Minister set up a Commission chaired by Lord Nolan which reported on the activities of MPs in July 1995 (see Minicase 7.1). The UK is not the only country where politicians have been brought into disrepute; the situation is not unknown in Europe. In Italy, for example, many politicians, including two former prime ministers (and the current prime minister), have come under scrutiny because of their close links with business and the Mafia. This type of relationship between politicians and businesspeople has been the subject of debate in many countries, not least in Japan, which has seen the resignation of a prime minister because of bribery allegations.

In summary, one of the key features of a democratic system of government is the ability of the judicial, legislative and administrative functions to operate in a reasonably autonomous way so as to be able to provide a system of 'checks and balances'. In the UK we have noted the willingness of judges to develop the concept of judicial review, perhaps to compensate for the lack of a written constitution.

The national scale

In the UK the leader of the largest party after a national (or general) election is, normally, appointed as Prime Minister. The Cabinet makes policy which is debated in the House of Commons and the House of Lords. Changes in policy often require legislation and much of the work of both Houses is in reviewing and debating the contents of new Bills. Policy is implemented administratively by civil servants and quangos. Bills become Acts of Parliament or statutes when given the Royal Assent. Every year a large number of new Acts are added to the statute books.

Minicase 7.2 shows how the actions and attitudes of government (at many scales) and society can impact on a particular sector.

Other legislation is also of key significance to organisations and consumers. The annual budget often has an impact on specific interest groups. After the 2003 UK Budget

Minicase 7.1   Standards in public life

The Nolan inquiry into standards in public life was set up in October 1994 following a wave of allegations about the behaviour of Members of Parliament. The inquiry comprised a permanent standing committee. In respect of the conduct of MPs the inquiry took evidence from a range of groups including ministers, public servants, experts, academics and pressure groups. The committee recommended that

- a Parliamentary Commissioner for Standards should be appointed to investigate complaints, complemented by a disciplinary panel of MPs whose hearings would be in public;

- MPs should not work for lobbying firms and must disclose details of any other parliamentary services performed;

- the long-established Register of Members' Interests should be made clearer and updated electronically;

- both MPs and ministers should be given new Codes of Conduct. Ex-ministers should wait three months before taking a job outside Parliament and all appointments should be vetted by the committee which currently deals with such matters for civil servants. Where there appeared to be a conflict of interest a delay of up to two years could be advised;

- a new Public Appointments Commissioner should be appointed to oversee the fairness of appointments to quangos.

In November 1995 MPs voted to

- appoint a Parliamentary Commissioner for Standards;

- ban paid advocacy by all MPs, including the tabling of questions, motions and amendments to legislation, and restrict the right of MPs to speak in debates on behalf of outside paid interests;

- require MPs to disclose their earnings from consultancy work arising from their parliamentary role and to register details of all contracts with the parliamentary commissioner from March 1996;

- approve a code of conduct.

Other important topics that the committee reported on include public appointments, national and local quangos and local government.

In November 1997 Lord Nolan was replaced by Sir Patrick Neill. The Committee's report was published in October 1998 and featured 100 recommendations, including those on

- the disclosure of large political donations;

- the amounts which should be spent at elections;

- strict rules requiring government neutrality in referendum campaigns.

These proposals were felt to be necessary to build public confidence in the system and reduce the feeling that political influence could be bought. The government has expressed its intention to legislate in line with the broad thrust of the proposals – but progress in many areas has been slow.

Questions

1. Do you believe that the reforms introduced as a result of the Nolan committee's report have been sufficient to restore the UK public's faith in the integrity of the national political system?

2. What further changes may be necessary to ensure that the UK government is both free from corruption and seen to be free from corruption?

the price of cigarettes was increased by a further 8p on a packet of twenty; this brought the retail price to around £4.60, of which some 80 per cent is tax. This change and further legislation at the European level (see below) mean that the Tobacco Manufacturers Association and their member companies had grounds for concern. Specific legislation, such as the National Minimum Wage Act 1998, established a legislative framework for the national minimum wage. Regulations arising from the Act are likely to have a significant impact on many organisations.

The local scale

In the UK, as in many other countries, local authorities are run by elected councillors, whose powers are laid down by parliament. They provide services and have regulatory responsibilities. Local government in the UK has traditionally been organised into a series of tiers such as County and District Councils. A Local Government Commission was set up in 1992 to investigate the structure of local government. Since then it has created a substantial number of new 'unitary' (single-level) authorities, for example by merging the responsibilities of former County and Borough Councils. Such changes may simplify the dealings of many organisations with local government, as there will only be one body with which to deal in a unitary authority. In the long term, efficiency gains may result in

Minicase 7.2   Advertising and the law

Advertising is a business activity that has a wide impact and requires a framework in which to operate to ensure an acceptable standard of behaviour. This framework may be self-regulatory or provided by statute.

The law impacts on advertising in a number of ways. The first statute passed in the UK to protect consumers from unethical advertising was the Advertisement Act (1889); now over a hundred statutes affect advertising. In June 1996, The Body Shop were cited by the Metropolitan Police for illegal flyposting under the Town and Country Planning Act 1990 and the London Local Authority Act of 1996 (Lee, 1996).

Legal and regulatory bodies have been established to monitor and control the activities of advertisers. In the UK these include the Advertising Standards Authority (ASA), the Independent Television Commission (ITC) and the Radio Authority (RA). In France it is the BVP, Commission for the Control of Advertising. Transnational bodies such as the European Advertising Standards Alliance (EASA) also have a role to play.

The ASA was established in 1963. Its role is to ensure that everyone who commissions, prepares and publishes advertisements in the non-broadcast media within the UK observes the British Codes of Advertising and Sales Promotion. The ASA codes state that advertisements should be 'legal, decent, honest and truthful, socially responsible and prepared in line with the principles of fair competition' (ASA, 1998a). In 1997 the ASA found that 98 per cent of poster advertisements, 96 per cent of press adverts and 85 per cent of direct mail advertisements complied with the code (ASA, 1998a).

If an advertisement breaks the rules, the ASA will ask the advertiser to withdraw the advertisement. Companies whose advertisements have provoked public complaints include Peugeot, Lee Apparel and Gossard (Boshoff, 1998). Benetton are (in)famous for their global advertising campaigns, which began in 1984. Their 1991 advertisement of a man, David Kirby, dying of AIDS was banned in the UK, and the BVP in France asked the media not to use it. As a result it was only published in the magazine *Max*. Virgin have also come under the regulatory spotlight. Virgin Interactive Entertainment (Europe) Ltd produced a poster for a Sony computer game 'Resident Evil', showing a bath full of blood. The ASA decided that the advertisement should only be allowed in adult magazines. In 1998 the ASA banned three advertisements produced for Virgin Cola Company Ltd (ASA, 1998b).

The Radio Authority came into being in January 1991 following the Broadcasting Act 1990. It is the responsibility of the authority to monitor the obligations of its licensees, all commercial radio stations, as required by the Broadcasting Acts of

1990 and 1996. One of these is to regulate programming and advertising. The ITC, established at the same time, undertakes the same task for commercial television.

There is also much reliance on self-regulation. The Committee of Advertising Practice (CAP), comprising twenty trade and professional associations representing all sectors of the advertising and media industries, gives direction and guidance to advertisers through regularly updated codes of practice. The EASA was cofounded by the ASA in 1991 and achieved legal status in January 1994. It is an alliance of 23 European self-regulatory bodies and has three principal aims:

- to promote and support self-regulation in Europe;

- to co-ordinate and administer the cross-border complaints system;

- to provide information and research on the self-regulation of advertising in Europe.

Questions

1. Investigate two recent decisions by the ASA as a result of complaints from the public. Do you agreee with their decisions?

2. Should the ASA be replaced by a statutory (government-appointed) body?

a lower business rate. The UK government also introduced a Local Government Bill in late 1998 which allows cities to elect executive mayors. It aims to reform local government and encourage greater participation in it. Despite some high-profile figures emerging from this process – most notably Ken Livingstone's election as the Mayor of London – the initiative has not, as yet, been greeted with great enthusiasm in many parts of the country.

It is paradoxical that many organisations, for example grant-maintained schools, NHS Trusts and civil service agencies, are managed at the lowest local level but funded and controlled at the highest, that is by central government (in these cases by the Department for Education and Skills, the Department of Health and Her Majesty's Treasury respectively). This is also the case for local authorities. The government controls what each local authority can spend; see Minicase 7.3.

Local authorities can, however, raise further funds by borrowing for major capital investment schemes. Despite recent moves towards devolution of power, some disquiet has been raised regarding the trend towards centralisation by the UK government and the use of non-elected bodies to administer policy. It is argued that excessive centralisation has resulted in many local initiatives being stifled. Some feel that the fact that quangos now do much of the work previously carried out by local councils has raised a serious question about democratic accountability. Members of quangos do not need to seek election, or re-election, as local councillors do.

Minicase 7.3   Northamptonshire County Council

Northamptonshire County Council's (NCC's) planned spending for 2003/04 was increased by 12.4 per cent from the previous year to a total of £552.4 million. The funds are raised via:

- Business Rates. These are charged on all non-domestic properties. An assessment is made by the national government and a uniform charge applied to all businesses. The charge for 2003/04 is 44.4p in the £ (rateable value), giving NCC an income of £169 million from this source.

- Revenue Support Grant. The amount received from this general grant is the amount that the government estimates that each authority needs to spend to provide a standard level of service. The amount is based on the Standard Spending Assessment (SSA) and is worth £211.4 million to NCC in 2003/04. Together the business rate and the revenue support grant fund approximately 69 per cent of the budget.

- Other smaller grants are received, but can only be used for specific purposes.

- The Council Tax provides the balance of funding. This is levied on every household. The amount collected in Northamptonshire in 2003/04 is around £169 million.

- Taken together, these sources of revenue provide NCC with the total funding needed to finance its £550 million spending.

Questions

1. Should local councils have more control over the revenue they raise, rather than being so dependent on central government?

2. What percentage of the electorate vote in local elections? Suggest ways in which this figure could be increased.

Changing attitudes to the role of government

As we have seen above, different individuals and indeed different cultures (see Chapter 5) have different attitudes to the role of government in controlling a country's affairs, in particular, how its economy is owned, controlled and regulated. What is notable over the last quarter of a century is how attitudes have changed within various countries and how this change is spreading around the world. In particular there has been a general move away from an interventionist approach towards laissez-faire, away from state planning and ownership of enterprises to the free market. This is reflected in the privatisation of many former state-owned enterprises and an increasing welcome for foreign investment. However, in most cases, despite these global pressures, nation states still possess considerable autonomy and the capacity to 'do things differently'. For example, the extent of government intervention in the economy varies enormously between countries.

This is not to say that the state no longer has an important role to play. The importance of government through public spending on infrastructure, such as roads, railways, educational establishments (such as schools and universities) and hospitals is still very significant. In countries throughout the world this sort of public expenditure supports a significant amount of economic activity. In Europe the EU is seeking to secure equality of treatment and opportunity for organisations bidding for public works contracts. European Commission public works directives require that all public contracts of more than €200 000 should be advertised in the *Official Journal of the European Communities*. The Commission is eager to ensure that companies from all member states have the same prospect of winning a contract as those from the home country. However, the vast majority of public procurement in the EU is awarded to companies from the home country.

Cuts in government expenditure are likely to have a significant adverse impact on businesses that supply those sectors. Increased private sector investment in projects may partially offset the loss of public works. More recently, projects in the UK such as the Birmingham northern relief road and the new Severn road bridge have been financed by the private sector.

Not all companies have to be limited by national boundaries and, therefore, by individual government decisions. When one government makes a decision to cut expenditure it is important for companies to look elsewhere for business. Key projects such as the construction of the new airport in Hong Kong or infrastructure building in Europe provided opportunities for companies from many countries to bid for business and gain valuable contracts. The international nature of the market has never been more evident, and nor has the need for effective monitoring of the wider environment. The changing attitudes in the UK are examined in more detail below.

The monetarist approach in the UK

The 1979 general election proved to be a significant political milestone, as the new government moved to a more free-market approach that was said to involve much less government 'interference' in running the economy. In other words, the interventionist approach that had characterised government policy since 1945 was replaced by a more liberal agenda.

The new government turned away from traditional economic thinking, based on the Keynesian approach, to controlling the economy by adopting a 'monetarist' philosophy. The Keynesian approach rests on the assumption that the economy is inherently unstable and in need of active government intervention, largely through fiscal policy (see Chapter 3), to control demand in the economy. It is believed that the level of activity in the economy can be controlled, business cycles smoothed out, peaks and troughs eliminated and unemployment limited. However, this orthodox Keynesian model was latterly unable to deliver a strong economy. The 1970s had seen increasingly high levels of unemployment and inflation which could not be explained by Keynesian theory or solved using traditional demand management policies. Keynesian theory was open to criticism, especially by the monetarists. The monetarist approach, in contrast, regards the economy as inherently stable and suggests that fiscal policy has no role in regulating the economy. In fact monetarists argue that fiscal policy can actually exacerbate instability and business downswings. Monetarists argue that changing tax rates and government spending has no beneficial effect on the business cycle and that policy should be targeted at the supply side of the economy. Minicase 7.4 takes a closer look at supply-side economic measures and how they may impact on organisations.

While we may support or oppose political decisions, depending on our political leaning, some important changes affecting managers and consumers have been made in the years since 1979. These will have a lasting effect on business. The change of emphasis and thinking in the 'corridors of power' has had some influence on the values and assumptions held by managers. In turn, this has affected the way managers consider customers, employees and other groups with an interest in their organisation (the stakeholders). In essence, the role of government intervention in the economy has been reduced and the importance of self-reliance emphasised.

The collapse of Communism

The collapse of Communist systems in the former Soviet Union and throughout Europe, the establishment of fledgling market economies and the opening of Communist China are bringing problems to some organisations and offering opportunities to others. The European Union itself seems to be undergoing an eastward shift as relations between Central and Eastern European countries have progressed significantly since the introduction of political and market reforms. The European Union is politically committed to enlargement, to embrace ten new members by 2004. These include: Estonia, Latvia and Lithuania (all formerly part of the Soviet Union); Poland, the Czech Republic, Slovakia, Hungary and Slovenia (all formerly Communist states); Malta; and Cyprus. If all goes according to plan and all these countries do join the EU, it will bring the total EU membership to some 25 states with a total population of 450 million, making it the largest single trading bloc in the world, ahead of NAFTA, the North American Free Trade Area.

Minicase 7.4   Supply-side measures

The goal of supply-side policy is to remove barriers which prevent or deter organisations and individuals from adapting quickly to changing demand and changes in production and, therefore, to increase efficiency and promote economic growth and employment. Conservative governments, from 1979, introduced a number of measures aimed at improving the supply side and giving organisations flexibility.

Taxation

Prime Minister Thatcher suggested that 'if people find too big a chunk of their pay taken away in tax they won't work so hard'. Measures have been introduced to ensure that people were better off in work: direct taxes such as income tax have been reduced, to be replaced by indirect taxes such as VAT; thresholds above which people start paying tax have been raised; and unemployment benefit is now taxed. Companies, particularly small and medium-sized enterprises, have also benefited from reductions in, for example, corporation tax.

The labour market

The government have introduced a number of training schemes designed to promote work skills, an example being the Youth Training Scheme. Whether these schemes have been successful is open to debate. Certainly the UK is still some way behind competitor nations such as Germany in the provision of quality training. Other measures have attempted to safeguard the interests of individuals in the workplace and to restrict trade unions. These measures aim to create a more flexible labour market and reduce unemployment.

Deregulation

Deregulation is the process of dismantling regulations governing the activities of business organisations. Deregulation has opened many other markets to greater competition and aims to make consumers better off by increasing competition. For example, the telecommunications sector was opened up to competition so that Mercury Communications could use BT's cable infrastructure to carry calls. Other sectors that were deregulated include road haulage, national buses and the capital market.

The capital market and financial sector

This is the market to which companies and the government turn when they need medium- and long-term funds. A whole range of controls have been abolished in the capital market. Foreign exchange controls were abolished in 1979; hire purchase controls in 1982; deregulation, the 'Big Bang', increased competition in the stock market in 1986, especially from foreign securities houses; the Financial Services Act 1986 and the Building Societies Act 1986 allowed non-banking financial institutions to provide services previously closed to them. These changes are seen as a way of encouraging competition and, therefore, improving the efficiency and competitiveness of UK businesses.

Privatisation

Privatisation usually implies the transfer of assets from the public to the private sector. The aims of privatisation are to introduce competition into previously monopoly-controlled public sectors and increase efficiency; to increase the extent of share ownership and to reduce government borrowing by raising revenue.

Questions

1. Do you think that the privatisation of the UK railway network has improved the quality of service to the public and/or made the industry more efficient?

2. How has the pattern of taxation in the UK changed over the past twenty years? How has this affected the relative incomes of rich and poor in society?

Over the last decade, many of the former Communist states have presented enormous opportunities to business. In particular, following the reunification of Germany in 1990, the former East Germany has succeeded in attracting substantial funds as it continues to rebuild its crumbling infrastructure. In 1991, Volkswagen secured a 70 per cent share of Skoda in the Czech Republic (then Czechoslovakia) for £480 million. In the following eight years Volkswagen ploughed in excess of £5 billion into the company. They have succeeded in turning a brand that was often derided as cheap and poor quality into one that now occupies a favourable position in the market, with strong consumer backing and sales growth. German companies have provided a substantial proportion, around 50 per cent, of foreign direct investment into the Czech Republic in the 1990s.

Foreign companies are being allowed access to China, particularly in the special economic zones such as Shenzhen. The reduced labour costs enjoyed by the incoming multinational corporations (MNCs) have enabled them to become more competitive on a world scale. However, other competitors outside of China and the other Newly Industrialising Countries (NICs) have found themselves unable to compete with the cost advantages enjoyed by these companies. This has led to redundancies or even complete closure of factories. The British shoe industry, which is still relatively labour dependent, has suffered because of cheaper Chinese competition.

Beyond the nation state

As we have stated earlier, the international political environment operates at a variety of levels; having examined national and local levels, we now turn our attention to the level above the nation state. There are many institutions that have been set up with some political power over sovereign, independent nation states, particularly since the end of the Second World War. Most of these bodies, if not all, require the states that are participating in them to give up some of their independent, sovereign rights, often by signing a treaty. This is a document which binds two or more countries to do something together, that is, a collection of commitments which are negotiated, agreed upon and signed. Treaties do not come into effect, however, until the governments concerned have ratified them, in other words, until each nation state has agreed to give up some of the sovereign rights it has in favour of closer co-operation. Only once the treaty is ratified will it be implemented. These institutions can be usefully split into two types: international (or global) institutions and regional co-operation agreements.

International institutions

The United Nations

The most well known of the international institutions is the United Nations. This body officially came into existence on 24 October 1945. Its purposes, as set out in its Charter, are 'to maintain international peace and security; to develop friendly relations among nations; to cooperate in solving international economic, social, cultural and humanitarian problems and in promoting respect for human rights and fundamental freedoms; and to be a centre for harmonizing the actions of nations in attaining these ends' (www.un.org). There are six major bodies that are the core of the organisation. These are the:

- General Assembly;
- Security Council;
- Economic and Social Council;
- Secretariat;
- Trusteeship Council; and
- International Court of Justice.

However, it should be noted that there are many more programmes, agencies and bodies which are part of the UN's overall presence and activities. These include such well-known institutions as UNICEF (the UN Children's Fund) and the UN Development Programme (UNDP), as well as many less high-profile organisations.

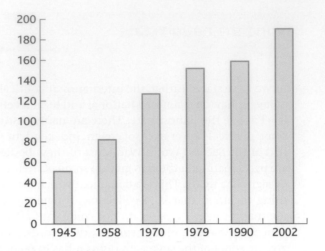

Figure 7.1 Membership of the United Nations, selected years (the figure shows the number of countries that were UN members at the end of each of the years)
Source: adapted from United Nations (2003), www.un.org/overview/growth.htm

The original UN Charter was signed by 51 nations. Many more states have joined over the years and the number has also fluctuated as the identity of member states has changed (see Figure 7.1). For example, both the former German Democratic Republic (communist East Germany) and the Federal Republic of Germany (capitalist West Germany) were admitted as separate members in 1973; the two states were reunified (as the Federal Republic of Germany) in 1990 and thus became a single member of the UN. Conversely, the splitting of the former Yugoslavia into five separate states has caused an increase in the number of members. By 2002 the total number of states in UN membership had become 191, with the admittance of East Timor, following its independence from Indonesia, and Switzerland, after that country decided to end a long period of non-involvement with international organisations.

As can be seen from the outline of its charter, above, the UN has a wide-ranging mandate to involve itself in many aspects of global life. The main, original, purpose was the promotion of world peace by providing a forum in which disputes between the governments of sovereign states could be settled by discussion rather than resorting to military means. In addition, if military intervention is thought to be necessary, the UN has powers to send in peace-keeping forces. It does not have its own troops, relying instead on member countries volunteering forces for specific instances of duty.

The main forum for discussion is the General Assembly (in which all 191 member states are represented) and the Security Council, both based at the UN buildings in New York City. The Council has five permanent members – the United States of America, the United Kingdom, France, the Russian Federation and China – with another ten seats being occupied by other members periodically. The five permanent members of the Security Council wield the most power, partly because of historical accident (they were the countries that were victorious at the end of the Second World War and the first five states to possess nuclear weapons) and partly because they each possess the power to veto resolutions that would otherwise be passed by either the General Assembly or the Security Council. This means that they are in a position to exert greater influence on the UN's policies and priorities than any of the other members and means that they play a vital role in all decisions, but especially those that are controversial in some sense.

It is relatively rare for the UN to play a direct role in influencing the business environment. Its influence is usually felt indirectly in influencing the actions of governments of member states, whose legislatures may, in turn, affect business more directly. However, there have been some instances where the UN itself has played a major role in influencing, if not determining, the political environment in which business operates. For example, the UN General Assembly has agreed on various occasions that sanctions should be imposed to prevent (or discourage) business from investing in and/or trading with particular countries. This was the case for Vietnam for some years after the end of the US/Vietnam war in the 1970s and for South Africa, whilst that country was controlled by the whites-only government during the apartheid years that ended with Nelson Mandela's election as President in 1994.

The most recent example of this can be seen in the build-up to the war in Iraq in early 2003. Following the first Gulf War, in which Iraqi forces were compelled to relinquish their occupation of Kuwait, the UN had become increasingly concerned about the nature of the Iraqi regime under Saddam Hussein and the possibility that it was developing what became known as 'weapons of mass destruction' (chemical, biological or nuclear) and the missile technology to deliver them over great distances. The General Assembly and the Security Council of the UN had passed a series of resolutions concerning Iraq since the early 1990s, mostly concerned with applying trade sanctions unless the country co-operated fully with weapons inspection teams appointed by the UN. President Saddam did co-operate, to some extent, for some years but not after 1998. The heightened tensions in the year after the events of 11 September 2001 caused many countries, especially the USA under President George W. Bush and the UK led by Prime Minister Tony Blair, to become increasingly concerned that Saddam's regime was developing weapons in defiance of UN resolutions. The Security Council unanimously passed a further resolution in the autumn of 2002, requiring Iraq to co-operate fully with UN inspection teams and threatening, unspecified, further action if it did not. As 2002 turned into 2003, the USA and UK continued to build up their military forces in the vicinity of Iraq in anticipation of war. At the same time, attempts were made to secure a further UN resolution that would specifically authorise the use of military force. However, when it became clear that various countries, including China, Russia and France, would not support such a resolution – indeed, France said it would use its veto – the UN found itself sidelined as the US and British forces attacked Iraq without specific UN authority, but with the support of what was termed a 'coalition of the willing'.

These events may come to be seen as a significant turning point in the history of the United Nations. The US (and the UK) have argued that for the UN to be effective it must be able and willing to back up its resolutions with actions and that by failing to do so in the Iraqi case it has lost much of its authority and power in the world of the early twenty-first century. Critics of the US and UK stance, on the other hand, argue that it is the actions of those two countries that are *causing* the UN to become sidelined and ineffective. They say that when it became clear to the US and UK that their argument would not be accepted by the rest of the Security Council, those two governments simply did what they wanted to do. Critics, therefore, are convinced that this unilateral action by the US and UK creates a dangerous precedent whereby countries may feel that they can act without the authority of the UN. It is apparent that the disagreements caused by these events linger on after the end of the war in Iraq, even though all the governments concerned are attempting to rebuild their relations in the post-war period – and all are still involved in the workings of the United Nations. It remains to be seen how long it will take to rebuild a successful working relationship. At a more populist level, one side-effect of the war was a call for Americans to boycott French products in protest at the French government's opposition to American actions. In some areas, French Fries were even renamed 'Freedom Fries' as part of the protest.

The Bretton Woods institutions

A further important influence on international politics – and economics – is provided by the trio of institutions originally proposed just before the end of the Second World War at a conference held in the mountain resort of Bretton Woods in New Hampshire in the USA. The motivation of the participants was to set up a system of regulation of world trade, exchange rates and international flows of capital. This was based on the belief that the isolationism and retreat from open trading that had occurred in the 1930s had not improved living standards for citizens in countries where there was depressed economic activity but had, in fact, worsened the situation. To avoid such disastrous political and economic decisions being taken again, three new bodies were proposed. These were the International Monetary Fund (IMF), the International Bank for Reconstruction and Development (IBRD), and the International Trade Organisation (ITO).

In the course of the negotiations and the subsequent ratification of the treaties it became evident that several countries harboured reservations about signing over powers that they held as sovereign states to these institutions. Although the treaties regarding the IMF and the IBRD – now known as the World Bank – were ratified and those institutions came into being, there were more problems regarding trade. In particular the USA did not ratify the treaty setting up the International Trade Organisation, fearing that there would be too great a loss of sovereignty and too little control over its own economy if it were to sign. As a result, the ITO was replaced by a different sort of body, the General Agreement on Tariffs and Trade (the GATT). This was a looser collection of states, in which all decisions had to be taken by agreement of all the members via a complex series of negotiations. The IMF and World Bank, in contrast, had their own powers assigned to them, meaning that they were able to adapt policies and take actions without continually having to get the agreement of all their members for each decision.

As globalisation and technology have progressed and political thinking has changed, so too has the role and impact of these organisations. The GATT negotiated itself out of existence in a lengthy series of meetings, known as the Uruguay Round, that lasted from 1986 to 1993. It was replaced by the World Trade Organisation (WTO), a body much more akin to the ITO originally proposed at Bretton Woods. Meanwhile the World Bank and the IMF continue to play a major role in regulating the world economy, in particular having a major impact on the processes of development in Asia, Africa and Latin America (see Case Study 7).

However, it is important to realise that economic decisions are also political decisions in many ways. For example, one of the functions of the IMF is to lend money to countries suffering from international debt problems, to enable them to pay for essential imports, to spend on development projects (such as schooling or health care) or to pay back some of the debt. However, over the years, the IMF has developed economic policies that reflect a liberal political agenda. Before lending money to countries, it requires a process of structural adjustment to take place. This usually involves reducing government spending, particularly on subsidies so that prices more closely reflect market prices, the privatisation of state-owned businesses, encouraging inward investment by foreign multinational companies and reducing regulations on business. All these do have an economic effect – but all are also political in nature, reflecting the views of politically liberal/conservative economists who favour free-market approaches to government intervention. This approach has also become known as the 'Washington Consensus', partly because it represents the general policy approach of successive US administrations (regardless of whether they have been run by the Democratic or Republican party) and partly because the IMF headquarters and World Bank headquarters are in adjacent buildings in Washington DC. Although detailed analysis of the impact of these institutions is beyond the scope of this book (see, for example, Stiglitz, 2002; Todaro and Smith, 2003; and World Bank, 2003), there have been many criticisms of the way policies have been devised and implemented. The impact of IMF/World Bank policies is examined more closely in Case Study 7.

Regional co-operation agreements

In addition to the United Nations and the Bretton Woods institutions, there are many other international bodies and systems that have been agreed by various governments around the world. One development that is becoming increasingly important is the growing tendency of countries to engage in closer co-operation at a regional level. Although this progressive integration is important economically (see Chapter 3) it is also important politically. Although there is no real economic reason for co-operating countries to be geographically close to each other, the vast majority of co-operation agreements are based on regional trading blocs. Probably the best known of these is the European Union (discussed below); other examples include:

- ASEAN, the Association of South-East Asian Nations whose members are Brunei Darussalam, Cambodia, Indonesia, Laos, Malaysia, Myanmar, Philippines, Thailand, Singapore and Vietnam;

- Caricom, the Caribbean Community, made up of twelve island nations and three on the mainland, namely Antigua and Barbuda, the Bahamas, Barbados, Belize, Dominica, Grenada, Guyana, Haiti, Jamaica, Montserrat, St Lucia, Suriname, St Kitts and Nevis, St Vincent and the Grenadines, and Trinidad and Tobago;

- Mercosur in Latin America, consisting of Brazil, Argentina, Paraguay and Uruguay;

- NAFTA, the North American Free Trade Area, including Canada, the USA and Mexico; and

- SADC, the Southern African Development Community, whose members include Angola, Botswana, Democratic Republic of Congo, Lesotho, Malawi, Mauritius, Mozambique, Namibia, Seychelles, South Africa, Swaziland, Tanzania, Zambia and Zimbabwe.

There are also many other groupings of states co-operating in various ways, some of which overlap with each other either in function and/or in membership. It should be noted that all these agreements are very different from each other and involve very different levels of political co-operation and integration. At the simplest level there are the free trade agreements like NAFTA, whose members are solely interested in the increased wealth generated by the increased efficiency that can result from reducing or eliminating trade restrictions. At the other extreme, we have the European Union, whose members are committed to growing political, as well as economic, integration.

The European Union

The origins of the European Union can be traced back to the Treaty of Paris in 1951, which established the European Coal and Steel Community (ECSC). There were six signatories to the treaty: Belgium, the Federal Republic of Germany (West Germany), France, Italy, Luxembourg and the Netherlands. The aim of the Treaty of Paris was to establish a unified market in those two commodities, within which all the countries could prosper from reduced barriers to trade. An important benefit, which should certainly not be overlooked, is that the establishment of the ECSC also had political effects, binding former wartime enemies more closely together.

Six years later, in 1957, the Treaty of Rome was signed by the same six countries. This created the European Economic Community (EEC) and the European Atomic Energy Community (Euratom). The Treaty extended economic ties by creating a customs union and common market. These three communities came together to establish the European Community (EC) in 1965. The first enlargement was in 1973 when Denmark, Ireland and the UK became members. Greece joined in 1981, followed in 1986 by Portugal and Spain. Further developments took place with the creation of the European Economic Area in May 1992 – the world's biggest free trade area. Austria, Finland, Norway, Iceland and Sweden joined the European Community twelve and established an integrated economic entity with a population of 372 million and enormous opportunities for trade and commerce. In 1995 Austria, Finland and Sweden became full members of the European Union; Iceland and Norway remained outside, preferring economic co-operation only to the increasingly political nature of the EU.

The Community has evolved largely through amendments to the original treaties, notably via the Single European Act (SEA) 1987, the Treaty of European Union (TEU) 1992, more commonly known as the Maastricht Treaty, and the Treaty of Amsterdam in 1997. Most recently the Treaty of Nice, paving the way for further enlargement of the EU by countries from the former Soviet bloc and the Mediterranean, came into force on 1 February 2003.

The SEA 1987 changed decision-making procedures within the Community. Prior to its adoption, decisions had to be agreed by a unanimous vote; this condition was replaced by the ability to adopt decisions subject to qualified majority voting, clearing the way for speedier decision making within the community. The Treat of Nice has extended this process to more areas and has also redesigned the rules relating to exactly how the 'Qualified Majority Voting' procedures will operate in the future. This is to take account of the fact that as the number of member states continues to increase (from the original six to a likely total of 25 in 2004 and even more later), the decision-making processes of the Union must be simplified and streamlined to avoid the entire system becoming paralysed in bureaucratic arguments.

The SEA 1987 also required that the Single European Market (SEM) should be in place by the end of 1992. Its objectives were to improve the environment for business by providing for the free movement of labour, capital, goods and services within the Community and to facilitate closer co-operation between countries on a range of other matters (see Table 7.2). It was anticipated that the benefits would include increased growth, higher employment, lower prices and wider choice for consumers. The most important non-tariff barriers that existed before the SEM are shown below. It is notable that there is a wide variation in both the types of barriers adopted by the various governments and their relative importance from country to country; in the table barriers are ranked from 1 (most important) to 8 (least important). The adoption of the SEM not only led to increased competition within the European Union, but also enhanced the ability of European business to compete in world markets by increasing the efficiency of EU-based businesses.

Table 7.2 The most important barriers to intra-EU trade before the SEM

Barriers	West Germany	France	Italy	UK	Euro 12
National standards and regulations	1	1	4	1	2
Government procurement	8	7–8	2	4	8
Administrative	2	2	1	2	1
Physical frontier delays and costs	4	4	3	3	3
Differences in Value Added Tax	5–6	3	7	8	6–7
Regulations on freight transport	5–6	5	8	5	6–7
Restrictions in capital market	7	7–8	5	7	5
Community law	3	6	6	6	4

Note: range of ranks 1 (most important) to 8 (least important)
Source: adapted from Paolo Cechini, The European Challenge, *Wildwood House, 1988*

The SEA 1987 represented an important supply-side initiative. Following the creation of the SEM it was envisaged that businesses would have unrestricted access to the European market and face lower costs and gain economies of scale. The UK industries that gained from the SEM include airlines, telecommunications and pharmaceuticals. However, a more open market also brings with it increased competition.

When the TEU 1992 came into force on 1 November 1993 the European Union came into being. The European Union comprises the European Community, a Common Foreign and Security Policy, and a common approach to Justice and Home Affairs: the so-called three-pillar structure (Thomson, 1995). The TEU 1992 was the focus for much internal disagreement in both the Conservative and Labour parties in the United Kingdom, and debate in Denmark and France where it was only ratified following referenda. Perhaps the most contentious issue in the TEU 1992, as far as the UK and Danish governments were concerned, was the Social Chapter, which included minimum requirements on:

- health and safety;

- consultation between management and employees;

- working conditions and the working week;

- equality between men and women regarding job opportunities and treatment at work.

The idea of applying regulations to the labour market was totally contrary to the supply-side approach that the government had adopted since 1979 (see above). The Conservative government felt that the costs to business would result in substantial job losses. By opting out of this part of the Treaty the government hoped that the low-cost environment it created within the EU would prove attractive to inward investment. As a result of the opposition by the UK government the Social Chapter was only included as a protocol annexed to the Treaty. The Treaty was ratified by the UK Parliament in 1993, though the UK (and Denmark) secured an opt-out clause on significant parts of the treaty, such as the section on Economic and Monetary Union that has led to the adoption of the euro in place of national currencies by twelve of the EU's current member states.

An agreement was made to revise the TEU 1992 around the middle of the decade, hence Article N was included in the treaty, providing for a conference to be convened in 1996. The inter-governmental conference lasted more than a year and came to an end in Amsterdam with the political agreement on the new treaty. The Treaty of Amsterdam has four main objectives:

1. To place employment and citizens' rights at the heart of the Union.

2. To sweep away the last remaining obstacles to freedom of movement and to strengthen security.

3. To give Europe a stronger voice in world affairs.

4. To make the Union's institutional structure more efficient with a view to enlarging the Union.

The changing nature of the EU is evident from these objectives. Remember that the original treaty dealt solely with trade in coal and steel; now the organisation is concerned with political, legal and social matters as well as economic. This process continues with the Nice Treaty, which came into effect early in 2003. As well as changing the areas and rules relating to qualified majority voting, as noted earlier, this treaty also changes and streamlines the political processes of the EU. The number of seats that each state has in the Parliament has been reduced, so as to allow for members from the new entrants to take their place without unduly increasing the size – and cost – of the institution. However, the number of parliamentary seats held by each state will still be proportional to its population as a percentage of the total EU population. In addition, there will be a restriction on the total number of commissioners, meaning that larger states will lose their current automatic right to have two individuals serving on the Commission at any given time. Finally the powers of the EU president are somewhat enhanced, though the position is still to be filled on a rotating basis, by each country in turn, for a six-month period.

This process now seems likely to be taken a stage further with the report of the Convention chaired by former French president Valery Giscard d'Estaing. This was set up to investigate and propose changes to three areas of activity in the EU, in the process producing what many, including those writing the report of the Convention themselves, regard as a draft European Union constitution. The highlights of the document are shown in Minicase 7.5.

The future development of the European Union will require further agreement – either on the lines suggested above and/or in other ways, so that more treaties are inevitable.

The powers, roles and, to some extent, conduct of the European institutions are set by the treaties. We will now examine their roles as they are currently specified.

The European institutions

The European Union has created a number of key supranational bodies. All the bodies of the European Union, particularly the four main ones, discussed in more detail below, have the power to influence the day-to-day activities of all European and other business organisations. The four most important such bodies (discussed below) are:

- the European Commission;
- the Council of Ministers (the Council of European Union);
- the European Court of Justice; and
- the European Parliament.

Readers should be aware that many more bodies, each with a specific role, do exist. Many of these are less well known, but still play an important role in the political and economic life of the EU. Examples of these include:

- the European Investment Bank;
- the Economic and Social Committee;

| Minicase 7.5 | The draft constitution of the European Union |

The Convention was asked to draw up proposals on three subjects: how to bring citizens closer to the European design and European Institutions; how to organise politics and the European political area in an enlarged Union; and how to develop the Union into a stabilising factor and a model in the new world order.

The Convention has identified responses to the questions [. . .]:

* it proposes a better division of Union and Member state competences;

* it recommends a merger of the Treaties and the attribution of legal personality to the Union;

* it establishes a simplification of the Union's instruments of action;

* it proposes measures to increase the democracy, transparency and efficiency of the European Union, by developing the contribution of national Parliaments to the legitimacy of the European design, by simplifying the decision-making processes, and by making the functioning of the European Institutions more transparent and comprehensible;

* it establishes the necessary measures to improve the structure and enhance the role of each of the Union's three instutions, taking account, in particular, of the consequences of enlargement.

. . . The Convention's proceedings ultimately led to the drawing up of a draft Constitution for Europe, which achieved a broad consensus at the plenary session on 13 June 2003. That is the text which it is our privilege to present today, 20 June 2003, to the European Council meeting in Thessaloniki, on behalf of the European Convention, in the hope that it will constitute the foundation of a future Treaty establishing the European Constitution.

[Signed]
Valery Giscard d'Estaing, President de la Convention
Giuliano Amato, Vice President
Jean-Luc Dehaene, Vice President

The above is an extract from the report of the European Convention designed to simplify and speed up decision making; the full text is available from www.european-convention.en.int/docs/Treaty/cv00820.en03.pdf.

- the European Training Foundation;
- the Agency for Health and Safety at Work;
- the Committee of the Regions;
- the European Environment Agency;
- the European Monetary Institute; and
- the Court of Auditors.

The inter-governmental conference (IGC) is another important EU forum. It is necessary for an IGC to prepare the ground for a new European treaty.

The European Commission

The Commission is headed by the Commission President and includes twenty members (commissioners), approved by the European Parliament and appointed by national governments to a specific portfolio for a period of five years (renewable). The Brussels based Commission is the civil service of the European Union. The Commission's role as the 'guardian of the treaties' is:

- to mediate between governments to secure agreement on legislation;
- to manage the technical details and day-to-day policing of agreed policy, for example the Common Fisheries Policy, and ensuring compliance by governments, companies and individuals;
- to represent the European Union in negotiations, for instance within the World Trade Organization (WTO), and to defend collective interests.

For administrative purposes the Commission is divided into four main branches. One of these deals with policy issues and is subdivided into various sections such as those dealing with agriculture, competition, energy and transport, and justice. The External Relations branch of the Commission is involved with such matters as development and trade. The other two branches of the Commission are providers of services.

One is concerned with services of a general nature (such as statistics and publications that are available to all), whilst the other deals with internal matters such as auditing and legal issues. Regarding policy, the Commission carries out preliminary research and makes proposals for directives and regulations in consultation with the Council of Ministers and the Parliament. It is, therefore, clear that the Commission is at the heart of decision making in the European Union. At the beginning of 1999 the Commission came under scrutiny because of allegations of corruption; tighter controls are now being introduced. New legislation must take account of three basic principles:

1. Subsidiarity: action at a European Union level must not be proposed if action can be more effectively carried out at the level of national governments.

2. Proposals have to be in the interests of the European Union as a whole.

3. The Commission has to consult widely before making a legislative proposal.

The Council of Ministers

The Council of Ministers is the main decision-making body of the European Union. It makes the final decision on adopting proposals from the Commission. Each Council meeting is attended by the national minister responsible for that particular subject (e.g. economics and finance, transport, agriculture). Much of the work of the Council is undertaken by the Committee of Permanent Representatives (COREPER) which screens proposals before passing them on to the Council. The presidency of the council is held by each member country in turn and lasts for six months. It is the role of the president to chair the meeting of the Council. The Council takes some decisions by a unanimous vote. However, more decisions are now being taken by qualified majority voting (QMV) following the provisions laid down in the SEA 1987 and the TEU 1992. As well as significantly increasing the speed of decision making in the Council, QMV also means that, because member states have lost their right to veto, the risk of unfavourable policy outcomes for business is increased. This has forced organisations to develop proactive and individual European lobbying strategies. The decision to ban tobacco advertising in December 1997 was approved by fifteen to eleven which is the narrowest margin acceptable under the QMV rules. The ban came into force on 14 February 2003, with cinema, hoarding and newspaper advertising being outlawed. The Council of Ministers should not be confused with the European Council, which meets twice a year. This is a forum for the heads of government of member countries which is important in the strategic development of the European Union; its proposals are passed on to the Council of Ministers for transposition into law.

The European Court of Justice

The European Court of Justice (ECJ), based in Luxembourg, is concerned with the application and interpretation of EU law. It follows directives and regulations and through its judgments ensures the compliance of member states. It interprets legislation and European treaties. The ECJ consists of sixteen judges (one from each member state), one nominee and six advocates-general. Cases can be brought to the court by individuals, companies, and governments as well as by the Commission. Member states are bound by the Court's rulings. It is likely that organisations and individuals will increasingly feel the effects of the judgments of the Court. A subsidiary court, the Court of First Instance, was established by the SEA 1987 to deal with certain cases, particularly those brought by companies.

The European Parliament

Since 1979, the European Parliament has been directly elected by member states on a five-year mandate. It is located in Strasbourg where it meets for twelve week-long sessions each year and Brussels where additional plenary sessions are held. Following the 1995 enlargement of the European Union the number of MEPs rose from 567 to 626, with 87 from the UK. The powers of the Parliament have gradually been extended, principally by the SEA 1987 and the TEU 1992, to amend and adopt legislation so that Parliament and the Council now share power of decision in a large number of areas. It retains control over the EU budget and must ratify proposals made by the Commission and the Council of Ministers. It has the power to amend or reject legislation and dismiss the Commission.

Political risk and international business

Political stability, corruption and terrorism

As we have seen elsewhere in this chapter, there are a great number of influences on the political process and many different forms of government. What is most important from a business perspective is, arguably, the degree of risk that organisations may face when undertaking investment, particularly, but not exclusively, in countries that are not their home.

Risk is difficult to define precisely. It includes the policies and attitudes of national governments and local authorities to business investment. This may be in the form of tangible factors, such as legislation that governs working hours, wage rates, health and safety conditions, trade union representation, the repatriation of profits from investments abroad and so on. Or it may be less tangible: does government welcome foreign investment? Or is its attitude hostile and unwelcoming? It must be remembered that firms, especially when investing internationally, are faced with choices, particularly the choice of where to invest. Firms have limited resources – they cannot do everything, sell or produce everywhere, that they may like to. What influences the decision? The answer is a combination of many factors, not least of which is one of desire and preferences as expressed by different stakeholders within the organisation.

One factor that is undoubtedly important for all organisations, however, is certainty. In other words, the fewer unknowns with which a firm is faced, the better. Firms like stability. It can certainly be argued that business does not care if a government is democratic or totalitarian, if it is liberal or communist, if it is legitimate or not. As long as the government is stable – and investment, therefore, safe – most businesses are happy. It is for this reason that many firms continued to invest in South Africa during the time of apartheid, the white minority rule period that ended with the election of Nelson Mandela as President in 1994. Similarly, the widespread reports of human rights abuses by the Chinese government have not stopped firms from taking advantage of that country's welcoming attitude to foreign investment in recent years. Indeed, the liberalisation of the Chinese economy (if not its political system) has been one of the major developments in the international business environment over the last ten years.

At a national level, one of the major deterrents to business investment is the level of corruption in an economy. That is not to say that the simple existence of corruption will, in itself, deter firms from investing. But it does make a location both more expensive and less stable – and therefore less attractive compared to possible alternatives. Transparency International, an independent agency based in Berlin, conducts annual surveys of perceptions of corruption, producing an index based on a variety of other surveys. This ranks 102 of the world's countries (they regard the data on the remaining countries as insufficiently reliable to be used) on a scale of ten (totally free from corruption) to zero (totally corrupt). Table 7.3 shows the results of the 2002 survey for a selection of countries; for the complete results and a full explanation of the methodology used visit www.transparency.org.

On a global scale, recent years have seen the emergence of a further destabilising influence, the increasing risk from terrorist activity. Since the al-Qaeda attacks on New York City's World Trade Center and the Pentagon outside Washington DC on 11 September 2001, the worldwide climate has undoubtedly changed. The USA, in particular, with its declared 'War on Terror' sees itself as both the main victim of such attacks and also as the main defender of the 'free world' against the terrorists. It should be remembered, however, that terrorism is not a new threat, even if the scale of the September 11th attacks was unprecedented. Many people and businesses in many countries have suffered from terrorist attacks for many years. Since 2001, attacks have taken place notably on the Indonesian island of Bali, in Saudi Arabia, Moscow and in Morocco, all resulting in a heavy loss of life. It is clear that the combined effect of terrorist attacks and the US response (especially given the lack of UN involvement, see above) is to make the world a more dangerous place. Whilst it would be facile to suggest that business is the major loser in these developments, it is nevertheless important to note that business does play a major role in society in countries around the world – and that terrorism (or the potential threat of terrorism) is one major determinant of investment decisions by multinational companies. In turn, those investment decisions help to shape not only production patterns, but also the distribution of jobs, incomes, consumption and standards of living. For example, many of the world's airlines have seen a sharp downturn in passenger numbers as a result of terrorist activity and various other external threats such as the SARS epidemic. This change in the public's desire to travel has an impact not just on the airlines, but also on the

Table 7.3 Corruption index 2002, selected countries

Rank	Country	CPI 2002 Score	Rank	Country	CPI 2002 Score
1	Finland	9.7	45	Brazil	4.0
2	Denmark	9.5		Bulgaria	4.0
	New Zealand	9.5		Jamaica	4.0
				Peru	4.0
5	Singapore	9.3		Poland	4.0
7	Canada	9.0	50	Ghana	3.9
10	United Kingdom	8.7	59	China	3.5
14	Hong Kong	8.2	68	Malawi	2.9
				Uzbekistan	2.9
16	USA	7.7	70	Argentina	2.8
17	Chile	7.5	71	Côte d'Ivoire	2.7
18	Germany	7.3		India	2.7
	Israel	7.3		Russia	2.7
				Tanzania	2.7
20	Japan	7.1			
	Spain	7.1	77	Pakistan	2.6
25	France	6.3	85	Georgia	2.4
	Portugal	6.3		Ukraine	2.4
				Vietnam	2.4
27	Slovenia	6.0			
28	Namibia	5.7	88	Kazakhstan	2.3
31	Italy	5.2	96	Indonesia	1.9
				Kenya	1.9
33	Hungary	4.9			
	Malaysia	4.9	101	Nigeria	1.6
	Trinidad & Tobago	4.9	102	Bangladesh	1.2

Source: adapted from Transparency International (2003), www.transparency.org

economies and living standards of the many countries whose tourist income has
dropped as a result.

Other sources of risk

Less dramatically, perhaps, organisations have to concern themselves with a variety of
other possible sources of risk. Countries, particularly developing ones, may be attractive
because they are potential sources of important natural resources and lower labour costs.

It is, however, also important to assess the stability of the political, financial, social and cultural systems when evaluating a potential investment in any given country. If companies export, or have production facilities outside their home bases, action by foreign governments may present both opportunities and threats.

Historically, the most important threat has usually been seen as that of nationalisation, that is the takeover of a firm's assets by the government. In some cases, for example when the UK Labour government nationalised the coal and transport industries in the late 1940s, compensation is paid to the organisations or individuals that had owned the assets before they were taken into state control. In other instances, for example, after the Cuban revolution in 1959, assets may be simply seized by the state leaving their former owners out of pocket. Although the risk of nationalisation is nowadays perceived to be small, it is one that cannot be ignored, as can be seen from the Russian example, in Minicase 7.6. In recent years the power of the Communists in the Russian parliament has waned, but companies are still fearful that the tide may turn again in the future.

In other instances, governments may freeze assets, curtail overseas sales contracts or impose exchange controls which can reduce the amount of money organisations can draw out of profit-making overseas subsidiaries. The last of these is a possible

| Minicase 7.6 | The Russian predicament |

The economic and political unrest in Russia following the devaluation of the rouble and the collapse of the Russian stock market in 1998 resulted in a considerable undermining of confidence in the Russian economy. The outcome of this was a rise in the popularity of the Communist party. The party, under the leadership of Gennardy Zyuganov, was the largest in the Duma (the Russian parliament). The Communist party pointed to serious consequences following the collapse, including hyper-inflation, mass unemployment and economic collapse. Possible solutions, under a Communist leadership, and proposed by Zyuganov, included nationalisation of private businesses. A policy of this nature is likely to have serious ramifications for both home-based and foreign-owned businesses.

Questions

1. How could companies reduce the threat of nationalisation?

2. Should the Russian government pay more attention to the demands of the Communists and modify its policies to take some account of their concerns?

response to a downturn in the domestic economy as happened, for example, as a part of the economic crisis which impacted on much of South-East Asia in the late 1990s. In June 1998 Japan, for example, announced that it was in recession and, with unemployment rising fast, the Prime Minister was replaced. The situation in Japan reflected the economic slump across Asia. Thailand went into recession in 1997. Malaysia's deputy prime minister was sacked and in September 1998 strict foreign exchange controls were introduced in an attempt to restore confidence in the economy and to prevent money leaving the country. In Indonesia the recession caused full-scale riots; President Suharto was deposed as unemployment rose. South Korea was also in recession and even Hong Kong, a few months after its return to Chinese sovereignty, experienced a contraction in the first quarter of 1998 (see also Case Study 3).

A further example of changes that may have a major impact is the raising or lowering of tariff barriers, making an organisation's product or service more or less competitive in a foreign market. For example, restrictions on the import of Japanese cars into the EU were largely lifted in 2000. As we have seen above in relation to the EU (see Table 7.2), there are a wide variety of other types of import barriers available to governments, including, for example, quotas (which limit the number of goods entering a market) and the imposition of technical requirements – for example, that a product must be of a particular standard or that it must not contain certain substances. Vehicle exhaust emission standards in the United States are such a case. These standards have placed an added cost on manufacturers exporting to the American market.

In other instances political decisions have forced companies to miss potential investment opportunities. American companies were left behind in the early rush to invest in Vietnam because of the trade embargo dating from the end of the Vietnam War in 1975. Companies from Singapore, Taiwan, Japan, France and Australia, in particular, took advantage. In the six years prior to American participation investment totalled in excess of £5 billion. It was only in February 1994 that the embargo was lifted and American companies were given the green light to enter a potentially fast-growing market.

Conversely, and much more commonly in recent years, the privatisation of former nationalised industries may present opportunities for investment and trade. This phenomenon began in the UK in the 1980s under the government of Margaret Thatcher when many state-owned industries were sold to private sector investors. This action was based on the ideological belief that greater business efficiency and, thus, a better service for customers can be gained from placing organisations in a competitive environment rather than their being a state monopoly provider. This change in political thinking, from interventionist to free-market, is now being followed in many economies around the world, including much of Africa, Asia and Latin America, and is opening up opportunities that were previously not available. For example, the Ghanaian government has recently privatised much of the country's water supply and the Brazilian government is encouraging foreign investment as part of a programme to extend and modernise the telecommunications infrastructure of that country.

Similarly, a change of policy by domestic governments can mean that opportunities that were previously not available to foreign firms may suddenly present themselves.

Although the specific conditions that attract investment will vary from firm to firm and decision to decision, the attitude of governments is a major factor in determining the level of inward investment. In Asia, the Indian government, after decades of being suspicious of foreign investment, has, since the early 1990s, been much more welcoming. This has resulted in many foreign companies taking advantage of the highly educated but relatively low-cost Indian workforce to establish themselves on the sub-continent. Many of the investments have been in manufacturing (for example, Suzuki has a major stake in the Indian car manufacturer Maruti). However, the major growth in recent years has been in the service sector as Western companies have taken advantage of the changes in technology to locate data processing facilities and call centres in India. This means that, for example, dialling a local number in the UK to enquire about an insurance claim or quote may result in your call being handled by an Indian call centre in Chennai or Delhi – without the UK consumer even realising that this is the case.

We must not forget that foreign investment has increasingly become a two-way flow, with companies based in Newly Industrialising Countries investing in production facilities in the Triad of North America, Western Europe and Japan, plus Australia and New Zealand. Certainly, before the recession of the late 1990s in Asia, the creation of new jobs in Europe, and particularly the UK, by Japanese, Taiwanese and Korean multinationals had led European governments to provide significant grants in many cases and to reduce obstacles to such investments by, for example, relaxing planning regulations. However, in 1998 Fujitsu announced the closure of its D-Ram microchip plant in Durham. This followed the closure of a similar Siemens plant on Tyneside and the abandonment of Hyundai's new plant in Scotland and that of LG in Wales. Job losses were substantial. This is another reminder, if one were needed, that the pattern of foreign investment is continually changing in response to changes in the political and other environments.

Even non-commercial organisations are increasingly having to operate against a background of changing political and economic issues. Although it has to be admitted that many firms do not greatly concern themselves with many of the issues that exercise various pressure groups, such as Oxfam and Greenpeace, these charities, and others, do work internationally and campaign to have an impact on political decisions at many levels. In the past they have run successful campaigns, targeting particular companies or governments. For example, Greenpeace successfully campaigned against Shell's decision to sink a redundant oil platform – the Brent Spar – at the end of its working life, by organising consumer boycotts of Shell's products. Nestlé, too has been the target of a campaign based on its selling of powdered baby milk in developing economies where clean water is in short supply. Oxfam is perhaps, *inter alia*, more concerned with lobbying governments and attempting to get them to legislate to improve living standards, by exposing what it sees as corrupt practices such as low minimum wages or long hours in 'sweat shops' producing goods for the multinationals. Mary Cherry, Oxfam's chair in 1993/4, has suggested that 'the constant challenge facing a charity was to change to meet the needs of the times and yet to retain our core values undiminished'. Charities, like all the other political actors, need to be aware of the constantly evolving environment.

Conclusion

Change and stability, liberalisation and privatisation

It is evident that organisations around the world are having to cope with rapid changes in the political (and other) environments that help shape their activities. It is only some fifteen years or so ago that the rival political philosophies of capitalism and communism, represented respectively by the USA and the Soviet Union, were dominating the global political environment in the so-called Cold War. This meant that hegemony, or influence, was split between these two superpowers. All that changed, amazingly rapidly, at the start of the 1990s, with the collapse of communism and the break-up of the Soviet Union, leaving the USA dominant as the world's only true superpower; hegemony had become unipolar. This change has been accompanied by many others, as can be seen elsewhere in this book. In the political sphere, the stability (albeit often tense stability) of the Cold War years has been replaced by a much more volatile situation. Political philosophy has changed from frequently interventionist to being more laissez-faire in virtually every country around the globe. This increasing liberalisation has had profound consequences for business. On the one hand, it means that new opportunities for expansion into new markets or new locations for production have arisen. On the other hand, as firms have scrambled to take advantage of these opportunities, the level of competition has undoubtedly increased.

Furthermore, it is notable that the role of governments and politics has changed. This is partly because of the changing attitudes already mentioned. But it is also to do with the actions that have resulted. Many governments have – and are still – privatising many formerly state-owned enterprises, thus providing yet more opportunity for private capital. The role of government, then, is changing from one of owning assets to one of regulating how those assets are used. Alongside this change in thinking, there have been changes in institutional arrangements, with the power of national governments arguably decreasing as the international institutions (such as the IMF, the World Bank and the WTO), together with the increasing importance of regional co-operation (most notably the European Union), have become increasingly involved at political and other levels.

Organisations are increasingly operating in a diverse range of countries. As we have seen, a large variety of factors are relevant when making decisions about the countries in which to locate any business activity. Many of these are specific to the company involved, as they assess their environment in the light of their stakeholders' aims and objectives. Clearly, for multinationals in particular, an awareness of political issues and tensions within all the countries in which a firm operates – or is considering operating – is of crucial importance. Such organisations will, therefore, want to ensure that appropriate staff have a good general idea of the multiplicity of factors that need to be taken into account in investment decisions, including people skilled in assessing the political risks involved in different countries or regions.

At the global scale a large range of interactions takes place, involving such groupings as supranational bodies, governments, multinational companies and international pressure groups. The activities of these groups will often result in new law or policy being formulated, which will have implications for organisations. Some of the political pressures which manifest themselves at the national and local scale will have their origins at this global scale. Clearly, therefore, it is important for managers in organisations to understand the levels (global, regional, national and local) at which different political decisions are taken in order that lobbying can be carried out effectively.

Taken together, all these changes mean that the environment in which organisations operate has become much more demanding, much more volatile – but, potentially, much more rewarding.

Summary of main points

This chapter has examined a range of political issues important to the context of the book as a whole. The main points made are that:

- Political change can occur at all levels which we have identified: global/regional, national and local.

- At the global scale there is a huge diversity of interactions which will cascade downwards to the lower geo-political levels and affect the activities of all organisations to a greater or lesser extent.

- There needs to be awareness by organisations which wish to compete across a range of countries that the interests of those countries may, on occasions, conflict with their own goals. As a result they must be prepared to respond flexibly when local political factors demand.

- Organisations can, and do, take action to influence political decisions at all political levels, for example by lobbying. In this way they can seek to neutralise political threats posed by political change or enhance their business opportunities.

- For any firms active in the EU, the roles of key European Union institutions need to be understood in order that organisations can understand the implications of developments at this level.

- In the UK the relationship between the judicial, legislative and administrative functions is in a state of flux. Here it is important for citizens and organisations to be aware of the possibility of bringing a claim for judicial review of certain administrative decisions.

- It is important to recognise corruption impacts on business in many countries and industry sectors.

- One of the key areas of concern for the future is the growth in international terrorism.

Discussion Questions

1. As some countries join together in supra-national organisations like the EU and others fragment into smaller units, how important is the nation state in the twenty-first century?

2. Does a laissez-faire (free market) approach to politics and economics necessarily bring benefits to all the citizens of a country?

3. Identify an issue and an interested lobby group (e.g. the Tobacco Manufacturers Association and the ban on tobacco advertising) and investigate how that group has used its influence on governments.

4. Research the impact of the IMF's policies on three developing countries. Compare and contrast the results of those policies.

5. When investing into foreign countries, should businesses be concerned about the social policies of the host government or merely its stability?

Web Links

http://www.un.org
This is the official homepage of the United Nations. It provides access to the full text of many archived documents as well as providing links to the sites covering the work of the UN's various agencies and departments.

The Bretton Woods institutions
The three organisations each have their own website. Although much of the information can be complex and technical in nature, there are also more accessible commentaries on the work of the organisations and many potentially useful statistics. The websites for the three organisations are:

International Monetary Fund: **http://www.imf.org**

World Bank Group: **http://www.worldbank.org**

World Trade Organisation: **http://www.wto.org**

http://europa.eu.int
This is the European Union's official website. As with the UN and the Bretton Woods institutions, it provides access to a large mass of information, some of which is, again, complex and/or technical. Nevertheless it is a useful source of information on many aspects of the EU, such as: historical development; institutions; policies; documents; political agenda; publications; news; governments online (which gives web addresses

for member states); updates on issues relevant to the EU; and a search engine to help you find specific EU-related information.

You should also be aware that the other regional institutions mentioned in the chapter also have a great deal of information available online. For example, the Southern African Development Community website can be found at http://www.sadc.int, whilst that for ASEAN is at http://aseansec.org (not at http://www.asean.com, which is a shopping site!).

http://www.open.gov.uk

This site is run by the Office of the e-envoy, part of the UK government's Cabinet Office. It aims both to promote Internet access in the UK and to provide links to government departments and local authority websites. As such it is a good starting point when searching for information and statistics relating to policies and priorities at various levels of UK government.

Media sites

The websites of many magazines, journals, newspapers and broadcasters provide valuable sources of information on many developments in the global political economy. However, it is important for you to remember that (virtually) all publications are not neutral in their approach. Although data may well be reported factually, articles will be based on the particular perspective of the publication concerned.

To see articles framed in a way that is generally supportive of a free-market, laissez-faire approach to economics and politics visit *The Economist*, a journal published weekly in the UK, at http://economist.com. For a different perspective on world events, one that is largely critical of current economic polices and political trends, see *The New Internationalist* (published monthly in the UK) at http://www.newint.org.

The broadcast media sites can be particularly valuable as a source of up-to-date news on political and economic events. Also, their archive material of stories from the (recent) past is often a major source of information and data. The BBC site is particularly useful; it can be found at http://news.bbc.co.uk.

Further Reading

Kegley, C.W. and Wittkopf, E.R. (2001) *World Politics: Trends and Transformations*, 8th edn, Boston, MA: Bedford St Martins.
This is a comprehensive look at world politics, political systems, priorities and problems, from a US viewpoint.
Todaro, M.P. and Smith, S.C. (2003) *Economic Development*, 8th edn, Harlow: Addison-Wesley.
A long-established book surveying global issues with an emphasis on a Developing World perspective. Some sections are rather heavy on economic theory for non-economists, but there is still much of value and interest to be found.
World Bank (2003) *World Development Report 2003*, New York, NY: Oxford University Press/The World Bank.

This is the latest edition of the World Bank's annual publication relating to global development trends and priorities. Each year's edition focuses on a different theme.

Stiglitz, J. (2002) *Globalization and its Discontents*, London, Allen Lane.

This book, written by a former chief economist at the World Bank, gives a devastating critique of the effects of many of the Bretton Woods institutions' policies in both economic and political terms.

References

ASA (1998a) http://www.asa.org.uk.

ASA (1998b) *ASA Monthly Report*, 14 (3), March.

Boshoff, A. (1998) 'Advert complaints show a shocking decline', *Daily Telegraph*, 31 March.

Cechini, P. (1988) *The European Challenge*, Wildwood House.

Electoral Reform Society (2003) http://www.electoral-reform.org.uk.

European Convention (2003) http://www.european-convention.en.int/docs/Treaty/cv00820.en03.pdf.

Lee, J. (1996) 'Body Shop faces fine over illegal posters', *Marketing*, 6, June.

Ohmae, K. (1995) 'Putting global logic first', *Harvard Business Review*, January–February.

Stiglitz, J. (2002) *Globalization and its Discontents*, London: Allen Lane.

Thomson, I. (1995) Editorial, *European Information Association*, January, pp. 5–20.

Todaro, M.P. and Smith, S.C. (2003) *Economic Development*, 8th edn, Harlow: Addison-Wesley.

Transparency International (2003) http://www.transparency.org.

United Nations, The (2003) http://www.un.org.

The Week (1998) 'Is Blair cool on electoral reform?', *The Week*, p. 9.

World Bank (2003) *World Development Report 2003*, New York, NY: Oxford University Press/The World Bank.

8

The Legal Environment

Rob McCusker

Learning Outcomes

On completion of this chapter you should be able to:

- understand the rationale for having a legal system and understand the key types of law within that system;

- be aware of the sources of law for England and Wales and the sources of European law;

- appreciate the importance of laws that directly affect business;

- understand the creation, application and role of ethical codes in underpinning the legal environment in which businesses operate;

- appreciate the role of ethical codes in dictating how multinational enterprises operate in the globalised economy;

- understand the impact of globalisation in creating danger within Internet companies and appreciate how that danger needs to be addressed.

Key Concepts

- sources of law
- consumer law
- codes of conduct
- stakeholder theory and business ethics
- multinational enterprises
- whistle-blowing
- e-commerce and Internet security

Introduction

This chapter will examine the purpose of law and will outline the sources of law in England and Wales and the European Union. It will then consider briefly the key parts of consumer law that businesses routinely need to consider in their everyday business dealings. The legal environment is concerned increasingly with the socially responsible behaviour of businesses as well as with its legal behaviour. The chapter will therefore consider codes of conduct in terms of their creation, value and enforcement.

Laws are incredibly difficult to create and enforce at the national, never mind the international, level. Businesses are being encouraged, therefore, to recognise and respond positively to the interests of the various stakeholders with whom they come into contact, often on a daily basis. Therefore, this chapter also considers stakeholder theory. Businesses who should be most conscious of ethical conduct and stakeholder interests are multinational enterprises (MNEs). We will consider, therefore, their impact upon and responsibilities to less developed economies in particular. Businesses who truly abide by their socially responsible principles should be affected by whistle-blowing employees, since in the majority of cases the employee is acting in the short- and long-term best interests of the business and all of its stakeholders. This chapter will consider the role and legitimacy of the whistleblower. Finally, we will examine the dangers posed by criminals to businesses and therefore to businesses' customers, suppliers and other stakeholders, in terms of the increased reliance placed by businesses upon computer systems during the rapid growth in globalisation.

The legal environment

Businesses are responsible for more deaths, injuries and cost the taxpayer more money in terms of damage and losses caused than all traditional crime put together. More than ever, businesses need to be aware that they operate, or should operate, within an environment in which abiding by the law is ever more important.

However, the legal environment is not concerned simply with the law itself in terms, for example, of Acts of Parliament, of cases, of rules or of regulations (of which the vast majority of businesses are aware) but also with the overall context in which businesses operate. This context is becoming increasingly international in scope and furthermore it is becoming based more and more in the globalised Internet economy of e-commerce.

Businesses are required to obey the law because failure to do so will have consequences, for example, for themselves, their customers, their workforce and their competitors. Serious breaches may also affect the economy or perception of the economy in which they operate. In the world of e-commerce, which is less well regulated, the potential for breaches is heightened.

In the Internet-driven economy the emphasis will be placed as much upon socially responsible behaviour as lawful behaviour. Companies will be required to think of their stakeholders more deeply, of their ethical behaviour in relation to less developed economies and of the potential dangers that lie within cyberspace. Although they might not seem business related, the events of September 11th indicate to government experts that the future targets of terrorists will probably be the computer networks upon which all major and minor businesses increasingly rely for their everyday operations and profitability. This fact alone gives us reason to ensure that businesses operate in strict accordance of the rules of law and codes of ethics that govern society.

The need for law and morality

The desire for a legal framework in general is self-evident. When a man lives alone on a desert island he is free to do whatever he wishes. There is no one upon whom he can have an effect. As soon as another person arrives on that island, however, both people are deemed to have certain rights and responsibilities. Laws are a finely tuned version of the same principle. The law consists of a body of rules imposed upon and enforced among members of society.

Laws can be viewed as a sort of contract. We each agree to obey the law (our part of the contract) and in return the government, via the police, the courts and the prisons, agree to protect us (their part of the contract). Clearly, anyone who disobeys the law breaches the contract and can therefore be tried or sued on our behalf by the government.

Law can be divided in a number of basic ways. The main division is between national law (sometimes called municipal law) and international law. National law is further subdivided into public and private law. Public law regulates the relationship between the public and the state and private law regulates the relationship between members of the public. So, for example, an example of public law would be Constitutional law which covers the relationship between the public and the government. An example of private law would be the law of tort which covers issues such as negligence. Thus, if I drive my car into the back of another car the law would hold me liable for the other car driver's injuries.

International law is further subdivided into private and public categories. Private international law (also known as the conflict of laws) is concerned with establishing which national law is to be used in a case which has an international element, for example a trade agreement between a company in the UK and another in the USA. Public international law is concerned with establishing the rules to be followed in our relationship with another state.

Two further subdivisions of law are substantive and procedural law. Substantive law is the name given to the rules of law, for example an assault occasioning actual bodily harm is a statutory offence under section 47 of the Offences Against the Person Act 1861.

Procedural law is the name given to the rules governing how laws are to be implemented, for example a legal action in relation to the assault mentioned above would begin with an arrest, then proceed to a prosecution.

It is important that both the law and the methods by which the law is enforced are clear. Only if each is certain can punishment take place. Punishment, in theory at least, is based upon four main concepts. The first is deterrence. Here, courts sentence the culprit in order to deter him/her from re-offending. If the aim of the sentence is to deter the culprit it is said to be specific deterrence. If it is to deter others it is said to be general deterrence. It is fairly widely accepted that deterrence does not really work effectively in preventing re-offending. The second principle of punishment is known as retribution. This is often misinterpreted as revenge. Retribution refers to the act of paying society back for a wrongdoing by, for example, serving a jail sentence, paying a fine, etc. The third principle is rehabilitation. This involves imposing a sentence that will allow the culprit to reform and learn from their experience. Finally, there is protection. This is where a sentence is imposed purely to protect society from the culprit.

Of equal importance to society, and in the context of this chapter, to businesses, is morality. Morality forms the basis of much of the law that we have today although many of us would not necessarily recognise the connection. Whereas laws are formal rules which are enforced by the state (via, for example, the police, the courts and the prisons) morals are informal rules which are enforced by members of society. Some behaviour is deemed to be a purely legal infraction. So, driving at 35 mph in a 30 mph zone is against the law but few people would be morally outraged at the driver. Some behaviour is deemed to be a purely moral infraction. So, committing adultery breaks no laws but is regarded by some as a moral breach. Some behaviour can be both a moral and legal infraction. Murder, for example, breaches both (see Minicase 8.1).

Minicase 8.1

A sailor is clinging to a piece of wood following the sinking of a passenger boat that he had been working on. As a passenger tries to grab hold of the wood the sailor pushes him away and the passenger drowns.

Questions

1. Do you believe that the sailor has broken any provisions of law or morality?

2. Would your answer be any different if the sailor had pulled the passenger from the piece of wood in order to save his own life?

The law has long debated whether, and if so to what extent, morality should be actively involved in the law. This has largely been concerned with perceived moral issues such as fox-hunting, homosexuality or abortion. However, supporters and opponents alike of morality's involvement with the law ignore certain problems. Many commentators who argue for an active involvement of morality with the law suppose that we all agree on what is moral and immoral and that our opinions never change over a period of time. Clearly, society changes and as it does so does opinion on moral issues. Forty or so years ago, both abortion and homosexuality were illegal in the UK. Today, they are not. Commentators who argue for a freedom of choice in terms of our moral behaviour, however, assume that everyone in society has the same mental capacity to make informed decisions about their behaviour. Clearly, children cannot know the dangers of certain activity which is why they are protected. Similarly, people who are mentally incapacitated may also be unable to reach an informed consent about their own or others' behaviour.

In the context of business behaviour, the word morality is seldom used. Instead, we talk of businesses being ethically, or more properly, socially responsible. This issue, crucially important in the legal environment, will be examined in greater detail shortly.

Sources of law in England and Wales

In the United Kingdom we have a system of common law, that is, law which is common to everyone. The primary sources of law in the UK are cases (or more formally, caselaw, which is the body of cases which have been and continue to be heard in our courts of law) and statute (or Acts of Parliament). In order to make our cases useable we have a system of precedent. Precedent requires courts to follow decisions laid down in preceding (hence the name precedent) cases. In order to do this, the principles of law in the case should be the same. So, for example, if a case in 1960 stated that all lions should be kept on a chain or a fine would be imposed, a case in 2003 involving a lion not being kept on a chain would follow the decision of the 1960 case and impose a fine. In order for precedent to work effectively, the law has created two characteristics of a case.

The first, *ratio decidendi* (which means the reason for the decision) is the legal principle behind the case decision. This principle can be applied in all cases dealing with a similar legal principle even if the facts in each case differ. For this reason it is called the binding precedent because judges in the future have to apply that decision. The second characteristic is the *obiter dictum* (which means an incidental remark). What this means is that in the course of a case the judges may make some general comments about the case. These comments do not form part of the legal decision but may be of use in the future. For this reason it is known as persuasive precedent because a judge in the future may be persuaded by a previous judge to decide the case in a different way. If we take our lion case again we can see persuasive precedent in action. Let us assume that in the 1960 case the judge had said that if the lion in question had not had any teeth the fine would not have been imposed for not keeping him on a chain because he could not have injured anyone. This did not affect the decision to impose the fine in the 1960 case because the lion in question did have teeth and was therefore dangerous. However, let us assume that in a case in 2002 a lion had not been chained up but did not have any teeth. The binding precedent from the 1960 case might suggest that a fine should be imposed. However, the judge's comment about what would happen in a case involving a lion with no teeth could be considered by the judge in 2002 and applied in his/her decision. If it is, then a new precedent concerned only with lions with no teeth would be created.

There are difficulties with precedent, however. Firstly, there are a vast number of cases to choose from and many of these are complex and the ratio (that is, reason) for the decision is not always neatly spelled out by the judge in the case. The system of precedent is also quite rigid. Precedent has to be followed by the courts unless the judge can distinguish an earlier case from a present case on the grounds that its facts are completely dissimilar. If the precedent has become outdated or unfair over the passage of time judges may often have to apply what they consider bad law. Some judges have argued that by having to apply bad case decisions, the law itself becomes stagnated and stuck in the past.

On the other hand, it could be argued that precedent provides a degree of certainty. The lawyer can inform his/her client that on the basis of previous cases their chances of success are good or bad. This can save lawyer and client a great deal of time and money. In general, each court is bound to follow the decisions of the courts above it. The court structure is divided in terms of the courts' criminal and civil responsibilities. Some courts have only a criminal or civil function, some have both. On the civil side we have the House of Lords at the top, followed by the Court of Appeal (Civil Division), the High Court (which has three subdivisions: Family Division, Chancery Division and Queen's Bench Division), the County Court and finally the Magistrates' Court. If there are issues of European law then the European Court of Justice takes priority over all other courts. On the criminal side we have the House of Lords at the top, followed by the Court of Appeal (Criminal Division), the Crown Court and finally the Magistrates' Court.

Statutes, more commonly known as Acts of Parliament, are the source of the majority of the law that governs England and Wales. Statutes are created in a long-drawn-out process that involves both Houses of Parliament, that is, the House of Commons and the House of Lords. All potential legislation begins life in the House of Commons as a Bill (a sort of draft version of the final Act). It then goes through an often lengthy process. The first step is the First Reading. Here, the title of the Bill is simply read out in the House of Commons and then it is printed. The Second Reading then begins and here the principles of the Bill are debated and a vote is taken as to whether it should proceed to the next stage. The next stage is the Committee stage. Here, a committee of MPs (Members of Parliament) go through each clause (section) of the Bill, making amendments where they see fit. During the next stage, the Report Stage, the head of the committee reports back to the House and at this point further amendments can be made to the Bill. The final stage in the House of Commons is the Third Reading. Here, a vote is taken as to whether the Bill should go to the House of Lords. In the House of Lords the same procedure is gone through again. Presuming that the House of Lords are happy with the Bill it goes forward to the Queen for Royal Assent (that is, her agreement expressed by her signature).

Sources of European law

European law is comprised of primary and secondary sources of law. The primary sources are the treaties that set up the three communities. These are the European Coal and Steel Community (set up by the Treaty of Paris in 1951), the European Economic Community (set up by the Treaty of Rome in 1958) and the European Atomic Energy Community (set up by the Treaty of Rome in 1958). These treaties have been updated over the years by the creation of other treaties such as the Treaty on European Union 1993, the Treaty of Amsterdam 1997 and the Treaty of Nice 2001. The treaties lay down the principles of Community law and give power to the European institutions (see below) to make laws on behalf of the European Union member states. The secondary sources consist of three types of legislation. Regulations are to be applied automatically throughout the European Union. Directives are addressed to certain member states which may, for example, be out of line with their fellow members on some particular issue. They have to introduce the directive into their legislation via, for example in the UK situation, an Act of Parliament. Decisions are similar except that they can also be issued to an individual or company within a member state.

European institutions

This legislation is created, implemented and enforced via a number of European institutions. Briefly these comprise of the European Parliament, the Council of the European Union, the European Commission and the European Court of Justice. The European Parliament consists of Members of the European Parliament (MEPs) who are elected by the people of each member state. The number of MEPs from each member state equates roughly to the size of its population. MEPs do not sit in national groups but in terms of their overall political allegiance, for example Socialist, Green, etc. The European Parliament is involved in the law-making process but in a far less direct way than our Houses of Parliament. Broadly speaking, they have the right to be consulted on any proposed legislation. Legislation is proposed by the Commission who pass it on to the Council who then pass it on to the Parliament.

The Council of the European Union (which used to be called the Council of Ministers) consists of one member from each member state and one observer from the Commission. The Council holds general meetings which the Foreign Secretary (or equivalent) from each member state attends and specialist meetings which the most appropriate government minister attends, for example agriculture, defence, etc. Because government ministers cannot attend the Council on a permanent basis they are assisted by the Committee of Permanent Representatives (COREPER) which is comprised of the member states' ambassadors.

The Council is responsible for creating European policy on issues covered by the Treaties, for passing legislation and in conjunction with the European Parliament agreeing the European Union's budget.

The European Commission consists of members from each member state with France, Germany, Italy, the United Kingdom and Spain having two members each. They are required to be completely independent of their own country so that they do not promote their own country's case above that of the European Union as a whole. Their key role is to ensure that the Treaties and all legislation passed under them are applied throughout the European Union. The European Court of Justice contains a judge from each member state. These judges, like members of the Commission, are independent from the government of their own countries. Actions are either started and finished in the Court (these are known as direct actions) or started in the Court and completed in the member states' courts (known as preliminary rulings). The Court can hear cases brought against member states for being in breach of Community law (which is binding on all member states) by another member state or by the Commission. Alternatively, action can be taken by the Court against institutions of the European Union on the grounds that a regulation, directive or decision is invalid.

The law-making process within the European Community is an often complicated and lengthy process even in comparison with UK legislation. In essence, the process involves one of a number of procedures which vary according to the type of legislation being created. Briefly, the main processes are the consultation procedure, the co-operation procedure and the co-decision procedure. The consultation procedure is only used occasionally. It provides that the European Parliament has the right to be consulted about legislative proposals and to express an opinion.

The co-operation procedure allows for greater involvement of the Parliament in the law-making process. It allows the Parliament to express its opinion on proposed legislation and to propose amendments where it sees fit. Although in this way Parliament may be able to influence new legislation it cannot in the end prevent it from being introduced.

The co-decision procedure is the most complicated and longest of the three. When the Council is considering legislation they reach a common position on it, that is, they all agree the way in which it should go forward. At this point the Parliament considers the common position. If they agree with the position taken the Council adopts the legislation and it becomes law. If they disagree, a Conciliation Committee consisting of an equal number of Council representative and MEPs tries to reach a compromise on the issue. If the Committee is unable to reach a compromise the proposal is dropped. Things become a little more complicated if Parliament suggests amendments to the common position. The Council can adopt the measure if it agrees all those amendments. If it does not the Conciliation Committee attempts to create a joint text that suits all the parties. If the text is agreed both the Council and Parliament have to adopt the proposal within 6 weeks. If they fail to do so the proposal will end unless the Council decide to adopt it. At this point, Parliament has the right to block the proposal if a majority of MEPs vote to do so. This, in a small way, gives the European Parliament a touch of real power.

Laws directly affecting businesses

Businesses are bound by a large number of statutes and industry regulations. This is not a business law text nor a business law chapter. However, within the context of establishing an awareness of the broad extent of businesses' legal environment, it is useful to provide a brief overview of the consumer law that could apply.

The main Acts worthy of mention are the Sale of Goods Act 1979, the Supply of Goods and Services Act 1982, the Supply of Goods (Implied Terms) Act 1973, the Consumer Credit Act 1974, and the Consumer Protection Act 1987.

Of greatest note, perhaps, at least in terms of consumers' everyday experience of business operations, is the Sale of Goods Act 1979. In essence the Act is concerned with how contracts are made, how the clauses within them should be interpreted and what remedies might be available to the wronged consumer. Primarily the Act implies that certain terms will be present in any contract covered by the Act (that is, one in which goods are sold). These are automatically deemed by the courts to be present in the contract whether or not the parties to the contract wanted them to be part of the contract. Briefly, the conditions provide a seller with a right to sell the goods in question. They provide that the goods should match their description, that they are of satisfactory quality, that they are fit for the purpose for which they were intended and finally, that if they are sold by way of sample the other goods will match the sample provided.

Part I of the Supply of Goods and Services Act 1982 deals with the supply of goods and Part II with the supply of services. More broadly, the Act is divided into three main parts. There are sections which deal with the transfer of ownership of goods, sections which deal with the hiring of goods and sections dealing with services.

The Supply of Goods (Implied Terms) Act 1973 implies a number of terms into hire-purchase agreements. These are the same terms as in contracts under the Sale of Goods Act 1979, that is, the right to sell, that goods will match their description, that those goods will be of satisfactory quality, that they will be fit for their purpose and that where goods are sold by sample the remainder of the goods will match that sample. The Consumer Credit Act 1974 regulates the provision of credit from personal loans to mortgages. It is an extremely complex piece of legislation but broadly covers the following aspects of credit provision. The Act seeks to control through licensing who may provide credit. It clarifies what information should be given to any consumer seeking credit. It seeks to regulate the terms of any credit agreement entered into and it seeks to restrict the remedies available to the creditor (that is, the person or company offering the credit). Finally, the Consumer Protection Act 1987 consists of two Parts. Part I deals with defective products and Part II with consumer safety.

Codes of conduct

Businesses, whilst bound by a range of consumer protection, employment, contract and tort laws, are also seemingly bound by a range of ethical or moral codes. Many businesses enshrine their ethical stance within a self-created code of conduct or mission statement. In the world of the Internet-driven economy in which it is difficult either to create and/or apply international binding consumer law, it seems likely that such codes will be one of the more likely routes of corporate control. Indeed, we are becoming, and will continue to be, increasingly reliant upon the goodwill of companies, especially in less developed economies, to resist the temptation to abuse their corporate power in the pursuit of economic gain.

There has been a proliferation of codes of conduct/ethics in recent years. Prior to codes becoming popularised, of course, there were rules of conduct and behaviour present, implicitly or otherwise, in companies and within industries. Without standards of some form or another, businesses could not operate for very long without transgressing national or international law.

Ironically, the current vogue for adopting and using a corporate code has led to a widely held belief that ethical standards are merely a publicity or marketing ploy.

The Institute of Business Ethics (2003) argues that although the existence of a code is undoubtedly a marketing advantage it has a number of other advantages as well. For example, formulating a written code encourages, or forces, a company's management team to consider what its values are and how best to promote them. Also, the code may assist the company in abiding by the law, since codes will reflect rather than contradict the prevailing legislation. Indeed, it may encourage organisations to apply higher than minimum legal requirements to their operations. In addition, the code enables an organisation to promote and adhere to universal standards of business behaviour and also allows disaffected individuals to complain about the unethical nature of any task their immediate line manager requests them to do. Finally, it allows a company to be able to inform and influence suppliers (by having, for example, an ethical position on prompt payment of outstanding bills), competitors (by having, for example, a code against unfair competitive practice) and stakeholders (by having, for example, a code promising safety and quality of products) (see Minicase 8.2).

Codes will only receive critical acclaim if it is readily apparent that the code is deemed to be important and vital to the well-being of a company. As with any enterprise entered into half-heartedly, a code that is not valued will soon be rendered valueless. So, for example, the company must have a clear purpose. Is it introducing the code for publicity purposes or because it wishes to become an ethical business?

Minicase 8.2

It is 1919. The Volstead Act has just been introduced across the USA. The Act has introduced Prohibition, which makes it an offence to supply, distribute, purchase or consume alcohol. The offences, if breached, will incur heavy fines and/or imprisonment. You are in the top tier of management within the Chicago Police Department. It has come to your attention that most of your officers (whose responsibility it is to enforce the Volstead Act) are actively consuming alcohol. You have decided to implement a code of ethics so as to dissuade, without alienating, those officers from drinking. Your tasks are shown below.

Questions

1. Establish why a code is necessary or desirable.

2. Establish how you propose to create the code, noting (a) *who* will be involved in its creation; (b) *why* those people will be involved; and (c) *how* those people will be involved.

3. Establish how the code will be disseminated.

4. Establish how the code will be maintained and enforced.

5. Establish the likelihood of the established code working.

Prepare your answers as if you were reporting directly to the Chief of Police who is awaiting your appraisal of the matter.

There must be a visible and accountable development process as far as the code is concerned. All of the people who are likely to be affected by the code should ideally be consulted at every stage in the process. Are there any existing rules or codes used in the company in particular or in the industry in which the company operates in general? Have they worked, have they been resented by all or some sections of the staff? If such issues are not resolved, the code will run into the same sorts of problems. There must be some fundamental values or principles, which will underpin the eventual code, for example honesty, integrity, loyalty, etc. The code should be particular to the company and its workforce. If the code is merely a general all-encompassing one, the workforce will deem it to be an irrelevant publicity stunt.

Once the code is in operation, it must be, and must be seen to be, monitored by the company. The staff must be asked for their feedback, positive and negative, and such feedback must be reviewed and the code updated accordingly.

The most important stage in the process of creating a code is the development/implementation stage. The company must create an awareness amongst its staff that the code will be introduced and that it will be introduced for a genuine reason and not simply because every other company possesses one. The company must identify the ethical issues of concern to their workforce, customers and stakeholders and not merely presume that they know what such people are concerned with. There must be involvement of everybody at every stage of the design process. Anyone excluded from the development of the code will feel justified in excluding themselves from its operation. Enthusiastic, specially chosen people must be appointed to create, implement and observe the code. The code should consider the international situation the company may operate in. A code on bribery may not seem particularly relevant in the United Kingdom with its multitude of laws and regulations, but may be of vital importance when dealing with companies in countries where corruption is seen as more widespread, for example Bangladesh or Nigeria (see Chapter 7).

The IBE suggest twelve steps for the successful implementation of a code of ethics:

1. *Integration* – the code must become part of the company's everyday activities.

2. *Endorsement* – the code must be seen to be endorsed (supported) by the senior management of company.

3. *Distribution* – the code must be sent to everyone who is expected to abide by, or is likely to be affected by, the code.

4. *Breaches* – the code must ensure that breaches of the code are punished and that breaches of the code can be reported safely and securely without the reporter suffering directly or indirectly for his honesty.

5. *Response* – all staff should be able to respond (critically if necessary) to the code. It should not, therefore, be deemed to be an unchangeable document.

6. *Affirmation* – management must be required to state for the record that they and their staff understand and apply the ethical code.

7. *Regular review* – the code must be reviewed regularly so that inoperative codes can be examined and situations recently arising can be incorporated into the document.

8. *Contracts* – all contracts of employment should have a requirement that the employee concerned must agree to abide by the code and suffer the consequences in a disciplinary sense if he/she does not.

9. *Training* – training at all levels should routinely involve a discussion of issues raised by everyday working under the guidance of the code.

10. *Translation* – the code should be translated for overseas use or indeed for use within UK companies where the workforce may not speak English fluently.

11. *Distribution* – all affected parties should have a copy as a matter of procedure. All other parties (customers, etc.) should be able to receive a copy if they request it.

12. *Annual Report* – the code should become a regular part of the Annual Report, so that the wider world becomes *au fait* with the ethical position of the company.

Arguably, the proliferation of codes of conduct produced by companies across the world could reflect a degree of dedication to ethical principles or it could simply be a form of camouflage whereby unethical behaviour is hidden behind a code of conduct which suggests that the company in question is being socially responsible. To expect a corporation to follow a code of ethics is perhaps to ask it to act against its very nature. Simply stated, corporations aim to make money. To make money they need to be in a stronger position in the market than their contemporaries. This may entail employees bending or breaking rules, regulations and laws for the good of the corporation.

Arguably, a corporation's close-knit group focus leads to the formation of a 'corporate subculture' in which the legitimate goal of competitive advantage cannot always be achieved through the observation of legal principles and practices. The market is a fluid, uncertain arena replete with other corporations vying for the same consumer base. The temptation either to fail to create a code of ethics or, having created one, ignore it, must be high.

Creating an ethical organisation requires more than simply adopting a code of ethics (though this is an important characteristic of an aspiring ethical organisation). In essence, it is essential that the whole organisation and everyone who works within it become ethical to the extent that the decision-making processes, the attitudes and the behaviour become automatically ethical, become second nature.

The first step is the creation of an ethical compliance programme. It is inevitable that within a company decisions are made by people at different levels of the company hierarchy. Consequently, these people will approach problems and issues with differing perspectives and, ultimately, with differing personal moral and ethical values. This situation creates a strong environment for ethical abuse. Under the Ethical Compliance Programme (ECP) the ultimate responsibility for misconduct of employees rests solely with upper management. The main rationale behind the ECP is that it should encourage companies to take stock of their ethical conduct and, by taking pre-emptive action, avoid being taken to court or losing public confidence. Court action can involve anything from a request to remedy a situation, to asset stripping fines to organisational probation (which involves on-site consultants). Slightly less severe, however, is the attempt to encourage ethical compliance through the use of codes of conduct. These codes must be more than general in scope. Thus, they should not simply say, 'Do not be dishonest', but rather they should be the catalyst for ensuring that employees simply do not act dishonestly. Codes of ethics ensure that, even if the company's ethical viewpoint is not perfect, there are recognised standards laid down by the company which can be shown to, and digested by, employees. Codes should be regarded as guidelines or principles. Naturally, they cannot reasonably cover every possible ethical dilemma or unethical action.

An ethical compliance programme can be rendered particularly effective if a high-level manager is put in direct control of its implementation and operation. This manager is generally referred to as an Ethics Officer or, more usually, Compliance Officer. The compliance officer is required to undertake and perform a number of tasks including co-ordinating the ethical compliance programme in conjunction with senior management, developing, updating and disseminating a code of ethics, developing methods of communicating ethical standards and establishing ethical audit systems to ensure that the codes and ethical standards are being maintained and that any breaches are being dealt with according to the compliance programme requirements. Underpinning the role of the compliance officer is the important role of communication. This role incorporates not simply a dissemination of ethical standards but also discussion with employees and managers in order to determine their viewpoints on what they consider to be ethical behaviour. It is clearly far easier to comply with a standard you already either ascribe to or deem to be worthy of compliance. Of equal, if not greater, importance is the ability of a company to determine whether this communication process has been successful. To this end, many firms have created 'hot lines' or 'help lines' which allow employees to voice ethical concerns they might have with their own or their fellow employees' conduct. This is, in effect, organised 'whistle-blowing'. In addition to this, many firms use role-playing exercises to train their managers. In observing how a manager solves or at least approaches an ethical dilemma a company can immediately rectify any deficiencies in his approach.

As far as the main workforce is concerned, questionnaires can be utilised which ask them whether, and to what extent, they perceive their fellow workers, their management team and ultimately their company as having a strong ethical conduct. The earlier such questions are posed, the better it will be for the overall ethical conduct and image of the company concerned. Thus, many firms require employees to sign a compliance form during their staff appraisals, which signifies that they are, or believe they are, complying with the ethical standards of the company. The standards the employee is required to abide by will often be placed in a mission statement – a broad outline of how the company wishes to operate and wishes to be perceived within the community, both social and business. The ultimate test of compliance, of course, is not to question one's own employees, since this is effectively 'preaching to the converted'. A cynic might argue that no employee is going to deny applying his company's ethical standards. Rather, it is of greater value to apply an objectively created set of criteria. This is usually known as an ethical compliance audit. Under this audit, the firm's ethical standards and achievements are measured against a pre-determined set of performance indicators.

Whistle-blowing

It is argued that drawing a salary from an employer places a responsibility upon the employee to remain loyal to the firm. Certainly, the majority of businesses faced with a whistleblower devote more of their resources to silencing and discrediting a perceived traitor than they do to the rectification of the issue he/she blew the whistle over. It is arguable that employees owe the corporation a moral obligation of loyalty in terms of keeping company trade secrets, of devoting all of one's efforts to the well-being of that company. However, breaching that loyalty may be deemed correct if:

- the corporation is involved in the production of some goods or services likely to cause serious harm to those using them or to the general public;

- the employee is in a privileged position to recognise the potential for such harm and has reported it through official corporate channels but no or insufficient action has been taken to remedy the situation;

- the employee has possession of full documentation of the dangerous product or services and has shared that data with his/her superiors in the corporation but without positive results.

It is a fact of life, in business perhaps more than in any other sphere, that mistakes are made. It is inevitable that those who make the mistakes (whether by accident or design) will wish to cover them up. At some point, however, such mistakes can reach the point that by their very nature, volume or extent the ethical employee finds them difficult to ignore any further. For such employees, the reaction from their organisations seems geared to deter others from whistle-blowing rather than to support the whistleblower and encourage others to do likewise. Given that the employee stands to lose, at the very least, his/her career, to suggest that the whistle-blowing in the majority of cases is some form of juvenile revenge rather than an attempt to save the company's reputation and colleagues' jobs is odd to say the least. If concerns can be raised and given an objective, non-stigmatised hearing and review within the company and where concerns justify it, behaviour can be changed, the need for whistle-blowing may decline. It is probably true, however, that for every genuine whistleblower there will be a few who are driven by thoughts of revenge at having been passed over for a promotion or pay rise, etc. It is precisely because of such people that the whistleblower collects a continuous bad press and uneasy reception within the corporation.

Unless the company encourages a controllable release of negative information about its activities though, it will lead to an unavoidable creation of disadvantageous publicity. A company that has no visible or plausible system of reporting leaves concerned employees with a range of options:

1. They could ignore the problem and continue working as usual.

2. They could try to raise their issues with someone of authority within the organisation.

3. They could simply blow the whistle anonymously on their employers to someone outside of the company.

4. They could blow the whistle publicly and risk the consequences from their employer.

5. They could simply resign in protest but effectively say nothing to anyone outside of the company as to why they did in fact resign.

6. They could resign and then blow the whistle.

The way in which to avoid or at least reduce whistle-blowing is through self-regulation by the company. This can only succeed if employers are willing to be scrutinised by their employees. Most companies have codes of conduct or mission statements but precious few stipulate that they welcome concerns being raised and more importantly will guarantee anonymity or protection for those who raise alarms. Naturally, in the absence of such a system the employee contemplating whistle-blowing should run through an actual or mental checklist before committing the act. Has the whistleblower got hold of all of the relevant facts and understood their actual import? Has the whistleblower considered the full consequences of leaking the information in terms of the company's situation and the situation of *all* of its stakeholders? Has the whistleblower considered the personal fall-out that may ensue?

Has the whistleblower considered what consequences non-action will cause? Will blowing the whistle solve or reduce these? Above all, the whistleblower should, wherever possible, exhaust all internal channels first. Whatever the consensus of opinion among companies regarding the rights and wrongs of whistle-blowing, the Public Interest Disclosure Act 1998 now affords the whistleblower protection albeit in certain circumstances known as protected disclosures. Briefly, an employee is protected by the Act if they disclose information about their company because they believe:

1. that a criminal offence is being, has been or is about to be committed;

2. that some legal obligation the company has is likely to be avoided;

3. that a miscarriage of justice has happened, is about to happen or is likely to happen;

4. that the health and safety of an individual is put in danger;

5. that damage to the environment is occurring, has occurred or is likely to occur;

6. that information relating to 1–5 is likely to be concealed.

It is regrettable that such a piece of legislation has become necessary to protect the interests of those who, in the main, have sought to improve, rather than undermine, the lot of the company and its stakeholders. It is also fairly certain that the Act fails to take into account the fact that there are many subtle ways in which an employee can be victimised for breaching company confidences without it appearing to the outside world that anything untoward has actually happened.

In short, therefore, whistleblowers can be viewed as a positive asset to a company whose commitment to socially responsible behaviour is based in practice rather than on rhetoric. Whistle-blowing occurs because few if any alternative, less damaging and less public alternatives are available (see Minicase 8.3). Mistakes undoubtedly happen within companies. The desire to hide rather than have these revealed, the lack of an organised structured and objective response to those who discover the mistakes will inevitably lead to an increase in whistle-blowing. Once the issue becomes public, its ramifications automatically gain in stature. A company which encourages controlled whistle-blowing within a structured context located in a widely disseminated code of conduct can only benefit from such action. If companies continue down their current path of victimisation and denial, they will lose stakeholder confidence and may well find themselves in the court system facing a charge under the Public Interest Disclosure Act 1998.

Minicase 8.3

Bob is an engineer for a leading airline. During an inspection of one of a new and expensive fleet of aircraft he notices that the seals in two of the windows are already corroding. He believes that at the aircraft's cruising altitude of 35 000 feet the pressure may cause the windows to break. He informs his supervisor who tells him that the last thing the company and its shareholders want to hear is that their new aircraft, upon which the airline is counting to save it from financial ruin, are potentially dangerous. He tells Bob to keep quiet about the situation. Bob decides to whistle-blow to a local newspaper.

Questions

1. Was Bob right to do as he did?
2. Did the supervisor act ethically?

Stakeholders

Businesses are faced with two conflicting beliefs. The first belief is that money and the pursuit of profit are good. The second is that having a positive effect upon the community is the business's primary obligation. Arguably, it is difficult to sustain both beliefs without affecting the business's corporate legitimacy. Stakeholder theory requires the business to consider all those who could be affected by the businesses' activities. This is based upon the fact that anyone who makes an investment (whether of time, labour or money) is entitled to have a voice. Each of these stakeholders, in other words, has a legitimate stake in the organisation. Some companies define a stakeholder as anyone who has an economic value. Arguably, stakeholders should be valued for their overall worth not just their economic value. Common stakeholders include customers, suppliers, local communities, competitors, employees, investors, shareholders, managers and so on. The list can of course be shorter or longer depending on the nature and size of the business concerned. The important factor, however, is that business leaders should provide an honest appraisal of the ethical issues connected with the businesses' relationship with their various stakeholders. If we take some practical examples of potential stakeholders we can perhaps see the nature of the appraisal:

- *Employees* – are the businesses' employees seen as individuals or merely numbers? Are they paid fairly relative to one another and relative to those outside? Are they treated as individuals and is their development in terms of training, education or promotion encouraged?

- *Suppliers* – do businesses treat their suppliers honestly and fairly or are they routinely exploited and abused? Are they paid on time?

- *Customers* – do businesses keep their promises to their customers? Are they honest about the quality and prices of their products or services?

- *Competitors* – do businesses steal secrets from their competitors or do they offer fair if rigorous opposition? Do they abuse smaller businesses simply because they are in a position to do so? Do they offer or accept bribes in order to increase their competitive advantage?

- *Society* – do businesses comply with all relevant legislation? Do they provide honest information on their business practices to the relevant authorities? Do they seek to avoid or evade taxation?

- *Environment* – do businesses consider the amount of waste they produce? Do they have a plan or strategy to deal with it and have they allocated the required resources?

There are some problems with the stakeholder model, however. First and foremost is that it politicises the decision-making process. Business is by nature dynamic and whilst a certain degree of planning is necessary the ability to respond rapidly to changes in the marketplace is also important. The stakeholder model requires business managers to be involved in a seemingly endless negotiation about the impact of their decisions upon a range of people and groups. In truth, there is no limit to the potential range of stakeholders who could be affected by any one business decision. As the business world continues to globalise and a range of social and business cultures emerge there are likely to be more instances of conflict over stakeholder theory than success.

Secondly, it seems that there is no clear decision-making process for deciding between different stakeholder interests. Furthermore, if stakeholders generally are placed above shareholders in particular the business will most likely witness a reduction in its share value and an increased reluctance of those shareholders to invest more capital into the business. This in turn could lead to businesses being unable to meet many if any stakeholder concerns.

It has been suggested that businesses might try to decide the relative value of stakeholders' claims for attention by comparing the interest shown by a particular stakeholder and then deciding how powerful they are in terms of the impact they could have upon the business. A further enhancement involves comparing the power of the stakeholder with the manner in which they are known to behave. So, for example, if a pressure group is one of the stakeholders and it has a strong public presence the business should take notice of its points of view if that pressure group is known to demonstrate publicly on a regular basis.

Some business commentators have attempted to create their own criteria. Thus, Mitchell *et al.* (1997), for example, argue that the business should look at three criteria in relation to any one stakeholder. First, the stakeholder's power to influence the business. Secondly, the legitimacy of the stakeholder's relationship with the business, for example a supplier, customer, etc. Thirdly, the urgency of the stakeholder's claim on the business. The authors argue that if a stakeholder possesses one of these three character-isics it should be deemed to be latent and of low importance. If the stakeholder possesses two of the characteristics it should be deemed to be expectant and of moderate importance. If, however, the stakeholder possesses all three of the characteristics it should be deemed to be definitive and of the highest importance.

Ironically, the upshot of each of these models or theories is that shareholders will always be deemed to be of the greatest importance. If shareholders' views are regarded as being paramount then all other stakeholder concerns, however valid, will always be given second place in the decision-making process.

The business that seeks to operate fairly and successfully within the business environment without flouting laws and regulations should bear a number of general criteria in mind when deciding where its loyalties and the direction of its policies lie. The business should identify its stakeholders. It should then identify each stakeholder's concerns and/or interests. The business should then attempt to identify the possible claims those stakeholders may make and identify the most important from the position of the business. The business should then identify the strategic challenges posed by their prioritised list. In short, the business should be attempting to meet the responsibilities it owes to its stakeholders and also to meet the expectations the stakeholders have of the business.

Businesses may ask themselves why they should be so concerned with stakeholder rather than shareholder interests. The answer, beyond the obvious one that it is simply right that they should do so, is that failure to do so will invariably lead to a loss of the businesses' reputation which will in turn lead to a loss of revenue. This will lead to further loss of reputation and further loss of revenue.

Multinational enterprises

Globalisation has inevitably meant that organisations become involved in overseas markets, increasingly in less developed economies. In reality, the most pressing concern within the international legal environment is the behaviour of Western Multinational Enterprises (MNEs) in these developing areas of the world. Globalisation requires international operations in a variety of countries and cultures (see Chapter 5). Issues of immediate concern include different employment practices where wages will often be below subsistence level, where there is little if any control over working hours, where the concept of holidays is non-existent, where child labour is routinely used, where health and safety controls are non-existent, where there are not always equal opportunities (in terms of gender) and where there is discrimination (on religious grounds), where bribery and corruption are rife and where environmental concerns come a long way down the list of the developing countries' list of priorities (see Case Study 8).

MNEs can respond to this situation in a number of ways. They could adopt the standards of the host country or they could adopt and attempt to bring across the standards of their home country. Morality varies from country to country and from culture to culture. MNEs which accept this fact may be tempted to use business practices which are acceptable or not according to the local culture. Other MNEs may decide to impose or follow the moral standards of their own countries.

MNEs have been subject to much criticism, not least of all from anti-globalisation protesters. MNEs have the power to control the economic, social and political nature of any country they attempt to invest in. They tend to pay lower wages in less developed countries than they would in their home country. They are able and willing to buy their raw materials locally at a reduced rate. They may build and operate cheaply and below accepted international standards because they can and the host country's government will be unlikely to risk their wrath by complaining about the fact.

Thus, a fundamental question for the MNE is should they abuse that dominant position or should they attempt to use their position of strength to do some good for the country as well as for themselves? MNEs would argue that the question is not as simple to answer as it might appear. For example, let us assume that an MNE decided that it was unethical to use 'slave' labour, for example as employed in 'sweat-shops'. The MNE might decide not to use any such labour in the manufacture of their products. However, using any resources at all from that country will invariably have involved 'slave labour' of some kind in the production of those resources. The MNE then has only one logical choice and that is to leave the country. The harsh reality of business, of course, is that MNEs aim to make a profit. The basis of that profit often lies overseas in less developed economies. MNEs take advantage of lower set-up costs and lower labour costs. There must be a temptation on the part of some MNEs to abuse (knowingly or not) their dominant position. The MNEs believe that they, like globalisation itself, are misrepresented in the media. They argue, for example, that they bring capital investment into a country. They facilitate less developed countries' access to international markets and they claim that they face a number of complications. For example, they maintain that the host country can require that MNEs use only locally sourced parts and materials and that they can require that a percentage of the MNEs' profit be re-invested in the host country's economy. Equally, the host country has its criticisms of MNEs. For example, they argue that MNEs destabilise the local economy by attracting the most skilled workers and by paying them more than the local average wage (see Minicase 8.4).

Whichever perspective one takes it seems evident that within the international legal environment principles of social responsibility will have more effectiveness than international laws on trade. However, principles of ethical behaviour have to be international in scope and universal in application. Is that possible? Certainly, it might be possible for all MNEs to agree upon basic concepts regarding human rights, for example, providing at least subsistence-level pay and not inflicting intentional direct harm upon the labour force or their local environment. The main problem with the concept of universal ethics is that the concept ignores the key reason for the presence of MNEs in less developed countries, that is, because it is relatively inexpensive to operate there. Furthermore, for the code to be effective, the development process would have to be inclusive and this seems an unlikely prospect. Even if it were possible to frame such a code we would then be faced with the difficulty of ensuring that every MNE applied the code rigorously. It seems likely that the bottom line would be more persuasive than a code of ethics. The closest to a code that we have is the Ethical Trading Initiative. This

Minicase 8.4

A well-known sports clothing firm has opened up a factory in a developing country. The firm accepts that local customs allow the employment of child labour and that the standard working day is 14 hours. They pay just above the national average wage to their employees but this is still 70 per cent less than they would pay an equivalent worker in their home country. In order to speed up the building process of their new factory the company bribes a number of local officials.

Questions

1. Has the company done anything wrong?

2. Is the company a full and deserving member of the legal environment?

consists of internationally agreed standards which ETI companies commit to adopting. The ETI operates a base code which requires the provision of freely chosen employment, freedom of association (that is, the ability to be in Unions), safe and hygienic working conditions, no child labour, living wages, working hours which are not excessive, no discrimination, regular employment and no harsh or inhumane treatment. The commitment also requires that those standards are monitored and that corrective actions are taken whenever those standards are not met.

The Internet, business and security

The growth of the Internet and security issues

There has been a revolution in the way in which products and services provided by companies are provided. The creation of the Internet and the pursuit of e-commerce throughout the world have made cyberspace *the* marketplace. The business community and the world's governments who support and encourage e-commerce development have not, perhaps, dealt appropriately with the question of whether they *should* be so quick to embrace these global changes in business practice. They assume that the electronic environment is simply an extension of the actual business world. It is not. The Internet has never been safe and the hackers and viruses that members of the public have heard about are increasingly concentrated within the business environment. Some of these dangers can either be reduced or eradicated if businesses take the appropriate precautions. Very few companies, however, have taken the time or trouble to protect their websites against intruders. To have done so during the initial dot.com boom would have led to lengthy delays which they believed would have been exploited by their less scrupulous competitors. Businesses' primary motivation, of course, is the creation of profit, and the delay caused by implementing protection for consumers would simply reduce their profit margin.

There is an ever-increasing growth in e-commerce. In the United Kingdom businesses are being encouraged to engage with the new emerging e-commerce markets or risk falling by the wayside. The Gartner Group estimates (*E-Commerce Times*, 2000) that e-tailing will grow to account for between 5 per cent and 7 per cent of total retail sales in North America by 2004, from the 1 per cent it represented in 1999. Analyst firm Forrester (2000) suggests that worldwide Internet commerce will be worth US$6790 billion by 2004. However, there are also dangers in this process. The stock market meltdown in the US in April 2000 saw the Dow Jones index falling by 616 points (5.6 per cent) in one day and the infliction of widespread suffering amongst Internet companies as a consequence. Bill Gates' Microsoft stock value was cut by $11.1 million and Jeff Bezos, the founder of Amazon.com, lost $2.4 billion. Even the debut share value of the much-hyped Lastminute.com fell from a floatation peak of 487.5p per share to 240p per share soon after (BBC, 2003).

A report from e-commerce solutions firm 'Cybersource' noted that e-commerce firms were reporting that up to 25 per cent of online transactions were fraudulent, the average being 5 per cent. Visa, and other credit card providers, have tended to de-emphasise the fraud perpetrated by the direct use of one of its cards or from information derived from it. They note (*Time*, 1999), for example, that approximately eight cents of every $100 spent online are lost to fraud. The comparative figure for ordinary non-cyber business is seven cents. The problem is that companies bear the brunt of that fraudulent activity. If the consumer loses money by dealing in e-commerce (even if that loss is then waived by their credit card provider) the likelihood of them purchasing goods or services online again is arguably reduced significantly. In addition to this fraudulent activity there is the possibility of identity theft (zdnet, 2000) in which the data derived from the credit card information held by the company (in a small file called a 'cookie') is used by a thief to obtain new credit, to borrow money or indeed to make further purchases. The pressure upon the e-company *not* to reveal that such losses have occurred will grow as the number of consumers using e-commerce grows. This is simply because if consumers find out about security breaches they will stop using the Internet in the same way that they would close their bank account if their bank kept on being robbed.

We have to recognise, of course, that companies are in a tricky situation. If they reveal that the breach has occurred consumers and credit card providers can be notified and the necessary action taken. However, revealing that a security breach has occurred undermines public confidence in the e-company in particular and in e-commerce in general. In addition, it may also sap the confidence of other businesses with which the compromised e-company has dealt.

The likelihood of security breaches becoming known in the public or business sector, therefore, will be slight. A study by the Computer Security Institute and the FBI (CSI/FBI, 2000), which surveyed 643 computer-security professionals at large corporations, revealed that 70 per cent of them had detected unauthorised use of their computer systems in the previous year. Only 273 of the 643 professionals were prepared to specify the amount of money lost, but for those 273 the losses were US$266 million for the year.

'Love Bug' was one of the most damaging and the most widespread virus outbreaks ever. The losses incurred in terms of lost work hours were estimated to be in the amount of US$10 billion. Eighty per cent of all US federal agencies, including the State and Defence departments, were infected by the bug. The fact that Microsoft Windows^{TM} runs on nine out of ten computers made the bug particularly powerful. The use of e-mail attachments is of course not new but Love Bug was particularly evil. Bugtraq argue that approximately 60 new vulnerabilities in software are discovered every month. Many e-businesses, especially Small to Medium Sized Enterprises (SMEs), are more open to hacking because rather than maintaining their own hardware storage facilities for important financial data, they often rely upon large website providers to maintain their business security.

The US Attorney-General Janet Reno has said (BBC, 2000) that the public and private sectors will have to co-operate if cyber-crime is to be tackled effectively. E-businesses seemingly recognise that consumer confidence is a prerequisite for the continued expansion of e-commerce. It is vital that financial transactions can be carried out securely over the Internet. The arrival of m-commerce (see below), that is, mobile commerce (which includes personal digital assistants (PDAs), third generation (3G) phones and laptops with an integral modem) will probably overshadow that rise quite considerably. Given such financial prospects, corporations may simply perceive that the delay caused by implementing e-commerce protection simply reduces their potential profit margin.

It is clear from the number of viral infections and the effectiveness of denial of service attacks their systems have been subject to that businesses are not very security conscious and/or prepared. In January 1999, one individual stole information on more than 485 000 credit cards from an e-commerce site. Some two weeks after that, data from 300 000 credit cards was stolen from the CD Universe website. In February 2000, a number of major e-commerce companies (including Amazon.com and Yahoo!) were subject to sustained denial of service attacks in which their websites were so inundated with requests for data that the sites' servers overloaded and could not deal with legitimate requests for information for a number of hours.

More generally, it is argued that the problem of security owes much to organisations' perception of security as an issue. Basically, businesses believe that security is a problem that can be solved by, for example, installing anti-virus software into their computers. However, security should be regarded more as a process. Security is best addressed by adopting a position of inevitability, that is, accepting that security breaches will occur and creating a security strategy that can attempt to reduce and/or deal with those breaches as and when they occur. This results in a proactive process of security rather than a reactive and ineffective panic.

Ironically, given the importance of security (in an environment in which security is perceived to be facing a very real threat), it is a function routinely delegated to already hard-pressed network or system administrators. Such administrators are tasked with keeping the computer network operational. They do not necessarily have the time or the expertise to keep that same network secure as well. Eighty per cent of security breaches are caused by a company's own staff (cited in Goodwin, 2000, p. 16). A survey

(*IT Week*, 2001a) found that organisations typically spend 80 per cent of their security budget protecting themselves against external threats, and only 20 per cent on implementing internal security despite the fact that 80 per cent of security breaches come from within companies. The Department of Trade and Industry in the UK reported in 2001 that only 14 per cent of UK companies had an information security policy (*IT Week*, 2001b).

Even if a password is not written down most can be established with a little deduction. This is because people tend to choose passwords that they can remember. Thus, family names, personal telephone numbers, favourite sports teams, etc., feature prominently. The most common password is, ironically enough, 'password'. The danger of over-reliance upon passwords as an essential part of a corporation's security measures was seen in the case of a merchant bank that laid off 5000 staff without deactivating their passwords. Research revealed that 40 per cent of the ex-employees had entered the network after their forced departure.

Effective security (in terms of both systems and processes) will never come cheap, and inevitably, therefore, financial commitment may also become an issue for corporations. Xephon indicates that corporations have a disturbingly lax attitude to security. Their report (Bennett, 2001a) examined the attitudes of IT managers worldwide regarding security issues and e-business success. One-third of respondents said that security concerns slowed down progress of their firms' e-business development. One in six IT managers felt that e-business was awarded greater importance than security matters. An exacerbation of the aforementioned factors may lie in the tendency of corporations to succumb to the pressures of joining the world of e-commerce at the expense of creating an adequately tested security system.

The Gartner Group reported (Neal, 2000a) that half of all small and medium-sized businesses would fall victim to Internet attacks by 2003. Smaller firms are driven to e-commerce conformity but lack the technical or financial know-how to do so safely. They further argued that smaller companies tend to rely upon part-time staff, or staff without appropriate qualifications, to run enterprise servers. In addition, they depend upon their Internet Service Providers (ISPs) to provide their security (see Minicase 8.5). This could open up their partners to intrusion. If, as seems likely, small firms are hacked or subject to viruses, they could become a weak link in the already weak chain of Internet security. Ironically, even if a large corporation has an effective security system in place, such corporations are now linked increasingly to small businesses with which they do business. If one of these small firms is subjected to a viral attack it could have a ripple effect upon all of the other firms in the chain.

A survey in 2000 (StPaul, 2000) of risk managers in large corporations in the US and Europe revealed that businesses did not really understand the risks posed by technology nor how those risks might be detected and effectively dealt with. More precisely, although computer/Internet risk was the number one concern of European companies and the number two concern of US companies, only 30 per cent of the former and 25 per cent of the latter had formal management structures in place to manage technology risk. Only 60 per cent of US companies and 56 per cent of European companies had implemented employee training programmes as part of their programmes to manage security risk. Furthermore, about 75 per cent of US executives and 60 per cent of European executives said their employees had only a 'fair' or 'poor' understanding of technology risks.

Minicase 8.5

A company has launched itself onto the Internet. It has had to rely upon its Internet Service Provider for the security of its systems. It utilises a password security system. It cannot afford to hire someone full-time to oversee security but it has managed to install an anti-virus package onto its computer system. It does not control employees' use of e-mail.

Question

1. Would you do business with this company? Why or why not?

Globalisation issues

Hand in hand with e-commerce and the Internet is the process of globalisation. We are undoubtedly living in a world of global economies. More accurately, and more worryingly perhaps, we are also living in a world of aspiring global economies. There are many countries who have, until now, been unable to enrich their economies through ordinary industrial growth. This has been partly due to the fact that they lacked the financial resources to do so and partly because we in the West did not wish to see the industrial revolution that created our wealth repeated with great environmental impact in the developing world.

The Internet-driven economy allows less developed economies to try to compete in the world market via e-commerce. The Organization for Economic Co-operation and Development (OECD) has maintained that e-commerce lies at the very heart of the future of globalisation (OECD, 2001). Equally, the OECD also argues that the computer network that supports e-commerce should be secure and reliable. Globalisation requires, and will continue to require, the connection of the world's computer, banking and financial systems. Globalisation has increased the free movement of capital between the world's developed and developing economies. Companies in the West will increasingly deal with less developed economies. This is simply because these economies provide cheaper locations for production of goods (and services) and also offer a potentially huge marketplace in which vast profits can be made. Globalisation operates in cyberspace, which is by definition extraterritorial, that is, without boundaries. This means that the regulatory practices which are supposed to exist and operate in the ordinary world are missing. A prime example of how that lack of regulation can impact upon the business world (even in an industrialised economy) can be seen in relation to an attempted fraud by the Sicilian Mafia in October 2002. This group created a digital clone of the Bank of Sicily's online site. Its plan, thwarted at the last moment by an informant, would have led to the diversion of US$400 million allocated to the Bank by the European Union for regional projects within Sicily (Williams, 2002).

Another more infamous example of weak security infrastructure is the Barings Bank collapse in 1995. In July 1992, Leeson, a trader, instructed a computer clerk in Singapore to create an error account (number 88888, referred to from now on as the 'error account'). He then instructed a systems engineer to amend the computer software so as to prevent the existence or contents of the error account from being divulged to the bank's headquarters in London. The fact that Leeson was able to instigate these changes without fear of contradiction or adverse consequences is the first point of concern. Leeson began to sell 'options' without authority from Barings. An option provides the interested party with the right, but not the obligation, to buy or sell a set quantity (usually of currencies or securities) at some stage in the future (for example in 6 months' time) in return for payment of a premium (a bit like a deposit). If the agreed price rises in the interim, however, the trader can start to lose money. So, for example, if he agreed to sell the product at £10 000 in 6 months' time but the price rises to £20 000 he will still have to sell at £10 000. He will have lost £10 000. This is what happened to Leeson – but he simply hid the losses in the error account hoping to pay them off by making better deals in the future. Just as a gambler often places more bets to recover losses, Leeson sold yet more options in a vain attempt to reduce his existing losses. As far as Barings were concerned, Leeson was, judging by the amount of premiums he provided them with, a raging success. In reality, he was bringing them closer and closer to collapse. By December 1994 he had accumulated losses on the error account of some £208 million, and by February 1995, the accumulated losses on the error account amounted to £830 million (Newsrisk, 1995).

The key problem for Barings lay in both its weak operational control and its weak application of its computer systems and processes. Leeson controlled the trading office and the office in which documentation relating to his trading was processed. This lack of effective segregation allowed Leeson to disguise his losses. Leeson's ability to achieve his deception lay in the simple fact that Barings never anticipated his actions. It was ironic, therefore, that despite his best endeavours, details of Leeson's error account *did* in fact reach London. In other words, the Barings Bank software *had* worked. The lack of control of the system, however, enabled Leeson's actions to continue to go unnoticed. The system in London could not correlate the contracts in the error account with existing account numbers and so, rather than raising a query, simply placed them in a computer suspense file. The suspense file was only noticed after Barings had collapsed. The suspense file should have been routinely and regularly audited. It was not.

The same ignorance of security protocol and the implicit trust placed in employees evidenced in the Barings fiasco can also be detected in the case involving FBI spy, Robert Hanssen. Hanssen helped to set up the FBI's Intelligence Investigative System into which agents placed the names, addresses, etc., of their Soviet targets. This gave Hanssen access to the true names of every FBI intelligence source in New York. He also worked with the intelligence specialists who installed bugs and cameras to watch over Soviet officials. Thus, he knew where every watching and listening device was placed. Aside from that, he was generally very inquisitive about every activity going on around him. A former colleague simply remarked that 'I just figured he was nosy' (McGreary, 2001). When he was posted to Washington Hanssen was given increasingly important assignments which allowed him access to secret information about government intelligence activities. The FBI trusted Robert Hanssen and therefore mistook his insatiable interest in the Agency's activities for keenness rather than espionage.

M-commerce

The flaws identified in existing processes and systems will arguably pale into insignificance if m-commerce begins to take effective shape. As mentioned above, m-commerce refers to the buying and selling of goods and services through wireless handheld devices such as cellular telephone and personal digital assistants (PDAs). M-commerce effectively provides for access to the Internet without the necessity of plugging directly into a computer terminal. The key technology for m-commerce is Wireless Application Technology (WAP). M-commerce will potentially affect a wide range of industries including financial services (including mobile banking, when customers use handheld devices to access their accounts and pay bills, and brokerage services where customers can see stock quotes and trade), telecommunications, in which bill payment can be conducted on the handheld device, and service/retail, where customers can place orders and pay for those orders from their handheld devices.

It has been predicted that m-commerce will be launched properly once third generation (3G) cellular services become routinely available. 3G services will provide a permanent Internet connection and data throughput will be higher, matching at least today's 56kbps modems. It is suggested that companies will be able to offer services and products to consumers via mobile handsets in much the same way as they can over the web today. The Gartner Group predicts that (assuming an ideal business environment) the global value of transactions by mobile device will rise to $1.8 trillion by 2005 (*IT Week*, 2000).

In order to be as successful as these predictions, however, the mobile phones and PDAs (Personal Digital Assistants) will have to be extremely rapid and efficient in data transfer and retrieval. The problem with wireless technology is of course that they have a limited memory. In terms of marketability manufacturers will dedicate memory to efficient utility rather than efficient, but memory depleting, encryption and authentication systems. If mobile phones and PDAs are stolen then the absence of effective security measures might be devastating for the individual and his/her corporation if those devices fall into even partly competent hands. A survey (Lemos, 2000) of 3000 people found that almost no handheld owners used anti-virus protection, even though 81 per cent of the sample stated that they were worried about future viruses that could infect their mobile devices. It is suggested that the threats to m-commerce will increase when, for example, such devices are able to receive and re-distribute e-mail attachments. These are of course perfect vehicles for transmitting viruses back into the company. In June 2000, experts intercepted Timofonica (a virus similar to the Love Bug) designed to attack mobile phones with text capability and, in September 2000, experts warned of the Liberty Crack virus, a PalmPilot virus that deleted files. A survey conducted by BindView (Neal, 2000b) noted that only 12 per cent of a thousand companies surveyed had a policy regarding communications over mobile networks. Twenty-seven per cent said employees used notebook PCs at clients' premises and 37 per cent said staff worked from home via remote access to the corporate network. Fifty-three per cent of managers said their IT department often had no idea where company laptops were and that, when in employees' homes, most were lent to friends or flatmates.

Cyberpayments, money and governance

The future of e-trading and globalisation lies in the utilisation and utility of cyberpayment systems such as electronic or e-cash. The more remote and automated banking systems become the more likely it is that criminals will be able to access and abuse business websites. With standard cheques and credit cards there comes a point (usually when statements arrive or credit card limits are reached) where criminal involvement becomes apparent. The cheques can be stopped and the credit cards cancelled. When banks and credit card companies become faceless it is much easier to cause financial abuse over a longer period of time. Faceless institutions rely more and more heavily upon computers. If those computers are not tamper-proof the dangers are obvious. If the supervision of China's banking system has been so lax as to permit the aforementioned criminal diversion of funds to occur, one cannot really place too much faith in its ability to adapt to the security challenges posed by cyberpayment systems at all, let alone in time to prevent mass infiltration and abuse of the global market.

The BCBS drew up specific e-banking principles in May 2001 (Schaechter, 2002). They concern themselves with risk management for electronic banking, clearly the future of e-commerce and, on the OECD's logic, globalisation. In broad terms, the fourteen principles alluded to necessitate, *inter alia*, 'effective management oversight', the establishment of an 'ongoing due diligence and oversight process' and the promotion of 'adequate segregation of duties within e-banking systems', and require the relevant banks to ensure that 'clear audit trails exist for all e-banking transactions'. It has to be acknowledged that even with the most optimistic of outlooks the likelihood of such criteria being met, given China's track record of adherence to the land-based Basel principles, is slim.

The Financial Crimes Enforcement Network (FINCEN) of the US Department of the Treasury argues that 'inadequately regulated or unregulated electronic banking systems may be used to conduct anonymous transactions and to obscure audit trails, acts that may facilitate money laundering and hinder traditional investigative techniques, especially those requiring the analysis of financial records' (US Department of the Treasury, 2000) The number and variety of crimes that might be committed through the use or abuse of computer systems is already vast. As far as money laundering in particular is concerned, it seems clear that if money continues to be paid online by remote computer systems the potential for abuse is high. Further, the FATF have noted the dangers inherent in new payment technologies and online banking. Less developed economies who are trying to bring as much money into their country as possible and are unlikely to screen for illicit proceeds are potentially huge targets for money launderers.

PowerGen, a UK electricity supplier, made a number of elementary errors in the process of security which served to undermine any security systems they had in operation. They held files of customer records on their web server rather than on a separate server. They failed to encrypt the data contained on those files. As a consequence, bank details of 2500 customers were accessible via their standard website.

The perceived inconvenience of obeying a system of security as it relates to communication has led to convenience above security becoming the driving force. Consequently, public key infrastructure (PKI) systems with digital certificates and digital signatures have promised to protect the sanctity of online communications. Public key cryptography utilises pairs of huge numbers used to encode and decode messages. One number (the public key) is published. The second number is a private key kept secret. One key is used to encode the message, the second key to decode it. Uptake of PKI systems is on the increase. In ordinary, land-based transactions, it is argued that handwritten signatures are not automatically acceptable for important transactions and that notarised signatures are used instead. In addition, of course, it is an accepted principle of ordinary consumer dealing that the credit card holder's signature is witnessed by the person they are purchasing goods from. The US National Notary Association argues that the same caution should be exercised in relation to digital signatures. They suggest that 'as industry becomes more digital, it becomes possible to reproduce and take-on the identity of another (person)' (Townsend, 2000).

Witherell (2002) has noted recently that 'recent high profile cases of governance failure and corporate misconduct . . . have shown that corporate governance mechanisms sometimes have not kept up with market developments'. In the USA, Enron overstated its profits by almost $600 million. Andersen, the supposedly objective auditors, shredded Enron-related documentation when it discovered that the Securities and Exchange Commission (SEC) had launched an investigation into Enron's accounting. WorldCom recorded losses over five quarters (from the beginning of 2001) as profits and Xerox overstated its profits by $1.4 billion over a five-year period (*The Economist*, 2002a). There were several other less high-profile admissions of corporate malfeasance and undoubtedly hundreds of others currently hiding behind the camouflage of corporate responsibility. Companies like these were already successful by-products of the globalisation process. They had already achieved dominance within their respective niches in the market. They were, theoretically, controlled by and accountable to a strict regulatory system.

However, corporate greed led to corporate malfeasance and whether such behaviour was caused by the apparent common denominator of business the world over – profit – or whether they were simply suffering from globalisation-engendered competitive stress does not matter. What really matters is that it raises the question as to the lengths companies will go and the size of the task facing regulators to devise and enforce laws that protect against such behaviour.

Georgy Satarov, president of INDEM, a Russian think-tank, noted in May 2002 that Russian companies paid £25 billion in bribes and unofficial charges, an amount equating to 12 per cent of Russia's Gross Domestic Product (*Independent*, 2002). The underground economy, grown large by dint of the collapse of the former Soviet Union, accounts for 35 per cent of the economic activity in Russia. The Russian Mafia purportedly runs 40 per cent of private business, 50 per cent of banks and 60 per cent of state-owned companies. Ironically, the USA maintained in June 2002 that Russia was now a fully fledged market economy and one with which they intend to trade. Not for the first time in the world of commerce in general, and e-commerce in particular, justifiable concern has given way to economic pressure. If the USA, and by definition, the rest of the Western global economies, are willing to trade with Russia whilst simultaneously condoning the rank criminality within Russia, it seems likely that they will also turn a collective blind eye to the widespread corruption that exists within China (see Minicase 8.6).

Minicase 8.6   E-commerce, crime and China

Although China has witnessed momentous changes it has not yet undergone Russia's *perestroika* (restructuring) or *glasnost* (openess). However, it is, particularly after its entry into the World Trade Organization (WTO), moving rapidly from a centrally planned to a socialist market economy. The corruption that pervades the former Soviet Union is present in China also. China can certainly boast one of the most dynamic emerging economies. The average annual growth rate of China's GDP between 1990 and 1999 was 10.7 per cent. For governments and MNEs outside China, China's population of 1.25 billion people and its strong manufacturing base, which accounts for 49.3 per cent of its GDP, represent a potentially lucrative opportunity. However, this trading must be carried out in an honest and secure environment. The Centre for Security Policy argues (conservatively perhaps) that corruption in China accounts for between 4 and 8 per cent of GDP. Such corruption pervades everyday life in China such that it, arguably, constitutes normality.

The culture of all-pervading corruption *per se* is unlikely to change as rapidly as the needs of the globalising economic system in China demands that it should. *The Economist* noted in February 2002 that the annual capital flight from China between 1991 and 2000 rose from $10 billion to more than $45 billion (*The Economist*, 2002b). In May 2002, Wang Xuebing, the Bank of Construction's President, was dismissed from office (BBC, 2002a) and is now under investigation for fraud. Wang had been at the Bank of China's New York branch but had been discredited by an American Treasury investigation (*BusinessWeek*, 2002). The Chinese government, it is reputed (*The Economist*, 2002b), must have known of his malfeasance. That fraud occurred was worrying. That it was systematically hidden was more worrying still. In November 2001 Ernst and Young found (BBC, 2001a) that almost half of the loans made by Chinese banks might never be repaid. Given that the four main state banks account for 66 per cent of lending and 60 per cent of deposits (Chang, 2002a) there is understandable and rising concern over the fact and consequences of such financial mismanagement. In February 2002 China's only private bank (with whom Western businesses might prefer to conduct business) was embroiled in a fraud scandal involving a loan for $43 million made to one of its own tellers (BBC, 2002b). China's national audit office found that $320 million of the Bank of China's funds had been diverted from a number of branches via a number of stratagems including unlawful loans (NYTimes, 2002). In March 2002, the Bank of China revealed the theft by five of its officials of $500 million (*Financial Times*, 2002). The OECD notes that the financial system in China 'performs inadequately in carrying out several of its basic functions in the economy'

(OECD, 2002). It has 'limited scope for transferring funds among financial institutions or regions' and 'the external discipline provided by the financial system has been a major weakness. Years of government-mandated lending and weak contract enforcement has created a distorted credit culture in which banks have had limited incentives – and even less ability – to maintain strict lending standards and enforce loan agreements.'

In January 2002 the Director of the Fund Management Division at the Chinese Securities and Regulatory Commission (CSRC) reprimanded fund managers on the Chinese stock market for speculative share-dealing on such a scale that the stock market itself could, in his view, have been destabilised (www.news.bbc.co.uk, 2002c). Ironically, in 2001, the CSRC had noted that 'the complexity of Internet technology greatly increases the difficulty of effectively monitoring on-line information. It is reported that the success rate for investigating and handling the fraud cases are relatively low . . . It will take some time for the current legislation to be adapted to the new technology' (Xiaochuan, 2003). To add to the difficulties posed by China's relatively slow development, the CSRC is also somewhat constricted by the Chinese government. Chang (2002b) argues that 'the nation's stock watchdog seems to be a captive of the industry it is supposed to regulate – this dog just watches all the problems and barks only when prompted.' More specifically, the OECD has noted generally that 'China's financial regulatory and supervisory authorities face especially great challenges given the adverse incentives inherent in extensive state ownership of financial institutions.' The OECD maintains further that 'supervisory authorities still lack full control over some basic prudential standards, such as the power to impose realistic norms for bank provisioning and loan write-offs.'

The fact that the CSRC has been given the responsibility but not the requisite power for regulating the stock exchanges, bond markets and securities and investment companies does not augur well for the soundness or security of a financial system which will eventually go online in response to the increased connectivity required by globalisation. Indeed, as things currently stand, Chang notes that 'the exchanges of Shanghai and Shenzhen are infested, plagued by market manipulation, insider trading, accounting fraud, outright theft, and a dozen other corrupt practices.' The Chinese government may believe that they are establishing, through entities like the CSRC, a market-based regulatory system. The point they are missing, however, is that regulation is not simply a collection of laws and regulations in individual areas but a process in its own right.

China, a relatively new, under-developed, under-regulated and quasi-capitalist economy, might go to great lengths in order to achieve the illusion of industrial parity. This is especially the case when increased trade in general, and the commitments made as a prerequisite of WTO membership (WTO, 2001) in particular, focus financial attention more and more upon the reality of China's economic stature. China suffers from poor oversight of a poor financial system and that combination of factors is destined to cause severe problems. Given that the International Monetary Fund (IMF) estimates (IMF, 2000) global laundering to account for between 2 and 5 per cent of global GDP ($600 billion to $1.5 trillion) it is a threat China needs to note carefully.

Those institutions which host (wittingly or otherwise) the money laundering activity are increasingly asked to create, enforce and adhere to a wealth of laws, conventions and regulations which operate nationally, regionally and internationally. The fact that such laws appear to treat the professional service providers who perpetrate the laundering as naïve and accidental malfeasants renders the overall global success of such intervention unlikely. More locally, if the way in which the banking sector in China is regulated is the litmus test for its prospective success in dealing with money laundering then money laundering control within China is likely to be poorly attended to. More generally, in a test of e-readiness, the extent to which an economy is conducive to e-business, of the world's 60 largest economies, China was ranked 45th (Perez, 2001).

The computer infrastructure in China is under-developed and, relative to the economies it seeks to business with, insecure. The Chinese government has, arguably, added to that security concern by insisting on attempting to control the availability and content of web traffic. Attempting to control the Internet *per se* and certainly within the context of a globalised economy in which Western companies will be loath to ignore the potential of the Chinese market, will undoubtedly lead to covert infiltration by those companies. Organised crime groups will exploit this level of uncertainty. Security within companies within Western economies is, relative to potential threat, a low priority. The security of China's computer systems is, given the state of its banking and finance sectors and level of corruption, unlikely to be a priority. Indeed, as with most Western businesses, if security breaches do occur they are unlikely to be reported. China, as a newly welcomed member of the WTO, could not afford the negative impact. In consequence, China could become one of the weak links in the already weak chain of globalisation security.

Questions

1. How should companies approach the difficulties of operating in China?

2. Should there be a new global authority created, similar to the World Trade Organisation, for the purpose of regulating financial movements across borders?

3. How could the Chinese authorities reassure foreign investors as to the safety of their investments in China?

Terrorism and anti-globalisation threats

Although not often discussed, the current global political climate may well render China an ideal target for terrorists and anti-globalisation protesters. Bin Laden saw the widespread economic impact of September 11th upon the capitalist economies of the world; it seems inevitable that the globalisation process will become his new focus. It seems equally likely therefore that fledgling globalising economies will constitute easier and, given increased Western investment in them, more devastating targets in the ongoing war against globalisation. Michael Vatis, a former head of the FBI's National Infrastructure Protection Center notes 'we have seen a clear decision by terrorist groups like al Qaeda to focus on critical infrastructures, financial networks and power grids' (Quinn-Judge, 2002).

Anti-globalisation protesters share, with Bin Laden, an unobtainable goal – the removal of capitalism or at least a minimisation of its perceived exploitative nature. If their protests continue to fall on deaf ears their firm belief in the correctness of their actions will undoubtedly spur them on to attacking the computer systems of those companies which participate in the globalised economy. China would present the perfect target for terrorists and anti-globalisation protesters – especially once the other WTO members have invested their billions of trade dollars and China supplies the world with a substantial volume of its products.

Conclusion

The legal environment used to refer simply to the various laws from contract to sale of goods to employment that businesses could be subject to on a daily or periodic basis. The legal environment has now evolved into a far more complicated system. Certainly, national and international law still applies to all businesses and it remains imperative that such law is followed. That much is accepted. Moreover, the lawful behaviour of businesses has begun to be concerned more with their ethical behaviour rather than their simple adherence to cases and statutes. Thus, codes of ethics or conduct have become a part of the most competitive companies operating at the national level.

The business that wishes to operate in the legal environment ought to ensure that its code is well formulated and well applied. Multinational enterprises that operate in the ethical shadows of the global economy are faced with the temptation of not abiding by the codes of conduct they follow in their home countries. It is crucial that the apparent trend for treating ethical issues in less developed economies differently than in Western developed economies is reversed. If it is not, there will be two legal environments which in reality means that there will be no legal environment at all. To ensure that this does not happen, it is vital that businesses start to treat all of their stakeholders as equally as possible. Should one of their key stakeholders, their employees, notice issues of concern and having exhausted all internal measures decide to whistle-blow, the business should recognise the fact that the employee may have prevented the business from moving away from the legal environment that is so crucial to its public credibility and to its financial viability. Finally, businesses need to recognise that, through no fault of their own, they have become an integral part of the defence against infiltration by criminal groups and terrorist factions into the computer infrastructure within which businesses increasingly ply their daily trade.

Businesses that continue to ignore security issues not only compromise their own financial stability but also that of their online business associates, competitors and customers. In a world in which computers are linked more and more frequently the net impact upon world trade of business apathy will be immense. The legal environment has become bigger than the mere application of national and international law. It has become a concept in which the legal and moral outlooks of businesses have to become further entwined. A business that obeys national laws and applies a code of conduct at the national level but leaves both law and conduct behind when operating in a less developed region is operating outside the legal environment. The business that has anti-viral software installed on its computers but relies upon a password system and/or does not control the opening of e-mail attachments is not secure. It allows infiltration by the few at the expense, in terms of loss, of the many.

Summary of main points

- Law may be divided into national and international law and both can be subdivided into public and private law. Sources of law include cases, statutes and, at the European level, treaties, regulations, directives and decisions.

- Laws, whilst important, need to be supported by effective codes of conduct.

- Businesses need to be aware of the various stakeholders who affect and are affected by the businesses' operations.

- Businesses that operate overseas in less developed economies need to apply ethical standards with even greater care.

- Businesses are one of the main targets of, and therefore one of the main protections against, criminal and terrorist infiltration of computer systems. It is vital that security becomes a proactive not reactive process.

Discussion Questions

1. How important is law in general, and to businesses in particular?

2. What is the value of a code of conduct and what steps must a company take in order to make a code effective?

3. Are whistleblowers a benefit or detriment to the company they inform on?

4. Do multinational enterprises bring prosperity or hardship to less developed countries?

5. Is stakeholder theory a practical way in which to run a company?

6. Are the Internet operations of businesses secure? Does it really matter whether they are secure or not?

Web Links

http://www.oecd.org
The Organization for Economic Co-operation and Development website contains a massive range of documents relating to all aspects of international trade and most importantly on trade within less developed nations.

http://www.csrforum.org/
The Corporate Social Responsibility Forum provides detailed information on the concept of CSR within different industrial sectors, countries and regions of the world. It also contains a news archive and a range of searchable databases.

http://www.pcaw.co.uk/
The Public Concern at Work website provides valuable information for individuals and businesses on whistle-blowing including a range of downloadable documentation and links to other pertinent sites.

http://www.vectec.org/researchcenter/list.html?category=36
The VETEC (Virginia Electronic Commerce Technology Center) website covers a full range of issues relating to e-commerce and e-commerce crime and deals with e-communications between businesses and consumers on a global scale.

http://www.google.co.uk
I would recommend the Google website for finding a massive range of sources on any topic you care to name. Searches can be by keyword or phrase. For any issue relating to the laws that affect business, for example, you will have more success with this site than via any other.

Further Reading

There are countless books on most of the topics addressed within this chapter. The following are designed to answer most of your questions relatively quickly and painlessly.

Keenan, D. and Riches, S. (2002) *Business Law*, 6th edn, Longman.

This text covers the English legal system, the types of business organisations and the law of contracts relating directly to business operation.

Vinten, G. (ed.) (1994) *Whistleblowing: Subversion or Corporate Citizenship?*, Paul Chapman Publishing Ltd.

This text uses a number of essays to cover general issues relating to the definition of whistle-blowing, perspectives from various professions including accountancy and nursing and a few personal observations from whistleblowers on their own experiences.

Fisher, C. and Lovell, A. (2003) *Business Ethics and Values*, Prentice Hall.

A good wide-ranging text in which the authors utilise a large number of case studies to illustrate ethical issues in business, whistle-blowing, organisational responses to ethical issues and the notion of corporate social responsibility.

Boatright, J.R. (2003) *Ethics and the Conduct of Business*, 4th edn, Prentice Hall.

A wide-ranging book which covers some of the less documented ethical issues such as gender discrimination, employee privacy and unfair dismissal. Each chapter has three case studies that assist in pushing the issues home.

http://www.hku.hk/crime/2ccgc/papers/mccusker.doc

This article discusses the relationship between e-commerce security, business and crime and addresses some of the issues raised in the chapter.

References

BBC (2000) Report on Stanford University Law School Conference on Cyber Crime, 8 April, available from http://www.bbc.co.uk/news.

BBC (2001a) 'Chinese Banks in debt crisis', 1 November, available from http://www.news.bbc.co.uk/hi/english/business/newsid/1632056.st.

BBC (2001b) 'Anti-globalisation clashes in Italy', 17 March, available from http://www.news.bbc.co.uk/hi/english/business/newsid_1226000/1226593.stm.

BBC (2002a) 'China banking chief under investigation', 15 January, available from http://www.bbc.co.uk/hi/english/business/newsid/1761242.st.

BBC (2002b) 'Fraud strikes China's only private bank', 24 February, available from http://www.bbc.co.uk/hi/english/business/newsid/1839576.st.

BBC (2002c) 'China steps up stock market crackdown', 10 January, available from http://www.news.bbc.co.uk/hi/english/business/newsid/1752758.st.

BBC (2003) 'More trouble for Lastminute.com', available from www.news.bbc.co.uk/1/hi/business/697058.htm [accessed 11 September 2003].

Bennett, M. (2001a) 'Strategies for fighting fraud', *IT Week*, 22 January.

Bennett, M. (2001b) 'Online firms must go global', *IT Week*, 22 January.

BusinessWeek (2002) 'The Bank of China's black hole', 4 February, available from http://www.businessweek.com/magazine/content/02_05b3768065.htm.

Chang, G. (2002a) 'China's banks: the only two things you need to know', *China Brief*, 2(6), 14 March, www.china.jamestown.org/pubs/view/cwe_002_006_001.htm.

Chang, G. (2002b) 'China's equity markets: floating with helium, Part 1', 25 April, available from http://www.china.jamestown.org/pubs/view/cwe_002_009_003.htm.

Commission on Crime Prevention and Criminal Justice (2003) 'Conclusions of the study on effective measures to prevent and control high-technology and computer-related crime', Tenth Session, 8–17 May, 2001, available from www.china.jamestown.org/pubs/view/cwe_002_009_003.htm.

CSI/FBI (2000) 'Computer crime and security survey', available at www.pbs.org/wgbh/pages/frontline/shows/hackers/risks/csi-fbi2000.pdf [accessed 11 September 2003].

Daily Telegraph (2000) 16 April, Ringshaw, G., 'Nasdaq crash wipes billions from fortunes', available from http://www.telegraph.co.uk.

E-Commerce Times (2000) 28 June, available from http://www.ecommercetimes.com.

Financial Times (2002) 'Bank of China reveals $500m theft by officials', 15 March, available from http://www.ft.com.

Forrester (2000) cited in Bennett, M. (2001), 'Online firms must go global', *IT Week*, 22 January, 2001, p. 25.

Fortune (2000) http://www.library.northernlight.com, 15 May.

Goodwin, B. (2000) 'Cybercrime – an inside job', *Computer Weekly*, 31 August.

IMF (2002) http://www.imf.org/external/pubs/ft/pdp/2002/pdp06.pdf.

Independent (2002) 23 May, p. 15.

Institute of Business Ethics (2003) http://www.ibe.org.uk/codesofconduct.html.

IT Week (2000) 18 September, Barrett, N., 'Hackers lose the game', p. 19.

IT Week (2001a) 26 March, cited in Street, M., 'Making security a user issue', p. 51.

IT Week (2001b) 19 February, p. 36.

Lemos, R. (2000) 'Handhelds: here come the bugs?', available from http://www.zdnet.com/zdnn/stories/news.

McGreary, J. (2001) 'The FBI spy', *Time*, 5 March.

Mitchell, R.K., Agle, B.R. and Wood, D.J. (1997) 'Toward a theory of stakeholder identification and salience: defining the principle of who and what really counts', *Academy of Management Review*, 22(4), pp. 853–886.

Neal, D. (2000a) 'Small firms raise insecurity', *IT Week*, 23 October.

Neal, D. (2000b) 'Firms fail to tackle mobile security risk', *IT Week*, 23 October.

Newsrisk (1995) 'Report of the Board of Banking Supervision Inquiry into Circumstances of the Collapse of Barings Bank of England', July, cited at http://www.ifri.co.uk.

NYTimes (2002) 'Bank of China's mounting problems', 1 February, available from http://www.college3.nytimes.com/guests/articles/2002/0/898075.xm.

OECD (2001) *Progress Report on the OECD's Work on Electronic Commerce*, 16–17 January, www.oecd.org.

OECD (2002) *China in the World Economy: The Domestic Policy Challenges Synthesis Report*, www.oecd.org.

Perez, B. (2001) 'Hong Kong seen as "e-ready", willing and able', *South China Morning Post*, 9 May, available from http://www.technology.scmp.com.

Quinn-Judge, P. (2002) 'Cracks in the system', *Time*, 17 June.

Regnier, P. (2001) *Changing Their Tune*, available from http://www.time.com/time/europe/specia/antiglobalization.htm.

Schaechter, A. (2002) 'Issues in electronic banking: an overview', *IMF Policy Discussion Paper*, PDP/02/6, available from http://www.imf.org/external/pubs/ft/pdp/2002/pdp06.pdf.

StPaul (2000) 'The e-frontier: new challenges to corporate risk management', available from http://www.stpaul.com/cyberrisk-survey.

The Economist (2002a) 'A guide to corporate scandals', 10 July, available from http://www.economist.com/adenda/displayStory.cfmStory_id=1223312.

The Economist (2002b) 'Something rotten in the state of China', 14 February, available from http://www.economist.com/displayStory.cfm?Story_ID=988457.

Time (1999) 2 November, http://www.time.com/time/digital/daily.

Townsend, K. (2000) 'Experts warn of PKI dangers', *IT Week*, 11 December.

US Department of the Treasury (2000) 'A survey of electronic cash, electronic banking, and Internet gaming', Financial Crimes Enforcement Network (FinCEN).

Williams, P. (2002) 'Organized crime and cybercrime: synergies, trends and responses', available from http://www.usinfo.state.gov/journals/itgic/0801/ijge/gj07.htm.

Witherell, B. (2002) 'Corporate governance and the integrity of financial markets: some current challenges', available from http://www.oecd.org/pdf/M00029000/M00029848.pdf.

WTO (2001) 'WTO successfully concludes negotiations on China's entry', Press Release, 17 September, available from http://www.wto.org/wto/english/news_e/pres01_e/pr243_e.htm.

Xiaochuan, Z. (2003) 'Securities market regulation in the Internet age', available at www.csrc.gov.cn/CSRCSite.eng/enews/efi20011121.htm.

Zdnet (2000) 17 March, http://www.zdnet.co.uk/news/2000.

9

Challenges and Changes

Ian Brooks

Learning Outcomes

Upon completion of this chapter the reader should be able to:

- appreciate the main characteristics of the international business environment and the prime themes identified within the text;

- understand the move towards greater dynamism, complexity and uncertainty (turbulence) in the international business environment of most firms;

- speculate about the future prospects for organisations, individuals, governments and groups in society as a result of environmental turbulence;

- outline the nature of chaotic and turbulent environments and the implications of these for long-term planning and flexible working;

- understand the characteristics of flexible firms and the advantages and drawbacks of flexible working;

- discuss the influences that the changing international business environment, and in particular the trend towards flexible working, have upon individuals and groups in the social community;

- explore environmental scenarios;

- discuss the future role of government and understand the environmental forces acting on public sector organisations;

- understand the nature of the drivers and resistors of organisational change within the public sector.

Key Concepts

- dynamism, complexity, uncertainty, turbulence and chaos
- long-term planning
- environmental scenarios and planning
- flexible firm and flexible working
- social inclusion and exclusion
- interventionist and laissez-faire government
- force-field analysis

Introduction

In this chapter we will outline the consequences for individuals, groups, organisations and governments of environmental and organisational turbulence. This will include analysis of the implications for long-range planning within organisations and of one major organisational response to environmental flux, that is, the growth of the flexible firm and of flexible working, which is impacting the daily lives of people across the world.

Throughout this text we have consistently suggested that the business environment is constantly changing, often in unpredictable ways. This implies considerable uncertainty for many organisations and can give rise to a near permanent state of internal flux as businesses attempt to respond to the changes in their environment. Broadly speaking, greater organisational change (dynamism), complexity and uncertainty (unsure how things are going to turn out) are common in turbulent business environments. Such environments demand considerable flexibility on the part of those organisations that wish to prosper. However, some evidence suggests that organisations operating in turbulent environments do not necessarily suffer a decline in profitability as the 'costs' of change are not always borne by the organisation initially influenced by such turbulence. Perrow (1986) argued that problems are often 'externalised' to dependent parts of the wider organisational system, such as employees (who may be made redundant or have to work more flexibly), suppliers (who will lose orders or change the way they do things to suit their customers) and other outworkers and persons responsible for non-core activities. This raises critical issues about how we define an organisation and where the boundaries lie between an organisation, its environment and its stakeholders. The organisation and its 'inner' or 'task' environment is itself undergoing major change and organisational boundaries are increasingly changing.

Changes in the international business environment

We have identified, by way of a summary or stock-take, a number of dynamic environmental issues which have been raised in this book. These critical environmental trends include:

- globalisation in manufacturing, and increasingly in service provision, creating international competition and the development of new markets for goods and services;

- large-scale geographical changes in the distribution of manufacturing (e.g. vast increase in parts of South-East Asia and stable, even declining, outputs in much of North America and Europe;

- increasing emphasis on free market economics, competition and managerialism including the privatisation, contracting-out and 'marketisation' of public services;

- widely varying and volatile economic growth rates: for example, rapid growth around 8 to 10 per cent in the NICs in South-East Asia in the late 1980s and early 1990s turned to decline from 1997 and increasing growth again from 2002;

- the prevalence of long-term unemployment in Europe, and economic stagnation or decline in many African countries;

- the continuing integration of Europe, with the establishment of the euro in 1999 and the broadening of the union to include many former communist Eastern European countries;

- technological advances in a wide range of fields, including information technology and communications, biotechnology and material sciences;

- growth in the power and influence of economic and political unions, such as the European Union, ASEAN and the World Trade Organisation;

- the demographic transition typified by declining fertility rates and increasing life expectancy leading to an ageing population in most countries – the so-called 'demographic timebomb';

- dynamic national and international cultures;

- increasing availability of information and ease of communication;

- changing attitudes towards the family and health, and rising crime, including internationally organised felony;

- atmospheric, water, space, land and noise pollution, resource depletion and other ecological concerns;

- the spread of biological/chemical and atomic weapons capability, religious fundamentalism and the ever-present threat of international terrorism;

- changing emphasis from multi-lateralism (e.g. power lying with the UN) to unilateralism (e.g. power with the USA);

- fundamental religious (also social, economic and political) divides between 'Western' and Arab/Islamic nations;

- ethnic divisions, such as those in Eastern Europe, the old Soviet Union and within Iraq and Turkey;

- increasing debate on the future role of government.

This list provides ample food for thought. Many of the issues raised have crucial implications for all governments and organisations, groups and individuals. Collectively, these environmental forces are fundamentally influencing, and being influenced by, patterns of economic growth, employment and investment. They will ensure that organisations are required to be dynamic and that change will be an omnipresent feature of human existence. However, it is not the intention of this book to crystal ball gaze or to explore, in detail, likely future events. If you have an interest in 'futurology' some 'experts' have written about likely changes which will impact society and organisations; www.skypoint.com/members refers to a number of writers including Toffler as well as Tapscott's *The Digital Economy* and Hamel's *A Point of View about the Future*.

Minicase 9.1 demonstrates some of the changes to key social and ecological global concerns over a ten-year period from 1994 to 2003 by way of illustration.

The nature of the business environment

In Chapter 1 dynamism and complexity were identified as two key factors in the business environment of many organisations. These are the prime characteristics of a turbulent environment. The models discussed there helped us to categorise environmental influences (using the PESTLE model) and to devise lists of key organisational opportunities or threats (the 'O' and 'T' in SWOT analysis). However, Johnson and Scholes (2002) argue that organisations need to understand the nature of their environments before they audit the individual environmental factors. Such an analysis might be expected to help an organisation decide upon the sorts of systems which are required to monitor and respond to environmental change.

If dynamism and complexity are key factors in analysing the nature of an organisation's business environment it seems reasonable to ask whether there are any academic models which may be of assistance to us. Miles (1980) devised a useful series of questions for evaluating the nature of an organisation's environment. The suggested process involves mapping an organisation's environment using a series of continuums, for example, from simple to complex and static to dynamic.

New technologies and increased globalisation of many markets encourage environmental turbulence, such that organisational planning cannot be seen as a continuous

Minicase 9.1   The pace of change

Over the last ten years (to 2003) world population has grown by about 800 million. That growth figure alone represents more than double the total population of the world at the time of the Romans or ancient Greeks (when it was about 300 million). It was not until about 1750 that world population actually reached 800m. So, in just ten years we have added to world population what previously had taken many millennia to produce and support. In many ways this might be considered a great achievement of the modern world but it has its negative consequences. About 80 per cent of that increase is accounted for by growth in the developing world, where living standards are far lower than in the developed world. In the same time period the concentration of greenhouse gases has increased from 362 to 372 parts per million and only a 60 per cent reduction in such emissions, it is thought, would stabalise concentrations. Chlorine concentrations acting with other chemicals in the atmosphere have opened a hole in the ozone layer above the Antarctic which is now three times the size of the USA. Ten years ago there were eleven cities with a population over 10 million, now there are eighteen. Deforestation of tropical forests (never, realistically, to be reversed) proceeds at about 1 per cent a year. Half of all mangrove forests have been lost. Fish stocks have collapsed in much of the North Sea and North Atlantic over the last ten years, possibly to irretrievable levels.

Almost all analysts predicted a large fall in global military spending after the end of the Cold War around 1990. In fact it did fall from about $922 billion to $811 billion over an eight-year period. However, it has now surpassed the levels of ten years ago and is rising, notably in the USA. Finally, in 1994 there were about 650 million motor vehicles while now there are over a billion, a rise of 350 million in just ten years, accounting for over 90 per cent of greenhouse gases.

Questions

1. To what extent are these trends predictable?

2. How might these trends continue?

3. Could currently unknown factors radically alter future trends?

'rolling out' of previous plans. If environmental factors are less predictable then planning needs to be seen as a more flexible, adaptive and responsive process. It is these two key areas, that is, the planning process and the need for organisational flexibility, which are given considerable attention in the next section. However, during this discussion we should be aware of the impact an organisation can have on its environment and the operation of the market by way of its strategic, tactical and operational actions.

Merely from scanning a quality daily newspaper, it is possible to catalogue a range of increasingly 'commonplace' surprises which threaten today's organisations, such as major global accidents, terrorism, kidnappings, hostile company takeovers, sabotage via product tampering, investigative journalism, equipment breakdowns, political upheaval and pressure group activity. There is a growing field of literature on crisis and shock event management. Underlying analysis of such 'shock events' in the business sphere, however, is the developing body of knowledge about the concept of chaos. Gleick (1988) offered some fascinating insights into the discoveries about the behaviour of things in the natural world. These included the graphically termed 'butterfly effect' in global weather forecasting: the notion that a butterfly stirring its wings today in one part of the world might transform weather systems next month in another far-off area. This effect underpins an equation written in 1963 by Edward Lorenz which seemed to predict cloud patterns. Gleick (1988) said that discoveries have begun to 'change the way business executives make decisions about insurance, the way astronomers look at the solar system, the way political theorists talk about the stresses leading to armed conflict'.

A number of largely American researchers have looked for such chaotic patterns in the movements of the stock market, in an attempt to predict its behaviour. However, this work has been criticised because:

- any small errors made at the start of the process would be likely to result in huge forecasting errors over time;

- huge amounts of data are required to model chaotic systems and these were unavailable in most markets; and

- the ability to spot chaotic patterns is small given the large number of variables which influence the markets – particularly if we think that new factors are now affecting performance.

Writers such as Stacey (2003) have looked at the business impact of chaos theory. He notes the tendency in many business cycles towards the sort of 'non-linear feedback loops' observable in the natural world. Although the value of chaos theory may be questioned it is possible that the mathematical models designed to explore non-linearity will generate useful analytical tools for managers in the future.

In Chapter 1 we briefly looked at scenario planning. We will now explore the implications of change at four levels – for organisations, individuals, groups and governments. Let us start by exploring an environmental change which has been unfolding in recent years and looks set to lead to quite different demographic characteristics between the two prime developed world regions, Europe and the USA. Minicase 9.2 explores these quite contrasting demographic trends.

Minicase 9.2   A parting of the ways

Demographic forces are pulling America and Europe apart. If the trend continues America's strong position in the world may grow further. As far as population counts can provide a shock, given the predictability of demographics, the census in the USA in the year 2000 certainly did. The population was/is rising faster than anyone had expected. The fertility rate in the USA is rising while in Europe it is low and decreasing. Even America's immigration rate is higher than in Europe and immigrants are reproducing faster than native-born Americans. The population of Europe is ageing, in the USA its median age is stable. It is estimated that the median age of Americans in the year 2050 might be 36 (very close to the current state at about 35) while in Europe it will be 52 (while currently it is about 38). This represents a stunning difference largely accounted for by the ageing of Europe's population. To move within just 50 years from a situation of near parity to a difference in median age of 16 years represents a major parting of the ways with far-reaching cultural, social, economic and political implications. If the trend continues, America's population will overtake that of Europe (excluding Russia) well before 2050. Unlike Europe, America's older people, their 'seniors', will remain a more-or-less stable proportion of the total population while in Europe over-65s are rapidly increasing in number and proportion of the total population and will continue to do so for many decades.

Europe claims at least equal status with the USA in trade negotiations based on its larger population size and similar sized economy. American's are about one-third richer than Europeans, their population is increasing, so by about 2050 the US economy may be twice the size of that of Europe providing a significant imbalance between these two powerful regions. The balance of global economic and political power may be significantly altered.

The fertility rates in most of Europe are below replacement level (about 2.1 children per woman are required for natural population to remain stable); in some countries, for example Germany, it is only 1.3, meaning that natural population change in Europe is rapidly downwards (the population of Germany and Italy, for example, is in decline). Inward migration does reduce such falls to an extent. Immigrant populations usually have higher fertility rates. For example, in the USA the non-Hispanic whites' fertility rate is 1.8 (below replacement levels) while for the black population it is 2.1 and 3 for the Hispanic population. In many areas in the south of the USA (e.g. Los Angeles and Houston), Latino groups account for over half of the under-14-year-olds. Whereas traditionally America's cultural ties with Europe have been strong, things might change. The majority of immigrants come from Latin America or south and east Asia and this might, in time, pull America's attention away from Europe.

> **Question**
>
> Discuss the likely implications of these changes on Europe, the USA and the rest of the world for:
>
> * organisations;
> * individuals;
> * any identifiable groups (such as people over 65 years of age; American Hispanics or 'whites'; immigrants);
> * governments.

Implications for organisations

Whatever their objectives and legal status, organisations have, almost without exception, changed over the last decade. Very many have restructured internally, realigned their business processes to improve customer service, made focused strategic changes to their management control systems, developed their staff, improved their technological positioning and adjusted their product market portfolio. Most of these changes reflect a conscious response to turbulence in the business environment and a deliberate effort to influence that environment. Many organisations have undergone fundamental change because the environment has itself transformed.

A number of researchers, among them some notable management 'gurus', have attempted to predict the ways in which organisations will change in the next decade and beyond. Such predictions are often based on current trends and collective expectations together with a pinch of 'educated' guesswork. To a large extent it is the changing nature of the international business environment that will dictate the nature of these changes and, in turn, the way organisations respond to change will alter the nature of the environment for all. The next section will first look at the implications of the changing business environment for long-term planning and will then explore one particular organisational response to environmental turbulence, that is, the growth of the flexible firm and of flexible working.

Implications for long-term planning

Operational plans have always been distinguished from strategic plans on the basis of the time period they cover and the scope and detail they contain. Strategic plans have tended to imply a planning horizon of about five years and to cover the organisation as a whole. To be able to plan over this sort of period implies a reasonable level of certainty about the environment in which the organisation operates. However, turbulence in the environment leads to an increasing lack of stability and predictability which, in turn, makes long-term strategic planning hazardous. This has led many writers on strategy to question whether organisations should adopt long-term, centralised approaches to planning. Authors such as Quinn (1978) and Mintzberg (1994) believe that incremental and emergent approaches to the process of strategy formulation should increasingly be considered by organisations. Increased environmental turbulence also suggests that systems of planning which devolve responsibility to individual business units are likely to make organisations more adaptable and responsive to environmental flux.

Stacey (2003) questions many of the underlying assumptions used by firms in the process of long-term planning. He points out that many of these assumptions are based upon a range of quantitatively based analytical techniques. These techniques contribute to an underlying assumption, on the part of some theorists and many managers, that there is a 'best way' to plan. However, as noted above, long-term organisational planning is becoming less and less reliable or valid in today's turbulent environments.

Perhaps we should not over-react; after all, Mintzberg (1994) reminds us that each succeeding generation tends to perceive its present situation as more turbulent than its predecessors'. He suggests the key factor is whether organisations can learn to think strategically and avoid inappropriately formal processes of planning. He reminds us that

> changes that appear turbulent to organisations that rely heavily on planning may appear normal to, even welcomed by, those that prefer more of a visionary or learning approach. Put more boldly, if you have no vision but only formal plans then every unpredicted change in the environment makes you feel that the sky is falling.

He also suggests that the perceptual filters discussed in Chapter 1 may operate differently in different countries. He notes that what was seen as turbulence in the USA in the 1970s and 80s was perceived as opportunity in Japan. Turbulence demands an organisational response. One such 'reaction' has been for organisations to attempt to develop far greater flexibility; hence the growth of the concepts of the 'flexible firm' and of 'flexible working'.

Flexible working

Many organisations have responded to turbulent environmental conditions by attempting to become more flexible. This real or perceived need for flexibility is increasingly influencing employment conditions. Within organisations, people are both the most vital and the most costly resource. Traditionally, however, they have been prone to inflexibility and inertia. As a consequence many individual employees and organisations have sought to achieve greater flexibility in employment conditions in recent decades. The trend in the UK, for example, is led by both employers and employees, with government supporting developments via legislation. That said, 'flexibility' often means different things for individuals as opposed to businesses.

The old 'industrialised' scenario of reliable employment, which allowed families shared times for shopping, travel, and leisure, together with patterns of work and retirement within the nuclear family, is metamorphosing into what some have called a 'post-industrial' age. Alvin Toffler (1985), a well-known writer about the future shape of work and of organisations, has termed such a society a 'super-industrial' age or a 'third wave'. Toffler likens this 'wave' to the Agricultural Revolution (the first wave) and the Industrial Revolution (the second wave). Others have referred to it as post-Fordism – that is, after or following Henry Ford's mass-production era. In this evolutionary phase certain types of work are in decline as other types of work are emerging. One could draw an analogy between the present period and a time in the UK between 1780 and 1830 when riots, arson and killings accompanied a shift from rural land-based jobs to industrial, factory work. Both are periods where two systems overlap and cause us to think again about our underlying assumptions about the nature of work.

Key characteristics of this new age are expectations on the part of employers that workers will be very flexible (examined in some detail below) and be able to adapt products and services, almost at will, to meet the particular needs of customers. The enhanced capabilities of many organisations to customise products and services has been strongly influenced by developments, for example, in microprocessor technology and management techniques. Computers enable us to process and communicate data and information extremely rapidly. Advances in telecommunications technology (telephones, faxes, multimedia computers, satellites and the Internet) have delivered significant improvements in the quality of data about life and work throughout the globe. These technologies have been harnessed by organisations which wish to operate in a range of countries. Quinn (1992) conceived of intelligent enterprises 'converting intellectual resources into a chain of service outputs and integrating these into a form most useful for certain customers'.

Bridges (1995) identified some 'new rules' which, a decade later, are still evolving and are becoming operative in some parts of the global economy more quickly than in others. The rules are divided into three key points:

- everyone's employment is dependent on the organisation's performance and, as a result, workers need to continuously prove their worth to the organisation and to behave more like an external supplier than a traditional employee;

- workers should, therefore, plan for career-long self-development by taking primary responsibility for health insurance and retirement funds and by renegotiating their compensation arrangements with each organisation when, and if, organisational needs change;

- wise companies will need to work closely with these new-style workers to maximise the benefits for both parties and to bring a range of projects to satisfactory completion.

Having looked at some of the assumptions which underlie recent trends we can now examine the different forms of flexible working which may be found. First, we can identify various types of 'numerical' flexibility, which generally affect employees' hours of work. These include long-standing practices such as overtime, homeworking, shift and part-time work and other increasingly common practices, such as flexitime, teleworking, annual hours and zero hours contracts, the use of temporary staff, and job-sharing. A few of these require some further explanation.

Zero hours contracts are similar to temporary work. For example, some companies have terminated the contracts of staff, some of whom were re-employed on part-time contracts but many others were offered work as and when required by the employer. These 'zero-hours' contracts enable the organisation to adjust staff levels in line with customer demand. Needless to say most of the employees concerned are less than satisfied with this arrangement as it introduced considerable uncertainty into their working lives. Another market-driven change is apparent in the electricity generating business. One company encourages some employees to engage in 'winter/summer stagger', where they work longer hours in the winter to accommodate demand. Hence people are employed on an annual hours basis. Employees of the Rover group agreed in late 1998 to accept annualised hours contracts and in early 1999 production of Land Rovers in Solihull was scaled down and workers' hours temporarily reduced. Many new NHS nursing contracts are also of this type.

There has been an increasing number of people employed as temporary and agency labour over the last few years. Table 9.1 estimates the numbers of 'temps' in various European countries. Temporary workers are employed in most sectors and at all levels including interim managers, industrial workers, administrative staff and medical workers.

Homeworking is not new, although the scale of this activity is increasing. However, teleworking goes a step further by connecting home-based employees by the use of computer modems to the organisation and/or other teleworkers. The availability of communications technology has also led to the 'virtual office' where laptop computers, modems, portable faxes and mobile phones enable people to work in any location. Linked with this is the practice of 'hotdesking' where employees 'touch base' at the office and use whatever

Table 9.1 Temporary workforce estimates

Country	Temporary Workforce 1995	Penetration (%) 1995	Temporary Workforce 2005 (estimate)	Penetration (%) 2005 (estimate)
UK	340 000	1.3	798 000	2.8
France	370 000	1.7	811 000	3.5
Netherlands	180 000	2.7	401 000	5.5
Germany	176 000	0.5	685 000	1.8
Spain	60 000	0.5	239 000	1.8
Belgium	41 000	1.1	105 000	2.5
Switzerland	26 000	0.7	62 000	1.5

work space is available, picking up messages on e-mail. Stanworth and Stanworth (1992) found that the most popular working pattern amongst teleworkers is a combination of home and office working which helps to overcome the inherent isolation of working from home and increases the feeling of belonging to a team. More recent research has supported these earlier findings. 'Telecottaging', where a local venue acts as a central point for teleworkers, may be one way of solving the problem of isolation. From an ecological perspective an increase in teleworking, which is particularly commonplace amongst management consultants, computing and sales personnel, may help reduce rush hour traffic and air pollution.

A second form of flexibility, referred to as 'distancing', is where employees are replaced by subcontractors and employment contracts are replaced by contracts for service. Again this has been commonplace in many industries, such as construction and manufacturing, for many decades. However, the process is increasingly popular in other types of activity, including service industries, and in the public sector.

A third form of flexible working is broadly termed 'functional flexibility'. Although in many organisations strict lines of demarcation exist between jobs, these are seen as offering little flexibility and often prove obstacles to effective teamwork and subsequent productivity gains. Hence multi-skilling, where individuals are trained to undertake a broader array of tasks, is becoming more commonplace. Minicase 9.3 illustrates one such attempt at flexibility in an NHS hospital.

A fourth form of flexibility, pay flexibility, is increasingly commonplace. This may involve the harmonisation of terms and conditions, including the removal of artificial barriers between white-collar and blue-collar workers, such as differences in pension, sick pay and holiday entitlements. This is an approach that the Rover Group, the motor vehicle manufacturer, has used to encourage the development of a teamwork culture. Many organisations have, however, taken a contrasting approach, offering personal non-standard contracts.

Many flexible working practices find their ultimate focus in the concept of a 'virtual corporation'. Virtual corporations have been defined by Davidow and Malone (1992) as

almost edgeless, with permeable and continuously changing interfaces between company, supplier and customers. From inside the firm, the view will be no less amorphous with traditional offices, departments and operating divisions constantly reforming according to need.

Such an organisation 'structure' is a clear culmination of a teleworking, information-based, constantly evolving enterprise.

Finally, there are a number of related concepts including career breaks, paternity and maternity leave, secondments, domestic leave for carers, childcare assistance and school holiday leave. Many of these measures may be considered as 'family-friendly' and are intended to help motivate and retain staff. In 2003 the UK Labour government's new employment law sought to promote family-friendly policies and introduced further statutory rights to, for example, maternity and paternity leave and flexible working rights.

There is strong evidence to suggest that flexible work practices are on the increase, although less agreement concerning whether this is part of a strategically planned reaction

Minicase 9.3   An NHS Trust: generic working

An objective expressed in the Trust's business plan is to 'produce a multi-skilled workforce'. The relevant objective is stated as 'to introduce teams of generic hotel service assistants at ward level so as to improve flexibility and responsiveness to patient needs by combining the role of porters, domestics and catering staff'.

At the hospital all domestics, unqualified nurses and ward clerks are to be based at ward level, a relocation which is involving severing many existing formal and informal relationships. Most of the 260 personnel are being trained in patient care, cleaning and portering skills in order to develop multi-skilled competencies. Staff will then undertake a wider array of tasks and be required to embrace flexibility and teamwork. There may be reduced role certainty. They will need to manage the interface with clinical and other staff groups on the ward. All existing formal status and pay differentials between the hitherto separate groups will be removed. Some staff will be required to change their shift pattern and the total hours they work within any one week.

It is argued that successful implementation will help to 'provide good value for money' and 'make cost savings'. It will ensure, for the time being at least, competitiveness with external commercial players. The single grade and pay spine will reduce status differentials and simplify the highly complex bonus schemes that had evolved. From an operational point of view it will bring benefits of flexibility and simplify work scheduling. It will serve to even out the workload for staff and improve efficiency by avoiding waiting-for-action time and duplication of effort. Managers believe it will improve worker motivation as people will feel part of a team. They will, it is believed, take a pride in their work at ward level.

In conclusion, the philosophy underpinning the care assistant concept is a familiar one. A multi-skilled, flexible workforce is thought to facilitate operational planning and enhance both the efficiency and effectiveness of service provision. The assumption is that employees benefit from the resultant job enrichment and co-operative teamwork, cost savings are there for the making, via enhanced efficiency, and patient care is improved.

Question

What are the benfits and drawbacks to (a) the employer and (b) the employee of these changes?

to changing environmental circumstances, including employee needs/wants, a result of short-term economic expedience or the outcome of a shifting balance between capital (employers) and labour (employees). Recent studies into flexible working in Europe suggest that, although there is an overall trend towards greater use of flexible working patterns, there is considerable variation in practice between countries, sectors and sizes of organisation. About 18 per cent of the workforce in the European Union works part-time, growth in this respect being most notable in Holland, Germany and the UK. Non-permanent employment has increased significantly in all European Union countries, as has subcontracting. Trailing the trend is Greece, where only 5 per cent of workers are part-time, compared to 8 per cent in Italy and 9 per cent in Spain. The equivalent figures for Britain and Holland are 28 per cent and 20 per cent respectively. In a survey of British part-time workers, 84 per cent suggested that they preferred part-time work. The majority of part-time workers are female. Around 50 per cent of women employees in the United Kingdom work part-time; the EU average is just 30 per cent. The trend in Europe follows earlier movements in this direction in the USA. It is not necessarily coincidental that in the UK and Holland, the two countries with the most flexible labour market in this respect, unemployment is amongst the lowest in the European Union.

The UK has the most flexible workforce in the EU with around 10 million people (almost 40 per cent of all employees) either part-time, temporary, self-employed, on a government training scheme or as unpaid family workers. This represented an increase of almost 2 million in a decade. Over 80 per cent of all medium-sized and large organisations in the United Kingdom employ some temporary staff. The BBC, for example, now offers the majority of new recruits only short or fixed-term contracts, as do many universities.

In the UK there has also been an increase in the number of men working flexibly, from 23 per cent in 1994 to almost 32 per cent in 2003, while the proportion of women in this category remained stable and high at 50 per cent. Men in this category were largely self-employed; women were mainly part-time or on temporary contracts. Additionally, over 12 per cent, that is 2.6 million people, work flexitime, while 2 million, or 9 per cent of the workforce, have annualised hours contracts. Over a million employees work school term-time only while about 200 000 people job-share. The Alliance & Leicester Building Society, for example, offer some employees, who are parents of school-age children (both mothers and fathers), the opportunity to work during term-time only, while Boots provide job-share 'partnerships' in positions from supervisor to pharmacy manager. These family-friendly measures attempt to motivate employees and help parents balance work and family demands. They also facilitate the retention of competent and well-trained staff.

Minicase 9.4 illustrates some interesting characteristics of the flexible firm and organisational change. Largely as a response to changes within its business environment, such as government directives inspired by wider technological and competitive conditions, the organisation has undergone a major restructuring. The result is a smaller, leaner, delayered and more flexible company. The organisation has moved from a 'mechanistic' to an 'organic' (Burns and Stalker, 1961) structure and from a 'defender' to a 'prospector' (Miles and Snow, 1978) strategic orientation (see Chapter 1). It also demonstrates that the boundary between the organisation and its 'task' environment is not fixed but rather dynamic and flexible.

Minicase 9.4   Melbourne Water

Melbourne Water was formed from the long-established Metropolitan Board of Works, a typical government bureaucracy which operated in a protected and stable business environment with guaranteed superannuated employment. Impending privatisation has encouraged management to structure the organisation along competitive commercial lines as it aims to become a market leader in the Asia Pacific region in the provision of water storage, purification and distribution capabilities.

Melbourne Water: the flexible firm

A layer of middle management has disappeared altogether. The executive and senior levels have been combined and supervisors have been reclassed as team leaders. The core workforce is now described as full-time and no one in the organisation is considered to have guaranteed life-long employment. All maintenance and construction activities are contracted out. Casual semi-skilled workers are employed as required on a daily basis and are recruited through specialist agencies. Much of the professional work is conducted by consultants. A number of major suppliers are now considered partners in the organisation as they are required to carry out some of the duties formerly conducted by employees.

Questions

1. It has been said that organisational loyalty (where the organisation remains loyal to its employees through difficult times) helped maintain organisational success. How has loyalty changed in recent decades?

2. Has the concept of organisational loyalty any relevance in modern organisations?

Changes in the external environment, which may have encouraged the moves towards flexible working, ensure that the flexible firm and flexible working will become an increasing reality. Summarised here, they include:

- increased national competition;

- globalisation and consequent competitive pressures;

- uncertainty created by market volatility and, in part, a hang-over from recessionary periods;

- government intervention to support and extend employees' and/or employers' rights;

- technological change, particularly in information technology and communications, which facilitates some forms of flexible working;

- investment in new plant requiring new and ever-changing skills;

- a move from Fordism to post-Fordism, from mass production to flexible specialisation;

- continued emphasis on costs and budgets and financial stringency in the public sector;

- political influence, particularly in the public sector;

- reductions in trade union power;

- increasing numbers of women and other employee groups 'demanding' alternative employment conditions; a change in attitudes to work and life, to levels of organisational loyalty (both ways) and responsibility for personal and career development.

In summary, it has been noted that as the business environment becomes more turbulent many organisations have sought ways of managing change. This has encouraged them to seek increased short-term operational flexibility and more adaptive approaches to long-term planning.

Implications for the individual

When environmental change demands organisational change, as it almost continuously does, then we as individuals have to respond. It is becoming increasingly uncommon for people to work within a stable environment and undertake similar tasks and responsibilities for any length of time. Individuals are required to change at least as rapidly as the business environment if they are to remain effective. They need to continually develop their capabilities in order to function effectively within changing organisations. As the now clichéd saying goes, 'standing still is not an option'. We have to develop new skills and behaviours and, perhaps more importantly, new attitudes and ways of thinking, as the environment demands flexibility and the capacity and willingness to seek personal development opportunities.

Moves towards greater flexible working and the growth of the flexible firm are of direct relevance to individuals in the workplace. It is individuals who are being made 'flexible' and it is they who will, or will not, cope with the changes in working patterns outlined above. Handy (1994) identified the 'portfolio career' which many people experience these days. This is multifaceted and may include holding a number of 'loose' employment contracts, with a number of employers. For example, a management consultant might work on a few short-term projects with a number of organisations, undertake to write a management textbook for a publishing company and work for a university business school as a part-time lecturer. Most individuals have been accustomed to regular 9 to 5, permanent, pensioned employment, so that new developments present personal challenges in balancing work and life patterns.

Increasing numbers of middle-aged and older people are having to adjust to changing employment patterns. The Organisation for Economic Cooperation Development (OECD) calculated that only just over a third of UK citizens aged over 55 years are in paid work despite there being near full employment in the economy as a whole. The equivalent figure for France is 27 per cent while for Italy it was just 15 per cent. Redundancy, early retirement opportunities and the lack of employment prospects for those over 50, together with youth unemployment and increasing numbers in higher education, ensure that the vast bulk of the workforce in Western Europe is between 25 and 55 years old. Many people's working life is restricted to just 30 years. In the 1960s the vast majority of young adults started work aged 15 and were expected to retire at 65 (male) or 60 (female) – a working life of up to 50 years. For some people changes in this regard have been unwelcome and have led to a reduction in their standard of living. Many have had to adjust their work-life expectations.

There is also a wider social implication for many millions who are not employed. They do not all do nothing! It is evident that many people have more time than they know what to do with, while others have far too little time to do what they want. Typical American and British citizens already work longer hours than they did in the 1980s. The average American works 164 hours a year longer than twenty years ago (equivalent to an extra month a year).

Successive Labour Force Surveys conducted in the UK by the Central Statistical Office have noted many significant changes including:

- a medium/long-term decline in full-time male employment;

- a significant increase in part-time employment for both men and women (see data above);

- an increase in the numbers of self-employed;

- an increase in the number of people with multiple jobs (approximately 1.4 million people in the UK have at least two jobs).

An increasingly 'flexible', self-employed and mobile workforce requires new forms of employment representation. Many trade unions are having to respond by providing different services and making different social responses. Increases in 'flexibility', which may often be forced upon employees, create personal uncertainty and anxiety about the future. Such uncertainties have complex implications.

Of concern for the management of organisations which are undergoing seismic change is the potential for loss of worker motivation and commitment. Stevenson and Moldoveanu (1995) argue that anxious employees will ensure that their curricula vitae are kept up to date in case they fall prey to the latest round of re-engineering or restructuring. However, with near full employment, employee complacency is also likely to be apparent. The authors contrast the mounting uncertainty for ordinary workers with improvements

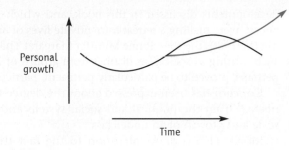

Figure 9.1 An adapted Sigmoid Curve

in certainty that senior managers gain from such things as golden parachutes, that is, the certainty of sizeable severance deals should their contracts be rescinded.

Previously predictable life-cycle patterns have, in the last two decades, changed considerably. Handy (1994) refers to the Sigmoid Curve (see Figure 9.1) as an analytical model for depicting a person's working life-cycle. He argues that people start life falteringly, then make steady and consistent progress before peaking and enjoying a 'decline' during retirement. However, the time-frame for the Sigmoid Curve, rather like many product life cycles, is now being squeezed. This, he argues, means people need to develop new options for a second or even third career during their working lives. Evidence suggests that an increasing number of people switch careers at least once during their working life and undertake a seemingly different occupation (e.g. from executive to management lecturer). Figure 9.1 shows this secondary curve superimposed on the Sigmoid Curve, indicating that many people can sustain personal growth by developing a second career.

This discussion has highlighted a trend in society towards greater life and employment uncertainty. For many people flexible working improves choice and freedom while for others it constrains or sidelines them. Unfortunately, as individuals we are powerless to change societal trends or governmental policy. Globalisation and technological change conspire to transform our social and working worlds. What we can do is exercise some control over our own patterns of living. The paradox is that fragmentation and flexible working can offer new freedoms for those able to take advantage of them.

Implications for groups

In this section we look at the implications of environmental change on a number of groups – under-25-year-olds, the socially excluded, women and racial minorities – and at the increasing economic vulnerability suffered by many families as a result of the growth of flexible working.

A generation ago Pawley (1974) considered that Western society was withdrawing from 'the whole system of values and obligations that has historically been the basis of public, community and family life'. He was of the opinion that the sorts of technological developments discussed in this book, and which he termed 'socially atomising appliances', were fuelling a retreat into 'private lives of an unprecedented completeness'. During the 1980s the then Prime Minister Margaret Thatcher famously denied that there was such a thing as society, as distinct from groups of individuals. Pawley's assessment has, perhaps, proved to be particularly pertinent, particularly so in Western countries.

Concern has been expressed about the degree to which young people feel 'disconnected' from the political and social system and about the generally acknowledged scale and growth of an underclass.

Moore (1995) draws attention to the fact that many young people have been attracted by single-issue campaigning on such matters as animal rights and environmental protection. She believes the attraction here is that the ethical basis of such campaigns contrasts sharply with the predominantly political atmosphere of parliamentary processes. She argues that,

> while the state has washed its hands of financial responsibility for the young, trapping them into economic dependence on their parents for longer and longer, it has intervened long enough to tell them that many of their leisure activities are illegal. The idea of voting once every five years is no compensation for the lack of say in the rest of their lives.

The use of the phrase 'underwolves' in the title of Moore's article reflects a feeling that increasing proportions of young people are not content to be 'underdogs' and are starting to fight back.

In the UK the Labour government launched the Social Exclusion Unit in 1997, bringing together the civil service, the police, business and voluntary sectors in an attempt to reduce homelessness and social exclusion, and address the problems of crime on many deprived housing estates. The emphasis is on trying to avoid one agency passing problems on to others and upon collaboration in order to try and prevent social exclusion from happening in the first place (Wintour, 1997). Crucial to the success of this policy was the extent to which the 'new deal' initiative can encourage the long-term unemployed to find jobs. Government statistics show that it has enjoyed reasonable success. Similarly, attempts to improve educational standards and embed life-long learning are in part aimed at reducing the growth and scale of social, economic and political exclusion.

In the UK there are ambitious targets for participation in higher education and it is recognised that these will only be achieved if a much larger number of students from middle and low-income families, together with those from under-represented minority groups, attend university. The White paper for HE in 2003 signalled the intention to provide significantly increased funding for universities to attract and retain what might otherwise be excluded (from HE) young people. It intends to reward and encourage greater participation rates among poorer families and certain under-represented minorities and expects all, even the elite universities, to recruit from this group.

We have noted the impact of the growth of temporary and contract forms of work on female employment. The proportion of working women increased from 44 per cent in 1971 to 53 per cent in 1994, to about 57 per cent in 2003 and is set to increase to 60 per cent by the year 2006. Just over a quarter of all women work full-time.

It can be argued that female job prospects have improved in the UK as a result of changes in the nature of work, the introduction of some more family-friendly policies and the increased availability of affordable childcare. Evans (1998) notes that only 9.8 per cent of mothers with children under 5 were unemployed in 1996, compared with 27.2 per cent in 1984. He argues that the availability of more part-time work, job-shares and the ability to work from home ease women's return to work after childbirth.

In the UK more women are advancing into higher managerial and professional work, passing through what has been termed the 'glass ceiling'. The female proportion of this group rose from 9 per cent in 1984 to about 23 per cent in 2003. However, about 11 per cent of the female workforce is engaged in highly routine low-skilled occupations; the comparable figure for men is just 5 per cent (Brindle, 1998).

Implications for government

This section explores some of the implications for government of environmental change before discussing the ongoing debate concerning the role of government. Government at local, national, regional and global levels is a powerful environmental force which influences the business environment of all organisations. However, there is a range of environmental phenomena which are themselves of major concern to governments at various levels. Many of these are listed in the introductory section of this chapter. We will look at just four of these changes and briefly assess the consequences for governments. These areas are:

- globalisation and consequent intense international competition;

- technological advances creating issues which many argue require a co-ordinated political and 'strategic' approach;

- the growth of the flexible firm and flexible working;

- conflicting pressures for both a reduced and an extended role for government.

Globalisation

Progress towards the globalisation of production and trade has been rapid in recent decades. It has been hastened by the successes of the General Agreement on Tariffs and Trade (GATT), now replaced by the World Trade Organisation (see Chapter 7), by market and political union, and by many genuine attempts on the part of world leaders to reduce 'distance' between nations and communities.

Despite the volatility in economic growth, notably in Asia, the last two decades have witnessed large increases in global income and in levels of international trade in both goods and services. Many protective barriers have been removed or reduced, such that competition between nations and companies is, by and large, more fierce than in previous decades. It is now important for companies and governments to consider the level of national and regional competitiveness. Undoubtedly, some countries enjoy political, social, technological and economic advantages which encourage multinational, transnational or global companies to invest in them. A number of organisations and researchers have attempted to calculate national competitiveness and produce 'league tables'. They consider such things as average wage rates, workforce skills and capabilities, income and corporation tax rates and the degree of political stability.

Many individuals, groups and organisations in most countries argue that government should play a major part in attempting to maintain or improve their national competitiveness. By so doing they may facilitate the achievement of comfortable economic growth rates, better and secure employment opportunities and improvements in standards of living. Although most governments actively pursue policies which they believe will enhance the competitiveness of their country and its organisations, there is considerable disagreement on how best to achieve this aim. Some argue for a heavily 'interventionist' policy in which government plays a major role, for example by directly investing in industry, providing training, building state-of-the-art infrastructure and facilitating international trade. Conversely, other arguments favour a more laissez-faire approach, such as was traditionally the case in the USA or Hong Kong. Broadly, government's role in this scenario is to 'free' private enterprise from many 'constraints', such as high social costs and taxes, and to allow it to compete in free markets. Government does not significantly intervene, for example, to subsidise public transport or to invest directly in industry.

Both broad schools of thought can claim successes. The USA and Hong Kong, for example, flourished by adopting a predominantly laissez-faire approach, while Singapore and Japan have, since the 1950s, experienced rapid economic growth, in part, it is argued, by active government interventionist policies; however, the latter of those two countries have been unable to sustain that growth, some say because government are unwilling to make the necessary but difficult decisions to change. Whatever one's views, it is clear that national and/or regional competitiveness is increasingly becoming an important determinant of the material well-being of a population. Consequently, government has an obligation to its citizens to ensure they share in global successes.

Technological change

Technological change has a significant influence over economic growth. Government, therefore, has a role to play in the development of conditions suitable for technological advances to be made and transformed into economic wealth-creating opportunities. The approach governments adopt will largely depend on their ideological stance, as indicated above. One government may, for example, invest a significant element of revenue collected from taxation into research which might lead to economic wealth-creating opportunities largely for private industry. Another may prefer to allow market mechanisms to dictate research and development spending levels within industry. Clearly, the role of government, although crucial, varies considerably across the world.

It is reported, for example, that in Hong Kong multinational organisations have for decades been invited to invest, irrespective of the technological benefits they might bring to the province. However, the government of Singapore has been somewhat more vigilant and active in encouraging companies which bring transferable technological advances to their country.

In addition to creating the 'right' conditions for technological development and diffusion, government also has a regulatory role to perform. This role may involve prohibiting, or otherwise regulating, potentially unethical research and technological development. Many countries are currently debating issues concerning the advances in genetic engineering which have been made in recent years. There are important and far-reaching ethical consequences of many technological advances. Although self-regulation, by researchers and professional bodies for example, is important, many people expect governments to adopt an ideological and regulatory stance in this regard.

Flexible working

There are a number of highly contentious issues associated with flexible working. For example, government policy in the UK may favour a reduction in the legal restrictions on the hiring and dismissal of workers, which would most certainly increase flexibility. However, this would have significant, often harmful, consequences for many groups and individuals. Beardwell and Holden (1994) have suggested that government might remove all state intervention in pay setting and further extend the law to curb trade union influence over pay and employment. However, these ideas often conflict with European Union legislation, which favours a statutory minimum wage and protection for workers, and takes a more interventionist, less free-market, approach. Additionally, the Labour government in the UK has introduced a minimum wage. They are 'mixed' in their support for the more focused pursuit of 'flexibility'. The introduction of new employment rights in 1999 suggested some attempt is being made to achieve a compromise between family friendly policies and the perceived needs of industry and in 2003 significant new rights of maternity and flexible working were introduced.

Changes in employment and career patterns have important and far-reaching consequences for pension provision (see Chapter 5 and Case Study 5) and some welfare payments. The government in the UK has responded to long-term change by increasing the age of retirement for women to 65 years, to match that for men, by strongly encouraging employees to take out additional private personal pension provision and by introducing new compulsory pension savings schemes. With an ageing population, government fears the rising burden of pension and welfare demands upon the public purse. The picture is even more pronounced in some Western countries with even lower fertility rates than the UK. By 2030, people over 65 in Germany, the world's third-largest economy, will account for almost half the adult population, compared with one-fifth now. Unless the country's fertility rate recovers over the same period, its population of under-35s will shrink about twice as fast as the older population will grow. The total population, now 82 million, will decline to 72 million while the number of working age will fall by a quarter, from 40 million to 30 million. The pattern is similar in Japan, Italy, France, Spain, Portugal, the Netherlands and Sweden. Curiously, China faces a similar concern due to its long-standing 'one-child' policy.

Dynamism in the public sector

Given the global context in which all organisations now operate it is not surprising that the nature of the public sector and its business environment has fundamentally changed in recent decades. This has created a state of flux where many organisations have changed ownership from public to private sector and others have been so transformed as to be virtually unrecognisable. There is little doubt that the complex array of political, social and economic objectives of governments over the last two decades have created enormous pressures for change within publicly owned organisations, creating a state of near permanent tension between different interest groups.

Both the scale of the public sector and the rate of change within its environment make it a valuable, but often neglected, field of study. Public sector organisations conduct government business, are largely funded from the public purse and are usually accountable to government at some level. As the vast majority of funding and support for most public sector organisations is provided from taxation, it is the duty of government to ensure that proper care is taken when dispensing these resources. Hence, government at local, national and international levels has a pervasive and powerful influence over public sector bodies, particularly in their role as legislators and resource providers.

A theme of environmental change or dynamism, together with ever-increasing complexity and uncertainty, prevails. The environmental changes are themselves part of a global transformation in the nature of public sector organisations. In most countries the public sector is a major employer and service provider. It also accounts for a significant proportion of Gross Domestic Product. In the United Kingdom, for example, in 2003 government expenditure represented about 43 per cent of total Gross Domestic Product (GDP) and over 5 million people were directly employed within the public sector. In much of Europe public expenditure accounts for between 45–50 per cent of total GDP, while in Japan and the USA it is a little lower at around 35 per cent.

Should government wish to rein back on its spending, this would be fraught with difficulties. There is considerable inertia from a series of built-in mechanisms which ensure future government commitment and a suitable tax regime. For example, the rapid growth in higher education in the UK and many other European countries is viewed as essential if these nations are to compete in the global economy. This has meant that government has had to increase expenditure in this area. The expectation will be for even greater numbers to experience higher education and for government to pay a significant proportion of the resultant university fees. Additionally, the criminal justice system has seen steady increases in the prison population with consequent increases in government expenditure in part as a result of rising crime rates, but also due to 'get-tough' government policies. Governments, especially in the old Western industrialised world, are increasingly concerned about the long-term social and financial costs of unemployment. An ageing population, as discussed above, continues to put increased demands upon the NHS, state pension and welfare systems, necessitating increased government expenditure. What is more, as the population ages there will be fewer people working and potentially fewer taxpayers.

It is estimated that improvements in life expectancy and medical care, combined with changing demographic factors, will mean that long-term care for the aged in the year 2020 may account for over 10 per cent of the GDP of the UK compared to a figure of just 7 per cent of GDP for the whole of the NHS in 2003. Despite the 'radical' changes that have occurred within the public sector, such as privatisation and compulsory competitive tendering, the fact remains that the level of taxation and the scale of the public sector have not declined, rather they have increased significantly since 2001.

The problem of potentially spiralling demands upon the public purse is certainly not unique to the UK. Many European Union countries experienced alarmingly rapid increases in government expenditure during the 1980s and 1990s and were obliged to reduce expenditure in order to qualify for first-wave euro membership in 1999. Business leaders, employer representative bodies, right-wing think-tanks and politicians frequently call for major reform.

The market system, public goods and change

It can be argued that the existence of the public sector is due to the failure of the free-market system to provide all the services required by the general public and by government. However, both the scope and scale of the public sector in any country are in part the result of prevailing political ideologies, or those that prevailed in the past. A multitude of other factors also influence both the level of government involvement in the economy and the scale of public expenditure. However, there is no indisputable law of economics which argues that the public sector should, for example, operate the full range of services found in most developed countries. Neither is there, at any time, a 'correct' or indisputable level of government expenditure.

There are a certain, strictly limited, number of services which most politicians, academics and the general public agree should be conducted by the government or at least under its tight scrutiny. Relatively uncontroversial examples include the judiciary, the police and the armed services. However, there are a large and growing number of activities which are the subject of considerable public debate in many countries regarding the most appropriate form of ownership and operation.

The trend towards a mixed economy, where economic activity is shared via both public and private ownership, proceeded apace in the developed industrialised world with the introduction and growth of government services throughout the nineteenth and twentieth centuries. The scope of government activity in most countries grew to include responsibility for education, health, law and order, defence and other services. Additionally, many industrial organisations were nationalised, meaning that they were not owned by private shareholders but by government on behalf of the nation, e.g. the steel, gas, railways, electricity and water supply businesses. There has been a major reversal of this trend since the early 1980s in the United Kingdom and in the 1990s across most of the world with the market economy once again becoming more dominant. In recent decades there has been a tendency in many countries for governments to move away from direct provision of goods and services and towards a focus on regulating more and producing less. The range of mechanisms which governments have employed in the past twenty years includes:

- privatisation;

- deregulation;

- contracting-out public sector services;

- quality charters, league tables and published performance targets;

- performance management and performance-related pay;

- more effective complaints procedures;

- tougher and more independent inspectorates;

- private/public sector financial partnerships.

Many politicians and some academics believe that private markets are capable of providing some services that are more usually regarded as 'public goods'. These include health care (supported by private insurance) and education (backed with means-tested student loans and private schools). Others argue that this would lead to a multi-tiered system and a restriction of access to high quality services for a significant section of the community. They further argue that the benefits of a healthy and well-educated population are shared by all, so the costs should also be shared. Additionally, objectors to the idea of a market economy argue that the conditions necessary for perfect competition rarely, if ever, exist and that competition in the provision of many public services, such as health care, is morally unacceptable and practically unworkable.

However, there is widespread recognition that in many circumstances the market is a sound and appropriate mechanism for the allocation of scarce resources (see Chapter 2). As such the marketplace, via the price system, allocates goods and services to individuals and organisations. Although the market economy is far from faultless, the alternatives are not necessarily guaranteed to be more efficient or effective in servicing the needs of society or individuals.

The political forces outlined above are themselves driven by powerful economic, social and technological changes within the global arena. Wider environmental changes inform political agendas and mould ideologies. However, the mechanism of influence between the wider environment and political activity is two-way as government decisions profoundly influence those environmental forces. For example, whereas changing social needs create dynamism to which government and public organisations have to respond, those same social changes are, in part, the result of government policy and behaviour. For example, the relative incomes of people in the poorest 10 per cent of United Kingdom society actually declined during the 1980s and 90s. This resulted from a lack of political will to address the problems faced by this sector of society through more progressive taxation or welfare policies, although the present Labour government have introduced employment and other welfare-related measures to tackle social and employment exclusion. The relative poverty of this group has contributed to many social problems such as urban deprivation, long-term unemployment, crime, drug abuse and social exclusion. As a result government and public sector organisations are faced with a social environment which is, in part, a consequence of their previous activity.

Public sector change: drivers and resistors

The business environment facing public sector organisations is in a state of flux largely, although not exclusively, due to changes in political ideologies and agendas. No public organisation is immune from change yet internal resistance is rife. There are within most organisations, not least publicly owned entities, both active and passive forces which encourage a state of stability and which serve to reduce the potency of the forces for change. Hence a dynamic balance exists between the forces which promote change and those that favour stability. Both sets of pressures comprise a combination of external environmental and internal organisational forces.

Lewin (1951) encompassed such tensions within a force-field model. He argued that the two sets of forces 'push' against each other. If the forces for change, the 'drivers' are more pervasive and powerful than the 'resistors' then change will occur. Conversely, if resisting forces are more powerful they may well scupper the intentions of change agents. Hence an intense, continuous and highly political process of change and stability is unfolding within the public sector. Figure 9.2 shows the force-field model.

Some of the forces for change and stability in the public sector are shown in Table 9.2. These are not ranked according to their potency. Nor is this an exhaustive list. The forces encouraging change are largely, but not exclusively, external to public sector organisations. These have been outlined within this chapter. Factors encouraging stability and other resisting forces are largely internal to public organisations.

Although the causal relationships between many of the factors are not shown in the force-field model it does indicate the complexity of the tensions that exists. It is also curious that some items, such as public accountability, can act as both a force encouraging change and reform and a pressure to guard against the flux and uncertainty which change often involves. This model could just as easily be applied to any single organisation or government department.

Just how much real change has occurred within the public sector over the past two decades is, like so many aspects of public policy, hotly disputed. There has been significant transfer of activity to private operators and major internal restructuring has altered patterns of responsibility and accountability. Whether organisational culture and workplace behaviour have or should alter radically within the public sector is far less certain.

Figure 9.2 Simple force-field model

Table 9.2 Conflicting forces for change and stability within the public sector

Forces for Change	Forces for Stability
Nearly two decades of Conservative government and the new right ideology	Organisational cultures: accepted practices & behaviours; taken for granted beliefs concerning how activities should be conducted; attitudes to colleagues, members of the public and politicians; fundamental public service values
Only moderate economic growth	
High levels of unemployment	
Increasing resource demands on welfare provision	Hierarchical organisational structures, formal reporting relationships and historically accrued bureaucracy
Ageing population	
Cultural change, e.g. increasing community expectation; power of the media; consumerism	Statutory and regulatory, duties and procedures
	Employee organisations, e.g. trade unions (UNISON), BMA and other individual or group vested interests
Technological advance, e.g. in medicine and information technology	
Globalisation, e.g. restructuring of industry; deregulation; increased competitive forces	Lack of 'ownership' of change, i.e. top-down imposed model is usually favoured
New blood, e.g. management trained/educated elites; managerialism; benchmarking	Resource constraint
	Individual and group overt and covert resistance
Public accountability	Public accountability
New Labour	
Social inclusion	

Conclusion

In this chapter we have focused on many of the environmental factors outlined in this text and on the increasing dynamism and uncertainty in the environment. We then explored the implications of this for organisations, groups, individuals and governments.

We have tried to resist the temptation to predict the future and have concentrated on examining currently developing trends which we expect to continue to have a significant impact. In so doing we hope to have created a book which does not date too quickly. The tendency with much factual data, however, is for it to become obsolete very quickly. This will, undoubtedly, mean that when you read this book there will be some points which no longer hold true. For this reason we trust that the most lasting impact of the book will be on the processes which you use to examine the business environment.

In respect of these processes we have placed strong emphasis on ways of evaluating the business environment. For example, we have stressed the importance of examining problems at a range of geo-political scales, that is, from international, through regional and national to local perspectives. It seems to us that a business environment textbook cannot confine itself to examining environmental factors at any one of these levels. We have also indicated that the methods which organisations adopt to monitor their environments will, to a large extent, influence both what is seen and whether changes are perceived as opportunities or threats. We have used the phrase 'perceptual filters' to describe this process. This, intentionally, placed the emphasis upon the human side of organisational activity.

Summary of main points

This chapter has focused upon the nature of change in the business environment and organisational, individual, group and government responses to environmental dynamism. The main points are:

- The international business environment is increasingly complex, dynamic, uncertain (turbulent) and even chaotic for many organisations, individuals, groups and governments.

- Major economic, political, technological and social changes have transformed the business environment in the last decade, necessitating organisational change and increased flexibility.

- There may be a trend towards high profile 'shock events' and non-linear chaotic patterns in many areas of the natural world (to some extent such patterns are also observable in the business world) which suggests that organisations might do well to make contingency plans.

- The nature of the international business environment calls into question the validity of organisational approaches to long-term planning and suggests the need for processes which build in flexibility and adaptability.

- There has been a rapid increase in previously considered 'non-standard' temporal and contractual patterns of work such as part-time work, teleworking, contracting-out, self-employment and temporary work.

- The position of many young people in the UK shows alarmingly large proportions are 'disconnected' from both the political system and from their local communities.

- Turbulent environments demand government attention.

- The future role of government is likely to remain a fiercely debated issue for some time.

Discussion Questions

1. What are the implications of increased turbulence and chaos in the business environment for the ways in which organisations plan for the future?

2. Discuss the opposing ideological positions concerning the role of government in encouraging national competitiveness and technological development.

3. Assess the implications for individual workers of the increased use of flexible working practices by organisations.

4. Contrast your parents' work-life experiences with those of your grandparents. How do you expect your work-life experiences will differ from those of your parents?

5. Conduct a force-field analysis for any public sector organisation using primary and/or secondary sources of information.

 Web Links

There are many sites which refer to each of the PESTLE elements. Reference to many of these can be found at the end of each chapter. Two additional sites that may be of interest are:

http://www.Bized.ac.uk/roads/busenv

http://www.Skypoint.com/members

(this 'futurology' site is worthy of attention).

References

Beardwell, I. and Holden, L. (1994) *Human Resource Management: A Contemporary Perspective*, Pitman.

Bridges, W. (1995) 'The death of the job', *Independent on Sunday*, 5 February.

Brindle, D. (1998) 'Teachers get more class in social shake-up', *Guardian*, 1 December.

Burns, T. and Stalker, G.M. (1961) *The Management of Innovation*, London: Tavistock.

Davidow, W.H. and Malone, M.S. (1992) *The Virtual Corporation: Structuring and Revitalizing the Corporation for the 21st Century*, Harper Business.

Evans P. (1998) 'Why has the female unemployment rate in Britain fallen?' *Bank of England Quarterly Bulletin*, 38 (3), August.

Gleick, J. (1988) *Chaos: Making a New Science*, Cardinal.

Hamel, G. and Prahalad, C.K. (1995), Competing for the Future', *Success* 42 (9).

Handy, C. (1994) *The Empty Raincoat*, Hutchinson.

Johnson, G. and Scholes, K. (2002) *Exploring Corporate Strategy*, 6th edn, Prentice Hall.

Lewin, K. (1951) *Field Theory in Social Science*, New York: Harper & Row.

Miles, R.F. (1980) *Macro Organisational Behaviour*, Sull Foresman & Co.

Miles, R.E. and Snow, C.C. (1978) *Organisational Strategy, Structure and Process*, New York: McGraw-Hill.

Mintzberg, H. (1994) *The Rise and Fall of Strategic Planning*, New York: Prentice Hall.

Moore, S. (1995) 'Beware of dances with underwolves', *Guardian 2*, 28 September.

Pawley, M. (1974) *The Private Future*, Pan.

Perrow, C. (1986) *Complex Organisations: A Critical Essay*, 3rd edn, New York: Random House.

Quinn, J.B. (1978) 'Strategic change: logical incrementalism', *Sloan Management Review*, Fall.

Quinn, J.B. (1992) *Intelligent Enterprise*, The Free Press.

Stacey, R.D. (2003) *Strategic Management and Organisational Dynamics*, 4th edn, FT Prentice Hall.

Stanworth, J. and Stanworth, C. (1992) *Telework: The Human Resource Implications*, IPM.

Stevenson, H.H. and Moldoveanu, M.C. (1995) 'The power of predictability', *Harvard Business Review*, July August.

Tapscott, D. (1996) *The Digital Economy: Praise and Peril in the Age of Networked Intelligence*, New York: McGraw-Hill.

Toffler, A. (1985) *The Adaptive Corporation*, Pan.

Wintour, P. (1997) 'Ghetto busters to tackle poverty in can-do mood', *Observer*, 7 December.

Part Two

Case Studies

Introduction

The nine cases that form Part II of this book illustrate aspects of the business environment. They have been carefully selected to include an array of organisational types and operating environments. They comprise three commercial companies, three themes key to any business, an international region and two countries. All cases are concerned with international organisations and/or issues.

The table below indicates the relationship between the case studies and each chapter in Part I. Each case study includes a number of questions. It may prove beneficial to refer to the relevant chapter(s) when answering them.

Indication of case studies' relationship with chapters

Case Studies	Chapters in Part I						
	2	3	4	5	6	7	8
Case Study 1: Cadbury Schweppes	***	*	*	**	**	*	
Case Study 2: Tourism in Greece	**	*		*	***		
Case Study 3: Global dominoes: the case of South-East Asia	*	***		*		*	
Case Study 4: Biotechnology: implications for business, society and individuals	**		***	**	*		**
Case Study 5: Ageing Europe and the growing pensions crisis		***	*	***	*	*	
Case Study 6: Carlsberg	*		*	*	***		**
Case Study 7: Tanzania: from socialism to capitalism	*	*		*		***	
Case Study 8: The Bhopal disaster	*					**	***
Case Study 9: The business of sport: Manchester United plc	**			**	*		

* = relevance   ** = significant relevance   *** = prime focus

Cadbury Schweppes
Jamie Weatherston

1

Background

The origins of Cadbury Schweppes go back 180 years. In 1783 Jacob Schweppe invented a system for the manufacture of carbonated mineral water, and founded the Schweppes Company in Geneva. In 1790 a factory was established in London. Schweppes was floated as a public company in 1897.

In Birmingham in 1824 John Cadbury opened a shop selling tea and coffee and later cocoa and drinking chocolate. The business thrived and the family moved from retailing into manufacturing in 1831. The business continued to grow and the Bournville factory and village was established in 1879. In 1899 Cadbury Brothers was incorporated into a limited company.

Throughout the first half of the twentieth century both companies continued to prosper and develop their operations on an international basis. The merger of Schweppes Ltd and Cadbury Group Ltd in 1969 created Cadbury Schweppes, a global giant in the confectionery and non-alcoholic drinks sector.

Cadbury Schweppes is structured on a regional basis, put in place in February 2003, comprising five business regions:

Americas Beverages

Americas Confectionery

Europe, Middle East and Africa (EMEA) Confectionery

Europe Beverages

Asia Pacific (including India and Pakistan)

In 2003 Cadbury Schweppes has a workforce of approximately 38 000. It has 57 subsidiaries, operational in 28 countries and is active in over 200 countries. In April 2003, following the purchase of Adams, the company was valued at around £7 billion. Table C1.1 shows the growth of sales and profits between 1998 and 2000.

Cadbury Schweppes' stated objective is growth in shareholder value, focusing on its core business of beverages and confectionery through acquisitions and sustaining its leading position in the global market. This expansion has allowed Cadbury Schweppes to exploit significant economies of scale in their distribution. It also launched its Managing for Value (MFV) process in 1997/1998 with an emphasis on improving returns through pursuing cost efficiencies and a low-cost strategy.

Since the early 1980s the soft drink and confectionery brand portfolio has been strengthened and extended considerably through a number of key acquisitions. These include notably:

Table C1.1 Cadbury Schweppes sales and profit 1998–2002

	1998	1999	2000	2001	2002
Net sales (£)	3999	4234	4118	4960	5298
% growth		5.9	−2.7	20.4	6.8
Operating profit (£)	551	634	713	831	866
% growth		15.1	12.5	16.5	4.2

Source: Euromonitor

- 1982 Duff-Mott Company;
- 1986 Canada Dry;
- 1989 Bassett's and Trebor;
- 1995 Dr Pepper/Seven Up Companies Inc.;
- 2000 Snapple Beverages Group;
- 2001 Slush Puppy Corporation;
- 2001 Orangina Pampryl from Pernod Ricard in France; La Casera from the Iberian Beverages group in Spain;
- 2002 Adams confectionery, its biggest ever acquisition, bought from Pfizer.

However, there have also been a number of significant developments and divestments during this period, particularly in the beverages side of the business.

Between 1987 and 1996, Coca-Cola and Cadbury Schweppes were in a joint UK venture, but this was dissolved in 1997. In 1999 Cadbury Schweppes decided to concentrate its efforts on key profitable soft drinks markets. Cadbury Schweppes moved out of 160 markets by selling its beverage operations to the Coca-Cola Company, which now sells Cadbury Schweppes brands in these markets. Cadbury Schweppes retained brands only in the US, South Africa, Norway and the European Union (with the exception of France, the UK, Ireland, Greece, Sweden, where the brands were sold). Cadbury Schweppes had planned to reduce its geographic coverage still further but regulatory barriers prevented it from selling to the Coca-Cola Company in a number of markets.

Corporate and social responsibility

Corporate and social responsibility (CSR) has been central to the activities of Cadbury Schweppes since its foundation. The Cadbury family were prominent members of the Society of Friends, or

Quakers. Quakers held strong beliefs and ideals that they carried into campaigns for justice, equality and social reform. Business and social reform often went hand in hand, as at Bournville. CSR is still a board-level responsibility. Indeed Cadbury Schweppes believes that a creative and well-managed CSR programme is in the best interests of all its stakeholders. Cadbury Schweppes is committed to strict compliance with the laws and regulations that apply to its business activities around the world. Cadbury Schweppes' ethical commitments include:

1. *Human rights and ethical trading policy*
   As a responsible corporate citizen, Cadbury Schweppes aims to act in a socially responsible manner at all times by:

   - respecting the economic, social, cultural, political and civil rights of those involved in its operations;

   - complying with all local human rights legislation;

   - implementing programmes across its worldwide operations and with its supply chain partners.

2. *Core labour rights and dignity at work*

   - preclude the use of forced labour;

   - respect the rights of employees to join legally recognised labour unions;

   - ensure that children are employed only under circumstances that protect them from physical risks and do not disrupt their education;

   - not tolerate any form of harassment in the workplace.

3. *Health and safety in the workplace*

   - create a healthy and safe work environment for each employee.

4. *Fair remuneration*

   - ensure that working hours and remuneration are reasonable and comparable to those offered by similar companies;

   - diversity and respect for differences;

   - manage diversity to promote and capitalise on cultural and individual differences to create competitive advantage through new perspectives and local market sensitivity.

5. *Opportunity for development*

   - recognise the value that employees create and reward them with opportunities for personal and career development;

   - provide employees with equal opportunities regardless of their gender, age, marital status, sexual orientation, disability, race, religion or national origin.

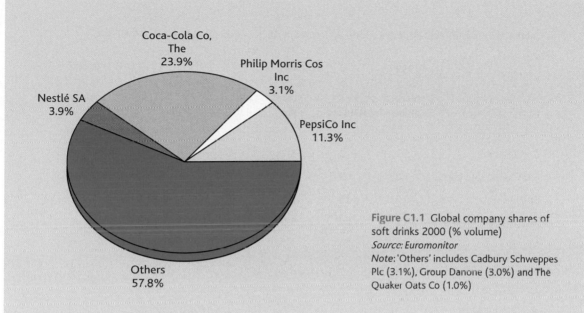

Figure C1.1 Global company shares of soft drinks 2000 (% volume)
Source: Euromonitor
Note: 'Others' includes Cadbury Schweppes Plc (3.1%), Group Danone (3.0%) and The Quaker Oats Co (1.0%)

To support its policy Cadbury Schweppes is committed to a continuous dialogue with stakeholders. In May 2002 Cadbury Schweppes produced its first CSR report. However, in spite of the stated policy in Nigeria in 2002 Cadbury Schweppes faced allegations that chocolate products have deliberately misleading safety and quality labels.

Soft drinks

In 2000 Coca Cola Company and PepsiCo jointly accounted for over 35 per cent of the global soft drinks market by volume. Figure C1.1 shows global company shares of soft drinks.

Table C1.2 shows Cadbury Schweppes' market share and ranking in the soft drinks market. It is responsible for a number of brands including five bottled waters, 31 carbonates, nine fruit juices and six functional drinks. Cadbury Schweppes is ranked number five overall. It is the global number three, in carbonates, after Coca-Cola and PepsiCo.

Between 1997 and 2001 growth in the carbonates sector worldwide was relatively sluggish at about 13 per cent. Beverage Marketing project a rise in worldwide carbonated soft drink volume of only 3.4 per cent from 1999 to 2004. Leading manufacturers have sought to diversify their portfolios, resulting in intense activity in the acquisition of companies (see above). Cadbury Schweppes is now looking to grow in high margin sectors such as functional drinks and ready to drink tea. Table C1.2 reflects this trend with growth in all targeted sectors, fruit/vegetable juice, functional drinks and ready-to-drink (RTD) tea, largely as a result of the acquisition of the Snapple Beverages Group.

Table C1.3 shows sales in the two biggest markets, Europe and North America, which accounted for 48 per cent of global soft drink sales in 2001, are growing.

Since 1998 the market for soft drinks in Europe has grown substantially, largely attributed to the increase in consumption of water, still drinks and iced tea. Average consumption in Western Europe

Table C1.2 Cadbury Schweppes Plc: world shares and rankings in soft drinks by sector 1999/2000

	1999 % Market Share	1999 Ranking	2000 % Market Share	2000 Ranking	2000 Actual Volume (million litres)	2000 % Volume Growth
Carbonates	5.2	3	5.7	3	7633.2	12.2
Fruit/vegetable juice	1.0	9	1.9	3	645	100.8
Bottled water	0.3	36	0.3	37	212.9	6.7
Functional drinks	0.3	20	1.0	12	74.8	319.4
RTD tea	0.2	30	2.7	11	289.4	1164.9
Total soft drinks	2.9	5	3.3	5	8855.3	20.2

Source: Euromonitor

is estimated to be around 206 litres per capita, compared to that of Eastern Europe of 50 litres per capita. In 2001 the soft drinks market in the US was 93 billion litres. However, demand in the US for Cadbury Schweppes drinks in the first half of 2003 was weak because of wet and cold weather, innovation from cola rivals and weaker consumer spending.

China is considered to be the future market with growth of almost 80 per cent in volume terms between 1997 and 2001. Zenith International forecasts worldwide growth of more than 50 billion

Table C1.3 Sales of Cadbury Schweppes soft drinks in North America and Europe (£ million)

	1998	1999	2000	2001	2002
Sales beverages North America	1129	1264	1179	1757	1811
Sales beverages Europe	436	470	443	515	717
Operating profit North America beverages	285	332	403	541	548
Operating profit Europe beverages	52	62	78	91	140

Source: Euromonitor

Table C1.4 Growth in R&D expenditure 1998–2001

	1998	1999	2000	2001
R&D expenditure (£m)	22	26	26	29

Source: Euromonitor

litres in the soft drinks market by 2003. Growth is expected to be strong in Asia and South America and moderate in the Middle East.

Keynote has identified a number of key trends that may have contributed to the increased consumption of soft drinks in the UK that may also apply to the global market. They can be summarised as follows:

- negative publicity surrounding the anti-social aspects of alcohol, including drink-driving restrictions;

- although there is concern over the amount of sweet drinks marketed to children, adults are increasingly using soft drinks with low or no sugar content as 'healthy' substitutes for alcohol or caffeine drinks;

- the use of soft drinks as a substitute for caffeine-based hot drinks, partly due to health consciousness trends. Sales of tea bags in the United Kingdom have fallen by 10 per cent since 1998, replaced by higher demand for fruit teas and canned ready-to-drink tea;

- demand from children for packaged drinks, driven by effective marketing by large companies, combined with the general 'snacking' aspect of British culture;

- wide distribution and availability – vast selections in superstores and corner shops, in bars, cafés and fast-food outlets;

- heavy marketing expenditure by multinationals.

These trends have also brought an increased emphasis on research and development to meet the new needs. An important aspect of this is new product development focuses on the addition of functional ingredients such as vitamins, minerals and herbal extracts and packaging innovation that concentrates on producing robust portable containers, such as single-serve plastic bottles. Table C1.4 shows how R&D expenditure has increased, albeit at a relatively slow pace.

Other significant trends relevant to developing markets are:

- increasing urbanisation eroding traditional, family-centred patterns of consumption;

- increasing number of women in the workforce, increasing levels of disposable income.

Sources:

adapted from '2000 Global soft drinks', available from http://www.beveragemarketing.com/news2p.htm [accessed 12 June 2003].

'Cadbury Schweppes brand history', available from http://www.cadburyschweppes.com/ [accessed 12 June 2003].

'Cadbury Schweppes corporate profile and brands', available from http://www.transnationale.org/anglais [accessed 12 June 2003].

'Cadbury Schweppes Plc: corporate summary and key events', available from http://www.euromonitor.com/ [accessed 12 June 2003].

'Cadbury Schweppes Plc: environment and society', available from http://www.euromonitor.com/ [accessed 12 June 2003].

'Cadbury Schweppes Plc: financial information', available from http://www.euromonitor.com/ [accessed 12 June 2003].

'Cadbury Schweppes Plc 2002. Euromonitor: Global market information database', available from http://www.euromonitor.com/ [accessed 12 June 2003].

'Cadbury Schweppes profile', available from http://uk.biz.yahoo.com/p/c/cbry.1.html [accessed 12 June 2003].

'Focusing on soft drinks', available from http://www.beverage-world.com/ [accessed 12 June 2003];

Jones, A. (2003) '7UP takes the fizz out of Cadbury', Financial Times, 11 June;

Pandya, N. (2003) 'Company Vitae', Guardian, 5 April. available from http://www.guardian.co.uk [accessed 12 June 2003].

Questions

1. Using the LEPESTC framework identify the key global trends in the business environment that Cadbury Schweppes faces. What are the opportunities and threats that the company is likely to face in the future?

2. Cadbury Schweppes' plan to reduce its geographic coverage was blocked by regulatory barriers. Explain this statement. What may have been the consequences if the plan had been allowed to proceed?

3. Roome (1992) suggests five possible environmental options open to organisations. Looking back to the company's foundation, use the model to explain how Cadbury Schweppes' environmental and ethical approach has evolved.

4. Use Michael Porter's five forces model to explain the increase in research and development expenditure between 1998 and 2001.

5. Asia and South America have been identified as key markets for the future. With reference to demographic and social change explain why this may be the case.

Tourism in Greece
Jamie Weatherston

2

In the summer or perhaps at any time when you have a break you may be considering a trip to recover from the rigours of student life.

The choice of where you go depends on a number of factors. The price that you have to pay is clearly a prime consideration. You may also have to consider the price of other goods that you buy. Will a trip to the sun be off set by the high price of food and drink when you arrive at your destination? The relative strength and value of currencies will play a part here as well. How will a trip impact on your ability to pay for things, for example your studies, during the coming year? Your income will be another factor. Can you afford to go? Do you have to work during your break to pay off debts or loans? Do you need to work to save money for the new semester? Other people's views may also be paramount. Is your planned destination a 'good' place to see and be seen in or is it stale? These are just some of the considerations that need to be taken into account.

Where to go?

The world is open to you. Greece is a popular destination providing for the needs: sun, sea and sand. You may choose to do a bit of hopping round the islands. Independent travel can be cheaper but it does present its own hassles.

Greece: an overview

Greece has a history stretching back more than 4000 years. In the second half of the fourth century BC, the Greeks, led by Alexander the Great, reached the height of their power conquering most of the then known world. In 146 BC Greece fell to the Romans. It remained under the control of the Byzantine Empire until it in turn fell to the Turks in 1453. In 1828, following almost 400 years of Turkish rule, Greece won its independence from the Ottoman Empire. Greece is divided into thirteen administrative divisions, named 'Peripheries' or regions. The country comprises over 1400 islands.

The 2001 census recorded a population of 10.9 million people. It is a parliamentary democracy, headed by a president who is elected for a five-year term of office. The legislature, a single chamber – the vouli – comprises 300 seats for which there are elections every four years.

The economy is a market-oriented economy with limited state intervention. Greece joined the European Union in 1981 and since 1 January 2001 has been the twelfth member of the European Monetary Union (euro-zone). On 1 January 2002 euro banknotes and coins were put in circulation, although drachma banknotes and coins could also be used for payments until 28 February. Drachma banknotes and coins ceased to be legal tender (i.e. generally acceptable means of payment) from 1 March 2002. Table C2.1 shows the conversion rate for drachma and other euro-zone currencies.

Map C2.1 Map of Greece

Table C2.1 Euro-zone currency conversion

Country	Currency	Euro
Greece	GRD	340.750
Austria	ATS	13.7603
Belgium	BEF	40.3399
Finland	FIM	5.94573
France	FRF	6.55957
Germany	DEM	1.95583
Ireland	IEP	0.787564
Italy	ITL (100)	1936.27
Luxembourg	LUF	40.3399
Netherlands	NLG	2.20371
Portugal	PTE	200.482
Spain	ESP	166.386

The Greek economy, from 1995 onwards, showed an annual average growth rate of 3.6 per cent (1995–2002), exceeding the average rate achieved by the EU. Growth in 2002 is expected to be around 4 per cent. Table C2.2 shows the key economic indicators in Greece.

Tourism in Greece

Tourism has grown substantially over a number of years and is Greece's biggest industry, accounting for approximately 15 per cent of gross domestic product. Greece lies in fifteenth place in the world classification of tourist destinations, receiving 14 033 378 tourists in 2001 (National Statistical Service of Greece, provisional data). The majority (92.25 per cent) originate from Europe, with 70.4 per cent from the EU (GNTO, 2003). The growth is due in large part to growth in other European economies and the trend in cheaper air fares (79.8 per cent of foreign tourists arrive by plane).

However, the heads of Greece's regional hotel chambers estimated a drop of up to 8 per cent year on year in foreign tourist arrivals in 2002. Economic slowdown in Europe, and travel fear after September 11th were to blame, they said (Athens News, 2002). Well-heeled Americans traditionally flock to the island of Santorini but the US market has collapsed since September 11th. Perhaps even more worrying for the Greek islanders is the significant shortfall in bookings from Greece's two biggest markets, Britain and Germany. Evidence suggests that tourist bookings worldwide fell by

Table C2.2 Greek economic indicators

	2000	2001	2002	Source
Gross Domestic Product per capita (rank: 23rd)	16.800			(1)
Growth rate (real GDP)	4.1%	4.1%	4.0%	(2)
Investments Fixed capital annual growth rate	9.3%	5.9%	7.7%	(3)
Employment Total	3.946.300	3.917.500	3.948.900	(4)
Primary sector	17.0%	16.0%	15.8%	(4)
Secondary sector	22.5%	22.8%	22.5%	(4)
Tertiary sector	60.5%	61.2%	61.7%	(4)
Unemployment (registered unemployment rate)	11.2%	10.4%	10.0%	(3)
Harmonised Index of Consumer Price	2.9	3.77	3.50	(4)

Source: available from the Greek National Tourist Organisation http://www.gnto.gr/1/01/0105/ea0105000.html [accessed 11 March 2003]
(1) OECD, National Accounts of OECD countries, Main Aggregates, vol. I.
(2) NSSG, February 2003.
(3) Ministry for Economy and Finance, Stability and Development Programme 2002–2006.
(4) NSSG, Greece in numbers 2002.
(5) Bank of Greece, Report of the Governor, Athens 2002.
Last update: 14.02.2003

20 per cent in the direct aftermath of September 11th. The bomb attack in Bali is expected to have a disastrous effect on tourism in South-East Asia but it could have a wider impact, including Greece.

Competition from cheaper rivals is also seen as a factor. Neighbouring Turkey is cheaper, and the revival of Croatian tourism is also challenging Greece's status as a top destination.

Another factor that may have an impact on prices may have been the move to the euro (to convert drachmas into euro we divide the drachma amount by 340.750 and then round to the nearest euro cent).

Getting there

The first decision that you need to make is how to get there. Flying is probably going to be at the top of your list, like the majority of tourists. The old bus from London used to take three days and was pretty uncomfortable, but good value. Olympic, the Greek national carrier, has regular scheduled flights to Athens from many European airports but if money is tight you may decide to choose a budget airline. Budget airlines have sprung up all over Europe in the past five years, offering very cheap fares to destinations all over Europe.

EasyJet, one of the pioneers, flies from London direct to Athens, the price of the ticket depending on the day you fly and the time of your flight. Weekends tend to be more expensive, as do school holidays, so you may want to avoid the last two weeks in July and all of August. Try flying at night or arriving early in the morning and compare the price to more convenient times.

Arriving early at Eleftherios Venizelos airport (Athens's new international airport) may have its advantages: 4.00am may sound early but with the day ahead you can plan to leave Athens straight away, without having to pay some high prices in perhaps shoddy accommodation. Check it out on the way home instead!

Ferry offices are open at the airport when you arrive. See where you fancy going and on what type of boat and buy a ticket. No haggling here. Those in a hurry can take the hydrofoil or high-speed catamaran, but they are more expensive. Deck class on the ordinary ferries is cheaper, though it can be wet! A bus runs regularly throughout the night to the ports of Piraeus or Rafina, where you will be able to pick up some provisions for your journey. The ferries are getting better at providing food and drink, with concessions held by outlets such as Goodies, but they can be expensive. You could get your first taste of a Greek hamburger or a club sandwich here.

A starting point for island hopping could be the Cyclades or Kiklades group (see Map C2.2), so named because they form a circle (kylos) around the island of Delos. Some islands, especially Mykonos, Santorini (Thira) and Ios, have eagerly embraced tourism. Other islands, such as Andros, Syros, Kea, Serifos and Sifnos, are less visited by foreigners but, thanks to their proximity to the

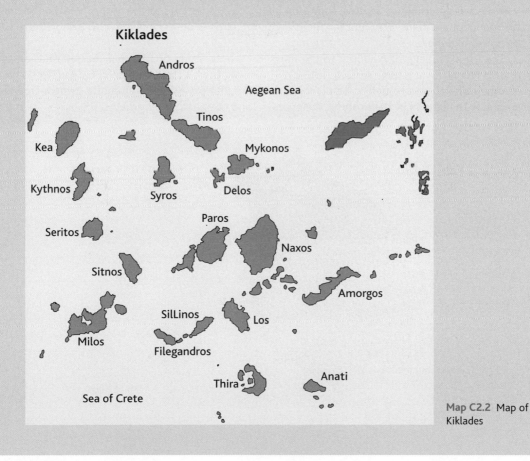

Map C2.2 Map of Kiklades

mainland, are popular weekend and summer retreats. The islands are very busy in July and August. This is particularly the case in the first two weeks of August when the population of Athens spills out all over the islands. Tinos is a place of pilgrimage (Willett *et al.*, 2000).

On arriving at an island on a ferry or stepping off a bus at a town or village you can immediately gauge the amount of accommodation by the numbers of hotel, apartment and domatia owners waving their boards to catch your attention. Domatia are the Greek equivalent to the British bed and breakfast. Timing your arrival may be crucial: leave it too late and there may be no rooms left. A midnight arrival at the height of the season is not recommended. Campsites can provide a good alternative. They will rent out all that you need. I suppose you could always try the beach!

The market at work

Prices for accommodation are officially fixed; every room has a guest notice displaying the room price. Three levels of price are available: high, middle and low season.

Syros is not a good place to come into port at midnight at the beginning of August. The scramble of people off the ferry and the lack of owners and hoteliers on the shore could signal an uncomfortable night ahead. Wandering around the town, a room may eventually become available. Is it a fixed price? Take it or leave it.

Paros has a number of centres, shown on Map C2.3. Ferries land at the port of Parikia, the main town and now a main ferry hub for the islands. Antiparos is only a bus ride and a short ferry trip away from Pounda.

The fishing village of Naoussa to the north is close to some pristine beaches and has an up-market French Riviera feel (Willett *et al.*, 2002). Arriving there in mid-August 2002 you would have assumed that there seemed to be plenty of accommodation available. Domatia owners crowded around with pictures of their rooms, their gardens and their astounding views. The prices per night at the Vassilis Domatia were:

Map C2.3 Map of Paros

- High season (1 August to 31 August) €55.00

- Middle season (1 June to 30 June and 1 September to 30 September) €30.00

- Low season (1 April to 31 May and 1 October to 31 October) €23.00

The price was fixed, or was it? A little bargaining made up for the extra paid in Syros; a room was available for €27.00, less than the mid season rate.

The room rate is only one part of the cost. Other prices may be driven up to compensate. Eating (and drinking) is a necessity too. Increasing the price of food in restaurants may offset the downward pressure on the price of accommodation. If you get tired of sitting on the same beach every day you can try hiring a scooter, a bike or a car. Prices are displayed on billboards and in offices, but be prepared to bargain.

Questions

1. Identify and list the number of times the mechanism of demand and supply comes into the case.

2. Explain and comment on the interaction of the forces of demand and supply at work in the case when booking rooms in Syros and Paros.

3. Why does demand and supply not operate when purchasing tickets for the ferry? How can you explain this?

4. Look at the easyJet website at http://www.easyjet.com/ for flights to Athens. Investigate prices at different dates and at different times of the day. Comment on the price differences and use demand and supply analysis to explain the differences.

5. How is it possible for the discount airlines to offer lower prices than their mainstream competitors?

6. Using Table C2.2 and the dataset from another country comment on the state of the Greek economy.

7. What is the likely impact of the adoption of the euro on Greek inflation? How will this affect the tourist industry?

References

Athens News (2002) available from http://www.athensnews.gr/athweb/nathens.print_unique?e= C&f=12987&m=A12&aa=4&eidos=S [accessed 11 March 2003].

GNTO (2003) Greek National Tourist Organisation, available from http://www.gnto.gr/2/01/ eb10000.html.

Willett, D., Barta, B., Hall, R., Hellander, P. and Oliver, J. (2002) Greek Islands, London: Lonely Planet.

Global dominoes: the case of South-East Asia

3

Mark Cook

The Asian 'tiger economies'

The annual growth rate of GDP in the ASEAN-5 economies of Indonesia, Malaysia, the Philippines, Singapore and Thailand averaged around 8 per cent in the decade up to 1997, and even before then their growth was fairly spectacular (see Table C3.1).

For some countries, in particular Korea, the move from developing nation to one of membership of the OECD – the world's richest industrial countries – can be described as impressive. In fact, in the 30 years up to 1997, per capita income levels in South Korea increased ten-fold; there was a five-fold increase in Thailand and a four-fold increase in Malaysia. In 1997, Singapore and Korea had per-capita incomes in line with many industrialised countries. Not only had per capita incomes grown in many Asian countries but they were seen as suitable sites for foreign investment (though not all countries sought this, for example Korea) and the region attracted about half of all capital flows into developing countries (approximately $100 billion in 1996). In addition, many of the countries had followed an import substitution and export orientation policy and in the decade 1987–97 they had doubled their share of world exports to around one-fifth of total world exports.

Table C3.1 Real GDP growth rates for selected South-East Asian countries up to 1997

Country	Annual Average Growth Rate 1984–91	GDP Growth Rate (%) 1992	GDP Growth Rate (%) 1994	GDP Growth Rate (%) 1997
Hong Kong	6.9	6.3	5.5	5.0
Singapore	6.8	6.0	10.1	8.5
Taiwan	8.4	6.7	6.5	6.7
China	9.8	13.2	11.8	8.8
Indonesia	6.0	6.5	7.4	4.7
Malaysia	6.2	7.8	8.5	7.3
Philippines	1.1	0.3	4.3	5.2
Thailand	8.9	7.9	8.5	−1.4

Source: World Bank, The World Bank Atlas 1995, *Asian Development Bank, and* World Economic Outlook, *May 1998 (IMF)*

Their economies had also been built on high savings and high (appropriate) investment. In addition they had achieved stable levels of inflation and a number of them, notably Thailand and Indonesia, were running budget surpluses. The South-East Asian economies also benefited the global community. They had become large consumers of foreign goods (19 per cent of all US exports in 1996 went to the region) and because of their incessant growth they were able to absorb the downturns that were experienced by the developed economies in the West, so damping the effect of any economic cycle.

It seems strange that the growth in these economies was never really investigated by the International Monetary Fund (IMF) so that the reasons for this growth in economic activity and performance could be more greatly appreciated. What went wrong with the tiger economies?

The South-East Asian crisis

The financial crisis in South-East Asia began in July 1997 following a speculative attack on the Thai baht. Speculators knowing about the short-term indebtedness in the economy believed that the currency would be devalued. They therefore began to withdraw money from the economy at the current fixed exchange rate against the US dollar. The Bank of Thailand, after defending the currency as it had done earlier in May 1997 and losing foreign exchange reserves, finally let the baht float on 2 July 1997. The baht immediately depreciated by 15 per cent and this was followed by the floating of the Indonesian rupiah, the Malaysian ringgit and the Philippine peso. By January 1998 the rupiah had depreciated by 80 per cent, the baht by 53 per cent, the ringgit by 42 per cent and the peso by 36 per cent. The South Korean won also suffered and this too depreciated by 42 per cent by January 1998.

But what led to this crisis? The traditional currency crisis does not really fit the Asian experience. There was no monetary or fiscal profligacy, unemployment was not high, and although current account deficits were large they were not overly so and were easily offset by foreign capital inflows. These capital inflows made the South-East Asian countries' real exchange rates appreciate. Due to pegged exchange rates and high interest rates money flowed into South-East Asia. The risk that could follow from this was reduced by the perception that governments guaranteed financial institutions. However, the structural weaknesses in financial institutions resulted in over-investment in excessively risky projects.

Export growth began to falter due to a downturn in the demand for electronics; the falling value of the yen gave Japanese exporters a competitive advantage and interest rates were required to rise. Faced with the need to get greater inflows of foreign capital and the bad debt issued by a number of financial institutions, confidence in the tiger economies began to wane. Investors began to move money rapidly out of South-East Asia. A net inflow into the region of $95 billion in 1996 changed to a net outflow of $15 billion in 1997. A number of South-East Asian currencies began to collapse. Because investors realised that there were going to be no government guarantees for investment, asset prices in the area burst. Falling asset prices resulted in insolvency of a number of financial intermediaries, leading to a fully-fledged financial crisis. The problems for South-East Asia were further compounded by the importance of intra-country trade between the tiger economies. The IMF attempted – and Stiglitz (2002) would say wrongly – to support the fixed currencies against the US dollar with a

$95 billion support package. This was to give the market a signal that the world financial institutions would support these economies. At the same time a number of conditions were attached to the financial support, which were supposed to stop the speculative attacks and persuade their creditors to extend the period of time for the loans that had been made earlier. One of the conditions was for a rise in interest rates that exacerbated the conditions affecting domestic firms in the South-East Asian economies that agreed to this IMF policy. Also, by agreeing to try and keep the exchange rate fixed, it allowed some rich people in the South-East Asian economies to exchange their local currency into US dollars and deposit this outside the country. Not all countries followed these damaging IMF policies – both China and Malaysia undertook their own policy initiatives.

The fall in raw material prices that affected the South-East Asian economies following their collapse was also felt in Europe. In 1998 Russia imposed a moratorium on some of its international debt payment and was forced to devalue the rouble. For Western European countries the impact of the South-East Asian crisis was being felt by exporters and through the freezing of FDI from a number of South-East Asian economies, such as that by Hyundai and Samsung of South Korea in the UK. The repercussions then moved on to South America. Countries such as Argentina and Brazil had, during the 1990s, reduced their inflation-prone economies by pegging their exchange rates to the US dollar. The net outflow of speculative capital that was seeking to leave the tiger economies was placed by speculators in what they considered a safer haven, the US dollar. This caused the dollar to appreciate in value. To continue to peg their exchange rates against the US dollar, both Brazil and Argentina were forced to raise interest rates. The rise in interest rates and the depreciation of the tiger economies' currencies meant that domestic producers in both Argentina and Brazil found trading opportunities difficult. The result of increased pressure in Brazil forced the Brazilian peso to be devalued in January 1999. Both the United States and the Europeans have responded to the global slowdown by reducing interest rates, and Japan, which has had its financial system mauled by bad debt provision, has also slowed. Thus what the South-East Asian crisis has shown is that changes in one area of the global economy can have major effects in other countries on the other side of the world.

The South-East Asian economies today

So how have the South-East Asian economies fared since the financial crisis and has the Asian miracle been reborn? Although Table C3.2 indicates that many of the South-East Asian economies have returned positive growth performances since 1999, many still have doubts about the strength of their economies. The macroeconomic outlook has stabilised, external finances are sounder, and much of the short-term debt has been either repaid or written off. Foreign investors are returning too and the stock markets in Indonesia and Thailand have outperformed most of those in 2002. The aftermath of the financial crisis has led to changes in political regimes in South Korea, the Philippines, Taiwan and Indonesia. Many of the countries' currencies are no longer fixed to the US dollar and better short-term finances and political stability have reduced the volatility that existed with their exchange rates. The resulting changes in their economy may not have overcome all their problems but have at least allowed them some breathing space.

However, there are still some serious banking problems and business lending is still poor throughout East Asia. But on a positive side the South-East Asian economies are less dependent

Table C3.2 The recovery of selected Asian economies – GDP growth rates 1998–2002

Country	1998	1999	2000	2001	2002
Republic of Korea	−6.7%	10.9%	8.8%	4.0%	6.3%
China	7.8%	7.1%	8.0%	7.4%	8.0%
Thailand	−10.8%	4.2%	4.4%	2.0%	5.2%
Indonesia	−13.1%	0.8%	4.9%	3.2%	3.7%
Malaysia	−7.4%	6.1%	8.3%	0.4%	4.2%
The Philippines	−0.6%	3.4%	4.0%	3.2%	4.6%

Source: Asian Development Bank, Annual Report 2002

upon overseas investment, principally that from the United States, to keep their economies running. Investors probably still need reassurance that they can lend for the long term rather than just the short-to-medium term. The decline of foreign money has forced a number of the South-East Asian economies to seek new trading partners, mostly within the South-East Asian trading area. The continued depressed state of the Japanese economy has not affected this trade since the rapid growth of the Chinese economy has been able to offset this. However, the growth in the Chinese economy also poses problems for the South-East Asian economies. China is receiving a very large share of total FDI to the region and since its entry into the WTO has been able to increase its level of exports. These exports are very price competitive since its labour resources are relatively inexpensive. South-East Asian countries who previously had used export growth as a means of securing their own economic growth are now being faced by a highly competitive Chinese economy. South-East Asian economies cannot rely, therefore, on exporting as a means to achieve further economic growth and so require other changes in their economies if they are going to return to long-term and sustained growth. In fact to treat all of the South-East Asian countries as though we are considering similar economies is a mistake. Countries like Taiwan, South Korea and Japan, which are more at the higher technology end of manufacturing, may well benefit from the growth in the Chinese economy by continuing to invest there and by producing the new services and high-technology products that complement production in China. Countries such as Thailand, Indonesia and the Philippines which have concentrated more on low-to-medium manufacturing may find export sales more difficult as they are now competing with a highly cost-competitive Chinese economy.

As for changes in the behaviour of their banking sectors, South Korea, whose banking system so favoured its own conglomerates, has now been overhauled. Banks have increased their activity in the area of consumer lending and developed a better relationship with small to medium-sized enterprises. At the same time the government has forced some of its conglomerates to sell off entire divisions or has put some businesses out of operation. Indonesia still, however, has still not really re-solved its banking crisis and it is still hard for a number of potentially profitable businesses in that country to raise capital. Other East Asian countries' banking systems lie somewhere in between.

Savers too have had to change. One of the reasons for the large investment boom before 1997 was that most of the South-East Asian nations had high savings ratios. As a result consumer spend-ing on imports was low and the investment that arose from the high savings ratio was used to im-port machinery that produced export-orientated products. External trade balances were good but the domestic economy was relatively neglected. What is needed now is for consumers to be more active in bonds and equities thereby expanding South-East Asia's capital markets and for con-sumers to begin spending.

The recovery after the 1998 period was quite rapid for a number of countries, as Table C3.2 indi-cates, yet in 2001 economic growth was the second lowest in decades. Singapore's economy shrank by 2 per cent following an expansion of 10 per cent in 2000. So have the South-East Asian economies shifted forever away from high positive growth records to one of fluctuating growth and when this growth occurs is it lower than that experienced before 1997? The answer to this is probably yes. They are now subject to even stronger ties to the global economy following their recovery after 1998. The downturn in the United States in 2000 was partly to blame for their poor performance in 2001 and indicates the growing interdependence between countries and trading blocs. Not only did the South-East Asian economies suffer, apart from China, but Europe also went into a lower growth phase in 2001. Part of the reason for this was the downturn in demand for high-technology products by both the United States and following on from that, Europe. Europe was an obvious region to be affected by the global slowdown, but what of the South-East Asian economies? Strong candidates to be af-fected by the global downturn in economic activity were Taiwan and Singapore whose exports are more skewed towards the high-technology products. Nonetheless, even countries for which high-technology products made up a smaller proportion of their exports suffered, such as Malaysia, South Korea, Thailand and Indonesia. In other words as the general demand for manufactured exports de-clined so did the demand for products from South-East Asia. Only the Philippines escaped relatively unharmed due to the size and importance of its agricultural sector. The five countries worst affected by the South-East Asian crisis – Indonesia, Malaysia, Thailand, South Korea and the Philippines – which provide around two thirds of the region's exports, saw the value of their exports fall by 11 per cent in dollar terms in 2001. The modest recovery by the United States after September 11th led to a recovery of the South-East Asian economies during 2002. It is hard, therefore, to consider how the South-East Asian economies can massively diverge from the growth performance elsewhere in the global community as they had done in the decades up to 1997. Greater consumer demand in their domestic economies may be able to offset partially some of the decline in the demand in the global economy and the threat of China to these export-orientated economies appears to be less than was first believed. Nonetheless, the Japanese economy is still in the doldrums as their government fails to take the structural reforms needed to expand the economy. Furthermore, the SARS (Severe Acute Respiratory Syndrome) epidemic has further damaged the South-East Asian economies, particularly where the SARS outbreak has been worst. Consumer demand has fallen as people have stayed at home. Tourism-related revenue, affecting hotels, airlines, restaurants, entertainment and the retail trade, has been hit, with those economies more dependent on the tourist industry hardest hit. Investor confidence has suffered and higher government expenditures are required to combat the disease. This will have a more significant impact on countries whose fiscal balances are weak. In fact the IMF predicts that the SARS outbreak will reduce economic growth in 2003 by around 0.4 per cent for South-East Asian nations and 0.2 per cent for China.

So what have we seen within South-East Asia over the past six years? The financial crisis of 1997 led to a ripple affect that first affected all the other countries in South-East Asia and then disturbed the economies of South America and Russia. The policies undertaken to reform their economies following the financial crisis, the growth of China and decline in growth of Japan have meant that the South-East Asian nations have become more strongly linked to the performance of many of the other economies of the OECD. The slowdown in the growth performances of these economies during 2001 and 2002 resulted in a further slowdown in the recovery process of the South-East Asian nations. The South-East Asian economies and the crisis that befell them show clear evidence of the interdependence between trading nations, and we will probably never see again in the region long periods of high positive growth independent of global forces.

Questions

1. How did the Asian financial crisis of 1997 affect Foreign Direct Investment from that region into Europe?

2. How did European and US companies benefit from the 1997 Asian financial crisis?

3. To what extent did the Asian crisis suggest that we now all belong to one global business community?

4. Could the Asian economies in the twenty-first century return to the growth performances that they experienced at the end of the last decade? Why? (Why not?)

5. What might be the positive and negative impact of the Chinese economy on the South-East Asian economies?

References

Asian Development Bank (2002) Annual report.

Economist (2002) 'Rousing Asia's Tigers', 12 April.

Economist (2002) 'Back from the brink', 1 July.

Fan, E. X. (2003) SARS: Economic Impacts and Implications, ERD Policy Brief No. 15, Asian Development Bank, May.

Roubini, N. (1998) 'Part 5: Money, interest rates and exchange rates. The collapse of fixed exchange rate regimes', The Asian Currency Crisis of 1997, Stern School of Business, New York University, available from http://pages.stern.nyu.edu/.

Stiglitz, J. (2002) Globalisation and its Discontents, London: Penguin–Allen Lane.

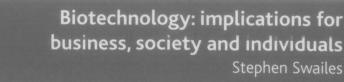

Stephen Swailes

> They are in you and in me; they created us, body and mind; and their preservation is the ultimate rationale for our existence . . . they go by the name of genes, and we are their survival machines. (Richard Dawkins, *The Selfish Gene*, 1976)

There is currently a big debate under way in which US organisations are arguing for much wider use of genetically modified crops and European and African nations are more cautious about the effects of genetically modified crops on the environment and on consumers. Clearly there are big commercial interests at play. The case draws heavily on a paper by William Rowley (2002) which you are encouraged to read.

What is biotechnology?

Think back to your school science classes when you learned that almost all living things are made of cells. The simplest organisms consist of only one cell (remember the amoeba?) whereas complex organisms (like us) have many different types of cells to carry out different functions, for example blood, muscle, and skin. Each living cell contains the 'instructions' for carrying out the tasks it is designed to do. These instructions, which exist in chromosomes in cells as a chemical called DNA, are passed from parent(s) to offspring in plants and animals. DNA is a string of genes and each gene plays a part in defining the organism it belongs to. Genes explain why children look like their parents, why some people are prone to particular diseases and why, by selective plant reproduction, corn cobs are much bigger than they used to be.

At this point I hope it is clear to you that genetic science, on which much biotechnology is based, is incredibly complex. Having realised the part that genes play in life, scientists set out to understand the human genome – the entire string of genes that makes us human. Genomes for some plants and simpler animals have already been mapped. Much progress on the human genome has been made and R&D work is now under way to understand how our health is influenced by our genes and to understand the genetic systems of plants and animals.

In order to create new products, biotechnology draws together knowledge from biology, chemistry and physics, it uses computer technology to process the complex calculations and simulations needed and engineering technologies to design systems for producing very complex chemical products on a large scale.

Some applications of biotechnology

Biosensors

For some years over-the-counter kits have been available to test for pregnancy or cholesterol levels. Many other tests are available in hospitals following referral from a doctor usually after a patient has presented with particular symptoms. Early identification and treatment is an important factor in raising survival rates after diagnosis of many conditions – how often have you heard of someone being diagnosed too late for treatment to be effective? Biotechnology offers the potential to develop sensors that continuously monitor a biological system – such as the human body. Perhaps placed under the skin, biosensors could monitor general conditions such as diabetes or more specific conditions where a person has a higher risk of developing a condition, for example a particular type of cancer.

Personalised and predictive medicines

Much medical treatment has been such that all people presenting with a condition get the same treatment, for example a course of the antibiotic penicillin. But, although most people benefit from the treatments offered, people respond differently to the same treatment and adverse drug reactions kill thousands of people every year (Schmidt, 1998). The ways in which we react to drugs are known to be associated with sex and ethnic group among other variables. It will be possible to screen individuals to see how they are likely to respond to a particular drug and this will lead to better informed medical treatments. Ultimately, drugs specifically designed for different genetic subgroups in the population will be available. This branch of medicine is called *pharmacogenomics*.

Predictive tests will be able to identify whether someone is genetically disposed towards developing a condition. Knowing this information could encourage a change in lifestyle or behaviour in order to help keep the condition at bay. Such tests, however, raise difficult questions about how such information should be handled.

While these tests do not exist now on a large scale it seems only a matter of time before they are widely available. Access to information about oneself is a key principle of modern times, and the UK Department of Health is concerned that people could misunderstand the results of predictive tests, either by causing unnecessary alarm or creating false security that in turn brings about inadvisable lifestyle changes (Department of Health, 2003). Another concern is that tests could be used on children or adults without their consent. In the UK it seems likely that the use of predictive tests will be strictly controlled and genetic information about people protected by law. There may be problems controlling test usage, however, if tests are freely available in another country.

Predictive tests would also cause problems for insurance companies and possibly employers in general. Life insurance is something that we commonly take out and insurers currently base policy charges on probabilities derived from many years of experience of insuring people of a particular age, sex and occupation. What if a simple test could show whether an individual was likely to develop an incurable disease and die young? Insurers might be less keen to offer a policy. On the other hand, young people who knew they had a high risk of dying naturally before retirement age might take out extensive life insurance to the detriment of the insurance companies. There are already concerns about the creation of an 'insurance underclass' (Kite, 2003) and regulation will be needed to cover the use of personal genetic information.

The costs of personalised drugs are likely to be very different to the mass produced drugs used now. It seems likely that, for the early years, personalised drugs will be relatively expensive and this leads to issues about the cost structures of the firms that produce them, the costs of private and public health care and hence the equality of opportunities for medical treatment.

New cures

Biotechnology will provide new cures for conditions. One way will involve gene therapy which is basically inserting a 'good' gene over a 'faulty' gene. This is massively complex but the first applications seem likely to occur soon. Other applications will be the production of vaccines and antibodies that are much more effective than existing ones and which have lower, even zero, rejection rates. AIDS and malaria are examples of the diseases that new cures could target.

Cell regeneration

Most human cells have specific applications but stem cells can be converted into different types of cell. They are formed in embryos and later develop into specialist cells (for blood or skin for example) but they also exist in adults. Research is progressing to find ways of using stem cells to repair damaged tissue, for example to the liver or heart. You will know of transplant surgery and the need to find organ donors – usually from an accident. In the long term it is possible that stem cells will be able to grow replacement organs thus reducing the need for human donors.

Cloning

Clones are cells or organisms taken from a common ancestor and which are genetically identical to the ancestor (Rowley, 2002). The science of cloning complete large organisms is hugely complex, as well as ethically problematic, but it seems likely that in the long term cloning science will be used. One application would be, following genetic modification, to create an animal with certain characteristics that benefit humans and then clone the animal. This could include a cloned animal producing natural medicines or producing organs, for example kidneys, suitable for human transplant. Conversely, cloning could produce an animal with a genetically engineered defect that is studied to help understand cures for the same defect in humans. Rowley (2002) mentions cystic fibrosis as an example.

Agricultural biotechnology

About 200 years ago, Thomas Malthus observed that, since the amount of land is fixed then the population that can be supported by food from the land is also fixed. What Malthus could not have foreseen was the massive increase in agricultural productivity in the nineteenth and twentieth centuries that produced more food from a given area. Biotechnology offers another massive productivity leap. By altering the genetic structure of plants it will be possible to:

- make plants more resistant to disease and attack by pests and thus help to move away from environmentally unfriendly pesticides and insecticides;

- make plants more tolerant of dry conditions so opening up new areas for agriculture;

- improve yields to produce larger, tastier and longer-lasting crops.

If these outcomes could be delivered on a large scale it would improve the productivity of agriculturally intensive regions like northern Europe and the USA and support increasing populations in difficult growing areas such as parts of Africa. But such 'progress' does not come without some risks and these require both continued research and ethical debates, including:

- Since the pollination of plants is hard to control in the open, what effects could genetically modified (GM) plants have on other plant species? What is the risk of creating GM vegetation in general and what would be the impact on insect and bird life?

- What are the risks to humans of consuming GM foods?

- Who owns the stocks of GM seeds? If large corporations are in control over distribution then the benefits to poorer regions may not occur.

Genetic modification of plants has occurred for thousands of years as farmers have selected seeds from the 'best' plants. GM is different to natural development in that it involves the transfer of just a few genes to a plant to address some specific improvement. GM foods have been grown for some years, particularly in the USA, and include corn and tomatoes (Brown, 2001). The key questions are how far can genetic modification of plants be taken and what safeguards need to be in place while development occurs? Plants do exchange genes with related plants and so fear of GM crops cross-pollinating other species and creating a 'gene flow' is reasonable. In the USA, most of the GM crops are soya bean and cotton that have no wild relatives – and so hybridisation is unlikely in those cases. But other crops, particularly cereals, do have many wild relatives. This is a technical problem that, apart from giving strength to the anti-GM lobby, is difficult to assess in small-scale field trials. One possible answer is to modify crops so that, as well as being enhanced in some way, they do not easily reproduce. This also has the attraction that it would prevent trade in unlicensed seed products and keep control over seed stocks securely with the owners of the technology (Brookes, 1998).

Genetic modification of animals and fish also offers the potential to produce better meat yields from more resistant species thus keeping down the costs of food supplements and medications. Genetically modified fish pose particular difficulties since, once escaped from fish farms to the wild, they are beyond detection. Interbreeding with the normal population could have drastic effects on the species and other species that they co-exist with. If its size and survivability have been enhanced, a species could threaten others to extinction by depleting food stocks and dispersing more widely than normal.

Other uses of biotechnology

Bacteria and plants may be developed to degrade particular forms of harmful wastes that are currently going to land or to costly chemical treatments. Land previously contaminated by wastes and pollution can be cleaned by GM plants that remove particular 'nasties' from the soil. Many industrial processes use large amounts of energy and use 'dirty' processes involving metals, plastics, acids and oil-based products that end up in water-borne, gaseous or solid wastes. Some industrial processes will be affected by biotechnology such that energy requirements will fall along with the use of environmentally unfriendly products and processes. Some materials, for example oil-based plastic packaging, that currently create environmental problems (where to put it and long degradation times) will be replaced with materials that degrade more quickly and are much less damaging.

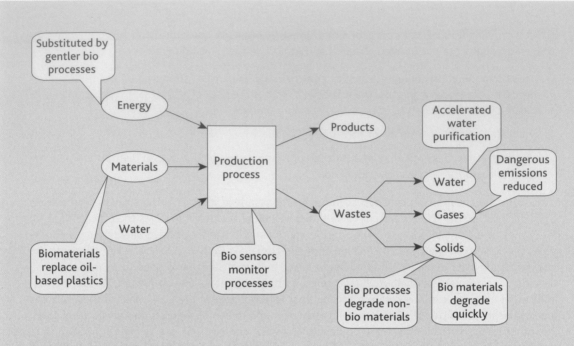

Figure C4.1 Impact of biotechnology on production processes

Figure C4.1 shows how production processes are being affected and how they will be affected in the future by biotechnology.

Issues raised by the case

As our knowledge of nature expands, what are the best ways to manage the production and sharing of that knowledge? If we are approaching a time when our understanding of genetics really could re-shape human society, then what systems are needed to ensure that knowledge and the innovations that derive from it are used responsibly and equitably? Poor people and poor nations could be effectively excluded from biotechnology advances given current economic structures that could concentrate the knowledge in the hands of a few technically advanced nations like the USA, the United Kingdom and Germany.

Like other major breakthrough technologies, investing in biotechnology projects is risky as projects have long lead times and uncertain outcomes. The same problem befell the early investors in the 'dot.com' sector in the 1990s. Because of the high risks, normal investment appraisal methods do not work very well. So, how can the returns on biotechnology projects, particularly those involving genetic engineering, be estimated?

Biotechnology appears capable of raising sector competitiveness and raising gross domestic product. But the dangers of a biotech productivity paradox, similar to that seen with ICT projects and explained in Chapter 4, are present. This could occur if the rate of biotechnology introduction to business enterprises is slow and the knowledge and technologies involved become widely available.

The complexities and risks of biotechnology mean that new 'models' of business will be needed to generate and apply knowledge. There are decisions about what R&D to conduct as part of core activities and what R&D to contract out to other, often much smaller but specialist, organisations. Decisions are also needed over what collaborative arrangements are needed and with whom. These problems raise questions about the relations between large firms, often multinationals, and small, localised firms with which they have agreements.

Funding for R&D comes from public (government) and private sources. Questions arise about how knowledge from the two scenarios should be treated. How should knowledge produced out of public money be handled compared to knowledge produced out of private funding?

Being based on new science and new applications of existing science, biotechnology has implications for education and skills as new occupations are created. How are the different regions equipped through schools and universities to provide those skills and what are the consequences of skill shortages?

In the long term, biotechnology will offer substitutes for many products and affect many production processes particularly by influencing production costs. The fundamental economic structures of some sectors will be affected – and can be modelled using Porter's five forces approach.

Because of the deep concerns about risks to humans and the environment and deep concerns about the ethics of genetic modification (playing God as some call it), new regulatory frameworks will be needed to govern the type of R&D projects that can be carried out. For example, strict controls on cloning research and on the use of knowledge generated by such projects.

Figure C4.2 shows the relationship between multinational companies and small companies in the biotechnology sector, three main application areas and society. Business enterprises collaborate to produce new knowledge, technology and innovations that affect health, agriculture and industrial processes. Society then adopts (consumes) products from innovations in these areas. The extent of adoption is moderated by the amount of trust that societies place in producers.

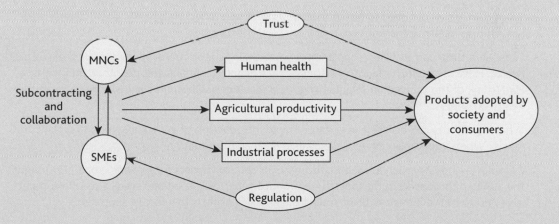

Figure C4.2 Key factors in biotechnology innovation

Regulation by governments also influences the type of development work that business enterprises can carry out and the ways in which innovations can be used.

What does this case show?

• The time lag from key scientific discovery to widespread commercial applications of the science can be very long – in this case about 50 years since the discovery of DNA.

• New technology leads to formation of new business start-ups. Investment in these is very risky and many fail but some survive and grow.

• Business start-ups provide jobs and the nature of the work affects the social make-up of the region.

• Technology affects existing sectors by both creating and destroying product markets and creates new sectors that may cluster geographically. There is a cluster of biotechnology firms around Cambridge, England, for example. Clustering in this region is partly explained by the linkage to world class research expertise at Cambridge University and university spin-off companies setting up locally.

• Technology is usually used to create processes or products that benefit mankind – often in incremental or marginal ways but occasionally in revolutionary ways.

• New technologies can fundamentally alter the economic structure of a sector.

• Some technologies bring with them complex questions about how they should be used.

Questions

1. What ethical concerns are raised by the prospect that all young children will have their DNA routinely tested for predictors of adverse health conditions?

2. What controls would need to be put in place if and when it becomes possible to diagnose a person's future health levels from quick and easy DNA testing?

3. Suppose a time comes when people know what their genetic make-up means for their future health. How might this affect the attitudes that people have and the way that they behave? Hint: think of the things that might change as a result of a widespread knowledge of our future health prospects.

4. What arguments can be made in favour of rapid introduction of genetically modified plants on farms? What arguments can be made against such an introduction?

5. Consider an industry such as that producing seeds sold to farmers for growing crops. How might the ability of producers in the industry to produce genetically modified seeds alter the competitive nature of the industry? (Hint: model the changes using a 'five forces' approach.)

References

Brookes, M. (1998) 'Running wild', *New Scientist*, 31 October, pp. 38–41.

Brown, K. (2001) 'Seeds of concern', *Scientific American*, April, p. 56.

Department of Health (2003) *Genes Direct*, Report by the Human Genetics Commission.

Kite, M. (2003) 'Insurance firm admits using genetic screening', *The Times*, 8 February, p. 6.

Rowley, W.R. (2002) 'Biotechnology overview – applications and forecasts', *Foresight*, 4 (4), pp. 4–12.

Schmidt, K.F. (1998) 'Just for you', *New Scientist*, 4 November, p. 34.

5

Ageing Europe and the looming pensions crisis
Jon Stephens

The objective of this case study is to look at how the ageing population trends in Europe are beginning to have serious impacts on future pension provision in Europe and how this throws up a number of future challenges for governments. The case will start by examining the trends towards ageing population (see also Chapter 5) and then will look at some of the aspects of pension provision in Europe and how the two of these when combined lead to the potential 'pensions crisis' mentioned in the case title. The case will then look at the particular issues facing one country, Greece, as a means of further illustrating the issue of future pension provision.

The pressure on future pension provision is essentially based around two key areas which are *the demographic effect* on pensions and *the eligibility effect* which reflects the various regulations and rules concerning eligibility for pensions such as age of retirement etc.

Demographic factors

The key demographic factor that is influencing future pension provision is the ageing of the European population. This has primarily been caused by falls in fertility rates across Europe (see Chapter 5) as women postpone having children until a later age and also tend to have fewer children for a mix of social and economic factors, such as the difficulty of getting part-time employment in markets with low labour flexibility.

The consequence of falling fertility and hence birth rates is that the proportion of younger people is falling in relation to the proportion of older people in the population. As the provision of state pensions derives primarily from contributions from the working population (between 15 and 64 years) which is meant to provide for the retired population (usually from 65 for men) then the proportion of people in these groups will be very significant when looking at future pension provision. Eurostat projections suggest that from 2000 to 2050 the EU's working population (based on the fifteen EU countries as of 2000) would decrease from 243 million to 203 million (a fall of 18 per cent) compared to an increase of the population aged over 64 from 63 million to 103 million (an increase of 60 per cent).

To look at this from another perspective, the United States currently has about five potential workers to support each pensioner compared to about four potential workers in the EU as the main effects of the ageing populations haven't yet been felt, with the main acceleration of ageing anticipated to occur between 2010 and 2030. However, by 2050 it is predicted that there will be about three potential workers per pensioner in the United States, compared to about two and a half workers in the UK, two workers in France and Germany and one and a half workers in Italy. The potential strain on the working population caused by increased taxes and insurance contributions to cover the cost of increased pension demands can be imagined and may well be unsustainable for governments, which is why the issue of pension reform is rising rapidly up the political agenda.

To reinforce the picture of the ageing population in Europe we can also look at the predicted average age of the population by 2050, see Table C5.1.

From the table above we can clearly see the ageing of the population in Europe, although the UK (with its relatively higher fertility rate and flexible labour market) appears to be ageing more slowly than some countries, especially the Southern Mediterranean countries of Italy and Spain. This suggests that the impact of the ageing population on pensions will be stronger in some countries than others.

Eligibility factors

The second key factor when looking at the potential pensions crisis is the *eligibility effect*. This reflects the mass of legislation as to the rules of eligibility for pensions in a country, particularly a pension provided by the state, as opposed to a private pension scheme run by the individual or a pension run as part of a company scheme, which reflects pension provision provided in addition to the state pension. One issue could be the determination of the age at which a person is eligible for a state pension. The ages in the UK were 65 for men and 60 for women, although women now have the right to work till 65 and indeed there is pressure to increase the age of retirement to 70 (see later). In Italy, the majority of Italian workers until recently were able to take retirement packages that allowed them to retire at 50. In fact, until 1995, Italian workers could retire at 50 on a salary-indexed pension valued at 80 per cent of their final salary. Although Italy switched to a contributions-based system in 1995, the government still has to cover all the people who retired before then and who will live well into their 70s and 80s. Sometimes there are special pension privileges for certain jobs or professions (such as early retirement) and these concessions are usually jealously guarded.

The problem has been that people have come to expect ever-improving conditions of eligibility for their pensions such as the right to retire earlier from work and to have secure and fairly well-paid pensions. This has led to more and more people taking earlier retirement and ever more generous retirement settlements (especially when final salary based rather than contributions based, such as in the UK, where relatively low national insurance contributions have led to one of the lowest rates of state pensions in Europe, although they are often index-linked to the rate of inflation). One of the major problems governments will face in the future is in changing expectations about improved eligibility for pensions, as earlier retirement ages linked to higher pension settlements does not make any economic sense when linked with a vast increase in the number of older people who are claiming pensions.

Although the crisis has been predictable for some time, it has never risen too far up the political agenda as the main impact will be felt from 2010 onwards when the post-Second World War

Table C5.1 UN population predictions of the median age of the population 2000–2050

Country	2000	2050
France	37.6	45.1
Germany	39.9	46.8
Italy	40.2	52.4
Spain	37.4	51.9
United Kingdom	37.7	43.8
United States	35.2	39.7
Japan	41.3	52.4

Source: United Nations

'baby-boomers' all start retiring and thus it could be postponed as any change in eligibility for pensions might be politically unpopular for the current government. However, there have been clear signs that the issue has taken on much more significance at the beginning of the twenty-first century with more and more countries looking at the issue of pension reform. The reason is clear as the maintenance of the current situation will mean that state pensions will take up an ever-increasing amount of the country's GDP, thus putting severe strain on economies and diverting spending from other areas.

If we look at OECD projections for 2050 we can see that the combined effects of the population effect and the eligibility effect will tend to drastically increase the pressure on some countries' GDP, although those with a slower-ageing population and a less generous pension system (such as the UK) will be less adversely affected. Thus the amount of GDP spent on pensions is predicted to rise in Germany from a figure in 2000 of 11.8 per cent of GDP to a figure of 16.9 per cent of GDP by 2050. Similar figures for Spain suggest a rise from 9.4 per cent of GDP in 2000 to 17.3 per cent of GDP by 2050, although the predicted change for the UK actually sees a decrease (5.5 per cent of GDP in 2000 to 4.4 per cent in 2050) for reasons suggested above.

The Greek experience

Before looking at some of the possible solutions that governments might take to reduce the impact of the pensions crisis, we will examine the demographic and eligibility factors for Greece to look at the potential impact of the pensions crisis in a specific country context.

Like many Southern Mediterranean countries, Greece has an ageing population with one of the highest life expectancies in Europe (75.1 for men and 81.4 for women). Like Italy and Spain it has a low fertility rate (1.2) and in 2002 actually had a decrease in natural population growth, although this was offset by some inward migration, especially from the Balkans. Pensioners are already a significant factor, equivalent to 60 per cent of the active population.

When looking at the eligibility factors we can see that the current retirement age for men is 65 and that the final pension is based on people's earnings over their last five years (being salary-indexed). It is possible in Greece to claim a full pension after 35 years of contributions (so a person starting work at 16 can claim a pension at 51), compared to 40 years of contributions in Germany and 49 years of contributions in the Netherlands. In addition certain jobs that are classified as 'arduous and unhygenic' qualify for a five-year reduction in contributions and this covers about 40 per cent of the working population (suggesting a possible retirement age of 46!) and in fact a minimum pension is available after fifteen years' work.

As before, if we put together the impact of the ageing population with the eligibility factors we can begin to see the impact that pension provision will have on the Greek economy. Current (2000) expenditure on pensions as a percentage of Gross Domestic Product (GDP) amounts to 12.6 per cent of GDP, compared to the EU average of 10.4 per cent of GDP. According to OECD estimates the pension expenditure in Greece by 2050 will amount to 24.5 per cent of GDP, compared to the predicted EU average of 13.3 per cent of GDP – that is to say that almost a quarter of the value of all the output in Greece will have to go to cover pension expenditure – a position which is clearly untenable for any government as it would put intolerable pressures on the working population through tax increases or lead to massive government borrowing which could have detrimental effects on the economy.

Solutions to the pensions crisis?

Like most governments, Greece has to find some solutions to the pensions crisis before it develops to the stage suggested above. One can look for solutions either from the demographic perspective or from the eligibility perspective.

In terms of the demographic perspective, it will already be difficult to offset the numbers of the ageing population as the people likely to retire in the future are already working at present. It will also be difficult to offset the relative sizes of the working population in relation to the pension-age population, given that fertility rates remain low. A longer-term solution would be to encourage higher fertility rates by offering incentives to have more children, such as higher tax relief or by providing better child-care facilities, enabling parents to return to work more easily. A shorter-term possibility could be to allow the amount of inward migration to increase significantly as economic immigrants usually have a lower age profile and thus would boost the working population in the short run. Whilst a potentially effective solution it may engender political and social problems in the country according to how well the immigrants are integrated with the society.

A much more likely approach to solving the problem will be to change the eligibility criteria for pension provision. One very likely solution (albeit one that may not be politically popular) would be to increase the age of retirement in the country as this would both reduce the population of pension age and increase the working population simultaneously. This has been done in the United States where they have raised the retirement age to 67 and recent (June 2003) propositions by the government in the UK have suggested raising the retirement age to 70 for those who wished to work until that age. One problem with this approach, identified by the UK government, is that any increase in the retirement age needs to be linked to a much more positive attitude by employers to older people, otherwise age discrimination may mean that the effect of increasing the retirement age is severely diluted.

Another element of eligibility that could be changed is the special pension privileges that go to certain groups. However, attempts to remove such privileges are likely to be severely resisted by the groups concerned and in June 2003 there were a wide range of strikes in the French public sector as they sought to resist government moves to get public sector employees to work beyond 60 – in fact previous attempts in France to resolve this issue in the mid-90s had led to the downfall of the government. Another way around the problem would be to encourage workers to take out private pension schemes or follow company schemes, although a number of concerns were expressed in June 2003 in the UK about companies who had used their workers' pension funds for other purposes, with many workers experiencing vastly reduced pensions when their companies went into liquidation. Another problem in this respect is that, increasingly, companies are only employing workers on short-term renewable contracts and this reduces the workers' confidence in joining the company pension scheme when they cannot be sure of their future with the company.

Thus, it can be seen that the solutions to the looming pensions crisis are not easy ones for governments and yet the dynamics of population change mean that it is a problem that can no longer be indefinitely ignored and difficult choices and decisions will lie ahead which will at some stage affect everyone working in Europe.

Sources:

PricewaterhouseCoopers European Economic Outlook (2003).

OECD Report on Greece (2003).

Questions

1. Why have governments tended to avoid the problem of pension reform? Why is it getting harder to avoid the problem in the twenty-first century?

2. Do a web search using search words like 'pension reform' in your country and evaluate the extent to which your government is tackling this problem (for the UK try: http://news.bbc.co.uk/1/hi/business/2580803.stm).

3. Critically evaluate the advantages of extending the retirement age to 70 in your country.

4. What do you see as the main problems likely to be encountered in reforming European pensions systems?

6

Carlsberg
Jamie Weatherston

Background

J.C. Jacobsen founded Carlsberg in Copenhagen in 1847. The brewery pioneered a number of new brewing techniques that set the scene for the modern brewing industry. Carlsberg's primary activities now are the production, sale and distribution of beer and soft drinks as well as related activities.

Carlsberg's international thrust began early on with the tentative export of one barrel of beer to Edinburgh in 1868. Carlsberg did not open its first overseas brewery, in Blantyre, Malawi, until 1968. It now operates in some 32 countries worldwide and is still expanding rapidly, with nineteen mergers and acquisitions reported since May 2000. The world famous Carlsberg logo was introduced in 1904. Special Brew was launched in 1950.

Social responsibility

Almost from the beginning, with the establishment of the Carlsberg Foundation in 1876, Carlsberg has been aware of its responsibilities and in 2002 Carlsberg expanded its principles for Corporate Social Responsibility with particular emphasis on responsible management, environment and alcohol consumption.

At the end of 2002, Carlsberg Breweries introduced a Code of Responsible Management. The code includes reference to business ethics and labour standards, extract below. Implementation is primarily through dialogue and continuous follow-up with business associates. Furthermore, a so-called 'legal compliance' programme was implemented in 2002 to ensure that as well as being aware of social responsibilities, competition regulations are always observed.

Extract from Carlsberg Breweries' Code of Responsible Management

Business ethics

Carlsberg Breweries does not permit bribes with the objective of winning business or other advantages in relations with actual or potential business partners and government representatives. Applicable local competition law shall be complied with and employees shall not conduct illegal industrial espionage.

Financial transactions shall be handled in a true and fair manner supported by accurate documentation in reasonable detail within the proper time period.

Labour standards

Carlsberg Breweries will actively implement the core areas in the United Nations' Universal Declaration on Human Rights, including:

*   equal opportunities;
*   regular reviews of proper work health and safety conditions;

- freedom of association;

- elimination of child labour and forced labour;

- fair employment terms, particularly as regards: remuneration, working hours and employee development in accordance with industry standards.

Environmental affairs

Carlsberg aims to operate in an efficient, economic and environmentally responsible manner. It works actively to reduce any negative impact on the environment and to optimise the use of natural resources. Although no major environmental accidents occurred in 2002 it was decided that Carlsberg Breweries' environmental activities would undergo improvement through internationally recognised standards for environmental management, ISO 14001. Carlsberg Breweries has focused its central environmental efforts on ensuring methodical streamlining of environmental management and reporting and on expanding knowledge of and training in environmental activities.

Carlsberg Breweries has adopted an environmental policy containing seven core goals, which are targeted at primary business activities.

The environmental policy states that Carlsberg Breweries will:

1. continuously minimise adverse effects on the environment, and optimise the use of natural resources;

2. protect and improve the environment in majority-owned subsidiaries and ensure that these subsidiaries, as a minimum, comply with all applicable local environmental legislation and regulations;

3. systematically and continuously measure and improve performance through an internationally recognised environmental management system, which will be supported by training and awareness programmes for relevant employees and by annual review of targets. ISO 14001 must be implemented in 37 production sites by the end of 2004;

4. prioritise environmentally driven investments higher than other technical investments;

5. implement its environmental strategy in joint ventures and in associated companies whenever possible;

6. encourage partners and suppliers to operate in an environmentally acceptable way;

7. be dedicated to an open and unbiased dialogue about environmental issues with their stakeholders.

The most important environmental efforts are carried out within the areas subject to substantial environmental impact. Carlsberg Breweries' environmental impact is most significant in malting, brewing and bottling of beer and soft drinks, as these require use of vegetable raw materials, water, energy

Table C6.1 Production of soft drinks as percentage of total output

Percentage of Total Production (%)	Year
14	2000
24	2001
28	2002

and packaging. Carlsberg Breweries seeks, primarily, the reduction of resource consumption, namely, water, electricity, and heat energy and the reduction of discharge, primarily CO_2 and wastewater. A total of 37 production sites participated in environmental reporting in 2002.

Several production units have achieved the environmental standard ISO 14001. Carlsberg Breweries plan that all production units should be ready for environmental certification by the end of 2004.

There has been a relative increase in production of soft drinks in recent years (see Table C6.1). This makes comparison of the current environmental impact with previous years more difficult given that soft drink production requires less energy consumption per unit of output. Between 2000 and 2002, however, the environmental impact of beer and soft drinks production appears to be significantly lower. Energy consumption is down approximately 15 per cent and water consumption and emissions of carbon dioxide have each fallen by about 20 per cent. In general, Carlsberg Breweries will promote environmental investments and prioritise co-operation with partners and suppliers who can demonstrate that their activities are environmentally responsible.

The activities at Carlsberg-Tetley show how the environmental policy is being implemented at plant level.

Carlsberg-Tetley

Since its introduction to the United Kingdom market, the Carlsberg brand has grown to become one of the most prominent lager brands. In 1992, the Carlsberg-Tetley merger created one of the United Kingdom's largest drinks companies.

Its strategy is to focus on its core brands and improved operating and distribution efficiencies. In 2000 Carlsberg-Tetley was the third largest brewer with a 13 per cent share of the 55.5 million hectolitres market. The strong brands (Carlsberg and Tetley's) constitute approximately 70 per cent of total sales. Carlsberg-Tetley successfully completed its restructuring plan with the commissioning of new plant and increased capacity at both the Northampton and Leeds breweries and the closure of the Wrexham brewery during 2000.

Subsidiaries are required to gather and report not only economic and operational data but also environmental data. They are required to prepare and set up goals and plans for local environmental activities on an ongoing basis and are obliged to make continuous efforts to improve environmental conditions. Carlsberg-Tetley is 'committed to achieving commercial success without detrimental impacts to the community, the natural environment and people.'

At the Carlsberg-Tetley Northampton Brewery the environment manager plays a key role within the system, providing:

• advice on, for example, legal compliance where necessary;

• corporate integrated management system;

- technical support for projects;

- environmental training;

- support for new technology and innovations;

- community public relations.

Under the EMS 14001 standard a number of key requirements have to be met:

- An environmental policy outlining the company's intent has to be produced.

- Potential environmental impacts have to be identified, ranked, documented, monitored and reviewed.

- A legal register of applicable legislation has to be maintained.

- Continuous targets and objectives have to be set and managed.

- Staff have to be trained.

- Audits have to be carried out.

- Environmental discharges have to be monitored and measured.

- A plan and response to potential emergency situations have to be in place.

When viewed from the level of the brewery, the individual activities required to comply with EMS 14001 may, at first sight, seem to be rather daunting and bureaucratic. However, the reality is that there are a number of potential gains that a company can make. Carlsberg-Tetley report that the pay-back period (the time it takes to recoup money paid out) for capital expenditure projects may be very short or immediate. Cost savings can be substantial. EMS 14001 is also compatible with other management systems, so requires little extra paperwork. The standard also contributes to improved housekeeping and health and safety as well as boosting customer and supplier confidence.

Progress at the Northampton brewery has been positive over a number of areas.

Wastewater

Effluent analysers have been installed to report on performance at all levels. Investments have been made in new plant and staff trained to minimise discharges into drains. An improvement group has been established to steer improvements.

Solid waste

Awareness campaigns have targeted waste minimisation and training is designed to optimise resources, e.g. photocopiers and the reduction of the use of packaging materials, and segregation initiatives, e.g. a paper collection scheme, have also been put into place. Waste is being diverted from landfill to recycling. Other waste is being compacted to reduce volume and frequency of collections. Audits of the production line are being carried out and suppliers appraised for environmental performance.

Energy

Refrigeration plant has been upgraded, resulting in a 10 per cent reduction in electricity consumption. New air compressors and air treatment plant that conform to industry standard benchmarks have been installed, resulting in a 5 per cent reduction in costs. Air leaks have also been reduced, saving £28 000 a year in kegging. Boilers have been re-insulated, reducing gas consumption by 2.5 per cent.

Benefits

Cost savings

A £1.5 million saving has been made over two years through improved waste and effluent management. Over five years there have been a 44 per cent fall in cost of electricity and a 31 per cent fall in the cost of gas to produce one litre of beer. Through their investment in a new CO_2 recovery plant the brewery has become self-sufficient in CO_2 production.

Environmental

There has been an 85 per cent reduction in waste sent to landfill; all by-products and all packaging wastes are recycled. The policy on reducing weight means that less material is being used. The reduction in the use of energy has clear environmental benefits and the CO_2 recovery plant has reduced emission of a greenhouse gas.

Carlsberg-Tetley has plans to progress this agenda still further. It is going to continue to improve partnerships with suppliers to minimise packaging and will eventually require supplier accreditation to ISO 14001. Ethical packaging will also come into the equation. Marketing will also come under the environmental banner with the adoption of eco-labelling and environmental advertising.

These initiatives are part of the overall strategy of Carlsberg-Tetley. Their primary aim is to generate profit based on competitive advantage. Environmental issues are viewed as a tool to reach this aim.

Sources:

adapted from Carlsberg A/S Report and Accounts (2002) Available from http://www.carlsberg.com/resources/letter+to+the+shareholders.pdf; http://www.carlsberg.com/main.asp?go=international [accessed 5 May 2003].

Wilson, J. (2002) Presentation to School of Business, University College Northampton, 6 December 2002.

Questions

1. Carlsberg Breweries states in its code of responsible management 'it does not permit bribes with the objective of winning business.' What are the ramifications that this action could have on the business?

2. Using appropriate sources from around the world gather evidence and comment on the use of bribes by business organisations.

3. Using the Taylor *et al.* (1994) schema categorise Carlsberg-Tetley. Summarise the externalities that Carlsberg-Tetley produces and assess how successful they are in limiting externalities.

4. Using the Roome (1992) continuum of environmental options identify, with justifications, which category Carlsberg Breweries falls into.

5. The European eco-label is the flower or daisy. Carlsberg-Tetley plan to adopt eco-labelling. What are the benefits that result from adopting such a policy? Have any other companies benefited from taking this approach?

References

Roome, N. (1992) 'Developing environmental systems', *Business Strategy and the Environment*, Sprint, part 1.

Taylor, B., Hutchinson, C., Pollack, S. and Tapper, R. (1994) *The Environmental Management Handbook*, London: Pitman.

Tanzania: from socialism to capitalism
Graham Wilkinson

7

Introduction

Tanzania, in East Africa, is one of the poorest countries in the world and the scene of a remarkable transformation in both political philosophy and economic policy in the 40 years since it gained independence from the UK. This case study aims to explore the political environment of Tanzania from the early days of independence to the early twenty-first century.

Background information

Tanzania (then known as Tanganyika) became independent from the UK in December 1961 under the leadership of President Julius Nyerere. It combined with the offshore island of Zanzibar in 1964, to form what is now officially known as the United Republic of Tanzania. The country is a republic, with the President (currently Benjamin Mkapa) serving as both head of state and the principal political leader in the legislature. Following a lengthy period of one-party rule, it is now a multi-party democracy with elections held every five years. It is organised politically in such a way that Zanzibar and the mainland are both semi-autonomous with considerable local powers. For purposes of local government, the country is divided into twenty-five districts, three of which are on Zanzibar. (For more information on government, and other matters, see CIA Factbook, 2003.)

The country has land borders with eight of its neighbours and has the Indian Ocean to the east. Despite being just south of the equator, it includes a wide variety of different terrains and climates, from the coastal plains to inland plateaus, including Kilimanjaro, the highest mountain in Africa. The largest city and commercial capital is Dar-es-Salaam, on the coast; the political capital is being moved from Dar to the town of Dodoma, situated at roughly the geographic centre of the country. Tanzania's economy is still largely reliant on agriculture, but tourism – often based on seeing wildlife – is also an important source of revenue. Table C7.1 highlights some important statistical data.

Basic indicators

The data in Table C7.1 provide some insight into major economic and social conditions in Tanzania; data for the UK are provided for comparison. Figures relate to 2000/2001 except (a) where otherwise stated and (b) when in *italics*, when they are for the nearest available year.

Independence

From the outset, the country adopted a socialist approach to politics and development. Nyerere believed that development should be a process that was led by (central) government, but one that must reflect the needs and priorities of ordinary people. In other words, he believed that the policies

Table C7.1 Economic and social indicators

	Tanzania	UK
Population		
Total population (millions)	35	60
Population growth (% per year, 1990–2001)	2.7	0.4
Land area (thousand square kilometres)	945	245
Population density – persons per square kilometre	39	249
Economic indicators		
National income and output		
Gross National Income (US$ billion)	9.2	1451.4
GNI per head (US$)	270	24 230
Average annual growth in GDP per head (%, 1990–2001)	3.1	2.6
Value of output as a % of GDP – agriculture	45	*1*
Value of output as a % of GDP – industry	16	*29*
Value of output as a % of GDP – services	39	*70*
International trade		
Balance of Payments (current account) (US$ million)	−998	−25 107
Merchandise trade – value of exports (US$ million)	780	273 462
Merchandise trade – value of imports (US$ million)	1660	332 523
Manufactured exports as a % of total exports	*15*	82
Net Foreign Direct Investment (US$ million)	193	133 974
Aid and debt		
Aid (Official Development Assistance, US$ per head)	31	—
External debt (US$ million)	7445	—
Present value of external debt as % of GNP	50	—
Social indicators		
Poverty		
% of population below national poverty line	*41.6*	—
% of population with an income below US$1 per day	*19.9*	—
% of income/consumption by top 10% of population	*30.1*	*27.7*
% of income/consumption by bottom 10% of population	*2.8*	*2.3*
Energy use		
Carbon dioxide emissions, millions of tons	*2.2*	542.3
Education		
Adult literacy	75	—
% of 5–11 age group in primary school (1991)	69	100
% of 12–16 age group in secondary school (1991)	5	86
Health		
% of population with access to safe water	*49*	*100*
% of population with access to sanitation	*86*	*96*
Infant (under 5) mortality per 1000 live births	85	6
Life expectancy at birth (years)	44	77

Source: World Bank, 2003, and author's calculations.

that government implemented should be designed not necessarily with conventional views of economic growth in mind, but rather that the basic needs of the population should be the priority. This emphasis on trying to meet the needs and expectations of the mass of the people meant that policy was to concentrate on the provision of water supplies, sanitation, health care and basic education, all based around the rural nature of what was (and still is) a largely agricultural society.

Nyerere argued, from the days before independence, that government and socialist ideas should play a major role in the affairs of the country. This political philosophy was expounded most succinctly and most famously in a speech given by Nyerere at Arusha in February 1967, in what became known as the Arusha Declaration. The main feature of the speech was that Tanzania should not attempt to develop in a conventional way, based on what Western thinking (and Western textbooks) had to say. Rather, Tanzania should be self-reliant, socialist and egalitarian. At one point, he even argued that it was stupid to depend upon money for development (Nyerere, 1967) when the one resource that the country did not possess was money. Instead of relying on money as *the basis of* development, he argued that money was *the result of* development. In other words, he turned conventional development thinking on its head.

A further element of this philosophy was Nyerere's rejection of money from foreign sources. He believed that if Tanzanians were to shape Tanzania's development, if they were to set their own agenda for the future, then foreign money had no part to play. This idea was founded on the simple belief, expressed by Nyerere at Arusha, that 'he who pays the piper calls the tune'. This means that he believed that if Tanzania accepted money from foreign governments or, worse, foreign companies, then it would be those bodies that shaped Tanzanian development, not the Tanzanian people and government. He thus urged Tanzanians to become self-reliant, depending only upon themselves and hard work as the basis of sustainable, if slow, development efforts.

Socialist policies

In pursuit of this socialist ideal, Nyerere's government instituted a series of policies designed to benefit the population as a whole. The emphasis was to be on rural development, based on a programme of reorganisation known as *Ujamaa*, the Swahili word for brotherhood or family. This was an ambitious programme which involved the development of new villages in rural areas, where production was to be based on communal ownership of land and any profits were to be used for the benefit of the entire community.

The thinking behind the plan was that replacing traditional, small and scattered settlements with larger, communal villages would bring benefits to all concerned. From the farmers' point of view, the cultivation of land on a larger scale was meant to bring cost reductions, greater efficiency and output and, thus, a better standard of living. From a government perspective, the provision of services to rural areas could be accomplished much more economically by supplying a smaller number of larger villages. Thus, the political philosophy was that the government should – and would – supply basic infrastructure and services, such as a primary school and teacher, basic health care via a resident paramedic, electricity and clean water. Overall Nyerere believed that the population would benefit, living standards would improve and development (and wealth) would gradually result.

These policies were put into effect from the late 1960s onwards. Initially there is little doubt that there was some degree of success and many people in the more remote and poorer rural areas were keen to embrace the new approach. Looking at the statistical evidence it can be seen that there were certainly successes in the field of social development. Adult literacy, for example, increased from 17 per cent of the population at independence to around 68 per cent in the mid-1980s. A similar percentage of the population had access to safe water supplies and life expectancy at birth had risen from 37 years in 1960 to 54 years in 1987. These figures compare exceptionally well with those for many other developing economies.

However, problems slowly became apparent. As government attempted to extend the Ujamaa programme to more prosperous regions, resistance to relocation increased. At the same time, it was becoming apparent that there was increasing corruption, that earnings from agriculture were not as high as had been hoped or expected and that other parts of the economy, notably industry, were being neglected. The lack of economic growth also meant that it became increasingly difficult for the government to fund the social services which were meant to be the cornerstone of development. Nevertheless, in what was essentially a one-party state, Nyerere remained in power as the economy stagnated and aid from foreign governments (notably Norway, Sweden, the UK and China) became increasingly important. By the mid-1980s, however, it was evident that major changes were needed.

After Nyerere

Nyerere retired from the presidency of his country in 1985. Although he remained active in politics for another five years, this move allowed his successor, Ali Hassan Mwinyi, to embark upon a new direction for what had become one of the poorest countries in the world, at least in terms of GNP per head. Mwinyi did what Nyerere could not: he approached the International Monetary Fund for assistance in coping with the country's stagnating economy and mounting debt. In response, the IMF, after long and sometimes difficult negotiations agreed to the release of funds to Tanzania, subject to various conditions.

In line with its usual approach, the IMF suggested (critics would say imposed) a reform programme based on fundamentally changing the economy. It can be seen that the IMF's Structural Adjustment Programmes in the 1980s and 1990s were all very similar policies regardless of the country involved. The prescription for all countries was based on the belief that reducing government involvement in the economy was the key to success, with success being defined as more rapid economic growth; Tanzania was no exception to this approach. The basis of the policies that Nyerere had embraced and implemented was thus swept away. Government subsidies were reduced and fees for schooling and medicines introduced. Spending on installing and maintaining clean water supplies and sanitation was cut as part of the implementation of cutting the Tanzanian government's spending. The value of the Tanzanian shilling was reduced on international money markets, making Tanzanian exports cheaper for foreign buyers and increasing the cost of imported goods for Tanzanians. The government was encouraged to reduce the amount of regulation faced by business and to encourage the investment of foreign capital by multinational companies. Politically, too, there were changes, with the development of multi-party politics and Western-style elections by the mid-1990s. In short, the whole emphasis of Tanzanian development changed from one of socialism to a more conventional, market-oriented approach.

Twenty-first century capitalism

At the start of the new millennium Tanzania finds itself in a position of transition. The old ways of Nyerere have largely been abandoned. This is despite the fact that the man himself, who died in 1999, is still revered by many (both inside and outside Tanzania) as a great statesman and a hero. His dream of building a socialist utopia has certainly failed, but many Tanzanians retain a lingering fondness for the dream that he held out for them. In reality, however, the current government, led by Benjamin Mkapa, is pursuing a much more conventional path. The liberal agenda, based on laissez-faire economic policies and extensive privatisation of government services and industries, is now in complete control as economic growth becomes the main priority. The Tanzanian government's national website (see http://www.tanzania.go.tz) and that of the London embassy (see http://www.tanzania-online.gov.uk) both emphasise the wide range of investment opportunities available to foreign firms in Tanzania. Indeed, the main emphasis of the London site would seem to be highlighting the business opportunities that exist.

Meanwhile, in the social field, many would argue that Tanzanians are now even worse off than they were. Defenders of the current approach would argue that it will bring long-term benefits to the population as a whole, even if those benefits are not yet apparent. They argue that the old, socialist, system was simply unsustainable: providing a (relatively) high level of social welfare may be what people want, but it is expensive. Without economic growth the money to sustain such spending simply is not there.

One further change that has resulted from the so-called new realism is that there is increased evidence of greater regional co-operation. As well as being a member of the Southern African Development Community (see Chapter 7), Tanzania is also one of three countries that make up the East African Community; the others are Kenya and Uganda. This move towards regional integration is based on historical foundations. While all three countries were under British control many services (such as posts and telecoms and the Civil Service) were provided in common and free movement of goods and people within the area was the norm. (This is perhaps to be expected, as the artificial nature of the colonial boundaries does not reflect the historical boundaries of the indigenous populations.) After all three countries' independence, attempts were made to continue this co-operation, but the increasingly different political views and policies meant that the community fell apart by 1977. However, as the political and economic ideologies of the three countries have converged again during the late 1990s, moves are now being made to more closely integrate the three once more. The benefits of closer integration (see Chapters 3 and 7) may well be one of the main benefits to Tanzania in the future.

Sources:

Africa Studies Centre, Tanzania page, http:// www.sas.upenn.edu/African_Studies/Country_Specific/Tanzania.html.

BBC News, http://news.bbc.co.uk.

Coulson, A. (1985) *Tanzania: A Political Economy*, Oxford: OUP.

Embassy of the United Republic of Tanzania, London, http://www.tanzania-online.gov.uk.

O'Neill, N. and Mustafa, K. (eds) (1990) *Capitalism, Socialism and the Development Crisis in Tanzania*, Avebury.

New Africa, http://www.newafrica.com.

Tanzania National Website, http://www.tanzania.go.tz/.

Tanzanian newspapers can be accessed directly online or via The Paperboy.com, http://www.thepaperboy.com.au.

Yeager, R. (1989) *Tanzania: An African Experiment*, 2nd edn, Dartmouth Press.

Questions

1. Outline the socialist policies and development priorities of Nyerere when he was President of Tanzania. What impact did these have on the environment for business during that period?

2. Why did these polices have to change? What changes have there been since Nyerere's retirement in 1985?

3. Discuss the effects of IMF-devised Structural Adjustment Programmes on development in Tanzania (and other developing countries).

4. How has the climate for foreign business changed in recent years in Tanzania? What, if any, are the benefits for companies and the people of the country?

References

CIA Factbook (2003) Available from http://www.cia.gov/cia/publications/Factbook/geos/tz.html.

Nyerere, J.K. (1967) *Essays on Socialism*, Dar-es-Salaam: Penguin.

World Bank (2003) *World Development Report*, OUP: Washington DC.

8

The Bhopal disaster
Rob McCusker

On the evening of 23 December 1984, a dangerous chemical reaction occurred in a methyl isocyanate (MIC) storage tank belonging to Union Carbide in Bhopal, India. The leak was first detected at 11.30 pm by workers whose eyes had begun to burn. They told their supervisor but he did not take immediate action. About 40 tons of MIC escaped from its tank over a period of two hours. It spread for eight kilometres over the city of Bhopal, which had a population of nearly 900 000. About 4000 people were killed by the gas as they slept. Current estimates put some 400 000 people affected by the gas over the intervening years. The most severely affected people were those living in shanty towns built immediately around the plant. Most of the victims were the poorest members of that community.

Although an unpopulated area outside the city had been set aside as an industrial area for hazardous facilities, Union Carbide decided to build next to the city instead. Thus, the plant was centrally located in an urban area, which contained a high number of potential employees, next to a large lake, which provided an essential water source. The site manufactured methyl isocyanate, a product used in pesticide production; it is extremely dangerous.

The impact of the gas escaping was made worse by the fact that there appeared to be no systems in place to care for and, more importantly, to compensate the victims. It was soon discovered that there had been a number of technical problems with the plant. These included the fact that the temperature and pressure gauges on the MIC storage tanks were deemed so unreliable that workers often ignored potential warning signs. The unit that kept the MIC at a low temperature had been shut down for quite some time. A device designed to neutralise any escaping gas (the vent gas scrubber) had been shut down for maintenance. It was shown, however, that even if it had been turned on during the fateful night of the escape it could only have coped with a quarter of the escaping gas. An additional device (the flare tower) designed to burn off the gas which escaped the neutralising device was also turned off, because a piece of corroded pipe needed replacing. However, this device too, even if it had been working, could only have handled a quarter of the gas escaping. The water spray system did not have enough water pressure to reach the points from which the gas was escaping. The alarm on the MIC storage tank failed to warn of the rising temperature of the MIC prior to the disaster. MIC should have been stored at zero degrees centigrade but the freon gas that ran the refrigeration unit was being used elsewhere on site. The unit had therefore been disconnected. Union Carbide's operational procedures required the MIC tanks to be filled only to 50 per cent of capacity. The tank in the Bhopal disaster was filled to between 75 per cent and 87 per cent capacity. Another storage tank which was designed to be used to carry excess MIC was already full. Between 1980 and 1984 the crew for the MIC unit had been cut from twelve workers to six and the maintenance crew from six workers to two. The maintenance supervisor role had been removed from the shift during which the disaster occurred. Many workers in key safety positions were not properly trained. Finally, the operating manuals were all in English.

It has been suggested that people living around the Union Carbide plant were warned of the potential hazards in a number of newspaper articles but they tended to ignore the warnings because they did not know how to respond, e.g. where would the people move to? Local officials made the situation worse by claiming that the warnings were sensationalist rather than realistic.

Ironically, a study conducted by a team from Union Carbide two years earlier, in 1982, noted that there was a serious potential for the release of toxic chemicals contained within the MIC. This could be caused by equipment failure, operating difficulties or maintenance problems. The report recommended that changes be made to the plant to make it safer. These were not apparently taken up by Union Carbide. There had in fact been a number of other accidents at the plant in the preceding years. Also, notably, in 1984, Union Carbide safety inspectors carried out a safety check on Union Carbide's MIC unit in West Virginia in the USA. That report warned plant managers that a reaction could occur which could lead to the gas escaping.

In addition to the deaths at Bhopal the injuries have taken on a new significance. The eyes and lungs were the first and most obvious targets of the gas but over the succeeding years the kidney, spleen and liver of the victims have been affected. There has also been evidence of genetic defects in the children of Bhopal survivors. Overall, the immune systems of the victims have been affected making it difficult to fight off disease – in an already disease-ridden society.

The Indian government registered more than 600 000 claims against Union Carbide. But, before these claims could be assessed by the courts, the Indian government accepted an out of court settlement from Union Carbide in February 1989 for $US470 million. Union Carbide did not accept liability for the disaster. More importantly, it is argued that just the healthcare costs for the survivors of Bhopal would cost at least $US600 million. This does not take into account the costs of sanitation, housing and ordinary compensation for loss that would be considered normal in Western society. It is argued that the settlement amount was based on an estimated 40 000 injured victims but that the actual total was more likely to be 400 000.

The victims suffered yet further because of the apparent tactics of Union Carbide of delay and denial. They attempted to delay payment to the victims and to deny anything other than moral responsibility for the disaster. Union Carbide spent $US35–40 million on legal fees in connection with Bhopal. In the Federal District Court in New York where the claims brought on behalf of the victims of Bhopal were lodged, Union Carbide argued that US courts were not the appropriate place to deal with the issues but rather that the Indian courts were better placed to do so. This tied up the litigation for a year. Once back in India, Union Carbide argued that the Indian courts were in fact unsuitable to try such a complex issue. Union Carbide appealed against every decision that went against them. The issue has never been decided in any court of law.

Union Carbide had previously utilised this neutralisation technique in relation to residents of Suffolk County, Long Island for polluting their local water supply with a chemical called Temik. Union Carbide's response to that situation could be observed in a number of discrete stages:

1. *Denying the problem existed* – Union Carbide maintained that only minute traces of the chemical in question were found at the site. This was untrue.

2. *Placing the problem in perspective* – Union Carbide argued that residues of several different chemicals had been located in the water supply over a period of many years. This was true, but did not detract from the significant presence of their own chemical.

3. *Blaming an hysterical public* – Union Carbide explained the decision of the Suffolk County's Department of Health Services to recommend that the local water should not be consumed (on the basis of its high chemical content) on the grounds that the Department was responding to an hysterical public rather than to a genuine health problem caused by Union Carbide.

4. *Blaming the victim* – responding to an allegation that the chemical had caused damage to the local population a spokesperson for Union Carbide argued that he had once fallen over a doorstep but that he did not know whether it was Temik or the large amount of scotch he had consumed.

5. *Dividing the victims* – Union Carbide suggested that real-estate developers were using the presence of the chemical to ensure that pesticides *per se* were banned. This would thus force the farmers to sell their land to them for future development.

6. *Settling out of court* – in exchange for installing and maintaining water filters and paying $US100 per poisoned well, Union Carbide were able to escape potentially crippling lawsuits and escape national and international adverse publicity.

In relation to Bhopal, Union Carbide had also sought to divert the moral responsibility it had accepted to a disgruntled employee whom they blamed for sabotaging the MIC gas tank and thus causing the accident. Union Carbide did not reveal who this employee was, even though they admitted that he was known to them. Even if this story were true, it has been argued that the ability of one person to act undetected in such a dangerous facility is itself an indictment of Union Carbide's standards.

The day the settlement figure of $US470 million was announced Union Carbide's stock price rose by $US2 a share. All but $US20 million of the settlement figure was covered by Union Carbide's liability insurance and money set aside each year of the litigation process. The remaining $US20 million was retrieved by taking a share of dividends paid to shareholders in 1988. That year Union Carbide recorded profits of $US662 million.

Source:

Dembo, D., Morehouse, W. and Wykle, L. (1990) *Abuse of Power: Social Performance of Multinational Corporations: The Case of Union Carbide*, New York: New Horizons Press.

Further sources

'Union Carbide: disaster at Bhopal', available from http://www.bhopal.com/pdfs/browning.pdf.

'TED case studies: Bhopal disaster', available from http://www.american.edu/TED/BHOPAL.HTM.

'Investigation of large-magnitude incidents: Bhopal as a case study', available from http://www.bhopal.com/pdfs/casestdy.pdf.

General (Union Carbide created) Bhopal site, http://www.bhopal.com.

Questions

1. What is your assessment of the degree of social responsibility shown by both Union Carbide and the Indian government in establishing the factory?

2. What is your assessment of how Union Carbide behaved after the accident had occurred?

3. What does the Bhopal incident tell you about the impact of the presence of MNEs (multinational enterprises) in less developed economies?

4. If you had to devise a code of conduct for Union Carbide in light of the Bhopal disaster what process would you have to undertake and what, in terms of issues, would your code cover?

5. Do you think Union Carbide acted illegally?

9

The business of sport: Manchester United PLC
Ian Brooks

Introduction

This case study explores the global business environment facing Manchester United PLC. It has to be said that some organisations enjoy international recognition and kudos well in excess of the size, in financial terms, of their underlying business activity. Nowhere is this contrast starker than in the case of Manchester United. In 2002 Manchester United PLC had a turnover of £146 million. That makes it a small to medium-sized business. Despite this, the club is amongst the most renowned organisations in the world.

Football's early days

Football began in English public schools in the mid-nineteenth century although it was not until 1951 that an English footballer made significant financial gains from the commercialisation of his talent. In that year Stanley Matthews received £20 a week from the Co-operative Society for wearing their football boots. The World Cup in 1966 was the first to gain such worldwide television coverage, and indeed to be shaped by that medium, and associated commercialisation – only older readers will remember 'World Cup Willy'. Since the 1960s football has enjoyed worldwide mass appeal boosted by television coverage. It is reported that 37 billion viewers watched games on TV during World Cup France in 1998 (clearly many viewers watched more than one game) rising to 50 billion who tuned into Japan and Korea in 2002.

Manchester United PLC: facts and figures

Manchester United had a turnover in 2002 similar to that of a medium to large British university; however, with the possible exception of England's Oxford and Cambridge, few if any universities enjoy United's global reputation. United's turnover looks set to increase. Figure C9.1 shows the growth in annual turnover and profits between 1998 and 2002.

The club's turnover in 2002 comprises 39 per cent from 'match-day' (such as gate receipts), 36 per cent from the media (e.g. BSkyB income for live UK rights; MUTV), 18 per cent commercial (e.g. hotels, financial services) and 7 per cent from merchandising. Although still important, the fact that United fill their 67,700 stadium to capacity for league and cup games accounts for a relatively small, and decreasing, proportion of their total turnover. Figure C9.2 shows the breakdown of activity in more detail.

The PLC chairman, Sir Roy Gardner, says that the '. . . strength of its football squad coupled with the appeal of the Club brand, the quality of its partners, and size of its fan base sets Manchester United apart from its competitors'.[1] Gone are the days when a focus on the playing field dominated the football club's energies.

---

[1] *Source*: all quotes taken from Manchester United PLC, *Annual Report 2002*, unless otherwise stated.

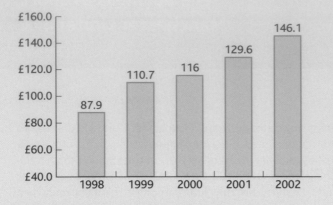

Figure C9.1 Manchester United turnover and profitability

Manchester United: 'business' strategy

Manchester United state four key strategic thrusts in their annual report (2002); just one directly refers to their core activity of playing football. They aim to maintain their playing strengths by a combination of transfer activity involving experienced players and developing younger players through their Academy (the new £8 million academy was opened in 2002). United will also 'leverage the global brand' and develop new products and services which appeal to their worldwide fan base. The new Nike deal (worth over £300 million over 13 years) is one of a number of strategic alliances with major international commercial organisations. This alliance brings together two global sports brands, that of Nike and Manchester United; other deals are with Vodafone and BSkyB, for example.

The PLC also seek to 'control and develop our own routes to market for media rights which can more effectively deliver value by exploiting the Club's own performance and reputation'. In other words, through initiatives such as MUTV (their own satellite/cable station), their website (now being extended with foreign languages) and a mobile phone service, they are delivering branded services to customers anywhere in the world.

Finally, Manchester United state that they are 'converting more fans to customers of the business and enhancing the value of customers through the implementation of customer relationship management (CRM)'. What is more, they are doing this in partnership with another sponsor, Dimension Data, who will implement a CRM process which will help to identify 'our most valued customers and grow the average revenue per customer segment'.[2]

The globalisation of the club

Manchester United is known across the globe. Even in the USA where European soccer clubs barely had any recognition a decade ago, Manchester United and a small number of their key players (most notably, of course, the new Real Madrid Player David Beckham) are increasingly supported or known,

---

[2]Fact sheet 11: 'Branding, sponsorship and commerce in football', Sir Norman Chester Centre for Football Research, www.le.ac.uk/fo/resources/factsheets/fs11.html.

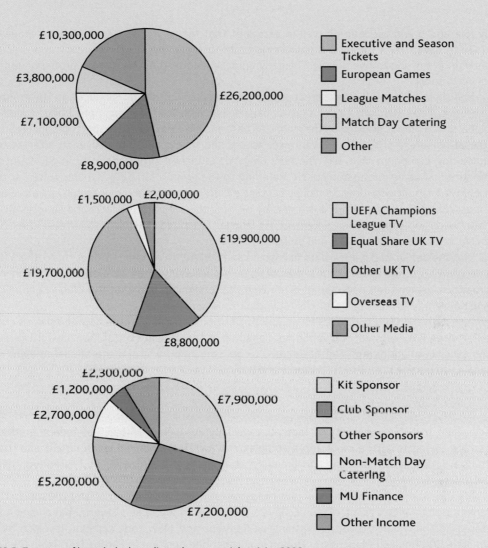

Figure C9.2 Turnover of 'match day', media and commercial activity 2002
Source: Annual Report 2002

particularly by younger people of both sexes. United mania and the strength of its fan base are strong in Asia, particularly in China, Japan, South Korea, Hong Kong, Thailand, Singapore and Malaysia. In some places it is said that the first words of English some children learn are 'Manchester United'. In addition, United enjoys a sizeable following across Europe, particularly in Scandinavia and Ireland. These supporters are often reasonably affluent and well informed thanks in part to the worldwide football TV coverage. It has been said that United enjoy a worldwide fan base in excess of 50 million people and brand recognition well in excess of that figure. In the UK and Ireland alone United claim to have over 11 million supporters (possibly using a liberal definition of 'supporter'); that's getting on for one in five people. The geographic spread of their fan base is probably unmatched in world sport.

Manchester United PLC take great pride in their global commercial connections. The group's chief executive, Peter Kenyon, argues that its partnership with Nike, for example, brings together two global sports brands drawing on the global fan base and Nike's expertise in sports product marketing – 'the combination of the Club's worldwide appeal and Nike's ability to deliver an integrated global marketing campaign that saw the new team kit launched simultaneously in 58 countries . . . produced a hugely successful launch'. Referring to the group's fan base, Kenyon writes 'at the moment we transact with only a small percentage of those fans. . . our aim is to convert more of them, especially from overseas, into customers by offering the content, products and services that meet their needs and capture the excitement of Manchester United'. They aim to increase their computerised database to include 3.5 million fans by 2005.

Manchester United games, both in England and Europe, enjoy larger ratings than other clubs and television coverage is set to increase for them. Additionally, they secured the rights in 2001 to broadcast delayed full coverage of every English Premiership game on the Club's channel, MUTV, and now enjoy similar rights for UEFA Champions league games.

Although the Club continues to work with UK sponsors, many of the new companies are global enterprises. For example, Budweiser has signed up as the official beer of Manchester United, Pepsi the official soft drink and Fuji has agreed to become a sponsor and the official imaging partner helping to pursue business-to-business and business-to-customer services.

Branding and merchandising

Television and the popularity of football, especially European football, has meant football clubs coming to terms with a much more complex and lucrative financial environment and many top clubs are turning to marketing and 'branding' as a means of maintaining and extending their competitiveness.

Manchester United probably enjoys the greatest brand recognition of any UK sports club and ranks among a select group of global players such as Real Madrid and Bayern Munich and American clubs like the Dallas Cowboys, Washington Redskins and New York Yankees. Research by Future Brand in 2001 placed Manchester United in number one position in Europe (see Table C9.1).

In estimating the value of the brand a series of factors was taken into consideration, including obvious ones such as income flows from sponsorship but also longevity of support. Certainly a feature of many sports clubs is the extent of loyalty which, to a significant extent, transcends the clubs' sporting performance in the short term. For example, Ferrari failed to win the driver's championship between 1979 and 2000 but was still the highest valued F1 team. The loyalty the club earned among supporters through the lean years of previous decades (including their relegation to Division Two) is testimony to the belief that brand loyalty for sports clubs probably stands the test of time far longer than that for other commercial companies.

Table C9.1 Top ten sporting brands

Position	Top Ten Brands	£m
1	Manchester United	175.7
2	Real Madrid	105.2
3	Bayern Munich	101.8
4	Ferrari F1	74.6
5	McLaren-Mercedes	71.9
6	Juventus	69.2
7=	Liverpool	57.7
7=	Barcelona	57.7
9	Arsenal	55.6
10	Williams BMW	53.6

Source: research by Future Brand, 2001

Shirt sponsorship now costs in excess of £5 million a year and, internationally, only one top club believes its shirt to be 'sacred' enough not to carry a sponsor's name (Barcelona). Many fans identify authentic club shirts by the sponsor's name, making 'product recognition' very high for many sponsors. Despite warnings of 'brand dilution' top clubs also engage in dual branding of a wide range of products. For example, there has been a Manchester United Nintendo game and Manchester United Monopoly as well as Manchester United mineral water, beer and even tomato sauce.

Manchester United, like most top clubs and many smaller ones too, enjoy a significant degree of 'brand loyalty' and 'brand longevity'. Football clubs do not need to spend great sums on their marketing efforts, unlike sports clothes manufacturers for example. However, if Manchester United's performance on the field drops significantly its brand strength may be tested.

Manchester United has made moves to develop branded financial services. They have enjoyed increases in the number of people holding MU finance saving accounts and credit cards and other financial products delivering £1.2 million of business in 2002.

Branding in football is not solely the preserve of the clubs. Top footballers are now major television and media icons and Manchester United have had their share; George Best, Eric Cantona and David Beckham to name but three. David Beckham's contract negotiations with United in 2002 were reported to involve recognition of the player's 'brand value' as a celebrity used to sell merchandise. Although in an historic sense or time frame his celebrity status will be of limited duration, he is, for the time being at least, probably the most famous Englishman. The marketing of David Beckham is another story[4].

Bosman and player power

One of the biggest challenges facing football clubs is controlling the cost of players' wages. Many clubs in the UK are in dire financial difficulty due, at least in part, to failure to keep wages to

[4]Factsheet 10: 'The "new" football economics', Sir Norman Chester Centre for Football Research, available from http:/www.le.ac.uk/fo/resources/factsheets.

manageable levels. Manchester United are among the most successful in this regard, maintaining their wage bill to about 50 per cent of turnover (of course that does not mean their players live on low wages, quite the contrary in fact – the average experienced university lecturer in the UK has to work for about 3–4 years to earn what David Beckham earns in a week!).

In 1995 the European Court of Justice decided that the existing transfer rules breached EU law on the free movement of workers. This 'Bosman' ruling (named after the player who brought the case) led to the free movement of players between EU countries with no fee payable when players' contracts have expired. Players are allowed to negotiate their own deals with a new employer when their previous contract has expired, putting top players in particular in a very strong position, particularly when their existing contracts are nearing completion. A top player who could offer his services without transfer fee would command a very healthy salary package and signing-on fee. It can be argued that this is to the detriment of the game overall. Previously wages were lower while transfer fees were, by and large, kept in the game – used to pay for further transfers, stadium improvements, youth schemes and so forth. The high level of player wages takes money out of the game as top players and their advisers pocket what in effect is a large proportion of the new TV income. The transfer market is increasingly driven from the top. The World Cup of 2002 undoubtedly raised the price tag on Rio Ferdinand for whom Manchester United paid £30 million in 2002.

Social, ethical and ecological considerations

It is clear that the exploitation of its fan base now forms a major plank of the PLC strategy. The wealthier and more devoted that fan is the better. Not long ago, certainly if one goes back 30 years, it was virtually unheard of to wear replica team kit, in fact most fans, after parting with modest entry fees to matches, were content with a meat pie or weak tea at half time. They largely stood, often in uncovered stands, and primarily comprised working men and their sons. Fans were squashed in, stadia were dangerous, frills were minimal but the experience was affordable for most working people and few expenses were borne other than entrance fees. Clearly, football is just one activity, albeit of central importance, of the PLC. Manchester United is now a range of businesses although the PLC would argue that these primarily aim to provide support for its core activity, football.

It can be argued that '. . . some "traditional" football fans – perhaps especially less affluent, teenage male fans – are probably being effectively excluded from today's "live" football audience at the top level either through the mechanism of price or because of their alienation from the new cultures which are being established around sport'[4]. At the same time, however, previously excluded fans, families, women and some ethnic minority groups may find the sport more appealing.

The PLC notes some of its achievements and ambitions on an environmental and social front in its annual reports. Manchester United were selected for inclusion in the FTSE 4 Good index which was launched in 2001, demonstrating progress made in working towards environmental sustainability, developing positive relationships with stakeholders and upholding and supporting basic human rights. The club has assessed the environmental standards of their major suppliers and contractors. They work with very many community-based and other charities, from local schools to UNICEF. Nevertheless, top clubs' ambitions have been questioned, not least by the UK Prime

Minister, Tony Blair who, in 1995, when asked to comment on the launch of Manchester United's third team strip in one season, said, 'There is a market, certainly, but there is a community too. Football clubs are part of it.'

Source:

Manchester United PLC, *Annual Report 2002.*

Questions

1. Conduct a PEST analysis for Manchester United PLC.

2. How is 'partnership' helping (or hindering) the development of the PLC?

3. What are the implications for the socio-economic composition of Manchester United's fan base?

4. Is a fan a customer?

5. What is the relationship between the PLC business activities and its football successes – how does the former give the club a competitive edge?

6. What problems might the PLC encounter in its attempts to exploit what might appear a highly favourable business environment?

References

Fact Sheet 10: 'The "new" football economics', Sir Norman Chester Centre for Football Research, available from http://www.le.ac.uk/fo/resources/factsheets.

Fact Sheet 11: 'Branding, sponsorhip and commerce in fooball, Sir Norman Chester Centre for Football Research, available from http://www.le.ac.uk/fo/resources/factsheet.

Guardian (1995) 16 January.

Williams, G. (2002) 'David Beckham, identity and masculinity', *Sociology Review*, 11 (3).

Index